Mainstreaming co-operation

MANCHESTER
1824
Manchester University Press

Mainstreaming co-operation

An alternative for the twenty-first century?

Edited by Anthony Webster, Linda Shaw and Rachael Vorberg-Rugh

Manchester University Press

Published by Manchester University Press
Altrincham Street, Manchester M1 7JA

www.manchesteruniversitypress.co.uk

British Library Cataloguing-in-Publication Data
A catalogue record for this book is available from the British Library

Library of Congress Cataloging-in-Publication Data applied for

ISBN 978 0 7190 9959 5 hardback

First published 2016

Typeset in Sabon and Gill Sans by
Servis Filmsetting Ltd, Stockport, Cheshire
Printed in Great Britain by
CPI Group (UK) Ltd, Croydon CR0 4YY

Contents

Figures, tables and boxes

Figures

Tables

Boxes

Contributors

Phil Considine is Principal Lecturer in the Nottingham Business School, Nottingham Trent University, where he leads the Executive MBA Programme. He specialises in sustainable strategic management and change management, and works across a wide range of sectors and organisations.

Philip Grant is Research Fellow in the Social Studies of Finance at the University of Edinburgh. He is a social anthropologist by training. He is also a director of Spirit of Lanarkshire, a community wind energy co-operative in the south of Scotland.

Rowshan Hannan completed her PhD in 2014 at the Sustainability Research Institute, University of Leeds. She is also an Associate of the Co-operative College in Manchester, and has worked with co-operative movements throughout east and southern Africa. Her article 'Participatory co-operative research: for the people, by the people, with the people' will appear in a forthcoming issue of *Development in Practice*.

Martin Hingley is Professor of Strategic Marketing at Lincoln Business School, University of Lincoln. He specialises in whole-chain business-to-business relationships, notably in agri-food-retailer channels, and the marketing of regional, speciality food-producer businesses and their network/community organisation.

Vern Hughes is Director of the Centre for Civil Society, and Convenor of the Consumer Co-operatives and Social Enterprise in Health Care International Working Group. He was previously CEO of South

Kingsville Health Services Co-operative Ltd, and a Director of the Co-operative Federation of Victoria.

Stephen McCusker is a registered architect and director at Loop Systems Ltd, an architects co-operative dedicated to delivering projects based on social, economic and environmental sustainability. His work in practice predominantly focuses on responses to existing buildings, including the extension and refurbishment of the Rochdale Pioneers Museum and the Unicorn Grocery Co-operative in Manchester.

Cliff Mills is a practising lawyer who advises on governance and writes constitutions for mutual, co-operative and member-based organisations. As a mutuals consultant with Mutuo, he designs new models of mutual ownership and governance, particularly in the context of public sector reform.

Virginie Pérotin is a Professor of Economics at Leeds University Business School working on the effect of employee, state and private ownership and worker participation on firm behaviour and performance. Her recent research on worker co-operatives has appeared in the *Journal of Comparative Economics* and the *Industrial and Labor Relations Review.*

Barbara Rawlings is Associate Lecturer at MIRIAD at Manchester Metropolitan University. She is a social researcher, and has worked mainly with public and third sector organisations, in particular with democratic therapeutic communities for people with personality disorders. She has authored a number of papers on these various research projects, and on the use of qualitative research methods.

Bruno Roelants is Secretary General of CICOPA, the sectoral organisation of the International Co-operative Alliance for industry and services, and of its regional organisation CECOP–CICOPA Europe. He co-authored *Cooperatives and Employment: A Global Report* (Brussels: CICOPA-Desjardins, 2014).

Claudia Sanchez Bajo was the Inaugural Chair in Co-operative Enterprises at the University of Winnipeg, Faculty of Business and Economics. Her current research is focused on co-operatives and development issues. Her most prominent publication (with Bruno Roelants) is *Capital and the Debt Trap: Learning from Cooperatives in the Global Crisis* (Basingstoke: Palgrave Macmillan 2013).

Carolin Schröder of the Technical University of Berlin is an urban planner who works on participatory and co-operative processes. Her most prominent publication is 'Chances and limits of co-operatives in times of socio-ecological transformation', in M. Freise and T. Hallmann, eds, *Modernizing Democracy: Associations and Associating in the 21st Century* (New York: Springer, 2014), with Dr Heike Walk.

Linda Shaw was formerly Vice Principal at the Co-operative College in Manchester, where she was responsible for research and international programmes. She has worked as both a researcher and practitioner in co-operative development with a focus on gender and education. Most recently she co-edited, with Hazel Johnson, a co-operatives issue of the *Journal of International Development* in 2014.

Ian Snaith was a senior lecturer at the University of Leicester Law School from 1979 to 2009 and still writes, researches and advises on legal aspects of UK co-operatives and social enterprises. His most recent publication is *Handbook of Co-operative and Community Benefit Society Law* (Manchester: Co-operatives UK and Jordan Publishing, 2014).

Keith Vernon is Principal Lecturer in History at the University of Central Lancashire. He has researched and published on the history of higher and technical education, education in the co-operative movement, and history in the school curriculum, mainly in the nineteenth and twentieth centuries.

Rachael Vorberg-Rugh is an independent scholar living in Fort Worth, Texas, USA. She has published widely on the history of the UK co-operative movement, including, with John F. Wilson and Anthony Webster, *Building Co-operation: A Business History of The Co-operative Group, 1863–2013* (Oxford: Oxford University Press, 2013). She has also worked with the Co-operative College, Manchester, on research and heritage initiatives.

Heike Walk is a post-doctoral researcher and head of section for social movements, technology and conflicts at the Centre for Technology and Society at the Technical University of Berlin. Her current research focuses on democracy, participation and co-operatives.

Anthony Webster of Northumbria University is a business historian who works on the history of the British co-operative movement. His most prominent publication, with John F. Wilson and Rachael Vorberg-Rugh, is *Building Co-operation: A Business History of The Co-operative Group, 1863–2013* (Oxford: Oxford University Press, 2013).

Angela Whitecross earned her PhD in history from the University of Central Lancashire in 2014, where she studied the history of the Co-operative Party in Britain in the 1930s–50s. She has worked on numerous projects with the National Co-operative Archive and Rochdale Pioneers Museum, and currently works with the Elizabeth Gaskell House in Manchester.

John F. Wilson is Director of Newcastle University Business School. He has published extensively in the fields of business and industrial history, covering subjects as diverse as management education, technology transfer and studies of firms such as Ferranti, BP and British Gas North Western, Recently, with Anthony Webster and Rachael Vorberg-Rugh, he published *Building Co-operation: A Business History of The Co-operative Group, 1863–2013* (Oxford: Oxford University Press, 2013).

Stephen Yeo is an historian and activist within the co-operative and other social movements. He is Chair of the Co-operative Heritage Trust, which looks after the Rochdale Pioneers Museum and the National Co-operative A rchive in Britain. He taught and wrote at the University of Sussex for many years before becoming Principal of Ruskin College in Oxford. Since 1997 he has been closely involved with the Co-operative College in Manchester in many different roles.

Ruth Yeoman is a research fellow at the University of Oxford. She researches the philosophy and organisational practices of mutuality and meaningfulness. Her most recent publication is *Meaningful Work and Workplace Democracy: A Philosophy of Work and a Politics of Meaningfulness* (Basingstoke: Palgrave Macmillan, 2014).

Acknowledgements

First and foremost, the authors would like to thank the many people and organisations who helped organise the conference from which this project developed: Mainstreaming Co-operation, held at the then headquarters of The Co-operative Group at New Century House, Manchester, 3–5 July 2012. The Co-operative Group's support for this major international conference was essential to its success. The entire staff of the Co-operative College in Manchester helped ensure the event ran smoothly, and have continued to be supportive of this book as it made its way towards publication. Our special thanks are due to Gillian Lonergan, Heather Roberts, Adam Shaw, Sophie Stewart and Mervyn Wilson for their assistance. A highlight of the conference was a tour of the Rochdale Pioneers Museum, then in the final phase of its renovation – an experience that would not have been possible without the welcoming and professional museum staff, Clare Hirst, Jenny Mabbott and Jonny Priestley. Our fellow members of the conference organising committee – Dr Alyson Brown, Professor Keri Facer, Professor John Schostak, Dr David Stewart, Professor John Walton and Professor John Wilson – helped craft a conference that brought together co-operative scholars and active co-operators from across the globe. While the presenters and attendees that made Mainstreaming Co-operation such a fruitful event for inspiration, education and debate are too numerous to include by name, we send our collective appreciation to them all.

We send particular thanks to the contributors to this volume, for their careful work and patience throughout this project's long gestation period. Finally, and most importantly, special thanks are due to Stirling Smith, Tim Smith and Leslie Webster, without whose constant encouragement and support this book would not be possible.

1

Introduction

Anthony Webster, Linda Shaw and Rachael Vorberg-Rugh

Early in July 2012 academics and active co-operators from across the world converged on The Co-operative Group's then headquarters at New Century House in Manchester, UK, to attend a major international conference entitled 'Mainstreaming Co-operation'. The theme was how co-operation internationally could renew itself and become once again the global force for positive economic and social change it had once been in the later nineteenth and early twentieth centuries. The central question was how co-operation could move from the fringes of orthodox economic, social and political thought to command a prominent position in the mainstream intellectual currents of the day. The conference was interdisciplinary, and focused on a wide range of historical and contemporary issues and themes in which co-operative models offered or had offered new ways of organising production, commerce and human society which became widespread and central to the wider functioning of societies.

The time for such an appraisal seemed particularly apt. In the later twentieth century co-operation as a business and social model had experienced retreat and defeats, especially in parts of the developed world which had been, a century or so earlier, the citadel of co-operative growth. This was especially evident in the field of consumer co-operation. Across Western Europe, in particular, consumer co-operative movements had lost market share to new investor-led and ruthlessly efficient and centralised retail chains, able to take advantage of large amounts of capital raised through the stock markets, and unhampered by the constraints of federal, regionalised business democracy which prevailed within the consumer co-operative movements.[1] In countries such as Austria, France, Germany and the Netherlands, major parts of the consumer movement were swept away in the 1980s and 1990s, while elsewhere, notably in Italy and the Scandinavian countries, strategies were adopted which enabled those movements to hold their own.[2]

In Britain, decline from the 1960s to the 1990s was arrested by new approaches in the first decade of the twenty-first century, but recent setbacks have resulted in all of the ground recovered being lost.[3] Accompanying business difficulties, consumer co-operation experienced membership declines in many countries, weakening the democratic credentials of the movement, and in some cases ultimately leading to loss of co-operative status and conversion to mainstream investor-led models, as occurred in Germany in the 1980s. But perhaps even more damaging than this was an ideological assault on co-operation which led to a widening perception that it was a form of business and social organisation whose day had passed. The 1980s saw the establishment of a new 'neoliberal' intellectual hegemony in politics, economics and business, exemplified by the Thatcher and Reagan regimes in the UK and USA. This dismissed the mixed-economy ideas of the postwar Keynesian consensus, and reasserted the free market and competitive ethos of nineteenth-century capitalism, with its emphasis upon a small noninterventionist state, low taxes, minimal welfare and the dominance of the investor-led public limited company (PLC) or corporation as the only really credible and durable form of business organisation.

The 'new' philosophy was intertwined with globalisation, financial deregulation and the development of a dizzying array of new financial instruments and assets which, for a time, seemed to offer the prospect of efficient, self-regulating financial markets which did not need the intervention of law or national state agencies. In this brave new world, co-operatives came to be seen as outmoded forms of business enterprise, destined to lose out to the investor-led paragons of economic rationality. Co-operatives might emerge to plug temporary gaps yet to be filled by superior investor-led models, but in the long run they would cede to the natural winners in this neoliberal version of economic Darwinism. This new orthodoxy had real consequences. The privatisation of state assets found a mirror in the policies of demutualisation which swept across the Western world, with new legislation to empower management teams and other interested parties to lead the way in converting building societies and other mutuals into investor-led companies. In Britain, the 1990s saw the vast majority of building societies converted to mainstream banks, and some of those which did not convert mimicked the more reckless and speculative behaviour of the new converts in an effort to retain membership and market share – as The Co-operative Group was to discover to its bitter cost following its absorption of the Britannia Building Society in 2009.[4] Meanwhile, the collapse of communism in

Eastern Europe and the former Soviet Union added to the discrediting of the co-operative model, as many of the 'co-operatives' in those regimes had been either absorbed into the communist state apparatus or set up by them. Thus neoliberal economic theory, combined with the failure of communism, served to inflict one of the greatest blows against the international co-operative movement in its history.

By the early 1990s, therefore, according to the mainstream of contemporary economic thought, co-operation was a dying form of business and social organisation.[5] Economic theorists wrote of numerous theoretical problems with co-operatives: the so-called 'horizon problem', in which individual co-operators struggle to put the collective interests of their co-operatives before their individual interests in the arena of long-term investment in the business; or the 'Illyrian problem' (mentioned in Grant's chapter 3 in this volume), in which members of co-operatives refuse entry to new workers in an effort to retain their share of the co-operative's earnings. This leads to the development of two classes of workers in the co-operative – member owners and employees – a state of affairs entirely inimical to the ethical aspirations of co-operation, and likely to constitute a slippery slope towards conversion to 'mainstream' investor-led status. In this way a new orthodoxy emerged in which co-operation had little or no place. This was reflected in the gradual fading of co-operation from the literature in academic business studies and economics. This fading of co-operation from important parts of the intellectual mainstream remains a problem, as will be made clear later in this introduction and the chapters in this volume.[6]

Yet, unexpectedly, the tide did begin to turn in the first decade of the twenty-first century. The dominance of the investor-led model began to be challenged, largely as a result of crises and problems in the international capitalist system, but also because of signs of durability and revival in the international co-operative movement. Even during the supposed heyday of neoliberal orthodoxy of the 1990s and early 2000s, many social observers of the globalised and market-driven economy noted that the corollary of the system was deepening divisions of wealth and power between the very richest elite and the rest, with potentially damaging consequences for social order and democratic legitimacy. To some degree, the emergence of new-style left-of-centre 'third way' strategies, such as that advocated by the Blair government in the UK after 1997, seemed to highlight that other business models than the dominant corporate investor-led template deserved a place in the capitalist hierarchy. The Blair government even sought to legislate for such alternatives, through the Community Interest Company Regulations of 2005 and the Charities Act of 2006, which established a legal framework for community interest companies, charitable incorporated organisations and the growing body of 'social enterprises' dedicated to the creation of a business sector with a distinctive remit to improve and strengthen society.[7] The warning signs that investor-led organisations were not without their weaknesses were evident when the Enron scandal erupted in the USA in 2001. This proved to be an ominous portent for the future, and when the great international financial collapse of 2008 occurred, with the failure of Lehmann Brothers followed by state bailouts of major banks across the world, shortcomings in the governance practices of investor-led companies and their underpinning structures began to move centre stage. As the crisis unfolded, an interesting phenomenon became clear. In countries such as Italy and France, co-operatives proved highly successful at riding out the storm, with co-operatives creating many more jobs at a time of crisis than the private sector (see Sanchez Bajo and Roelants' chapter 2, this volume). In Britain, The Co-operative Group had been steadily recovering following the Lanica crisis of 1997 and its reorganisation in 2000–01, and was not proving to be the failure once predicted. Consumer co-operatives in the Scandinavian countries were also holding their own, with quite spectacular levels of success being achieved in Finland. In addition, in Britain, the 'liberalisation' of education from local authority control, which had been gathering pace for some time, created new opportunities for schools organised on 'multi-stakeholder' co-operatives lines, a model that had enjoyed considerable success in Italy.[8] By 2015, over 700 such schools had been created through reorganisation or were in the process of converting.

There were also signs of ideological reassessments amongst political bodies not traditionally favourable to co-operation. In the UK the Conservative Party, once the architect of the demutualisation and privatisation drives, rediscovered the benefits of co-operatives, mutuals and social enterprises during its long period in opposition from 1997 to 2010. Problems with privatised public services and the spectacular failures of many demutualised building societies (especially in the 2008 crisis) persuaded some Conservatives that there was room, after all, for co-operatives, mutuals and other non-investor-led organisations to flourish – especially in public services from which the state would have to retreat, following the massive financial retrenchment resulting from the debts arising from the huge state bank bailouts of 2008–09. From this emerged the 2010–15 Coalition government's 'Big Society' strategy, in which co-operatives, mutuals, social enterprises and other 'third sector' organisations were to 'spring into being' to take over key services (libraries, leisure centres, playschools) previously provided by the local state.[9] The idea of a non-state, non-capitalist third sector emerging in the wake of the crisis also informed European Union strategy, with an important plank of its future plans defined as 'social innovation', with the object of increasing citizen participation in society and democracy via more direct engagement with the voluntary and social enterprise sectors.[10]

Thus the Mainstreaming Co-operation conference in 2012, which coincided with the United Nations International Year of Co-operatives (itself a sign of renewed global interest in co-operative models), seemed to catch a changing intellectual *milieu* on the brink of readopting ideas of co-operation and mutuality more or less rejected by the mainstream a generation earlier.[11] Notably, the original impetus for the international year came from the developing world, as Mongolia was the resolution's original sponsor in 2009. The first wave of support for the resolution also came from the countries of the developing world.[12] After the resolution passed, Mongolia hosted the initial meeting of UN experts to plan for the year.[13] The aim of the Mainstreaming Co-operation conference was to explore the possibilities of moving co-operative models of business and social organisation from the margins to which had been relegated, back into the mainstream of intellectual debate about business, social organisations, and the wider field of public and commercial ethics. It was recognised that while a new openness to such ideas was in evidence, this did not constitute a wider awareness of or acceptance that co-operatives and mutuals might have a continuous and substantial role to play in developed and developing societies. Business and economic textbooks remained firmly wedded to the investor-led business paradigm.[14] The conference therefore explored how co-operative models had succeeded in the past in breaking down intellectual and political barriers, and had 'won the high ground' – often against entrenched, self-interested opposition. It sought to identify fields in which co-operatives were once again beginning to win ground – how they had achieved this, and what could be learned from it. The conference also focused on general strategies (historical and contemporary) for co-operation to win its place in the intellectual mainstream – and in fact changing that mainstream itself.

But no sooner had the conference happened, and the editors had set to work turning the conference proceedings into a publication, that events overtook them. The crisis in the British consumer co-operative movement, which began with the near failure of The Co-operative Bank in 2013, threatened to destroy all of the advances made since the difficult years of the 1980s. For a time even the survival of The Co-operative Group itself seemed in doubt. Realising that any book exploring the position of co-operation in relation to the mainstream which did not analyse the most recent and serious crisis in the history of British co-operation and its ramifications would be obsolete before it got into print, the editors decided to allocate a chapter to examine the roots and results of that crisis, something which had to await the completion of the major reviews of The Co-operative Group's affairs undertaken by Sir Christopher Kelly and Lord Myners during the course of 2014, and the outcomes of their recommendations.[15] As a result, a volume originally planned for publication in 2013 has taken substantially longer to produce. But we think that, in this case, it is a substantially stronger and more relevant volume for its extended gestation period.

So what are the main themes of the book? Firstly, the ways in which co-operative ideas have won support in the past, and clues as to how they might do so again in the future, figure very prominently. Here it is necessary to sound a note of caution. The aim is not to offer examples of successful and expanding co-operative practice as blueprints or approaches to be universally replicated. A resounding aspect of co-operativedevelopment has always been its adaptation to social and economic conditions which are specific to particular social, cultural and historical contexts. The editors reject the notion of a simplistic co-operative blueprint or approach as something which can be universally transplanted, and few of the contributors to this volume seek to proselytise specific models. Of course, it may well be that co-operators reading this book will draw their own conclusions and adapt ideas to local circumstances – but it is not the intention of the editors to actively campaign in favour of this or that model. Furthermore, the question of 'mainstreaming co-operation', in the sense of winning wider intellectual, legal and political acceptance of co-operation across the world, is not merely a question of developing successful models. Sanchez Bajo and Roelants' chapter demonstrates that it is not merely a question of co-operation and mutualism *adding* to the mainstream of economic ideas and business models, but of their substantially *changing* many of the underlying assumptions behind the mainstream; not least in the replacement of the hegemony of neoliberal ideas and the investor-led organisational model with a *plurality* of models, in which a wide range of potential forms of organisation might coexist. They point to the continuing success of co-operative models during the post-2008 crisis in which 'mainstream' capitalist organisations struggled, offering the example of co-operatives such as Desjardins in Canada and Mondragon in Spain. On a similar theme, Grant, in chapter 3, pinpoints the central problem of *how* co-operative ideas might not only dominate in the intellectual mainstream, but also exercise greater purchase over the popular imagination. For him, it is a central question of *agency*, of how co-operative ideas might gather sufficient momentum to challenge neoliberal orthodoxies. For Grant, this requires the development of effective networks of co-operative advocates and institutions, able to promote co-operative ideas in a co-ordinated, self-supporting and coherent way. He points to the effectiveness of such networks in promoting feminist ideas since the 1960s, and how they have moved the interests of women into the mainstream of modern thinking.

This question of championing co-operative ideas is also a very strong theme in the historical chapters. Yeo's chapter on G. J. Holyoake (chapter 4) is a classic study of one of the movement's most successful nineteenth-century proselytisers. Yeo celebrates Holyoake's ability to project co-operation to a diverse range of audiences, including politicians as well as the educated middle class more generally. This was achieved not through writing alone, but through a variety of media, including graveside speeches! Yeo contends that Holyoake was probably the most effective proponent of a non-Marxist, non-revolutionary socialist alternative to the prevailing capitalist order, and that his skills as a highly flexible and creative communicator were complemented by his ability to combine practicality and moral purpose in the construction of his messages. Holyoake's argument was not just that co-operation offered a more rational and materially beneficial way to organise society, but that it was also *ethically* superior. Yeo argues that one of the most powerful ways in which the co-operative idea can have modern appeal is by stressing this ethical as well as rational foundation. Yeo argues that here lies the way, in particular, to appeal to the young, through a set of ideas which can offer a moral and social dimension conspicuously absent from the selfish and profit-maximising individualism of neoliberal theory. That such an appetite exists for an ethical economic alternative is evidenced by the growth of support for Green movements across the globe in recent decades, and arguably in the UK by the surge of support for Jeremy Corbyn for the Labour leadership in the summer of 2015. Vernon's chapter (chapter 5) also explores an important past example of how the British co-operative movement sought to maintain the currency of its ideas through education. Vernon explains how, by the 1890s, the Co-operative Union, the political and educational wing of the movement, had become concerned about the decline of educational opportunities provided by retail societies. This decline was in response to the growing role of the state in the provision of education – especially for children – as exemplified by the 1902 Education Act. The Co-operative Union was deeply concerned that co-operative values and history were likely to be marginalised in state curricula which focused on mainstream beliefs – in history in particular, there was especially strong concern that this would lead to new generations filled with a patriotic, imperialist and nationalist perspective of the country's past, with little or no awareness of working-class history and the place of co-operation in it. Vernon explains how, to combat this, the Co-operative Union developed and promoted a range of accredited courses aimed at adults and children to offer an alternative view of history, with working-class movements and co-operation firmly embedded in it. Vernon contends that its impact, though difficult to measure with precision, was substantial and, until 1930 at least, helped ensure that new cohorts of co-operative members had some sense of the ethics and historical origins of the movement. Here was a national initiative which sought to *keep* co-operation as part of the educational and cultural mainstream.

But other chapters offer worrying examples where opportunities were missed – and are being missed – to keep co-operation as a solid component of the intellectual and popular mainstreams. Vorberg-Rugh's chapter (chapter 6) and that by Rawlings and Shaw (chapter 7) expose a historical failure to address issues of gender inequality within the British co-operative movement which arguably have contributed to its marginalisation. Vorberg-Rugh shows the largely negative response of the British movement in the nineteenth and early twentieth centuries to the efforts by the Women's Co-operative Guild and others to increase women's participation in co-operative democracy. She demonstrates that, despite co-operatives' longstanding commitment to gender equality in membership, in practice many women were excluded from membership and leadership positions despite the movement's dependence on a predominantly female customer base. Nor was this solely a British phenomenon. Rawlings and Shaw's comprehensive survey of women and leadership in the global movement reveals similar historical and contemporary inequalities, though there is also evidence from some parts of the world that these are being challenged. What is notably worrying and disappointing, however, is the lack of academic research into this area – which is surely essential if it is to be tackled systematically. The basic question here of course is how will it be possible to mainstream co-operation if it fails to mainstream women into leadership positions within the global movement? How will it be possible to fulfil the mission of co-operation to provide a vehicle for deeper democratic participation in societies through economic control, as cited in Sanchez Bajo and Roelants' chapter, if it perpetuates the gender inequalities of the existing mainstream?

Whitecross, in chapter 8, exposes another historical failure to promote co-operation in a key arena. Her study of the failure of the Co-operative Party to significantly shape the economic policies of the Labour Party in the 1930s and 1940s, fashioning for co-operation a firmer position within Labour's overwhelmingly statist version of democratic socialism, reveals that it was not merely a result of Labour's strong predilection for state socialism over voluntary association, but also an unwillingness on the part of the wider co-operative movement itself to press the more assertive strategy favoured by many Co-operative Party activists. An important opportunity to stake out a significant claim to the political legitimacy of co-operation, as a movement worthy of serious consideration as part of the mainstream of state economic policy, was largely missed. One might reflect that this frequently sterile political alignment with Labour also served to alienate the main Conservative opposition party which, after all, dominated government for much of the twentieth century. Somehow, the movement contrived to fashion for itself a 'lose–lose' situation in parliamentary political terms. Parliamentary and party politics, after all, are also part of the mainstream. These historical and contemporary failures to promote co-operation in fields such as parliamentary politics and gender illustrate that, at times, the movement can be its own worst enemy. One might add that the Co-operative Union's efforts to sustain a sense of co-operative history and culture in the first half of the twentieth century also seems to have atrophied in later years.

A second important theme in the book is to explore where contemporary co-operatives and other forms of collective enterprise seem to be offering new opportunities for the movement, and fresh forms of organisation which might be adapted to new contexts. A pivotal chapter in this respect is by Mills and Yeoman (chapter 9), which offers a review of some new forms of mutual organisations in Britain, especially in the provision of public services, which might be adapted to a wider range of enterprises and organisations. They cite the development of 'polyvocal' or 'multi-constituency' forms of mutual organisation to bring together different (sometimes opposing) interest groups in joint representation on the governing body. The examples they cite include Rochdale Boroughwide Housing and NHS Foundation Trusts. They see this as a model capable of much wider application, resulting in public services which are much more responsive to consumer needs and interests. One might add that the co-operative school movement of recent years in Britain has very much followed this multi-constituency approach.[16] Some even advocate it as a possible model that The Co-operative Group might emulate. Hughes' chapter on co-operative approaches to health care (chapter 10) fleshes out some of these themes of using co-operative models to engage patients in the development of their own care, and offers several major examples of how this works in practice in Australia, the USA and elsewhere. McCusker (chapter 11) focuses upon the spread of the co-operative model among professional architects, arguing that this is a model which is attractive as it both helps architects to adapt to a frequently difficult economic climate and offers collegial forms of work relationships which are beneficial for the working patterns of the profession.

Schröder and Walk's study (chapter 12) of the role of co-operatives in promoting environmental protection, most notably in German housing co-operatives, focuses upon the role of the co-operative model in promoting education and member participation – both crucial ingredients for embedding environmental sensitivities and awareness in modern organisations. Hannan's chapter (chapter 13) makes a similar point about the beneficial aspects of the participatory behaviours which co-operatives promote. She discusses the role of co-operatives in addressing poverty in the developing world. Rejecting assertions by some scholars that co-operatives are not inherently poverty-reducing organisations, Hannan's study of dairy co-operatives in Kenya shows that they do have important, if indirect, poverty alleviating qualities. She makes the point that it is the changes in wider behaviours which co-operatives inculcate which are crucial in bringing these wider benefits. Active dairy co-operators were much more likely to engage with other collaborative poverty-reducing initiatives, because they had become accustomed to participatory practices. Democratic participation, collaboration and network building were all by-products of co-operative formation and involvement which brought wider benefits.

Pérotin's timely reassessment of worker co-operatives (chapter 14) is one of the most significant and revealing chapters. She points out that a number of key assumptions are commonly made about these types of co-operatives by economists and business academics. The orthodoxy suggests that they are smaller than most firms, and frequently under-capitalised – essentially small, niche firms which do not offer a credible alternative to 'mainstream' small and medium enterprises (SMEs). But Pérotin's review of worker co-operatives across a range of countries is revelatory. In fact, she demonstrates that worker co-operatives match 'mainstream' firms for durability, and that they are found in most industrial sectors. She rejects the notion that they are systemically under-capitalised, and asserts that there is strong *prima facie* evidence that many are more productive than their mainstream equivalents, largely because of their capacity to motivate workers through their control of the enterprise. Her conclusion is portentous for the subject of this book – worker co-operation *is* a viable alternative to private ownership for SMEs, suggesting that the model could be much more successfully mainstreamed in Britain, as it has been in Italy and Spain.[17]

Considine and Hingley's chapter (chapter 15) provides an encouraging example of a contemporary British co-operative, the Lincolnshire Co-operative Society, where conscious and strenuous efforts have been made to sustain a commitment to the wider values of co-operation among employees and members, and to promote wider awareness of their benefits. The results of this have been impressive, not just in terms of commercial performance, but also in the wider benefits which these values have brought to the community, through engagement in a wide variety of educational, charitable and community-oriented activities. They present the society as an example of the creation of 'shared value' whereby a commercial organisation engages in activities which both enhance the well-being of the wider community and the commercial prospects of the organisation. Considine and Hingley demonstrate that the co-operative model is especially well placed to fulfil this function of shared value, and that as an objective it is almost uncannily compatible with the values and principles of co-operation. Lincolnshire Co-operative Society provides a potent example of how co-operation can recapture an important part of the mainstream of wider public awareness of co-operation and its benefits. The organisation is seizing an opportunity to move co-operation firmly into the mainstream of 'Big Society' thinking about social and economic regeneration, and the way is open for others to follow.

What emerges in total from this volume is a sense of the ways in which the opportunity presented by the more promising climate presented for co-operatives which has emerged might be turned to lasting advantage – how it might be consolidated into an era in which co-operative and mutual forms of organisation are not only grudgingly accepted, but seen increasingly as a viable alternative to the neoliberal consensus which has dominated since the late 1970s. There are ideas here which offer much for further thinking and development. But the final chapter is included as a hedge against hubris. The Co-operative Group crisis in Britain is a sobering reminder that co-operatives are always vulnerable to a multitude of types of failure – whether through commercial incompetence or a loss of co-operative ethics and direction. Such problems are not new, and many co-operatives in many countries have experienced crises, from which some have not recovered. The chapter seeks to offer some thoughts on how such catastrophes have been addressed in the past, discussing the specific origins of the British crisis and its potential legacy for the future. For while the scope for co-operation to break into and even dominate the intellectual mainstream is real enough, so also is the danger of overreach and loss of focus. Co-operation still has enemies as well as friends. If it is to truly become the new intellectual force of the twenty-first century it must learn from past mistakes as well as create new and novel approaches to a fast-changing global environment.

Notes

1 P. Krampfer, 'Why co-operatives fail: case studies from Europe, Japan and the United States, 1950–2010' in P. Battilani and H. G. Schröter, eds, *The Co-operative Business Movement, 1950 to the Present* (Cambridge: Cambridge University Press, 2012), pp. 126–9; especially pp. 132–7.
2 E. Ekberg, 'Consumer co-operation and the transformation of modern food retailing: the British and Norwegian consumer co-operative movement in comparison, 1950–2002' in L. Black and N. Robertson, eds, *Consumerism and the Co-operative Movement in Modern British History* (Manchester: Manchester University Press, 2009), pp. 51–68; Ekberg, 'Organization: top down or bottom up? The organizational development of consumer co-operatives' in Battilani and Schröter, *The Co-operative Business Movement*, pp. 222–42.
3 For details of these initiatives see J. Wilson, A. Webster and R. Vorberg-Rugh, *Building Co-operation: A Business History of The Co-operative Group, 1863–2013* (Oxford: Oxford University Press, 2013).
4 Sir Chris Kelly, 'Failings in management and governance: report of the independent review into the events leading to The Co-operative Bank's capital shortfall' (30 April 2014) at: www.co-operative.coop/PageFiles/989442031/kelly-review.pdf (accessed 27 January 2016).
5 For a summary of some of these criticisms see E. Furlough and C. Strikwerda, 'Economics, consumer culture and gender: an introduction to the politics of consumer co-operation' in Furlough and Strikwerda, eds, *Consumers Against Capitalism: Consumer Co-operation in Europe, North America and Japan, 1840–1990* (Lanham, MD: Rowman & Littlefield, 1999), pp. 29–30.
6 P. Kalmi, 'The disappearance of co-operatives from economics textbooks' *Cambridge Journal of Economics* 31:4 (2007), 625–47.
7 R. Ridley Duff and M. Bull, *Understanding Social Enterprise: Theory and Practice* (London: Sage, 2011), p. 17 and p. 177.
8 S. Sacchetti and T. Ermanno, 'The social value of multi-stakeholder co-operatives: the case of the CEFF system in Italy' in T. Mazzarol, S. Reboud, E. Liminios and D. Clark, eds, *Research Handbook on Sustainable Co-operative Enterprise: Case Studies of Organisational Resilience in the Co-operative Business Model* (Cheltenham: Elgar, 2014), pp. 285–300.
9 Big Society, Not Big Government: Building a Big Society (London: The Conservative Party, March 2010); P. Blond, *Red Tory: How Left and Right Have Broken Britain and How We Can Fix it* (London, Faber 2010); and Building the Big Society (London: Cabinet Office, May 2010).
10 See European Alliance for Innovation, 'Social Innovation Europe: An Introduction', http://eai.eu/organization/social-innovation-europe (accessed 27 January 2016).
11 On the UN International Year of Co-operatives see Resolution adopted by the General assembly of the UN, on the report of the Third Committee, 64th session Agenda item 61 (b) (18 December 2009), www.un.org/en/ga/search/view_doc.asp?symbol=A/RES/64/136 (accessed 27 January 2016).

12 Personal conversation with Dame Pauline Green, President of the International Co-operative Alliance.
13 See UN Expert Group Meeting, 'Cooperatives in social development: beyond 2012', www.un.org/esa/socdev/social/meetings/egm11/documents/Aide-Memoire_EGM_Coops_2011.pdf (accessed 27 January 2016).
14 P. Kalmi, *The Disappearance of Co-operatives from Economics Textbooks* (Helsinki School of Economics, Working Paper 398, 2006); P. B. Whyman, 'Co-operative principles and the evolution of the "dismal science": the historical interaction between co-operative and mainstream economics' *Business History* 54:6 (2012), 833–54.
15 Kelly, 'Failings in management and governance'; Paul (Lord) Myners, 'The Co-operative Group: report of the independent governance review' (7 May 2014), www.co-operative.coop/Corporate/PDFs/Myners/Report_of_the_Independent_Governance_Review.pdf (accessed 27 January 2016).
16 On British co-operative schools, see T. Woodin, ed., *Co-operation, Learning and Co-operative Values: Contemporary Issues in Education* (London and New York: Routledge, 2015).
17 See also V. Pérotin, 'The performance of workers' co-operatives' in Battilani and Schröter, *The Co-operative Business Movement*, pp. 195–221.

2

Mainstreaming co-operatives after the global financial crisis

Claudia Sanchez Bajo and Bruno Roelants

The following discussion is mainly based on our presentation at the Mainstreaming Co-operation conference on 3 July 2012, organised by the Co-operative College UK in Manchester, and on our book *Capital and the Debt Trap: Learning from Cooperatives in the Global Crisis.*[1] This chapter brings in an institutional focus: it discusses the mainstreaming of co-operatives against the background of the global financial crisis that burst in 2008.

After defining the concept of mainstreaming, we examine whether co-operatives are indeed marginal, and, if so, in relation to which mainstream. We then move to the global financial crisis, examining the 'debt trap' and the issues of control which, according to our analysis, are related to it. Then, based on studies demonstrating co-operatives' resilience to the crisis and considering the shortcomings of measures put in place to solve the latter, we ask ourselves whether the 'one-size-fits-all' economic organisation is the solution for our future. We next argue that we are at the right moment to discuss the mainstreaming of co-operatives, and we provide a tentative framework to monitor such mainstreaming. We end up by focusing on the need to mainstream co-operatives also in the field of development goals, and on the relationship between mainstreaming and leadership.

What is mainstreaming?

Mainstreaming is neither an end in itself nor the loss of identity or specificity into a larger mass. It is important to keep this in mind because co-operatives, before the start of the global financial crisis, were under pressure to adopt the features of conventional enterprises. The clearest signs of the trend of some of them to turn into investor-led enterprises, also called 'isomorphism', were the loss of democratic control, of joint ownership and of reserve funds earmarked for the mission of the co-operative.

As far as entrepreneurship is concerned, the first goal of mainstreaming is that all decision-making and activities (programmes, policy, projects, funding etc.) take into account the plurality of entrepreneurship. But, in the case of co-operatives, the process of mainstreaming actually goes beyond this goal in so far as it necessarily involves three complementary processes. Firstly, it entails reshaping the currently predominant way of thinking, still based on an entrepreneurial model which is fundamentally different from the co-operative one: this process entails embeddedness in attitudes and mind-sets. Secondly, the mainstreaming of co-operatives carries an institutional dimension expressed through social and economic organisation as well as policy and regulation: indeed, the entrepreneurial model of co-operatives – with all its standards linked to corporate governance, financial management and relations among the enterprises belonging to this model and with the community – calls for a focus on institutional building, as well as consequent policies and regulation. Thirdly, it requires a process of re-embedding the economy into society, as citizens are – and should be – at the centre of co-operative enterprises. The third point calls for the question: why would mainstreaming be necessary? Do we really need co-operative enterprises? Why not simply accept having a 'one-size-fits-all' type of economic organisation for all human beings on earth? But, first of all, are co-operatives really marginal and why, if at all, is there a need for mainstreaming them?

On co-operatives being marginal to the mainstream, and to which mainstream

In the field of enterprises, co-operatives offer an entrepreneurial model that is coherent and stands out by itself, namely without any need to refer to any other existing entrepreneurial model. Firstly, with around a billion human beings as members of co-operatives active in all economic sectors and all types of activities, co-operatives are certainly neither a marginal phenomenon nor just a sector of the economy.

Secondly, as enterprises *of* (owned and controlled by) citizens and *for* (aimed at satisfying the needs and aspiration of) citizens, co-operatives have a mainstreaming basis which is far stronger than any competing entrepreneurial model: citizens.

Effective participation of ordinary citizens (or commoners, as they were first called) in civic life began in the UK with the gentry's revolution and on the European mainland with the French revolution. It gradually found its concrete application with the implementation of the universal suffrage (whose extension to women first occurred in the UK in 1918), and with a body of rights embodied by the UN Universal Declaration of Human Rights and by the constitution of virtually every country in the world which, in addition, establishes the idea of 'three powers' (executive, legislative and judiciary) of modern nation-states as a way to protect citizens from the abuse of power. We should remember that co-operatives' emergence has often been linked to social movements, such as the Chartist struggles for democratic voting that linked citizens to co-operatives: then, voting rights belonged only to men with property, and co-operatives provided the opportunity to access both property rights and political voting rights.

Before incorporating as an enterprise of producers, workers, consumers, users or any other type of stakeholders, a co-operative is 'an autonomous association of persons united voluntarily to meet their common economic, social and cultural needs and aspirations through a jointly owned and democratically controlled enterprise',[2] therefore an association of citizens, the latter figure being the common denominator among the various types of co-operative members–stakeholders.

The crisis, the debt trap and the issue of control

The crisis that flared up with the fall of Lehman Brothers in September 2008 brought about a plethora of consequences that are far from being over yet. What was initially a national financial crisis connected to falling housing prices in the USA between 2006 and 2007 extended to the rest of the world through the banking sector in 2008, unleashing a debt crisis domino effect. At the start of 2009, the steep plunge of the real economy led to rescue packages that weakened public finance and nation-state budgets. One year later, at the start of 2010, we began to see a string of EU member states undertaking structural reforms and falling under transnational supervision. Since mid-2011, currencies like the euro as well as the European social contracts in most European nations have been at stake. In 2014, at time of writing, currency fluctuation and devaluation have become tools to increase exports and restart national growth. The 2009 monetary policies are still in place with the expectation that interest rates may rise in 2015 or after, while many developing countries, African ones in particular, have fallen once again into unsustainable debt with foreseeable negative effects on how the future needs of those countries will be addressed.[3]

This crisis is probably the first truly global financial–economic crisis in history, understanding 'global' in the sense of a circular and closed world system, which goes beyond the sole concept of 'worldwide', and with inter-linkages making things come back as through a revolving door. This situation attracted our attention. In *Capital and the Debt Trap*, we first looked at the crisis as it developed and its consequences in the real economy (homes, jobs, pensions, enterprises etc.). Among the main mechanisms at its roots, we then identified three traps: a consumption trap, having its roots in inequality; a liquidity trap as a crucial moment in the crisis; and a 'debt trap' which the other two traps feed into. We observed that individuals, firms, regions and countries alike fell into these traps. At an even deeper layer, we then found out that the increasing debt practices seemed to be linked to a shift between ownership and control, where control had become more important than ownership, with increasing control by some actors while the stakeholders in the real economy (producers, consumers, workers and ordinary investors) were increasingly losing control.[4]

We then turned to co-operatives, where, by contrast to the dominant trend, we found a lesser tendency to fall into the 'debt trap' and a closer correspondence between ownership and control ('joint ownership and democratic control' by the same stakeholders, as the international co-operative definition mentioned above states). We selected the examples of two co-operatives – namely, Ceralep in industry in southern France and Natividad in fisheries in northern Mexico – and two co-operative groups – Desjardins in Canada's Quebec province and Mondragon in the Spanish Basque country.[5]

On the 'one-size-fits-all' economic organisation for all human beings

Our hypothesis to explain the higher resilience of co-operatives to the crisis rested on the co-operative operational principles and their practice as a coherent business model based on the strong association of personal wills and motivations. Yet, as pointed out by Stephen Yeo in chapter 4 of this book, these principles have been put in doubt by some.

This trend to put in question the co-operative principles is related to a wider view on the crisis itself and its causes. Although many scholars and public figures, and not least UN Secretary General Ban Ki Moon at the Rio 20 meeting in 2012, have acknowledged that the previous model of economic and social development is broken, not everybody takes such a wide-ranging view. For many others, debt is a circumstance that can be solved by more demand, more austerity or more investment on the supply side. Keynesians such as Skidelsky[6] and Krugman[7] believe that it is due to poor demand and liquidity. Austerity voices, in particular from

Germany, believe it to be a regional crisis of some European countries led astray by clientelism and lack of market discipline. Others, like Natixis, a French company providing excellent market analyses, take the view that Europe's problem is in fact the lack of supply of competitive export goods and services.[8] In the meantime, citizens bear the brunt of enduring recessions and lack of employment opportunities, while enterprises lack credit and markets. Still, the urgency in Europe has been to first bring down the interest rates that some EU countries must pay to refinance themselves while, at the global level, new regulation has sprung up to raise bank equity.

Increasing evidence has shown that debt, far from being a conjuncture, has become an intrinsic part of the system through various instruments and mechanisms that link together the financial and the real economy spheres, the world of production and that of consumption. 'Debtism', as we call it, touches upon all: public and private, states, local authorities, firms and households. The real economy is evaluated on the basis of liabilities and/or the capacity to claim back debts, and this on the basis of fair value carrying short-term expectations.[9]

Thus, when examining the debt phenomenon, we asked ourselves: why is it so, and how did it happen? Why do all actors use so much leverage, such as 30 to 40 times to 1 if not more? Even investment for innovation has been financed with little equity, as Stiglitz pointed out.[10]

Why? We found out that debt is functional in many ways: for example, to pass the risk onto others; to raise capital; to acquire firms without disbursing a penny; to avoid taxation; to remove liabilities from the balance sheet in order always to look good and better; to enforce restructuring by pouring debt onto acquired or invested companies, in particular shedding labour with the famous 15 per cent requested return to investors, and possibly closing these firms and taking them out of the global competition.[11]

And how has this been possible? We have observed a substantial shift in terms of control and ownership. Control has become more important than ownership itself. The word that comes along is control: control of global chains; privileged control of, and access to, resources; and control of information. As a result, ownership has shrunk to something almost residual. Besides, we have analysed how technological change was also affecting control,[12] arguing that technification is

> the necessary and progressive manifestation of a programmed determination over life. Technification of decision-making can adapt to continuing change because it functions on the basis of hypotheses. On such basis,

> machines can automatically relay orders to the 'market', to which humans should constantly keep adapting. In turn, human beings feel that they are losing control.[13]

Indeed, stakeholders in the real economy are scrambling to retain some share of control. When turning to the macro level and analysing how the market is being built, through competition for business scale within globalisation, we can observe that the building of global chains of production and distribution since the mid-1990s has been leading to structural control instead of direct control, thus blurring the line between ownership and control.[14]

In turn, in this crisis as well as in previous ones, co-operatives have demonstrated higher resilience compared to other enterprises. Since *Capital and the Debt Trap* was first published in 2011, this resilience has been demonstrated through a number of studies, both sectoral and inter-sectoral, at national, regional and world level. For example, the *Annual Report on Co-operation* in Italy produced by the Italian research institute CENSIS states that employment in co-operatives in Italy increased by 8 per cent between 2007 and 2011, compared with a decrease of 2.3 per cent in all types of enterprises. In 2012, employment in Italian co-operatives grew by a further 2.8 per cent, creating 36,000 new jobs compared to 2011, reaching a total of 1,341,000 jobs.[15]

In France, worker co-operatives and multi-stakeholder co-operatives (called collective interest co-operative societies) experienced a 4 per cent net employment increase in 2013 compared to the previous year and a 12.5 per cent one compared to 2009.[16] During the crisis, the survival rate of these co-operatives after three years has been 82.5 per cent compared to 66 per cent for all French companies, and 66.1 per cent after five years compared to 50 per cent for all French companies.[17]

In the banking sector, co-operative banks and credit unions have not only shown resilience, but have also continued to provide SMEs with credit, taking a more important role in this field than other banks.[18] In industry and services, resilience has been observed in terms of a lower level of enterprise bankruptcy, lower unemployment and lower indebtedness.[19]

The resilience of co-operatives to the crisis has been formally acknowledged by the European Parliament through a report adopted in July 2013, *On the Contribution of Cooperatives to Overcoming the Crisis*. The report underlines co-operatives' resilience in terms of both employment rates and business closures, and points out that, despite the crisis, 'cooperatives have been created in new and innovative sectors and that there is considerable evidence of this resilience, particularly in relation to cooperative banks and industrial and service cooperatives (worker cooperatives, social cooperatives and cooperatives formed by SMEs)'.[20]

The material gathered since the crisis began has also enabled us to understand more clearly the mechanisms behind such resilience. The study conducted by CECOP CICOPA-Europe in the industrial and service sectors in Europe suggests that this resilience relies on three levels and is stronger when all three levels are strong: at the micro level, rapid and democratic (and thus legitimate) decisions taken by worker-members when faced with the crisis; at the meso level, the creation and development of horizontal groups and mutualised entities such as business support institutions, consortia and federations; at the macro level, an effective national legal system for co-operatives with specific provisions that are particularly conducive to the development of such enterprises.[21]

From a more general and intersectoral viewpoint, since they are made up of stakeholders (producers, consumers, workers, apartment-dwellers, account-holders, credit-seekers, communities etc.), co-operatives necessarily tend to have a long-term vision and strategy, having a stake and interest in the generation of wealth, which is not only financial, but comprises all types of public and private goods and has a distributive dimension. Cross-checks and balances appear to be vital to build trust and legitimacy, being enacted through participation and education, not only information. This means not only 'assembleistic' democracy under the Athenian 'agora' component of democracy but also division of powers under the Roman 'res publica' one.

Co-operatives' comparatively higher difficulty in raising capital has led them to build expertise in how to prepare for crises beforehand and thus to value what they do, above all their human capital and their resources. In *Capital and the Debt Trap*, we considered cases that had experienced earlier and diverse crises, to try to find out whether this current crisis was different for them. Desjardins had survived the 1929 crisis, Mondragon had gone through crises during the 1980s and Spain's entry into the EU, Ceralep had been subject to a series of aggressive buyouts, and Natividad in Mexico had faced an environmental crisis. Their renewed resilience under this global financial crisis has been verified, and seems even stronger in horizontal groupings like Mondragon and Desjardins, which allow their constituent co-operatives to innovate and venture down new paths.

The case of Mondragon is particularly interesting to examine in terms of resilience, as the group is active in a series of industrial, service, agricultural, financial, retail, educational, and research and development (R&D) activities, many of which are globalised ones. Thanks to

Mondragon's common services, the pursuit of the internationalisation drive in the midst of the crisis has enabled most of its constituent co-operatives to firmly maintain their economic sustainability and position in the market, while the group's co-ordinated system of temporary or permanent redeployment of staff from one co-operative to another and welfare insurance for pre-pensioners has made it possible to not resort to layoffs.[22] Even in the case of the only major co-operative of the group (out of over 100) which has been liquidated as a consequence of the crisis in Europe, Fagor Electrodomésticos, the Mondragon group has succeeded in organising the redeployment of most worker-members from that co-operative to other ones within the group and in providing sufficient income compensation through Mondragon's own social security system. At the end of July 2014, eight months after the beginning of this co-operative's bankruptcy process, the group had already found solutions for 76 per cent of its worker-members: out of 1,895 worker-members of Fagor Electrodomésticos, 1,050 had been redeployed to other co-operatives within the group and another 400 individual solutions had been found, such as early retirement schemes. A solution was found for the remaining 24 per cent of the co-operative's worker-members before its liquidation.[23]

Now, let us go back to the crisis in Europe and to the measures that are put in place to sort out problems. Two models of financing are competing against each other; we can call one private equity and the other traditional banking. The Italian bank Monte dei Paschi di Siena is the symbol of this historical crossroads. This was the first bank in the world, created in the fifteenth century. Due to changes in accounting, globalised competition calling for enlarged business scales and the intake of toxic debt, at time of writing in 2014 it is failing after five centuries of existence.

The collapse of Bankia in Spain is another case in point. Formed in 2010 as a merger of seven Spanish financial institutions, Bankia was until recently Spain's fourth-largest bank and third-largest lender, with 12 million clients. In May 2012 it became insolvent, wiping out many small investors' assets. It abruptly revised its 2011 results from a 300 million euro profit to a 2.98 billion euro loss, and asked the state for 19 billion euros, making it the biggest bailout in Spanish history.[24]

The European Union's solution to the crisis has been to promote a transition from European economies where credit is primarily (generally more than two-thirds) provided by banks, also called 'intermediated', and in particular to SMEs, towards a US-style financing called 'disintermediated'. For example, private equity and other funds from the USA are providing liquidity to Europe through crowdfunding or in partnership with European banks, but these amounts are minimal compared to what SMEs require. Examples of partnerships have included Avenue Capital and JZ Capita, while other funds have bought the real estate platforms of Santander, CaixaBank, Bankia, Popular and Catalunya Banc in Spain. Yet, as the main goal is to help capital markets, this significant process may overhaul the entire economic system as economic entities will be required or forced to alter their practices and organisation.[25]

And yet, whereas the EU is trying to imitate another model, it does not want to copy the solutions to repair its side-effects, such as the Troubled Asset Relief Program (TARP, a US government programme to purchase assets and equity from financial institutions which takes toxic debt out of the balance sheets of the banks), or directing help to banks and firms with the US Federal Reserve System taking an active role to revamp the economy, to name just two.

The Bank of International Settlements said in the summer of 2014 that we were only halfway out of the crisis and that a new Lehman Brothers scenario could take place at any time.[26] Measures and outcomes seem to tread the old path and are not working. We need to face the harshest hypotheses: what if we find ourselves in a situation with no credit and little cash, if exports dwindle as the global economy has little growth, if the state further reduces its presence and if consumption, investment and savings keep falling? What if most banks in Europe go bust?

On the other hand, the model in place leads us into recurrent crises and an increasingly implosion-prone economic environment. Will we accept that we have to depend mostly on private angel investors that will control things at a distance? Will we become accustomed to continuous volatility because that is where the exchange traded funds and machines linked to the stock markets make most of their profits? Will we accept working conditions that can change instantly on an individual basis, because they will be accounted for as service units and liabilities? Are we ready to exchange our role as money-savers to become shareholders under the fair value regime and lose everything, like thousands of Spanish citizens did with Bankia? Is this the way forward?

Why it is so important to discuss the mainstreaming of co-operatives now

With the crisis, the situation has changed profoundly. Before looking for a new path, it would be wise to acknowledge that growth, as it is now understood and measured, is not tantamount to wealth generation for the long term, that capitalism today paradoxically does not seem to truly value any type of capital, that we should distinguish investment from pure financing, and above all that control is not the same as ownership.

Between the 1990s and the mid-2000s, the approach to co-operatives was somewhat similar to what may have also been applied to women and gender issues. Co-operatives were being left out of frameworks and policies; they were said to be lacking the same level of education and credit rating compared to those that investor-led companies could enjoy. The problem seemed to be the co-operative model itself and, thus, co-operatives were expected to change their attributes in order to be integrated into growth.

Since the crisis flared up, a new thinking in economic theories has appeared and the old concept of growth, based on gross domestic product (GDP), is being increasingly brought in question.[27] Indeed, GDP only indicates the transactions of goods and services (the multiplication of disease treatment brings about a rise in GDP), but gives no indication about inequality (even though the economic cost of inequality has been widely acknowledged after the global financial crisis), and provides no clue about looming debt crises, as occurred just before this one.[28] In addition, the GDP-based concept of growth tends to favour the entrepreneurial model based on stock markets (even though evidence has been given that growth and stock market returns were negatively correlated).[29]

In turn, the co-operative model's contribution to economic growth would be far better demonstrated if other indicators, such as local and regional capital accumulation, savings that are then reinvested or circulated in the economy, taxes, investments, local purchases, sustainable employment and demand, contribution to equality, resilience to shocks and so on, were included to measure growth.

Co-operatives, as explained above, can do much in times of crisis. They are comparatively more resilient and can be innovative and efficient. They can contribute to equality, job creation, livelihoods and wealth generation, sustainable resources management and lower levels of indebtedness, among other things. The previous tendency of casting co-operatives in a bad light was due to certain processes and structures. The solution is to change institutions, ideas and practices in support of plural and equal choices and opportunities.

With a plural and inclusive approach, co-operatives could mainstream their unique expertise in resilience, development and innovation to inspire others to adopt more resilient practices. In particular, clusters of SMEs could create synergies in horizontal groupings inspired by co-operative governance, or even in co-operatives of SMEs. Artisans, liberal professions and other self-employed producers of goods and services are increasingly opting for this co-operative form in order to mutualise common services (purchases, commercialisation, inputs, technology etc.) and therefore reinforce their economic sustainability and jobs.

This period is not for blindly following but for building a new future. Solutions may not come from old theories, policies and behaviour that have demonstrated their inefficiency, but from building a new path on the basis of shared ethical values that are then mainstreamed into structures and organisations akin to co-operatives' experiences. Co-operative entrepreneurship allows citizens more qualitative control over their lives and opportunities. In addition, the current system seems to be regulated on the basis of debt and leverage, raising the question of whether to call it 'capitalism' or 'debtism'. It is in this context that we must rethink what co-operatives offer to individuals, families and communities: which values, mechanisms, instruments and expertise can be mainstreamed to inspire, raise awareness and build a better future for all?

How can mainstreaming be monitored?

What should the mainstreaming of co-operatives cover? Elements to be considered include decision-making and other institutional practices, the monitoring and evaluation of co-operatives' value in accordance to the nature of the entity, access to resources including finance that respect co-operatives' principles, policy design and so on.

There is no defined framework of analysis yet to monitor the mainstreaming of co-operatives. The following is a tentative framework.

Meeting members' needs and ensuring members' control

- What is the activity profile of members, including volunteers, based on labour and economic sector, and activity by sex, age and other factors, as well as time spent on economic activities, and percentage of transactions with the co-operative compared to the member's transaction elsewhere of the same product or service?
- How are members' needs assessed in co-operatives, in terms of processes, priorities, participation and control?
- Access and control profile: can the access and control over resources, services and benefits be identified?
- Can factors influencing access and control (social, cultural, economic, gender, race etc.) be described?
- How are human needs interrelated through co-operatives so that response to one need strengthens the other? This can be related to health, education, nutrition, transport, employment, credit, balanced gender roles and so forth. For example, in some co-operatives women

artisans receive support to save, in both individual accounts and common funds, for a rainy day.

Internal management

- Liabilities and assets, equity and capital: who carries liability; who carries the assessment and forecasting scenarios; how do co-operatives enhance various types of capital at individual, household, and community levels? Is the entity fully and fairly represented in accounting and financial reporting?
- Relations with staff: is the staff of co-operatives sufficiently aware and sensitive towards the needs of co-operative members and co-operatives themselves? Are co-operatives and their members involved in the delivery of goods and services, are they involved in assessments? Is the staff sufficiently trained?
- Within the co-operatives and their networks, how are delivery, time and location, management information systems, flexibility and mediation designed, monitored, evaluated?

External environment

- Is there any certification or evaluation available for partners working with co-operatives and their members?
- Can members and co-operatives rely on adequate support in terms of resources and capabilities?
- Have institutions, both public and private, included co-operatives when they regulate or develop standards; do co-operatives appear in policy frameworks? Are co-operatives included in meetings, celebrations, recognition, assessments, dialogues, negotiations?

Mainstreaming co-operatives in the development goals

Co-operatives' mainstreaming in development goals will be as critical as their mainstreaming in other fields, such as education and research. Whereas previous approaches to development have shown their limitations, very substantial contributions to development goals can be brought about by recognising that co-operative enterprises are embedded and participative; that they create and maintain durable jobs; that they provide timely information, education, training and a skills upgrading path to their members; and that they are resilient and characterised by long-term accumulation and wide distribution of wealth.

Given its widely recognised role in development, the issue of employment, in particular, is worth underlining. CICOPA's *Co-operatives and Employment: A Global Report* estimates that co-operative employment, both full time and part time, involves at least 250 million people in the world, including self-employed producers who organise their production together within the scope of co-operatives. Co-operative employment makes up almost 12 per cent of total employment in the G20. In addition, the report points out that such employment tends to be durable and to be well distributed between rural and urban areas, two fundamental elements in appraising the contribution of employment to local and regional development, beyond sheer employment numbers.[30]

In regions where co-operatives have attained a particularly important critical mass, such as the Basque country in Spain (with the Mondragon group alone making up around 3 per cent of the region's GDP) and Emilia Romagna in Italy (where co-operatives' contribution to both GDP and employment is around 15 per cent), we also find a particularly high GDP per capita (the second highest in their respective countries after Madrid and Milan in 2007).[31] Even more importantly, co-operatives' contribution to regional development is due to the fact that 'co-operative systems create and maintain locally innumerable transactions that provide transparent access to flows of information, create socialized knowledge and innovation, all of which, in turn, generate collective visions, strategies and systemic capabilities'.[32] This is linked to Putnam's notion of 'social capital', which he developed precisely in studying the Emilia-Romagna model.[33]

Co-operatives' role in gradually transforming informal economic activities into formal ones is also a fundamental contribution of co-operatives to development, not only because formalisation is linked to more social and legal protection to workers and members, but also because it is linked to long-term economic sustainability and the fight against indebtedness and debt bondage. Since their origin two centuries ago, co-operatives have generally provided their members with the highest level of formality that the members could possibly attain considering their national conditions. In the Self-Employed Women's Association's women's co-operatives in India, the gradual formalisation of the members' jobs and economic activities has clearly improved the economic sustainability of their co-operatives.[34] In Southern Italy, some co-operatives manage assets confiscated from the mafia. This legalisation drive is fundamental as it 'links together civil engagement, employment and entrepreneurship'.[35]

Another fundamental dimension of development is the environment. As enterprises based on the association of people embedded in the community, which do not delocalise and are open to all as long as they remain sustainable, co-operatives are among the best economic organisations to deal with scarce resources. They can manage resources sustainably and peacefully because all are involved and control is thus attainable through active participation and accountability.[36] The Natividad fishermen and divers co-operative in Mexico is a very valuable case, showing that limited de-growth was actually not such, as it led to industrialisation and development soon after.[37]

The need for leadership

Is co-operatives' mainstreaming only an issue of cultural transformation or is leadership necessary to achieve it? This is another question with no easy answers. Leadership could be seen as a field of power aimed at building co-ordination. The idea of a 'field of power' enables us to overcome individualistic assumptions. By focusing on both the sources of power (personal or institutional, individual or collective) and representation, we can see leadership as a relational quality within a field in which power may be potentially exerted. This can be applied to individuals, coalitions and institutions. This conceptualisation could be applied to a co-operative environment.

The first function of leadership is co-ordination, both in decision-making and in conflict resolution. In addition, leadership carries both an element of consensus, since it must be able to obtain compliance from others, and sometimes the option of coercive power to enforce sanctions. Leadership pertains to the person or institution that is able to take an active role in structuring the priorities (issues and means) of the prevailing agenda in which normative rules are usually embodied, while the capacity to structure and decide the priorities depends on the possession of important information, usually based on a privileged situational point in the flow of data and communication.

As Elinor Ostrom said in 1990:

> What is missing from the policy analyst's toolkit – and from the set of accepted, well-developed theories of human organisation – is an adequately specified theory of collective action whereby a group of principals can organise themselves voluntarily to retain the residuals of their efforts. Examples of self-organized enterprises abound. Most law firms are obvious examples … . Most cooperatives are also examples … . But until a theoretical explanation – based on human choice – for self-organized and self-governed enterprises is fully developed and accepted, major policy decisions will continue to be undertaken with a presumption that individuals cannot organize themselves and always need to be organized by external authorities.[38]

Mainstreaming in the business world may be seen as a proactive process or strategic approach to raise equality and benevolent regard from others towards plural forms of enterprise, including co-operatives. It is undertaken by all peaceful means of dialogue, advocacy, education, information, training, policy development, research, planning, implementation and monitoring. Freedom of entrepreneurship entails the existence of different types of enterprise and various ways in which human beings can organise themselves. Beyond the utilitarian goals of development, wealth generation and distribution, the solidarity and resilience which co-operatives have delivered throughout their history and across the world, striving to satisfy the needs and aspirations of human beings and carrying the values of sustainability and embeddedness, will prove to be their lasting promise.

Notes

1 C. Sanchez Bajo and B. Roelants, *Capital and the Debt Trap: Learning from Cooperatives in the Global Crisis* (Basingstoke and New York: Palgrave Macmillan, 2013).
2 ILO (International Labour Organization), *R193: Promotion of Cooperatives Recommendation, 2002*, art 2, www.ilo.org/dyn/normlex/en/f?p=NORMLEXPUB:12100:0::NO::P12100_INSTRUMENT_ID:312531 (accessed 2 February 2016).
3 Jubilee Debt Campaign, *Don't Turn the Clock Back: Analysing the Risks of the Lending Boom to Impoverished Countries* (10 October 2014), http://jubileedebt.org.uk/reports-briefings/report/dont-turn-clock-back-analysing-risks-lending-boom-impoverished-countries (accessed 2 February 2016).
4 Sanchez Bajo and Roelants, *Capital and the Debt Trap*, chapters 1 to 3.
5 Ibid., chapters 4 to 8.
6 R. Skidelsky, *Keynes: The Return of the Master* (London: Penguin Books, 2009).
7 P. Krugman, *The Return of Depression Economics and the Crisis of 2008* (London: Penguin Books, 2008).
8 'La crise selon Patrick Artus' (The Crisis by Patrick Artus), interview with Patrick Artus (Director of Natixis), *Le Monde* (13 February 2010).
9 Fair value is a valuing system based on 'market assessment of future short-term expectations, and no longer on the system of historic book accounting. In a crisis, the fair value brings about a vicious pro-cyclical circle through which, every three months, a new financial assessment takes place in a context of uncertainty and falling value of the business, leading to further sales of assets in order to keep the enterprise alive. Thus, banks started hoarding cash and reducing their balance sheets by selling assets, leading to fire-sale prices. In addition, banks reduced credit availability, required more collateral and raised interest rates. As a consequence, firms largely depending on credit lines had to cut costs by reducing investment and laying off workers' (Sanchez Bajo and Roelants, *Capital and the Debt Trap*, p. 15).
10 J. Stiglitz, *Information and the Change in the Paradigm in Economics*, Nobel Prize

Lecture (8 December 2001), p. 513, www.nobelprize.org/nobel_prizes/economic-sciences/ laureates/2001/stiglitz-lecture.html (accessed 29 February 2016).
11 Sanchez Bajo and Roelants, *Capital and the Debt Trap*, chapter 2.
12 U. Galimberti, *Psiche et techne, l'uomo nell'età della tecnica* [Psyche and techne: man in the age of technology] (Milan: Feltrinelli, 2002), p. 712.
13 Sanchez Bajo and Roelants, *Capital and the Debt Trap*, p. 86.
14 W. Ruigrok and R. van Tulder, *The Logic of International Restructuring* (London: Routledge, 1995).
15 Censis, *Primo rapporto sulla Cooperazione in Italia* [First report on co-operation in Italy] (Rome: Censis, 2012).
16 See CG Scop's press release, 2013: Dynamisme et pérennité économique pour les Sociétés coopératives et participatives [2013: Dynamism and economic sustainability for cooperatives and participatory societies] (5 June 2014), www.les-scop.coop/sites/fr/espace-presse/Bilan_chiffre-2013 (accessed 2 February 2016).
17 CECOP (European Confederation of Workers' Co-operatives, Social Co-operatives and Social and Participative Enterprises), *Business Transfers to Employees under the Form of a Cooperative in Europe: Opportunities and Challenges* (Brussels: CECOP Publications, 2013).
18 J. Birchall, *Resilience in a Downturn: The Power of Financial Cooperatives* (Geneva: ILO, 2013).
19 CICOPA (International Organisation of Industrial, Artisanal and Service Producers' Cooperatives), *A Qualitative Analysis on the Economic Situation of CICOPA Members, 2012* (Brussels: CICOPA, 2012), www.cicopa.coop/A-qualitative-analysis-on-the-1196.html (accessed 2 February 2016); B. Roelants, H. Eum, E. Terrasi and D. Dovgan, *The Resilience of the Cooperative Model* (Brussels: CECOP Publications, 2012).
20 *On the Contribution of Cooperatives to Overcoming the Crisis*, European Parliament report (July 2013), www.europarl.europa.eu/sides/getDoc.do?type=TA&reference=P7-TA-2013-0301&language=EN&ring=A7-2013-0222 (accessed 2 February 2016).
21 Roelants et al., *Resilience of the Cooperative Model.*
22 Sanchez Bajo and Roelants, *Capital and the Debt Trap*, chapter 8.
23 B. Roelants, H. Eum and E. Terrasi, *Cooperatives and Employment: A Global Report* (Brussels and Lévis: CICOPA and Desjardins, 2014), pp. 94–5; and personal communications from J. Marcos and M. Lezamiz in 2015.
24 'Spain's loss-making Bankia vows transparency', BBC News website (26 May 2012), www.bbc.com/news/world-europe-18216793 (accessed 2 February 2016).
25 J. de Portillo, 'La financiación no bancaria a pymes se abre camino' [Non-bank financing to SMEs on its way], *Cinco Días* (30 November 2014), http://cincodias.com/cincodias/2014/10/02/mercados/1412273056_056147.html (accessed 2 February 2016); see also I. G. Zuriaga: 'La financiación de pymes y la crisis' [The financing of SMEs and the crisis], www.fef.es/new/publicaciones/papeles-de-la-fundacion/item/download/865_db1acd5b1de6a32fb829302cead2ba63.html (accessed 2 February 2016).
26 A. Evans-Pritchard, 'BIS chief fears fresh Lehman from worldwide debt surge',

Daily Telegraph (13 July 2014), www.telegraph.co.uk/finance/markets/10965052/Bank-for-International-Settlements-fears-fresh-Lehman-crisis-from-worldwide-debt-surge.html (accessed 2 February 2016).

27 Dēmos, *Beyond GDP: New Measures for a New Economy* (New York: Dēmos, 2011).

28 C. Sanchez Bajo, 'Placing cooperatives in up-to-date theoretical debates' in B. Roelants, ed., *Cooperative Growth for the 21st Century* (Brussels: International Cooperative Alliance and CICOPA, 2013), p. 15.

29 S. Johnson, 'Rising GDP not always a boon for equities', *Financial Times* (14 April 2013), www.ft.com/intl/cms/s/0/8b5ae298-a065-11e2-a6e1-00144feabdc0.html (accessed 2 February 2016).

30 Roelants et al., *Resilience of the Cooperative Model.*

31 Eurostat Newsrelease, 'Regional GDP per inhabitant in 2007' (18 February 2010), STAT/10/25.

32 Sanchez Bajo and Roelants, *Capital and the Debt Trap*, pp. 219–20.

33 R. Putnam, *Making Democracy Work: Civil Traditions in Modern Italy* (Princeton: Princeton University Press, 1993).

34 Roelants et al., *Resilience of the Cooperative Model*, p. 87.

35 C. Sanchez Bajo, *Cooperatives in the Post-2015 Millennium Development Framework*, presentation for the UN Expert Group Meeting on 'The Role of Cooperatives in Sustainable Development: Contributions, Challenges and Strategies' (Nairobi, 8–10 December 2014) (Mimeo), pp. 7–8.

36 Ibid., p. 6.

37 Sanchez Bajo and Roelants, *Capital and the Debt Trap*, chapter 5.

38 E. Ostrom, *Governing the Commons* (Cambridge: Cambridge University Press, 1990), pp. 24–5.

3

Our agencies: persuasion and the value of a concept to mainstreaming co-operation

Philip Grant

What is to mainstream, if not to persuade? From the straitened circumstances of his fascist prison cell, Italian Marxist thinker Antonio Gramsci famously argued that contemporary intellectuals, 'the organic intellectuals' he saw as necessary to the success of a communist workers' and peasants' movement, ought not to be orators in the classical mould, but 'permanent persuader[s]'.[1] Today the principal agent of a transition to a better world cannot be 'the Party'. Nonetheless, in an age of austerity, menaced by multiple forms of violence, from aggressive wars to gender violence to the ongoing structural violence of increasing inequalities of wealth and income, in a world threatened with massive environmental degradation, the need for permanent, effective persuasion is overwhelming.[2] Co-operatives and co-operative movements across the world have a major role to play, in word and in deed, as exemplars of how things not only might, but *can* be done differently.

This much is simple; the trick, of course, is to know how to persuade. When I began thinking about co-operatives as agents in the struggle to address the multiple injustices that beset us, I was naively optimistic. It was 2012: the United Nations' International Year of Co-operatives. Preparing to move to the UK from the US, and reflecting on what forms of social organisation might best redress inequalities of wealth and power, I read up on various initiatives in co-operation. In the UK, it seemed, there was a wave of official encouragement for co-operatives. Both the governing Conservative–Liberal Democrat coalition and the main opposition Labour Party (long allied to the country's Co-operative Party) had, since the financial crisis, been talking enthusiastically about co-operatives and mutuals as an important part of the solution to the problems the crisis had revealed, created, and exacerbated. A gate of opportunity had opened up, I felt, and with a bit of a push, co-operatives would swarm through it. At the time of writing, over two years later, I am a director of a small consumer co-operative wind energy company in southern Scotland, and a member of a rapidly growing political party among whose policies are a workers' 'right to buy' businesses up for sale, in the expectation they be turned into producer co-operatives. Despite this, I am now pessimistic.

One reason is the local context. The promises of the major political parties have not led to a dramatic transformation in the organisation of commerce. Meanwhile, The Co-operative Bank is no longer entirely owned by The Co-operative Group, the world's largest consumer co-operative, but majority owned and controlled by hedge funds which provided funds to prevent it going bust (see Webster et al., chapter 16, this volume). The Bank's ambitious expansion plans were stopped in their tracks after it posted massive losses, mainly stemming from its takeover of a mutually owned financial institution, the Britannia Building Society. This is a tale more reminiscent of the world of joint-stock corporations chasing the illusion of ever-increasing short-term profitability than of the sustainable, ethically superior alternative co-operatives are supposed to provide.

Another reason for my pessimism is the continuing drive worldwide towards the harmonisation of trade rules through treaties such as the Trans-Pacific Partnership (TPP) and the Transatlantic Trade and Investment Partnership (TTIP), treaties whose presupposition is that the central agents of the prosperity and well-being of humanity are transnational corporations whose shares are traded on stock exchanges. Thousands of column inches are devoted to the analysis of disparities of wealth and power, but policy action to end them is scarce indeed. Where there are signs of successful insurgencies – the election of Syriza in Greece, for example, and the subsequent referendum rejection of EU bailout terms – these are met with the familiar refrain of 'capitalist realism': it cannot be any other way. Either austerity, or bust.

Against this background, if pessimism is justified, is there no space for (to speak with Gramsci again) an optimism of the will? Might not co-operatives of various kinds still be part of the solution? At least in the UK, mainstreaming has not proved as straightforward a task as it had seemed to some a few years ago. What I offer here in response is a possible path towards the formation of co-operators as permanent persuaders. Part of the problem co-operators face is that in many parts of the world they operate in an environment where what they advocate flies in the face of common sense. This common sense holds that the best way to innovate and create prosperity is through the joint-stock company, funded through capital markets, controlled and owned by shareholders whose goal is simple profit maximisation. This idea has become common sense because it has long benefited from political, legal, media and other forms of institutional support. It is true that co-operatives, benefit corporations and social enterprises increasingly challenge this received wisdom, but their voice remains marginal. To counteract the ossified common sense of capitalist enterprise, a massive counter-hegemonic effort is required, one which will, however, be made up of many smaller initiatives.

Here, therefore, I offer the concept of 'agency' as a tool with which to map, to persuade and to implement: one part of a Gramscian 'theoretical–practical nexus' in which theory and practice constantly inform and transform each other.[3] Having explored how agency in its multiple meanings can help generate relevant questions for co-operators, with these questions in mind I then discuss an ongoing challenge to the viability of producer co-operatives in the UK.

Why 'agency'? The varieties of a concept

Agency has been one of the keywords of the human sciences in the English-speaking world since the mid-1980s. Befitting a concept that has migrated through various disciplinary and interdisciplinary fields, its meaning is plastic. Generally 'agency' refers to the human 'capacity to act', to which, however, there are important exceptions. It is this range of meaning that makes it so valuable. Certainly, it conveys a sense of empowerment, an ability to effect change, to shape the world in the way agents would like, and often in a manner that challenges prevailing norms. Yet this concept also contains a variety of complementary and sometimes contradictory meanings. These include the imposition of limits on action; the necessary contingency of the word, and the need to take this into account when planning action; and an orientation to others, an orientation that may require mutuality rather than the assertion of an autonomous individual will. A brief review of these multiple meanings generates a series of questions that could be of value to advocates of co-operation seeking to advance their cause. At its most basic, the concept refers to the relative weighting of human initiative as determinant of the course of history on the one hand, and forces beyond human control on the other. The latter may be environmental, climatic, material or socio-economic. Notwithstanding debates over the exact relationship or specific formulations of the problem,[4] most analysts tend to assume a balance of some sort between structure and agency, something not too dissimilar to Marx's famous observation about humans making history, but not under circumstances of their own choosing.[5]

A related usage is the feminist insistence, especially in second-wave feminism, on women's agency, an insistence that women not be written out of history, nor portrayed by historians as passive, downtrodden victims unable to shape their own ends in a world where only men matter.[6] Here, agency has a positive ethical value, the ability of women to resist or undermine the structures of patriarchal domination. This continues to be the case even in third-wave feminism and queer theory with their focus on the instability of gender identities and the possibilities for subversion and transgression of dominant gender norms.[7] Feminists have also complicated the picture of the human agent as someone who exercises her will in resisting dominant values and structures. She may equally be someone who cultivates a sense of virtuous selfhood in submitting to patriarchal norms, as Saba Mahmood argued provocatively in relation to the Egyptian women's mosque movement of the late 1990s, thus decoupling agency from resistance.[8]

More pertinent for co-operators, however, is the argument that agency should not be equated with individual autonomy, but that it may also be understood in a mutual sense, as implying other agents as part of one's own agency. Thus working-class women in England between 1750 and 1850 did not seek inclusion in liberal citizenship, but exercised a deeply political agency that was rooted in extended ties of (fictive) kinship, and an emphasis on a collective life, group action, and values of compassion and love that undermined the bourgeois divide between the 'private' sphere of family and the 'public' sphere of paid work and politics.[9] For all their differences, these versions of agency have in common the assumption that agency is human agency. There is an important strain of contemporary social thought, however, which insists that to see agency as an exclusively human characteristic is to engage in an 'asymmetrical' analysis.[10] It is not only human 'subjects' that are agents, but non-human 'objects' too. Paradoxical as it might seem, non-human objects can also be subjects of an action.

While attributing agency to objects might seem counter-intuitive, it is important to remember that the agency involved here is not a question of conscious, rational, pre-planned action. Bruno Latour's study of the spread of Pasteur's microbiology in late nineteenth-century France offers a lucid explanation of what the agency of the non-human can involve.[11] He compares Pasteur with the Russian general Kutuzov in Tolstoy's *War and Peace*: far from his defeat of Napoleon's forces being the result of following a pre-determined battle plan, it was the consequence of mistakes, accidents, muddles, lost orders, under-preparation and various other contingencies. Similarly with Pasteur and the spread of his techniques for combating microbial infection: it was never a case of a single genius patiently putting to work a single rational scientific method until the problems he and his contemporaries in the medical profession faced were solved. Rather, for a transformation to be effected in medical science, a whole array of forces combined in ways that no one could foresee exactly, let alone plan: microbes, diseases, scientists, doctors, patients, science as an idea, networks of funding, researchers, parliamentarians, periodicals, laboratory equipment.

This, and related work in the fields of economics and finance,[12] not only breaks down the subject/object, human agent/non-human non-agent split, it also reminds us there is no corresponding split between, on one hand, the messy and contingent world of politics and ethics, and, on the other, the rational objectivity of science. This should not lead to the conclusion that, since everything is contingent and complicated, nothing can be done to effect change – in the present case, mainstreaming co-operation. Rather it is a reminder that, while the only thing guaranteed is that the future will not unfold according to even the best designed of rational plans, those forces that resist the mainstreaming of co-operation, that hold co-operatives to be at best marginal, are no less contingent and messy. The task, then, is to mobilise the same kinds of networks of people, ideas, models, institutions and funding that the mainstream currently mobilises.

Finally, it is important to remember that the original sense of the word 'agency', as it emerged in late seventeenth-century philosophy, had nothing to do with humans at all. Rather it referred to the setting in motion of something by an agent. Agency is the 'acting force', the 'efficient' or 'effective' cause of action.[13] While here agency is a property of human and non-human indiscriminately, its form is simpler than the agency of the actor-network theorists: here the agent is an instrument, something by means of which an action causes an effect. In this sense, 'agency' is not dissimilar to the agency of contemporary economics. Here, an agent is an individual or firm acting at the behest of a principal, another individual or firm;[14] the authority to act is thus delegated by the principal, even as she expects to benefit from the action of the agent, who usually therefore requires remuneration. The widespread contemporary nature of this phenomenon has spawned a branch of rational-choice economics, 'agency theory', itself involving a number of different approaches, designed to analyse problems of control where authority is delegated in this way.[15]

A classic case of a principal/agent split is the joint stock company, where shareholders (principal) employ management as their agents in order to carry out the day-to-day running of the business. Consumer co-operatives also exhibit a principal/agent split, but unlike joint stock companies are able to mitigate weaknesses (diffusion of responsibility, lack of oversight) through practice of the ethical principles of co-operation, for example in having flatter internal structures, or being able to internalise externalities. As examples of the latter may be cited: providing services where markets have otherwise failed, employing marginal populations, undertaking costly practices to protect the environment, or introducing fair trade into the supply chain.[16]

Bearing in mind these various dimensions of the concept of agency permits the generation of a series of questions that all those wishing to mainstream co-operation might ask of themselves and of the situation they find themselves in. Who and/or what are the agents here? What capacity for action do they have? What are the limits on that capacity? On whose behalf do they act? What motivates their actions (where motivations can be ascribed)? For whose benefit do they act? To what other agents are their actions oriented? What are the moral dimensions of their agency? With this in mind, I now turn to an ongoing situation in the UK whose resolution would involve righting an injustice done to people being exploited by the worker-owners of a large business. Being able to demonstrate that this situation is not inevitable would be of great value in advancing the cause of co-operation.

Inevitability: problem and solution

Many analysts of the international financial crisis of 2008–09, and accompanying recession, have pointed out that there is a consensus among politicians, policymakers, central bankers, economists, bankers, journalists and others, that while the globalisation and financialisation of the world economy over the past generation have had at times unfortunate effects, notably during the crisis, 'we' have no choice but to deregulate commerce and deepen and strengthen financial markets; such an approach is proven to be the best way to generate economic growth, and the nature of international competition is such that if one country tries to opt for a different path, it will quickly fall behind and find itself adopting the very policies it initially rejected.[17]

The concept of agency demonstrates its usefulness when faced with this discourse of inevitability. A drive to mainstream co-operation with agency at its centre can contest and neutralise these claims to inevitability, by insisting that alternatives cannot only be conceived, they can be designed and operated successfully too. The spectre of inevitability has long been present in critiques of co-operation. Take, for example, an ongoing controversy in the United Kingdom, to do with the employment by the country's largest worker-owned business, the John Lewis

Partnership, an operator of middle- to upper-market department stores and supermarkets in the UK's major cities and towns, of contract labour to clean its premises, this labour therefore being excluded from the distribution of the co-operative's profits in the form of its annual 'bonus' to its 'partners' (employee-owners).

This controversy first entered a wider public consciousness in September 2012 when a prominent left-of-centre journalist, Polly Toynbee, drew attention to this issue in the *Guardian* newspaper,[18] pointing out that, besides being excluded from the bonus and other benefits accruing to the partners of the business, most of the cleaners were being paid only £6.08 an hour, well below a living wage, and had recently begun to organise to demand a living wage of £8.30 an hour.[19] The advocates of inevitability have argued that this situation is what naturally happens to worker co-operatives. A few months after Toynbee's article had stirred up controversy, an economist called Frederick Guy explained that John Lewis had fallen foul of the weaknesses of something called the 'Illyrian model'.[20] He summarised the problem thus:

> Since the 1950s, economists have speculated that a profitable employee-owned business would not grow as much as the same business would if it were owned by capitalists, because the incumbent workers would not want to dilute their individual shares of profits by adding new worker-owners. This argument is known as the Illyrian Model ... Within a capitalist economy, workers who happen to own their business can try to have the best of both worlds. By hiring non-owner employees whenever an opportunity for growth presents itself a two-tier system is produced – owners and non-owners – and this has been widely seen as leading to the degeneration of the worker-owned company, marking its gradual descent into capitalist ownership. Notice that the Illyrian model is both a prediction about the fate that will befall worker-owned enterprises (they will either stay small, or stop being worker-owned), and an explanation for why worker ownership is not more widespread.[21]

This argument harks back to debates between Eastern and Western bloc economists in the 1950s. Applying their models to non-capitalist economies, neoclassically trained Western economists developed typologies of capitalist and socialist economies based on the same assumptions that had originally developed within the anti-socialist neoclassical economics of the late nineteenth and early twentieth centuries, eventually engaging in dialogue with their Soviet and Eastern European counterparts.[22] One of these was a US economist, Benjamin Ward, who, after research in Yugoslavia, published an article in the *American Economic Review* in which he explored different types of firm in the Eastern bloc.[23] He was particularly impressed by what he termed the 'reformed

Yugoslav model' of the firm, a neoclassical 'market socialism' similar to that described theoretically by earlier economists Enrico Barone and Oskar Lange. He argued that this model was legislated for in a 1954 Yugoslav law, but in practice was unfortunately distorted because of state intervention. His article on what he dubbed the 'Illyrian model' was broadly in favour of this unrealised version of market socialism, with its nationalised means of production, workers councils managing firms, and individual workers working to maximise their own income from their equal share of firms' profits from a competitive market.

At the same time, he also argued that the system had a dangerous flaw, namely that it ultimately incentivised workers to maximise their own incomes, which would mean that it would be more advantageous for them not to take on more employees for their enterprises, diluting their share of the profits. This is the problem that Guy refers to above in the context of John Lewis and its outsourced cleaning operations.[24] It seems that the company, despite being a worker-owned firm, now acts like a capitalist principal, employing others as its less-well-remunerated agents in order to maximise the owners' returns. Toynbee offered anecdotal evidence of this in her article, remarking that one partner had indicated that many colleagues believed 'taking in another 3,000 partners will dilute the value of the bonus and perks paid to the existing 70,000', while others even believed cleaners do not deserve 'the status of partnership'.[25]

Ward's argument, and Guy's invocation of it,[26] while sympathetic to the idea of worker-owned and -managed businesses, nonetheless imply an inevitability to the problem: reach a certain size, and a worker co-operative cannot grow any more, since its employee owners start, selfishly but rationally, retaining their increasing profits for themselves. The business grows, if at all, only through exploiting non-owners' labour. This inevitability is implied by the abstract nature of the 'model', whose workings start from clearly stated premises and follow a logical order consistent with neoclassical economics' description and justification of itself as a science. It is also implied by the contemporary economist's employment of it: don't be surprised, he seems to be saying, that the few maximise their incomes at the expense of the many – it's exactly what the model predicts.

The problem is, in the first instance, with the model of human behaviour this presupposes. That is to say that human beings will always seek to maximise their own wealth, income or possessions; indeed, the very definition of rationality being that they do so. Whereas a corporation owned by outside shareholders will seek to maximise profits, and therefore constantly seek to grow, a corporation owned by its employees will only seek to maximise profits accruing to each individual member.

In both cases they act rationally, whence the supposed inferiority of the Illyrian model. The trouble is, as anthropologists, sociologists, geographers, and heterodox, behavioural and political economists have pointed out for decades now, this one-dimensional model of human rationality does not accord with our empirical observations of human action in the world.[27] This is not to say that many, if not all, of us do not act in this narrowly self-maximising way some of the time, under certain conditions; indeed, there is some evidence to show that economists' models and their take-up by various firms and institutions may contribute to the production of self-maximising individuals.[28] Nonetheless, even in societies dominated by capitalist organisation of production and consumption, all of us act in other ways much of the time too – in a spirit of mutual aid, for example, or sacrificing our time or ourselves for others' well-being.[29] Monetary incentives, even in our hyper-individualised society, are far from the sole driver of our actions.[30]

Here is not the place to explore the wide range of human behaviour that falls outside neoclassical economics' base assumption of self-maximising rationality; it is important to note that it exists, and is widespread. Note also that in the quotation from Toynbee above, while many John Lewis employees fear dilution of their profit share, by implication many others do not. The problem also lies in the assumption made by users of economic models generally, namely that taking a set of premises (rational actors, supply–demand equilibrium) from one context (the late-nineteenth-century neoclassical economics that developed out of utilitarian philosophy) and transplanting them into another (postwar Yugoslavia) allows for the development of general rules about the viability or otherwise of all worker-owned businesses. This lack of empirical context was later criticised by Yugoslav economists like Branko Horvat, who called for more empirical studies to test the validity of the model.[31]

One dimension of the problem that Guy and others miss, moreover, is that it did not originate with the Yugoslav debates of the 1950s, but goes back to British socialist organising and theorising at the end of the nineteenth century. Amid debates within the British co-operative movement over whether consumer or producer co-operatives were the best form of organisation, Beatrice Potter (later Webb) argued that 'associations of producers' would all inevitably degenerate into associations of 'small masters' exploiting wage labour hired outside of their original democratic, self-governing corporate form, an argument she first advanced in 1891, before making it more forcefully in 1921 alongside her then husband, Sidney Webb.[32] The Webbs (as they became known) were influential figures in early twentieth-century British socialism, and their views coloured approaches to co-operation for decades subsequently. Yet

Derek Jones long ago showed that, contrary to the Webbs' arguments, producer co-operatives in Britain from the late nineteenth century until the 1960s demonstrated increasing employee ownership, and that the median age of majority worker-owned firms was higher than that of comparable capitalist businesses.[33] The Webbs' antipathy to worker co-operatives stemmed from their experience of the failure of earlier associations, and also from their unflinching support of vertically integrated co-operatives dominated by retail businesses over other forms of co-operative organisation.

Read in this light, the John Lewis case presents a double challenge. On the one hand, it is a challenge to advocates of worker co-operatives, as an example of the phenomenon that first the Webbs and then the Illyrian model economists had identified: an association of producer-owners excluding some of their colleagues from the benefits and responsibilities of ownership, while exploiting their wage-labour to grow their own profits. On the other, it is a challenge to co-operators to show that this phenomenon is by no means inevitable.

The concept of agency addresses these problems. It does so firstly by being rooted in an anthropological tradition of holistic enquiry, adapted to the contemporary world, and drawing on other, related scholarly traditions. Its premise is that it is impossible to isolate economics from law, culture, society, ethics and politics, with all their intrinsic dynamism. Against this background, agency asks us: what kind of ethical selves and frameworks exist in the world, and what kind of selves and frameworks would we like to see in the world? It helps us challenge the dismal vision of inevitably self-maximising worker-owners, pointing to plausible alternatives.

Our politics then becomes a question of how to bring this transformation about, how to persuade John Lewis partners, for example, that seeing individuals' profit share diminished is nonetheless worthwhile, because it is in keeping with the ethos of worker-owned businesses: an ethos which rejects the idea that some should control, others be controlled, the former richly rewarded, the latter not. It is worthwhile, too, because it does not necessarily harm the financial health or growth prospects of the business, but even potentially enhances them, by making John Lewis an attractive place to work for all who contribute to its success, including cleaners. A focus on agency, the capacity to change things for the better under given conditions, would propose solutions: not just taking cleaning in-house, as Toynbee suggests, but also having John Lewis help cleaners set up their own worker co-operative cleaning company, in accordance with the principle of mutual aid between co-operatives.[34]

More generally, agency can be used to map out the contours of the controversy and draw conclusions both for present activism and future planning. Cleaning remains a poorly remunerated form of labour performed mainly by women, often immigrant women. The feminist senses of agency are therefore highly pertinent. Agency as directed towards other agents suggests the forging of alliances for mutual ends: most obviously between the cleaners themselves, but also with sympathetic owner-partners of the business whose votes will be necessary to rectify the situation, as well as with external campaigning organisations. Agency as confrontation and subversion of patriarchal norms is also highly relevant: the most feminised parts of the workforce are the least well paid; and the better paid a particular segment of the workforce is, the greater the number of men involved, in a hierarchy beginning with retail staff, rising up through middle to senior management and finally to the extremely well-remunerated male chairman.[35] The struggle to achieve at least a living wage for outsourced cleaners, and by extension the challenges posed by the Webbs and the Illyrian model, are therefore feminist issues.

When it comes to agency as including non-human actors, advocates of co-operation may ask which of these are most important here. Which agents contribute to the sense of inevitable failure of worker-owned businesses? They surely include the authority of economists and economics, and more specifically their models. They also include the failure of the old Eastern bloc as socio-economic alternative, and the corresponding entrenchment of the assumptions of neoclassical economics as common sense: formal economic rationality as a dominant value, and the idea that profit maximisation necessarily helps all in society, in a context where the highest end of politics is gross domestic product (GDP) growth.

If, in order to generate a counter-hegemonic movement, co-operators then ask what networks of agents they can activate, and how to generate positive surprises out of all the messy contingency of the world, it is helpful for them to think of themselves as *designers* rather than *ex nihilo* creators, not as designing something from scratch, but inevitably working with pre-existing materials and systems – as redesigners.[36] In this case, non-human agents include the values of mutuality and sympathy, the critique of selfishness, the slogan 'people not profit', examples (not necessarily the most prominent ones) of co-operative businesses that do 'work', solidarity campaigns,[37] and ultimately a cogent, rigorously justified vision of human flourishing that builds on but goes beyond contemporary distrust of finance and large corporations, or critiques of growth- and profit-dominated economics already enjoying some public acceptance. These materials are to hand, but need to be carefully and imaginatively assembled in order to render void the assumptions that underpin the discourse of inevitability.

Finally, understanding agency as instrumentality contributes additional moral force to co-operators' arguments. Across the world millions of people, as employees of large, companies owned by external shareholders, are viewed as little more than agents-as-instruments, at best 'intangible assets', 'human capital' or 'human resources', part of an overall asset base which can generate good returns if deployed wisely; at worst merely a cost item in the profit and loss account, as Jaroslav Vanek pointed out long ago.[38] The promise of co-operatives, particularly producer co-operatives, is that they challenge this instrumentalisation through their radically different practices. In the John Lewis case, this promise has been betrayed.

Mapping agencies and agents thus achieves the following: assessment of the relative strengths of the forces involved, illumination of the moral contours of the controversy (selfish individualism versus mutuality), highlighting of its gender dynamics, analysis of why the justifications of the doubters of co-operation seem inevitable, and how this seeming inevitability might be countered. This is no magic bullet, but a systematic focus on agency can contribute to the formation of co-operators as permanent persuaders, and mainstreaming co-operation as permanent persuasion. Permanent, and increasingly successful.

Notes

1 By 'organic intellectual' Gramsci simply meant intellectuals who had emerged from the ranks of those they wished to influence and organise, thus sharing their concerns and class position, as opposed to the 'traditional intellectual' who lectures and writes and makes public pronouncements without maintaining any close ties to a particular class or group, and whose activities therefore help legitimise and perpetuate the status quo. A. Gramsci, *Quaderni del carcere* [Prison notebooks], 4 vols (Turin: Einaudi, 1975), p. 1547.

2 T. Piketty, *Capital in the Twenty-First Century* (Cambridge, MA: Belknap Press, 2014).

3 Gramsci, *Quaderni del carcere*, p. 1386.

4 P. Bourdieu, *Outline of a Theory of Practice*, trans. R. Nice (Cambridge: Cambridge University Press, 1977); Bourdieu, *The Logic of Practice*, trans. R. Nice (Palo Alto: Stanford University Press, 1992).

5 K. Marx, 'The Eighteenth Brumaire of Louis Bonaparte' in D. McLellan, ed., *Karl Marx: Selected Writings* (Oxford: Oxford University Press, 2000), pp. 329–67.

6 J. W. Scott, *Gender and the Politics of History* (New York: Columbia University Press, 1988).

7 J. Butler, *Gender Trouble: Feminism and the Subversion of Identity* (New York: Routledge, 1990).
8 S. Mahmood, *Politics of Piety: The Islamic Revival and the Feminist Subject* (Berkeley and Los Angeles: California University Press, 2005).
9 R. L. Smith and D. M. Valenze, 'Mutuality and marginality: liberal moral theory and working-class women in nineteenth-century England', *Signs* 13:2 (1988), 277–98.
10 B. Latour, *We Have Never Been Modern: Towards a Symmetrical Anthropology*, trans. C. Porter (Cambridge, MA: Harvard University Press, 1993).
11 B. Latour, *The Pasteurization of France*, trans. A. Sheridan and J. Law (Cambridge, MA: Harvard University Press, 1988).
12 F. Muniesa, Y. Millo and M. Callon, 'An introduction to market devices', *The Sociological Review* 55:s2 (2007), pp. 1–12.
13 B. Cassin, ed., *Vocabulaire européen des philosophies: dictionnaire des intraduisibles* [European vocabulary of philosophies: dictionary of the untranslateable] (Paris: Le Robert/Seuil, 2004).
14 Ibid.
15 K. M. Eisenhardt, 'Agency theory: an assessment and review', *Academic Management Review* 14:1, 57–74; E. Kiser, 'Comparing varieties of agency theory in economics, political science, and sociology: an illustration from state policy implementation', *Sociological Theory* 17:2 (1999), 146–70.
16 S. Novkovic, 'Defining the co-operative difference', *Journal of Socio-Economics* 37 (2008), 2168–77.
17 D. Graeber, *Debt: The First Five Thousand Years* (New York: Melville House, 2012); D. Harvey, *The Enigma of Capital and the Crises of Capitalism* (New York: Profile, 2011); and L. Panitch and S. Gindin, *The Making of Global Capitalism: The Political Economy of American Empire* (London: Verso, 2012).
18 P. Toynbee, 'The John Lewis motto should be "Never Knowingly Underpay"', *The Guardian* (13 September 2012), www.theguardian.com/commentisfree/2012/sep/13/john-lewis-model-ethical-cleaners (accessed 3 February 2016).
19 At time of writing in 2014, the UK Living Wage Foundation calculates the living wage for London to be £9.15/hr in London and £7.85/hr outside of that city, the UK's minimum wage for under 21s being £6.50/hr. In 2012 these rates were slightly lower: £8.55/hr for London, £7.45/hr for the UK outside London, and a statutory minimum wage of only £6.19/hr – still slightly above what John Lewis cleaners were being paid. See www.livingwage.org.uk/calculation (accessed 3 February 2016).
20 F. Guy, 'Outsourcing and employee ownership: growth versus equity?', *Open Democracy* (8 March, 2013), www.opendemocracy.net/ourkingdom/frederick-guy/outsourcing-and-employee-ownership-growth-versus-equity (accessed 3 February 2016); and Guy, 'Employee ownership meets outsourcing' (3 April 2013), http://frederickguy.com/2013/03/04/employee-ownership-meets-outsourcing (accessed 3 February 2016).
21 Guy, 'Outsourcing and employee ownership'.

22 J. Bockman, *Markets in the Name of Socialism: The Left-Wing Origins of Neoliberalism* (Palo Alto: Stanford University Press, 2011).
23 B. Ward, 'Firm in Illyria: market syndicalism', *The American Economic Review* 48:4 (1958), 566–89.
24 The John Lewis case is not exactly an illustration of the problem as Ward delineated it. The business has grown considerably since its founder gifted his business to its employees in 1929, in terms of number of stores, range of business activities and number of employees – not to mention turnover, profits and assets. As Guy acknowledges, for this reason it is often advanced as a counter-example to Ward's claim about the weaknesses of the Illyrian model. At the same time, he argues that it is an example of how the model does eventually reach limits to its growth.
25 Toynbee, 'The John Lewis motto'.
26 He also discusses the even more celebrated case of Mondragon, the Basque worker-owned co-operative, and its 'capitalist' employment of non-worker-owners in its overseas subsidiaries. For a good discussion of the strengths and shortfalls of Mondragon in this regard, see J. K. Gibson-Graham, *A Postcapitalist Politics* (Minneapolis: University of Minnesota Press, 2006).
27 F. Dobbin, ed., *The New Economic Sociology: A Reader* (Princeton: Princeton University Press, 2004); C. Hann and K. Hart, *Economic Anthropology: History, Ethnography, Critique* (London: Polity, 2011); and M. Mauss, *The Gift: Forms and Function of Exchange in Archaic Societies*, trans. I. Cunnison, with an introduction by E. Evans-Pritchard (Eastford, CT: Martino Fine Books, 2011).
28 M. Callon, 'What does it mean to say that economics is performative?' in D. MacKenzie, F. Muniesa and L. Siu, eds, *Do Economists Make Markets? On the Performativity of Markets* (Princeton: Princeton University Press, 2007).
29 Graeber, *Debt*.
30 M. Sandel, *What Money Can't Buy: The Moral Limits of Markets* (London: Allen Lane, 2012).
31 As Bockman also points out in regard to Ward's typology of economies, neoclassical models in general assume, questionably, that knowledge about the firm provides knowledge about the entire economy, and vice versa. Bockman, *Markets in the Name of Socialism*, pp. 94, 98–9.
32 B. Potter, *The Co-operative Movement in Great Britain* (London: Swan Sonnenschein, 1891) and B. Webb and S. Webb, *The Consumers' Co-operative Movement* (London and New York: Longmans Green, 1921).
33 D. C. Jones, 'British producer cooperatives and the views of the Webbs on participation and ability to survive', *Annals of Public and Co-operative Economy* (1975), 23–44.
34 The International Co-operative Alliance's principle number six, 'Co-operation among Co-operatives', reads thus: 'Co-operatives serve their members most effectively and strengthen the co-operative movement by working together through local, national, regional and international structures'. See http://ica.coop/en/whats-co-op/co-operative-identity-values-principles (accessed 3 February 2016).
35 Chairman Charlie Mayfield's basic pay was sixty times that of the lowest-paid employee in 2012, and his total pay including bonuses was over £1.5m in 2013.

See G. Mackie, 'John Lewis chairman paid 60 times average salary', *The Scotsman* (10 May 2013), www.scotsman.com/business/retail/john-lewis-chairman-paid-60-times-average-salary-1-2925585 (accessed 3 February 2016), and S. Butler, 'John Lewis chairman's pay goes above £1.5m for first time in 2013', *The Guardian* (25 April 2014), www.theguardian.com/business/2014/apr/25/john-lewis-chairman-charlie-mayfield-pay-above-one-and-half-million-first-time (accessed April 2015).

36 B. Latour, 'A cautious Prometheus: a few steps towards a philosophy of design (with special attention to Peter Sloterdijk)', keynote lecture, Design History Society meeting (Falmouth, Cornwall, UK, 3 September 2008), www.bruno-latour.fr/sites/default/files/112-DESIGN-CORNWALL-GB.pdf (accessed 3 February 2016).

37 Such as the one mobilising through a petition website that as of the beginning of April 2015 had claimed almost 144,000 signatories. See www.change.org/p/tell-john-lewis-to-pay-cleaners-the-living-wage/u/10329301?tk=d12r-8WpkgH4xryWoMVZ9cRJjZgGywe2HjjRV22ZT4g&utm_source=petition_update&utm_medium=email (accessed 3 February 2016).

38 J. Vanek, *General Theory of Labour-Managed Economies* (Ithaca, NY: Cornell University Press, 1970).

4

G. J. Holyoake (1807–1906): a resource for a journey of hope?

Stephen Yeo

For Ian MacPherson (1939–2013)

Questions

What could the life and work of George Jacob Holyoake have to do with the subject of this book: mainstreaming co-operation in the modern world? For whom could this idiosyncratic agitator, moralist and journalist, who was born in Birmingham in 1807, the son of a whitesmith and a horn button dealer, and who died in Brighton in 1906 as the 'Grand Old Man of Co-operation',[1] be a resource? For modern co-operators? For whoever is left in active membership of the associations, including co-operatives and mutuals, which once were part of a labour *movement*?

Mainstreaming co-operatives as modern businesses is one thing. To see the movement to which co-operatives belong as the 'world-making' (Holyoake's phrase) alternative to global capitalism is quite another thing. My suggestion is that Holyoake's work could still help.

Remembering in Rochdale

I arrived at these questions in Rochdale during 2012,while celebrating the United Nations International Year of Co-operatives. I was enjoying Holyoake's notoriously untidy *History of Co-operation* (1908 edition, 'revised and completed') when I remembered that this book, like many of his others, is as much a collection of essays in social ethics or morality as it is a conventional history. As such, it is at least as useful for the future as for the past, reminding us, as Philip Grant does in his chapter 3 of this volume, of the 'moral contours' of the movement: 'selfish individualism versus mutuality'.

Beyond his part in the Owenite socialist and then the co-operative movement, Holyoake is best known by historians as a pioneer of secularism (a term he invented) and for his self-defence in the last trial for blasphemy in Britain.[2] He never cut and ran from any movement but, in summary, his life journey ran: from Owenite co-operative socialist to sceptical Chartist, to campaigner for fair trade in knowledge to secularist, to radical co-operative Liberal to radical Liberal co-operator. As soon as secularists looked like they might become as dogmatic in their atheism as their opponents were in their theism, he turned his attention back to co-operation. Animating the co-operative movement occupied much of the last twenty years of his life. His book, *Self-Help By the People: The History of the Rochdale Pioneers* was first published in 1857 and had gone through ten editions by 1907. It became an icon, as did its subjects.[3] He put the idea of a Rochdale 'tradition' on the map, for co-operators across the world to work through and contest, because he believed it could come to matter more than anything else. He wrote other notable histories, of the Halifax Industrial Co-operative Society in 1867, the Leeds Industrial Co-operative Society in 1897 and the Derby Co-operative Provident Society in 1900. His aim was to address members and potential supporters rather than professional historians. A copy of the Derby book was presented to all 14,000 members of the Society, each of whom was also given a commemorative teapot. In a long life, Holyoake was energetic as author, publisher, journalist, debater, autobiographer, 'explainer', grammarian, proprietor and editor of no fewer than eighteen radical journals, the most lasting of which was the *Reasoner* (1846–61).[4]

The best way of seeing him in the round, perhaps, is as an epitome of Antonio Gramsci's idea of the organic intellectual. Again, Philip Grant uses this concept in his contribution to this book, arguing for the need the movement has for 'permanent persuaders'. An organic intellectual in Gramsci's sense is a thinker–activist devoted to the career of a class – or in Holyoake's case a specific combination of classes – rather than to any idea of his own professional advancement, of which he was always careless. Edward Owen Greening thought that Holyoake's 'career was one long conquest of self, in remarkable ways'.[5] Perhaps this is why he has never been celebrated as a prophet, even within the co-operative movement, in the way that his mentor Robert Owen (1771–1858) still is, or in the way that his French and German contemporaries Jean-Baptiste Godin (1817–88) and Friedrich Wilhem Raiffeisen (1818–88) are, or in the way that the twentieth-century prophet of the Mondragon complex in Spain, José María Arizmendiarrieta (1915–76), is now. A full Life and Times is overdue, for which this chapter will hopefully serve as a provocation.[6]

'A new Order of Labour'?

Enjoying Holyoake's work in Rochdale, I saw that behind their lack of conventional literary or academic shape, there is another kind of coherence to Holyoake's numerous books. There is something, he insists – always addressing readers as if he knew them personally – which is elevated and contagiously attractive, almost sacred, about the *idea* of co-operation with its essential links to the practice of co-operatives. The history of any movement, he thought, is the history of its idea.

Co-operators, he argued, belong to a very ordinary but at the same time extraordinarily *social* movement. The word 'social' carried weight among early co-operators, meaning more than the term 'social co-operatives', as used among European co-operators today to describe the mutualisation of welfare programmes. Holyoake used the phrase a 'social society' to oppose the antisocial, competitive society which surrounded him.[7] Co-operators, he argued, were developing their own moral tradition concerning matters like debt, equitability (a characteristic Rochdale Society word), independence and unity. A new practice or ethic of *association* was abroad. Holyoake thought that the co-operative movement had discovered ways of arranging human potential uniquely adapted for transforming a new industrial age in the interests of Labour rather than Capital, both of which he often capitalised, as he did Co-operation as opposed to Competition. Holyoake opined that: 'Co-operation creates a new person, a new character, and a new policy, and the new knowledge required is as extensive and various as that which has perfected the science of antagonism which we call "civilization".'[8] Such epochal terms encourage one to think of Max Weber on *The Protestant Ethic and the Spirit of Capitalism* (1904, translated into English in 1930).[9] Holyoake would have welcomed the thought of a twenty-second-century Weber, using his work to trace the emergence of the co-operative ethic and the spirit of associationism.

Labour and capital ... but also 'character'. 'Capital', he thought, 'is always aggressive', while the 'character' of labour should not and need not be. He kept reminding his readers that the conflict between labour and capital, which is sometimes violent and always disabling for labour, can be countered by harmonious forms of 'unity' – as in the Manchester Unity of Oddfellows. Unity is not the same as homogeneity.[10] There 'can be no unity save among equals', he explained in 1887, but equality means freedom for individual differentiation as well as common action. Differences and commonalities were being fused in new forms of working-class association. Holyoake celebrated these, particularly in his Histories, written to open up possibilities in the present rather than to define what happened in the past. His prize-winning lectures on Charity, Truth, Knowledge, Science and Progression, written for the Oddfellows in 1846, were an exercise in applied, associational philosophy.[11] The lectures were used for more than fifty years by members progressing within the Unity, of which Holyoake was a member.

The Manchester Unity of Oddfellows, like the Ancient Order of Foresters, was a giant international federation of self-governing branches of working people taking care of what we would call their own welfare. Holyoake's idea of 'Co-operative Associations'[12] is that they constitute a practice, a way of living 'abroad and at home' which includes distinct ways of behaving. He knew that co-operatives were unique: in their insistence on financial rewards for members based upon *use* and hence member-loyalty; in their democratic, delegate-based self-government; and in their 'no more than equitable' returns for capital. Ordinary, necessary things, made by the membership which uses them – 'candles and treacle'[13] – properly exchanged, properly produced by human beings (seen by other people as 'the labouring classes'), carry 'world-making' potential.

The fact is, Holyoake suggests, labour *already has* power: the power which belongs to making (production) and doing. This is not a theory of value of the kind political economists produce. For Holyoake, it is a plain fact about human agency. His readers did not need to capture, seize, still less vote representatives into power, but to 'arrange' the powers they already had. Think what masters would do, he asked, if working people ceased to produce. He liked to describe their impotence.[14] Holyoake largely ignores the language of 'masses' much used to describe ordinary people from the 1840s onwards, including by one of his hero figures: William Gladstone. It is words like 'people', independence, association, self-help, self-government, unity, equitability, character, morality, social, secular and Order (a Friendly Society word for a whole society) which recur in his work as Great Facts.

'Such sweet courtesy and consideration'

Holyoake is remembered in Manchester with a fine art deco plaque on Holyoake House, the Co-operative Union (now Co-operatives UK) building erected in his memory in 1911. Holyoake House was built by subscription, and 794 co-operative societies, all members of the Co-operative Union, contributed. For an English co-operator he was also unusually well known internationally. His work was translated into several languages. At its best, his writing style recalls that of Charles Dickens, sometimes epigrammatic, sometimes delightfully convoluted and always full of wit and fable.

Holyoake liked to celebrate other people in the movement, giving graveside addresses – a characteristic practice among radicals – for many co-operative heroes.[15] He was committed to equal citizenship for women, going beyond the Chartists in this respect; full property rights for women were achieved in co-operatives before they existed elsewhere. His intended address at Robert Owen's funeral had to wait until 1902, when the Newtown monument was completed. Priests never liked graveside addresses by lay leaders of working-class social movements. So when the rector prevented Holyoake's encomium to Owen in 1858, there was anger among mourners that Owen was buried in the context of a church service. Holyoake's ironic comment was typical: 'better ten popes officiated at his funeral than disturb it with a broil'.[16]

Holyoake was committed to continual debate, with humour when possible and over many days when necessary. Rather than denunciation, he saw open debate as the way to deal with disagreements. He suggested to members of co-operative societies that 'associative animosities' should be closed every quarter, like their societies' accounts: retaliation was a waste of time and energy and, as with debts, there was a limit in law to the time within which wrongs could be recovered. 'The Co-operator does not rail at wrong, his business is to make it impossible.'[17] Epigrams like this stud his work, as he looked for memorable ways of explaining to his readers *how* to associate so as to make it easier for co-operators to influence everyone else in society to do right.[18]

> Society does not recognise that morality has material conditions. Sacred motives have their place and power. Nevertheless, a philosopher or divine without a meal, will think more of his dinner than his principles. After a few days at sea, foodless in an open boat, a vegetarian will reconcile himself to devouring his grandmother.[19]

Holyoake spoke in public a great deal. He wrote a book on the *Rudiments of Public Speaking and Debate* which went into thirteen editions between 1849 and 1906.[20] But he was no orator. His voice was small and his stature – like that of John Stuart Mill, whom he introduced to his first popular public meeting – was less than commanding.[21] He had a nose for rhetoric in allies as well as in opponents. Imperialism, or 'paramountcy' as he sometimes called it, was a personal as well as a political or class issue for Holyoake. He claimed to have coined the term 'jingo'. His class background meant that he understood and resisted masters and mastery with his whole being as well as in his consciousness. 'The ordinary governing mind', with its 'passion for supremacy' was to be found among 'Tory socialists', among whom he included Robert Owen and Edward Vansittart Neale. Such people worked from above, through state and system rather than through solidarity and self-government.[22]

Co-operators should, he thought, behave differently from their rivals in the competitive system. Details mattered, in ways modern progressives might be tempted to laugh at. But why? He saw divisions of labour as a social problem for co-operators rather than as the economic opportunity they were for Adam Smith's pin manufacturers. It needed a Minute from the committee of the Rochdale Pioneers in June 1854 to allow 'that Cooper, the cashier, be exempt from coffee grinding'.[23] Committee members were expected to work with their hands. And can this passage from a paper by Holyoake on *Moral Errors which Endanger the Permanence of Co-operative Societies*, published by the Bury Co-operative Society in 1862, be dismissed as merely moralistic?

> The moral obstacles which constantly frustrated co-operative success, and dissipated it when achieved, were the difficulty of acting with, and tolerating, people one disliked, trusting those in whom one had no confidence, the difficulty of creating personal authority and prohibiting offensive imputations, as well as the difficulty of viewing with satisfaction, and personally promoting, the growing prosperity and influence of those considered to be unworthy.[24]

For Holyoake, good manners and openness to opposed points of view, particularly towards those who failed to show them towards him, were cardinal virtues: 'I love the picturesqueness of personal opinion.'[25] His friend Edward Owen Greening remembered how he 'treated all his opponents in debate with such sweet courtesy and consideration as are not easy to describe'.[26] Minds closed to opposites were unhelpful in co-operatives. Holyoake admired the way in which one of the Pioneers, a Swedenborgian, would linger in the store, not to convert others but to be open to their arguments. Trouble began in co-operatives when beliefs and opinions got caught up with power structures in such a way that they could not be exchanged freely. This had happened, definitively, in Christian churches. So religion, in Holyoake's opinion, now needed to be 'rescued from the tyrant and the policeman'.[27]

At the same time he was no relativist. He was full of fine discriminations. There was a difference between 'hostile' and 'generous' toleration.[28] Holyoake believed that toleration need not imply an absence of strong convictions. The same was true of political and religious neutrality in co-operatives. For Holyoake, neutrality meant testing truths in action and with evidence. He argued against what we might call entrism: people joining co-operatives to further extraneous political or religious objectives. He was not afraid to confront powerful patrons of the movement like the Christian Socialists with exactly this charge. He warned against truths becoming vested interests and celebrated co-operatives as associations in which individual beliefs and external commitments could contribute to, rather than obstruct, dynamic social construction.

One of the excitements of reading his volumes of autobiography is their sense that his times (like ours) were far from normal. Times like the first industrial revolution generated and needed eccentrics. So Holyoake delighted in the story of the Ham Common Concordium and in the life of Peter Baume. The *History of Co-operation* is full of such entertaining and instructive examples. Holyoake was convinced that 'the first duty of man is the maintenance of his own convictions, the next is respect for those of his neighbours'.[29] As part of his annunciation of an idea which, like other religions, was also a way of life within an inventive form of association with its own (co-operative) catechism, he coined his own words for many things, including for his agnosticism. 'Limitationism' was one of these, 'netheism' another. In 1858 he called himself a 'cosmist'.

During the second half of his life, Holyoake liked to distinguish between those Liberals he criticised as 'stationary' and the 'deliberate' ones like himself who saw no end to democratic invention, detail by detail. It was Holyoake who gave Samuel Smiles his best-selling strapline 'self-help'.[30] Collective or associated self-help was a bedrock value *and* principle. For Holyoake, this meant self-government and free association for an excluded class of people rather than for a few escapees from poverty. Social mobility was not the point, although Holyoake certainly achieved it in his own life. Changing the destination by the very nature of the vehicle was the task.

Historians writing during the second half of the twentieth century tended to get him wrong. Labour historians in particular became too preoccupied with the second half of the nineteenth century as a period of 'labour aristocratic' incorporation of 'respectable' working people. A hitherto 'revolutionary' working class was somehow tamed, adopting 'middle-class values'. This is to 'mainstream' Holyoake and the co-operative movement too comfortably. 'Character' was indeed a keyword for Holyoake, as it was for Samuel Smiles and for Victorians in general.[31] But character, in Holyoake's opinion, could not act independently of 'circumstances', a keyword for everyone influenced by Robert Owen. Circumstances meant material determination. And it was precisely such determination that co-operatives were designed to overcome, by victims acting for themselves to become the subjects of their own destiny rather than the objects of other classes' benevolence. Once a lasting ecology of co-operative associations existed – which it visibly did by the 1860s – it would be possible that the 'credit note', as Holyoake called it, for co-operative behaviour, with which everyone was born, would be redeemed rather than cancelled by selfish, competitive predators.[32] The moral art of association was the art of making co-operative behaviour more likely among more people than selfish, competitive behaviour. In this way a new order would replace an old one, in the same way that capital had won through, but in labour's case it could be done without violence. In an equal society it might be understandable to resist the introduction of the secret ballot as John Stuart Mill did, on the grounds that individuals should stand up in public for their opinions. But in the prevailing circumstances protection from patronage was essential. So Holyoake chided Mill and Herbert Spencer for 'not thinking that self-help has its limits'. He went on: 'There is no sense in telling a man whose legs are broken he ought to walk unassisted.'[33]

Too readily patronised from the left in our own times as a 'Gladstonian Liberal', Holyoake respectfully – face to face as well as in letters – disagreed with the Grand Old Man on fundamental matters of theology as well as on equality of opportunity, both showing and winning respect, from one intellectual to another. He considered it a personal duty as well as a class strategy to relate to people in, or likely to be in, high office, acting episode by episode rather than through an 'all at once' revolution. As a journalist, he asked questions, wrote and organised wherever the front line was on any single day, shifting the frontier between his values and principles and those currently ruling the roost whenever possible. He was not afraid of inconsistency. By appearing to fellow-travel with powerful enemies, for instance in the Reform League demonstrations in 1866–67, he lost face with friends and allies.

Equity was at stake: the *Equitable* Society of Rochdale Pioneers. Rather than 'the economy' – an abstraction he did not use – it was inequality between whole classes of people that was wrong. At his most Liberal, some would say starry eyed, in his relationship with Gladstone, he was also most deeply and cleverly committed to his class. After a breakfast meeting in 1876 he wrote to the great man about 'the conditions of association among the people'. These were, after all, 'the same as among gentlemen':

> In a club gentlemen have refreshments according to their taste: read what books they please: discuss what topics they choose. The working people want to do the same. Being crowded in their daily lives, they have no sense of distinctness and deference to each other as gentlemen have. To allure them into association and compass its pleasant perpetuity, it is only needed to concede them the liberties of gentlemen.[34]

Only! But a start had been made in Rochdale, where microscopes and telescopes were added to the Society's 3,000-volume Library in 1861 'so that the co-operator can look into things small and great, far and near'.[35] The gentlemen of Rochdale had no such institution for their use. In his celebration of the Pioneers, Holyoake played with what would happen 'if workmen were gentlemen' so that he could make subtle points on behalf of his class which we have still not caught up with. 'In this place and elsewhere', he wrote in his history of the Rochdale Society,

> I prefer to use the phrase *claim* of the workman instead of the term 'right'. A right of labour, like a right in politics, is what can be got to be ruled or conceded. A claim is what ought morally to be conceded. But the claim holds good, and is to be persisted in. If workmen were gentlemen in means no employer would dare to disallow it.[36]

Playfully, often archly, modest about himself, Holyoake took public pride in the movements he helped to generate. In a manner unusual among cultural critics to the present day, he understood social movements as forms of human creativity or 'moral art' as intricate and learned as any other cultural achievement or work of art: 'The art of association has no professors and no literature.'[37] His writings deliberately held a mirror up to parts of social life rarely seen elsewhere. For example, the aura created by Cassandras in progressive organisations 'who predict to everybody that the thing must fail, until they make it impossible that it can succeed'; or a social movement as a river that 'moves through society as the river does through the land ... new outlets seem to open of themselves, and in an unexpected hour the accumulated torrent of ideas bursts open a final passage to the great sea of truth'.[38] An anthology of these cameos would be entertaining and instructive for modern activists. For instance: 'The middleman ... is like the Australian rabbit, very well for cooking purposes; but when he multiplies, and is everywhere eating up every green thing growing in the fields of profit, he becomes a pest.'[39]

Holyoake loved to coin metaphors to describe co-operators. His fellow co-operator J. T. W. Mitchell's face was 'as radiant as a jubilee' and Alexander Campbell's voice 'sounded like a truce'. By contrast, one opponent came across in debate as a 'moral rhinoceros'. As a teacher, he was fond of Bunyanesque dialogues between archetypes, such as Tom Seekout and Jack Tellall. He insisted that while co-operation was old, Co-operatives were new. To see them as otherwise was to sell out to the political economists, eager to vaccinate society against a revolutionary form by saying that co-operation with a small 'c' had always been there. Co-operators' sense of history, not only their own, deserves a study in its own right.[40]

But it was their existence as recent social inventions by working people which made co-operatives world-making, the term Holyoake used to contest the familiar 'utopian' put-down:

> Gibbon Wakefield says: 'Co-operation takes place when several persons help each other in the same employment, as when two greyhounds running together kill more hares than four greyhounds running separately.' This is the nature of the Co-operation chiefly known to political economists. But industrial co-operation unites not merely to kill the hares but to eat them. The greyhounds of Wakefield run down the hares for their masters – the new co-operative greyhounds run down the hare for themselves.[41]

Holyoake attributed unnecessary wars to standing armies, bloated states and secret decision-making. He was convinced that only the free, mutual, fully equitable, universal (the Owenite word for global) exchange of knowledge and ideas could produce peace. It was the lack of open, shared 'intelligence' – a word he often used to mean education and knowledge – which produced war. So he campaigned against government taxes on all forms of communication, whether on railway travel or newspapers. Backhanders between tradespeople or 'clandestine commissions' in business were intolerable, particularly between co-operative societies.[42] Intelligence was a primary product for co-operatives. 'Associative intelligence' was as material as groceries: at one time Holyoake was prepared to advocate education or 'knowledge' as a qualification for extending the franchise to working people: consciousness was that important.

But peace was more than freedom *from*. It was part of the 'positive moral and social culture' for which Holyoake stood.[43] Peace was a way of life with its own associational loyalties, solidarities and state formations within 'the state'. These were already replacing the human deformations of the capital–labour relation. Labour had started to employ capital rather than the other way round. Capital should be paid a fair wage and no more; 5 per cent was the maximum interest capital should receive. Prefigured in co-operative societies and their federal formations, co-operation would constitute – already was constituting – an utterly different state of affairs. It was the epochal nature of this difference, combined with their immediate economic rewards which made co-operatives uniquely attractive. The new 'Order of Industry' which was to replace the 'Order of Capital' was to be as different from capitalism as feudalism had been. Holyoake shared this sense with Marx. But whereas the transition to capitalism had required the 'organisation of arms', the transition to Industry (Co-operation) could only endure through 'the organisation of ideas'. In January 1906, shortly before he died in Eastern

Lodge near the sea front in Brighton, he was still observing 'the growth and trend' of nothing less than a 'new Order of Labour'.[44]

An invitation: three possibilities

To invite a man like Holyoake into a twenty-first-century, global mainstream – if there is one other than market fundamentalism – may be eccentric. But this is what I want to do, as a preface to bringing his life into our times in a more comprehensive way. Holyoake's theory and practice in his chosen social movements needs to be reappraised in the light of three possibilities. The first is that the co-operative movement – and here I focus mainly on Britain – remains central to the making of a coherent, but unfinished, associational-socialist alternative to the Marxist revolutionary tradition of c. 1848 to c. 1959.[45] More than *alternative*, the period which Holyoake called 'the constructive period' in co-operative history from 1845 onwards was powerfully *oppositional*.[46]

The second possibility is that the co-operative movement, as understood by Holyoake, is central to the emergence of a distinct, coherent and to some extent self-regulating, ethical or moral *tradition*. The Catholic philosopher Alasdair MacIntyre specifies different circles within which 'traditions' operate, some wide, some narrow:

> A tradition is constituted by a set of practices and is a mode of understanding their importance and worth; it is the medium by which such practices are shaped and transmitted across generations. Traditions may be primarily religious or moral (for example Catholicism or humanism), economic (for example a particular craft or profession, trade union or manufacturer), aesthetic (for example modes of literature or painting), or geographical (for example crystallising around the history and culture of a particular house, village or region).[47]

Could the co-operative movement be seen as a tradition in one or more of these settings: most ambitiously as a moral *and* economic tradition in its own right? Having stated 'the values of self-help, self-responsibility, democracy, equality, equity and solidarity' on which 'co-operatives are based', the 1995 International Co-operative Alliance 'Statement of co-operative identity' goes on to list 'the ethical values of honesty, openness, social responsibility and caring for others' which '*in the tradition of their founders* [my emphasis], co-operative members believe'.[48] What is the strength of that usage?

The third, more speculative possibility is that it could become attractive to young people across the twenty-first century world to articulate a 'religion of co-operation' as an ethic or set of values, which are inseparable from a set of organising principles concerning the moral art of association. A movement of this weight and sense of belonging was anticipated in Holyoake's work, even if he never quite named it as a religion. His 1840 lectures for the Worcester Socialists, in their Hall of Science, were 'imbued with a highly moral, and truly religious tone of sentiment, which it was his most ardent desire and endeavour to inculcate among his audience'.[49]

An associational-socialist alternative to the Marxist revolutionary tradition?

The 'moral force' strand in Chartist and post-Chartist 'social radical' and secularist politics, to which Holyoake committed himself, has commonly been seen as a subtraction from the 'revolutionary' ambition of its 'physical force' opponents. It may now be time for would-be world-makers to examine moral force as a useable, transformative, revolutionary tradition in its own right. Although moral force has had a long history since Holyoake and remains of great interest to modern radicals who have their roots in anti-imperial movements on the Indian subcontinent, civil rights movements in North America and anti-globalisation movements such as 'Occupy', Holyoake and post-Owenism more generally as a resource for the further development of 'moral force' movements remain to be explored politically as well as academically.

'Socialism' is now predominantly seen as a dead, odious, impossible failure and, when used by existing regimes to describe themselves, as a fiction. Throughout 'the West', the word is feared by those in power more than it is longed for by those out of it. Its surviving proponents see it either as in some scientific way inevitable, or as the capture or taking of power at some future date, whether by communist revolution or social democratic election, followed by the introduction of policies by political parties, which may or not carry the 'socialist' label on their tins.

Holyoake was never a systematic thinker. Like Dickens, he saw 'system' as a modern phenomenon, putting it in inverted commas and thinking aloud about whether co-operation amounted to one or not.[50] Socialism's negative presence in 2015 is as far from Holyoake's way of seeing things as could possibly be. He believed in an entirely new order which was already on its way, to be realised by means of non-violent construction and voluntary association. He believed in working people 'arranging' the powers inherent in their work (production), and in the multiplication of knowledge and education. Production and distribution did not determine or take precedence over government and education. Contrary to later Marxist emphases, all four were seen as 'powers' on the same plane and mete for equitable 'arrangements' made by working people on their own behalf. Such a folding into one another of the material and the ideal, the 'base' and the 'superstructure', was something to which Holyoake returned repeatedly, in some of his most original writing.

A whole way of living well, ethically as well as economically, was available *now* rather than after the revolution or the next election. Incidentally, this made him appreciative of early nineteenth-century Evangelicals like Shaftesbury, though not of their Christology. How co-operative associationism related to emergent forms of socialism after 1848 was a theme in his writing for the rest of his life. In so far as socialism came to mean a smothering state, he opposed it. In July 1843 in his journal *The Movement* he had attributed to 'socialism' 'the capacity … to build up individual as well as general character, to serve as *a complete body of moral, political and social philosophy*' (my italics).[51] After the mid nineteenth century it was the co-operative movement which, with Holyoake as a leading protagonist, put such a philosophy into practice. By then, socialism had fallen into statist hands.

Holyoake subscribed to the 'political anti-politics' or 'social radicalism' of what he later called 'the enthusiastic period' of co-operative socialism, which lasted until the mid nineteenth century.[52] He then carried its structures of thought and feeling with him for the rest of his life. They informed the 'constructive period' and then 'the modern period' into which *The History of Co-operation* was divided. They also informed his secularism and his Liberalism. His insight that Liberals should realise that liberalism was not 'already self-regulating' speaks directly to today's neoliberals and neoconservatives. He saw how party and single interest politics got in the way of social movements and social construction. Vested interests, with social classes as their prime example, were obstacles which co-operators had to take care not to reproduce in their own societies. Hence the importance not only of dividends based upon *use* but also of rewards for producers as well as consumers and limited payment for capital which stopped well short of feeding capital*ism* as system.

Holyoake's interests during much of the second half of his life were indicated by a lecture he gave on 9 April 1848, on the eve of the last great Chartist meeting, to a large audience at the John Street Institution, an old Owenite venue. The title paints a backdrop to the rest of his life's work: 'The chances of obtaining an English Republic by moral means'. Not very great, but worth trying? Like most other co-operators between the mid nineteenth and the early twentieth centuries, Holyoake resisted the label 'socialist' and the 1789 type 'revolutionary' connotations which were to carry 'socialism' and 'communism' through 1917 in Russia, to

China in 1948, Cuba in 1959 and now to its North Korean parody. He anticipated how quickly would-be progressive, all-at-once, state-led changes could turn sour. Self-help by means of getting together was his constant reference point: a discipline in the intellectual as well as practical sense. 'I maintain always and everywhere that the people should keep the State, not the State the people.'[53]

People already had power. The question was how can they (we) best help themselves (ourselves) to articulate it? People make value. How best to share this reward of labour? There would, he knew, be vicious counter-attacks. The interests of 'private traders' needed to be considered, and emergent chains (copying the co-operatives) needed dealing with, as the antagonists of small private traders (independent grocers etc.) as much as they were also the enemies of co-operatives. Holyoake spent time on this matter in his old age.[54] Not-quite co-operatives like the Civil Service Supply Associations, which were today's 'social enterprises', also needed to be considered. Holyoake pointed out their limitations. He knew them as 'London Co-operation' or, 'another form of Co-operation [which] has grown up among the middle and upper classes, very useful in its way'.[55] The real task was to build capacity as 'a state within the state', as Lord Rosebery told the 1890 Glasgow Co-operative Congress the movement had already become. Holyoake wanted to raise the stakes still further, to 'influence the State, cover the State, and eventually change the "system" prevailing in the State'.[56]

A distinct, ethical or moral 'tradition'?

As a social philosopher who does much more than acknowledge Marx, MacIntyre is alert to the material as well as the moral direction and social provenance of thought and practice in our times. In and against the incoherent (as he sees it) post-Enlightenment world outlined in his now classic work *After Virtue* (1981), MacIntyre subscribes to an Aristotelian, Thomist, Catholic tradition.[57] He defends this philosophically, against all comers, as a precondition of his own theological and practical commitment. Although not cited by MacIntyre, the Spanish co-operative Mondragon may best be seen in light of this perspective.[58]

The question arises: might it become possible in the future to subscribe, with equal rationality and commitment, to a co-operative tradition of which Holyoake would then be seen as one of the makers? It goes without saying that this would be to elevate what is at stake in the history of the co-operative movement, quite considerably. MacIntyre understands Buddhism, Liberalism, Marxism, Catholicism, Utilitarianism and other philosophies as distinct and entire traditions. Traditions grow and yield to other traditions by asking questions of a real world, of its social formations and of each other's presence and practice within them. The answers given by rival traditions are adequate or empty, hold together or fall apart in ways which are, or should be, open to reasoned analysis and sustained philosophical argument. Could co-operation invite itself into such a discourse?[59] Can a single co-operative tradition, in the fullest sense of the word, be called out as such, with the 1995 'Statement of co-operative identity, values and principles' at its core? If so, it would need to include the various virtues, values and principles displayed in the French, the British, the German, the producer, the consumer, the credit and the common-land-ownership movements across the world.

I cannot answer this question here, but believe it to be worth asking. Traditions 'differ in their catalogs of the virtues'. MacIntyre is a philosopher against whose work co-operators could learn to measure themselves. A tradition in his sense is a body of enquiry into 'what practical rationality is and what justice is'.

> In each [tradition] intellectual enquiry was or is part of the elaboration of a mode of social and moral life of which the intellectual enquiry itself [is] an integral part, and in each of them the forms of that life [are] embodied with greater or lesser degrees of imperfection in social and political institutions which also draw their life from other sources.[60]

MacIntyre is particularly interested in what 'plain people' do to sustain associative, civil, ethical, mutual, productive and communal practices, in order to resist the pressures of dominant state and markets. In his reluctance to commit to any reformist programme (patiently waiting, as he famously was at the end of *After Virtue*, for a new amalgam of St Benedict and Leon Trotsky), MacIntyre may even be read as a proto co-operator and mutualist. He resists the late twentieth-century 'communitarian' label while favouring working people's practices like those of the first half of the nineteenth century in Europe and America, to which the label 'communitarian socialism' was first applied.[61] He also defends 'present utopianism' against utopianism 'of the future' in a way which chimes with Holyoake's preference for the phrase 'world-making'.

A religion of co-operation?

Why would I, at some risk of inflation, want to promote the co-operative movement and its 1995 'Statement of co-operative identity, values and principles' in a 'religious' as well as in an ethical setting? Surely mainstreaming 'member-owned businesses' as economically rational in a competitive world is difficult enough? Birchall, among other modern experts, has warned against inflated claims for what he prefers to call 'member-owned businesses'.[62] Cool it, he seems to be saying. And many advocates of co-operation and mutuality now prefer the looser term 'social enterprise', or what Holyoake saw as lesser or 'London', rather than 'Rochdale' co-operation. The precise organisational form that co-operatives take (specified as Principles in the 1995 'Statement of co-operative identity') now takes second place, among some would-be mainstreamers, to their benevolent intentions.

I take the risk for two reasons. Firstly, because it might be helpful to propel the movement further out into the open spaces of the modern world and to give it more of what Holyoake called an *outside*.[63] Secondly, it might encourage modern members of co-operatives to present themselves to potential enthusiasts with the conviction of nineteenth-century prophets like John Stuart Mill and John Ruskin. In his *Principles of Political Economy*, Mill argued that 'there is a capacity of exertion and self-denial in the masses of mankind which is never known but on the rare occasions on which it is appealed to in the name of some great idea or elevated sentiment'.[64]

Communicating a sense of co-operatives and mutuals as ideas to win the world as well as economic facts which complement capitalism could turn out to be as inspiring for future generations as the business rationality which professional advocates of co-operatives currently favour. The idea of linking the general idea – the hope – of co-operation to the very particular ownership and democratic forms co-operatives take, could be the biggest as well as the clearest 'heritage' or asset that ailing societies like The Co-operative Group, to take one example, possess. 'Member engagement' might then be energised from below rather than as a policy to be implemented by managers in corporate affairs departments. In December 1878 the Southern Section of the Central Co-operative Union resolved that a 'manual' on *Foundations: A Study in the Ethics and Economics of the Co-operative Movement* be commissioned by the Union. An outline by Thomas Hughes and E. V. Neale was approved in February 1879 and referred to the United Board and thence to the Co-operative Congress of 1879. In the first edition of the resulting book, revised in 1915 during the First World War, Hughes and Neale observed that:

> Co-operation, as it is presented in these pages, is an attempt made by men profoundly convinced of the eternal reality of moral truth, to embody the high ideal of duty in institutions applying to the daily events of our ordinary lives ...
>
> Our Societies have come to acknowledge that the mere fact of membership in a retail store involves more than paying ready money, attending

> once a quarter, and drawing dividends. As the years pass they find themselves constantly brought into new and more intimate relations with their fellow-members, in their own association and in the Union. In the primary sense of the word, *id quod religat*, 'that which binds together', they have already found that co-operation has been a religion to them.[65]

This was written at a time when the movement was flourishing. Religious idealism is very much alive in the modern world. But it is at some distance from the co-operative movement. It inspires numerous intelligent young men and women who are prepared to sacrifice their lives for a cause. Could it be unearthed as one of the greatest buried assets the co-operative movement has? For decades now there have been calls for socialists to dig down to their moral and ethical roots. In my socialist lifetime, such calls go back to E. P. Thompson's revised work on William Morris. They continue into the work of Robert Unger, among many others who challenge a sense that 'the academic' nowadays, 'does not seek to be in any sense a prophet of hope; indeed the very notion seems to him pretentious and vulgar'.[66] Rational commentators still wonder what glue could be capable of holding co-operative and mutual enterprises together during the twenty-first century as strongly as it held together during Holyoake's time, helped by its strong Nonconformist, Anglican and other religious – and secularist – binding. The simple fact is that at the height of the 'Age of Capital' (1848–75) and then the 'Age of Empire'(1875–1914), large numbers of working people were growing a large-scale, confident, oppositional, productive, non-capitalist 'system'. And the party-political left, whether social democratic or communist, has either patronised or ignored it.

The burden of the conference from which this book grew was to mainstream a *business* form, that of co-operative and mutual enterprises (CMEs). Is it also time to mainstream 'religious' attachment to mutually respectful, *social* forms – *id quod religat*, that which binds? By this I mean 'open and voluntary' co-operative societies with the capacity *now* to remake a whole society worthy of the name. Could modern advocates of CMEs invite loyalty not only to economic rationality but also to gods other than today's trinity: the individual, the family and the nation? I like to imagine Holyoake's work in progress entering the practical and theoretical mainstream in future books with titles like 'The Co-operative Ethic and the Spirit of Associationism'; 'The Association of All Classes of All Nations' would be at the centre of early chapters. This was the Owenite society which Holyoake joined in 1838. In the second decade of the twenty-first century, why is such an association so easily condescended to nowadays as quaint? Holyoake's sense of the injustice of the wage as the limit of the employer–employee relationship whether in co-operatives or in private companies, which he came back to all through his long life, had a 'religious' flavour to it, both in its zeal and in its carefully controlled, self-consciously ethical behaviour towards those who disagreed.[67] As a secularist he was obsessed with 'the religious question'. He thought it mattered, seldom passing priestly believers by without engaging them in debate, calling their attention to this world rather than the next.

Holyoake was not an 'and then' thinker, in political or religious terms. He did not deal in the politics of promissory notes. Seize goods and power from the rich and powerful, vote for progressive representatives, concentrate on the material base, organise around a single demand or interest group as a fulcrum for everything else, kill tyrants, borrow money to generate employment ... and all will be well. These were not his ways, although he carefully considered the morality of all such instruments, including tyrannicide for which he saw that, in the case of some regimes, a case could be made. Debt was ethically abhorrent in individuals and organisations because it meant they could no longer own or govern themselves, let alone anything else.[68] One of Holyoake's most original contributions to the 'moral art of association' was his critique of all agitations – whether for the repeal of the Corn Laws, an Independent Labour Party or Votes for Women – which turned into organisations, now known as pressure groups, predicated on 'pressing a single political purpose to the extent of over-riding other just reforms'. Evaluating such agitations was a matter of 'political morality' to Holyoake; Cobden's stance on the Corn Laws, for instance, however right in itself, was a subtraction from 'being the change', which was Holyoake's ambition long before Gandhi coined the phrase. Long after his secularist biographer, Joseph McCabe, thought that the times had made it impossible, Holyoake persisted in his quest for unsectarian, prefigurative, mutual ways of socialising economics as well as politics. He wanted to hold co-operation, education, secularism and politics together, working for forms of 'unity' in each area which could allow them to travel together in this world rather than the next, and today rather than tomorrow. He wanted great differences to be held as well as divided, in a uniquely 'social' movement which it might be worth trying out all over again – mainstreaming – in the twenty-first century, using his work as one of its major resources.[69]

Notes

1 *Co-operative News* (27 January 1906). This would have been understood as Holyoake having a similar stature within 'the co-operative state' in Britain as Gladstone (known as the Grand Old Man) had in the wider, British nation state.

2 This was celebrated in John Osborne's 1960 TV play, *A Subject of Scandal and Concern*, in which Richard Burton played Holyoake. At his trial Holyoake spoke for nine hours and was rewarded with six months in prison. See G. J. Holyoake, *The trial of George Jacob Holyoake, on an indictment for blasphemy, before Mr Justice Erskine and a common jury, at Gloucester, August the 15th, 1842, from notes specially taken by Mr Hunt* (London: The Anti Persecution Union, 1842).

3 G. J. Holyoake, *Self-Help By the People: The History of the Rochdale Pioneers, 1844–1892*, 10th edition (London: Swan Sonnenschein, 1907). A legend grew up that 'the gracefulness of his story led to its reproduction in every European language – creating quite a sensation among the workmen of Lyons – while in England it was a seed from which sprang 250 co-operative societies in two years', C. W. F. Goss, *A Descriptive Bibliography of the Writings of George Jacob Holyoake, With a Brief Sketch of His Life* (London: Crowther & Goodman, 1908), p. xlviii. Modern historians have enjoyed correcting this legend, as they do, while not always appreciating the interest of it *as* a legend of the kind of which serious social movements are made. As Holyoake wrote, 'the real peril of the historian is that he may paralyse his readers by tameness, or kill curiosity by monotony', *The History of Co-operation, Revised and Completed* (London: T. Fisher Unwin, 1908), p. xiv.

4 He founded or was on the executive or equivalent of twenty-two progressive leagues and associations; see J. McCabe, *Life and Letters of George Jacob Holyoake*, vols 1 and 2 (London: Watts and Co, 1908), vol. 2, pp. 284, 327.

5 Ibid., vol. 1, p. vii.

6 L. Grugel, *George Jacob Holyoake: A Study in the Evolution of a Victorian Radical* (Philadelphia: Porcupine Press, 1975) does not replace the earlier work cited in my chapter, although McCabe's accuracy over details cannot be relied on.

7 Holyoake, *Self-Help By the People*, p. 46.

8 G. J. Holyoake, *The Co-operative Movement Today*, 1st edition 1891 (London: Methuen, 1903), p. 86.

9 M. Weber, *The Protestant Ethic and the Spirit of Capitalism* (London: Allen and Unwin, 1930).

10 For the violence of the 'never-ceasing conflict between Labour and Capital' and how 'there was murder in the march' of unmitigated competition, see the 1879 Preface to vol. 2 of Holyoake, *History of Co-operation*, p. xviii. For the 'war of Industry against Capital' which will not cease until Co-operative Industry is established, see Holyoake, *Co-operative Movement Today*, pp. 6–15.

11 G. J. Holyoake, *The Lectures Used by the Manchester Unity of the Independent Order of Odd Fellows, Sanctioned and Approved by the Bristol A.M.C., June 1846* (London: John G. Hornblower, 1846).

12 Holyoake, *Self-Help By the People*, 1893, preface to 1907 edition, p. vii.

13 'It was a great descent from the imperial attitude of world-making to selling long-sixteen candles and retailing treacle. Doubtless, if only we knew it, the beginning of civilized society was not less absurd.' The 'first co-operative society motto I have found', wrote Holyoake, 'came from the Economical Society in 1821. It consisted of Milton's lines "Our greatness will appear/Then most

conspicuous, when great things of small/Useful of hurtful, prosperous of adverse/ We can create"', Holyoake, *History of Co-operation*, vol. 1, pp. 40–1.

14 Holyoake, *Co-operative Movement Today*, pp. 112–13.

15 'He spoke over the grave' of the Pioneers' Cooper and Smithies, and of Thomas Livesey, John Bright's schoolfellow and a friend of the Pioneers. G. J. Holyoake, *Bygones Worth Remembering* (London: T. Fisher Unwin, 1905), vol. 2, p. 118.

16 McCabe, *Life and Letters*, vol. 1, p. 294.

17 Holyoake, *Co-operative Movement Today*, p. 142.

18 G. J. Holyoake, *The Jubilee History of the Leeds Industrial Co-operative Society from 1847 to 1897 Traced Year by Year* (Leeds: Central Co-operative Offices, 1897), p. 191.

19 Holyoake, *Co-operative Movement Today*, p. 74.

20 G. J. Holyoake, *Rudiments of Public Speaking and Debate: Or, Hints on the Application of Logic* (London: J. Watson, 1849).

21 Holyoake, *Bygones*, vol. 1, p. 263.

22 Holyoake, *Co-operative Movement Today*, pp. 6–15.

23 Holyoake, *Self-Help By the People*, p. 160.

24 Goss, *A Descriptive Bibliography*, p. 31. In chapter 6, pp. 53–66, of Holyoake, *Co-operative Movement Today*, there is a masterpiece in this mode. 'The Store as an Institution' is an essay which mixes morality with management and social analysis with methods of social advance. There is another version in G. J. Holyoake and A. Scotton, 'Distinction between store-keeping and shop-keeping', *The Jubilee History of the Derby Co-operative Provident Society Limited 1850–1900* (Manchester: Co-operative Printing Society, 1900), pp. 178–83.

25 Holyoake, *Bygones*, vol. 2, p. 114.

26 McCabe, *Life and Letters*, vol. 1, p. vi.

27 Ibid., vol. 2, p. 176.

28 G. J. Holyoake, *Hostile and Generous Toleration (a New Theory of Toleration)* (London: E. W. Allen, 1886).

29 Goss, *Descriptive Bibliography*, p. lxxvii.

30 The first chapters of *Self-Help by the People* appeared in the *Daily News* in 1857, two years before the first publication in 1859 of Samuel Smiles' *Self Help*, modern edition P. W. Sinnema, ed., (Oxford: Oxford University Press, 2008).

31 S. Collini, 'The Idea of Character in Victorian Political Thought', in *Transactions of the Royal Historical Society*, 5th series, 35 (1908), pp. 29–50.

32 Holyoake, *Jubilee History, Derby*, p. 33.

33 G. J. Holyoake, *Sixty Years of an Agitator's Life*, 2 vols in 1 (London: T. Fisher Unwin, 1906), vol. 2, p. 181.

34 McCabe, *Life and Letters*, vol. 2, p. 164.

35 Holyoake, *Self-Help by the People*, p. 135.

36 Ibid., pp. 135, 113.

37 Holyoake, *Co-operative Movement Today*, p. 86.

38 Holyoake, *Self-Help By the People*, p. 21; *History of Co-operation*, vol. 2, p. 579.

39 Holyoake, *Co-operative Movement Today*, p. 145.

40 P. Gurney, 'George Jacob Holyoake: socialism, association and co-operation in nineteenth-century England' in S. Yeo, ed., *New Views of Co-operation* (London: Routledge, 1988), pp. 111–42.
41 Holyoake, *History of Co-operation*, p. 300.
42 G. J. Holyoake, *Against Clandestine Commissions, Mainly in the Interests of Co-operative Societies* (London: Gay and Bird, 1899), originally published in *Co-operative News* (25 November–9 December 1899).
43 McCabe, *Life and Letters*, vol. 1, p. 96.
44 Holyoake, *History of Co-operation*, p. xi.
45 S. Yeo, 'State and anti-state: reflections on social forms and struggles from 1850' in Philip Corrigan, ed., *Capitalism, State Formation and Marxist Theory* (London: Quartet Books, 1980), pp. 111–41; S. Yeo, 'Notes on three socialisms – collectivism, statism and associationism – mainly in late nineteenth and early twentieth-century Britain' in C. Levy, ed., *Socialism and the Intelligentsia* (London: Routledge, 1987), pp. 219–70; Yeo, 'Towards co-operative politics: using early to generate late socialism', *Journal of Co-operative Studies* 42:3 (2009), 22–35.
46 R. Williams, *Culture* (London: Fontana, 1981), pp. 71–4.
47 S. Mulhall and A. Swift, *Liberals and Communitarians* (Oxford: Blackwell, 1992), p. 90.
48 See 'Statement of co-operative identity, values and principles', adopted by the International Co-operative Alliance (ICA) in 1995, http://ica.coop/en/whats-co-op/co-operative-identity-values-principles (accessed 3 February 2016).
49 Goss, *Descriptive Bibliography*, p. xxiv.
50 The *Leader*, for which Holyoake wrote under the pseudonym 'Ion' during the early 1850s and for which he was one of the editors, called itself 'Socialistic' and liked the 'doctrine' but had no 'system' of socialism. The task was to give the people, by means of 'equality of intelligence', 'the power to develop a system' (McCabe, *Life and Letters*, vol. 1, p. 166). Holyoake commented on Robert Owen's predilection for 'system' and how it lost his readers; 'it was said of Montaigne that his sentences were vascular and alive, and, if you pricked them, they bled. If you pricked Mr Owen's, when he wrote on his system, you lost your needle in the wool'; quoted in McCabe, *Life and Letters*, vol. 2, p. 276. In Holyoake *Self-Help By the People* (p. 8), there is a fine sense of how capitalists become trapped in their own 'system'. If 'system' (and chapter 10 of Holyoake, *Co-operative Movement of Today*, pp. 88–96, is called 'The Rochdale System'), it had, for Holyoake, to be a system which affirmed rather than denied associated, human agency or self-help by the people: it was not, as it were, an automatic or self-acting loom.
51 McCabe, *Life and Letters*, vol. 1, p. 181.
52 For the roots of 'social radicalism and the politics of anti-politics', see G. Claeys, *Citizens and States: Politics and Anti-politics in Early British Socialism* (Cambridge: Cambridge University Press, 1989) and Yeo, 'Towards co-operative politics'.
53 A letter to Gladstone in 1881, quoted in McCabe, *Life and Letters*, chapter 23,

pp. 161–83, 'Corespondence with Gladstone and Chamberlain' is a rich source for Holyoake's ideas and ways of expressing them.

54 G. J. Holyoake, *Anti-Boycott Papers* (Manchester: Co-operative Union, 1903).

55 Holyoake, *Co-operative Movement Today*, p. 59.

56 Ibid., p. 53.

57 A. MacIntyre, *After Virtue: A Study in Moral Theory*, 3rd edition (London: Duckworth, 2007).

58 F. Molina and J. K. Walton, 'An alternative co-operative tradition: the Basque co-operatives of Mondragon' in A. Webster, A. Brown, D. Stewart, J. K. Walton and L. Shaw, eds, *The Hidden Alternative: Co-operative Values, Past, Present and Future* (Manchester: Manchester University Press, 2011), pp. 226–50.

59 I broached such questions of wider intellectual contexts for a *sui generis* co-operative tradition in 'The identity of co-operative and mutual enterprises and the political sociology of Emile Durkheim: an introduction' in L. Black and N. Robertson, eds, *Consumerism and the Co-operative Movement in Modern British History* (Manchester: Manchester University Press, 2009), pp. 86–107, and in 'Theorizing co-operative studies: obstacles and opportunities for twenty-first century co-operative and mutual enterprises' in I. Macpherson and E. McLaughlin-Jenkins, eds, *Integrating Diversities Within a Complex Heritage: Essays in the Field of Co-operative Studies* (Victoria: University of Victoria New Rochdale Press, 2008), pp. 345–90.

60 A. MacIntyre, *Whose Justice? Which Rationality?* (Notre Dame: University of Notre Dame, 1988), pp. 349–69.

61 A. E. Bestor, *Backwoods Utopias: the Sectarian and Owenite Phases of Communitarian Socialism in America 1663–1829* (Philadelphia: University of Pennsylvania Press, 1950).

62 J. Birchall, *People-centred Businesses: Co-operatives, Mutuals and the Idea of Membership* (Basingstoke and New York: Palgrave Macmillan, 2011), p. 210.

63 Holyoake, *Jubilee History, Leeds*, p. 60.

64 J. S. Mill, *Principles of Political Economy*, 7th edition (Clifton, NJ: Augustus M. Kelly Reprints, 1973).

65 T. Hughes and E. V. Neale, *Foundations: A Study in the Ethics and Economics of the Co-operative Movement, Prepared at the Request of the Co-operative Congress Held at Gloucester in April 1879, revised by A. Stoddart and W. Clayton* (Manchester: The Co-operative Union, 1915), pp. 87, 24.

66 The quote is from an early essay by A. MacIntyre, 'Breaking the chains of reason' in E. P. Thompson, ed., *Out of Apathy* (London: New Left Books, 1959), pp. 195–240, p. 196. See also S. Critchley, *The Faith of the Faithless: Experiments in Political Theology* (London: Verso, 2012), reviewed by S. Kelly: 'Rather than seeing modernity in terms of a process of secularisation I will claim that the history of political forms can best be viewed as a series of metamorphoses of sacralisation.' Oscar Wilde dreamed of a 'confraternity of the Faithless … where on an altar, on which no taper burned, a priest, in whose heart peace had no dwelling, might celebrate with unblessed bread and a chalice empty of wine', *Saturday Guardian* (4 February 2012). Critchley's question is: 'how can

those who *cannot* [his emphasis] believe reclaim from the vestiges of religion the moral authority and political radicalism it once had?' 'Everything to be true must become a religion', said Wilde. So the question is, how can secular societies find a binding mechanism that effectively replaces traditional forms of unity? Alain de Botton is in this territory too, in his *Religion for Atheists* (Harmondsworth: Penguin, 2011), as is much of Terry Eagleton's recent work.

67 Notably, Holyoake disagreed with his fellow socialist missionary John Watts. About the muscular-Christian Thomas Hughes' behaviour, with whom he often agreed on substantive issues, Holyoake felt quite differently. He could be quite explicit about Hughes' patronising class position as it contrasted with his own. But he could also be uniquely generous about more modest Christian Socialists, insisting, for example that the Co-operative Congress honoured the life and death of the great theologian F. D. Maurice.

68 Holyoake, *Jubilee History, Leeds*, p. 86.

69 The quotations in this paragraph are from McCabe, *Life and Letters*, vol. 2, pp. 178, 149.

5

History, citizenship and co-operative education, c. 1895–1930

Keith Vernon

A strong sense of the past pervades the co-operative movement. With the origins of the modern movement traced back to 1844, discussions of the nature and principles of co-operation routinely return to their foundations in the grim industrial conditions of the hungry forties.[1] Aspects of this historical culture have been analysed, primarily, through selected writings on the history of co-operation, such as those by G. J. Holyoake (see Yeo, chapter 4, this volume). The crop of jubilee histories written at the beginning of the twentieth century were also an opportunity for local societies to record, and reflect on, their several pasts, achievements and struggles.[2] Another important component was the educational activity that grew enormously from the turn of the century. It was recognised at the time, and has been acknowledged by historians subsequently, that educational work within the movement embraced a diverse set of activities.[3] Among key educational spokespeople of the movement, however, increasing emphasis came to be placed on the more formal and structured classes and courses on the history and development of co-operation. Although accepted as having a place in the formation of co-operative culture and identity, these more formal classes have not been considered at any length by historians. So, while not wishing to downplay other elements, this chapter focuses on this feature of educational activity. It seeks to show that these classes operated on a remarkable scale, reached a substantial number of people and, arguably, constituted a significant form of historical education in Britain in the early twentieth century.

From the early ideals of the Rochdale Pioneers, a commitment to education has been presented as a central feature of the co-operative movement.[4] Indeed, much endeavour was devoted to broadly educational purposes and several auxiliary organisations, such as the Women's

Co-operative Guild, also saw education as a central concern. At the end of the nineteenth century, however, the central educational department of the Co-operative Union, responsible most directly for education within the movement, felt that there was more lip service than real effort afforded to education among local consumer societies. Funds designated for education were being diverted into miscellaneous, and often largely social, occasions, ostensibly for propaganda purposes, rather than serious study. It was more than an academic interest: the co-operative movement faced significant new demands, and a return to the core principles of co-operation was seen as fundamental to revivifying the membership. Thus, from the mid-1890s, there was a concerted campaign to re-launch educational activity, and set some clear guidelines and standards, especially through diligent study in taught classes. A Herculean effort, sustained over several decades, resulted in an impressive array of courses on a range of subjects.[5] At the heart of the educational programme were courses on the nature and principles of co-operation, designed to encourage and enhance the commitment of co-operators to the movement. Courses were geared to all age groups and abilities from juniors of about ten to advanced-level instruction for adults. The approach was essentially an historical review of the emergence of co-operation and some of the key figures of social reform through the nineteenth century. Alongside were courses specifically on industrial history, citizenship and complementary social sciences, intended to fit co-operators for positions within the movement and as informed and engaged citizens in modern municipal society.[6]

These initiatives within the co-operative movement paralleled a wider national concern to promote good citizenship through education – particularly, historical teaching.[7] In 1900, the Board of Education stipulated that elementary schools should include history in the curriculum, primarily to instil moral and civic virtue, and enhance character development among the working classes. Teachers were advised to present a predominantly Whiggish tale of national progress, increasingly infused with aggressive imperialism and militarism. Through a triumphalist narrative, revolving around heroic leaders and daring exploits, children would be imbued with a sense of patriotism, obedience to those in authority and duty to the state. It was intended as a homogenising story, avoiding or glossing over social and political friction, in which all might share in the benefits and glories of England. Where ordinary people featured at all they were at best supporters to leaders, at worst actively denigrated. What exactly elementary school children took from these lessons is uncertain, but the aims were pretty clear, and not necessarily to the liking of committed co-operators.

This chapter seeks to explore a series of issues around the nature and place of history and citizenship within formal co-operative education around the early twentieth century. We begin by considering the emergence of an educational campaign at the end of the nineteenth century, which put the teaching of the history and principles of co-operation at the core of the movement's educational endeavour, supplemented by complementary historical, civic and social science subjects. We then examine the kind of history being expounded in the movement during the early years of the twentieth century. To get some appreciation of the scale and significance of co-operative historical education we move on a generation to the middle of the interwar years, when the educational programme had expanded considerably and was reaching substantial numbers, especially of young people. Juxtaposing these figures with their contemporaries studying history in school raises some potentially interesting issues, with which we conclude.

New directions in co-operative education

Through the 1890s, there was growing concern around education within the movement, and a conscious reorientation of its aims and emphasis. The movement itself was quite different from the pioneering days; it was much larger, more complex and more successful, and the end of the century naturally prompted some introspection about priorities and direction. On education in particular, significant changes in state involvement led to some important rethinking.[8] Almost all aspects of education were under state review; elementary provision had been reviewed by the Cross Commission and MP James Bryce was leading an investigation into the expansion and reorganisation of secondary education. Coming out of these inquiries was the fundamental revision of national education through the 1902 Education Act. In addition, state-sponsored technical education was growing and more working-class people had access to literature through free public libraries. While this expanding provision raised questions about the necessity for co-operators to continue to provide education, the nature and orientation of state education raised considerable qualms about its implications for co-operators as working people.

By the mid-1890s, co-operative education was in the doldrums. Although committed in principle to education, and having done a great deal to promote and provide the resources for working-class self-education, practice had rather drifted away. At the 1895 annual congress, the Committee on Education reported that only nine societies had held formal classes on the history and principles of co-operation, with 104 students taking examinations, while fourteen societies ran courses on bookkeeping with a total of 146 examined.[9] Bemoaning a general lack of interest in educational matters, the committee lamented that few even turned up to debate their report. A recent controversy, however, had begun to raise the profile of education.[10] When the President of the Board of Education, Arthur Acland, advocated the study of co-operation in evening continuation schools, there was a wave of protest from private shopkeepers, who successfully banned the teaching in some areas. Margaret Llewellyn Davies took up the issue of education in a strongly worded speech to the Women's Co-operative Guild, to which the education committee gave much attention.[11] She argued that the movement's whole educational apparatus was out of date and ineffective. There needed to be a much stronger and vigorous central organisation to support local activity. In visionary mode, she suggested that educational bodies could investigate a range of economic, industrial and municipal questions, ultimately perhaps resulting in a National School of Industrial Science analogous to what was being established as the London School of Economics. Although intrigued, the education committee felt that these ambitions were somewhat beyond their remit in promoting co-operative education within the movement. Nevertheless, the committee seized the opportunity to launch a full-scale review of the current state of affairs. Llewellyn Davies offered her support and her services: 'we need a training ground in our movement, so that members may be educated to do the duties of citizenship as well as possible.'[12]

A special committee on education was appointed, which sent a circular enquiry to every local society, followed up by visits to a selected number.[13] Responses were received from 402 societies, of which 133 had no educational fund at all. From the rest, a total of £36,336 was spent on educational activities, of which £16,500 went towards maintaining reading rooms and libraries. A little was spent on lectures, classes and local publications, and some societies offered scholarships, but most of the remainder, some £17,000, paid for entertainments, concerts and so forth, ostensibly for propaganda purposes. Closer inquiry suggested that it was not mere apathy gripping the local societies, but that wider educational change had overtaken them. Local authorities routinely provided technical education, which in any case was becoming beyond the capacity of co-operators to provide. Other organisations now had extensive programmes of talks and lectures, and several co-operative societies actively worked with neighbouring cultural and literary societies to promote these activities. Free libraries had to a large extent rendered co-operative libraries and reading rooms redundant, although in some cases co-operative libraries had flourished alongside municipal ones. In other instances, however, it appeared as if local societies continued to maintain a library as a convenient and appropriate outlet for their educational fund, in the absence of any other ideas of what to do with it.

Out of their survey of the markedly changing educational landscape, the special committee recognised the need to enunciate a new policy and direction for co-operative education with clear objectives for local societies. With laudable insight and ambition, it fixed on the absence of any positive teaching about industrial and municipal subjects, not only within the co-operative movement, but by any other body, and pronounced: 'Here, in *the teaching of industrial economics and of the duties of citizens*, is the new pioneer work lying at the doors of co-operators.'[14] To put the new mission into effect the administrative structure managing and co-ordinating co-operative education would have to be overhauled. Once this was achieved, its work would be to promote the study of economic theory and practice, which would, naturally, be based on the detailed, scientific teaching of co-operation, including the history, theory and practice of co-operation and its context. Secondly, citizenship was presented as having always been the essential aim of co-operative education, which now needed to be addressed more directly. Lastly, co-operative societies would continue to have a role in technical education, but in conjunction with other local bodies. Although the educational committee was initially rather cautious about Llewellyn Davies' vision presented to the Women's Guild, there was a good deal of her ethos in their proposals. While firmly based on co-operation, the scheme was outward facing; co-operators needed to take their part in the great contemporary debates about citizenship, labour and democracy.

From the end of the nineteenth century, the education committee put a huge effort into devising courses, writing syllabuses and developing organised programmes. As will be discussed further below, an impressive educational programme was issued each year with a progressive series of offerings in a diverse set of subjects.[15] Giving substance to its announcements, the education committee worked hard to establish citizenship as central to co-operative studies. One interesting innovation was to set a special subject in the educational programme on 'aspects of citizenship' that could serve as a focus for meetings, lectures and discussions at local societies.[16] The first one was 'The Housing Question', which was carried over into the following year. Subsequent topics included 'The Land Question', 'National Education', 'Co-operation and the Poor', 'Municipalisation' and 'The Temperance Problem'.[17] A list of recommended speakers was circulated and the topics were discussed at the annual educational conference. More familiarly, a syllabus and reading list were devised for a course on citizenship.[18] Various incentives were offered to encourage engagement with the more advanced classes in co-operation, industrial history, bookkeeping and citizenship. Scholarships were offered in all four subjects, and arrangements were made with the Oxford Delegacy to examine those students taking the higher-level classes. As with many other aspects of the educational work, however, the committee was somewhat disappointed with the take-up. The special subject in aspects of citizenship lasted until 1904 then disappeared from the programme. Classes in citizenship continued but, for many years, struggled to muster more than a handful of classes or more than a hundred students.

These initiatives were aimed at adults, and this was the main focus of attention through the latter years of the nineteenth century. From the beginning of the twentieth, there was something of a shift in direction, with several interrelated strands. One was to move away from general training for active citizenship to refocus more explicitly on co-operation as the chief object of education within the movement, with a notably more historical approach. There was also a greater concern with reaching children. At the educational conference of 1901, W. R. Rae, one of the most vigorous spokespeople on co-operative education maintained:

> Co-operators ought to be conversant with the evil conditions of the past and the lives of men and women who strove to better social and industrial surroundings ... We must keep the record of the past before our members, many of whom know nothing of the history of co-operation, which had an important bearing upon the success of the present undertakings.[19]

This statement was made in the midst of the bitter and protracted debates surrounding the introduction of the 1902 Education Act.[20] The political, religious, social and cultural implications of the Act were far reaching and profound, and only those elements pertaining to co-operative education can be outlined here.[21] Most directly, the Act abolished the locally elected School Boards, replacing them with a uniform system of Local Educational Authorities, and made rate support available to voluntary, primarily church-led, elementary schools. Although some aspects of the Act were welcomed as progressive measures, such as the first state support for secondary education, the co-operative movement, alongside most other working-class organisations, deprecated the new Act for undermining the democratically elected School Boards and allowing rate support to religious education without local authority control. Other measures restricted access to evening classes for adults. Thus, state education had been distanced from popular control, made less accessible to working people who had missed out earlier in their lives, and efforts to liaise with other municipal bodies to promote popular engagement with issues of the day had been dealt a considerable blow.

Moreover, a lifeline had been offered to predominantly Tory-supporting Anglican educational bodies, at a time when labour movements generally were under increasing assault. Not for the first time, the co-operative movement would have to look to its own resources to shore up their organisation and maintain a sense of cultural identity.

In the wake of the Act, Rae returned to the current situation and future direction of co-operative education.[22] In many respects, it was a reprise of his mid-1890s review, but issued with rather more force and thrown into relief by the national educational reconfiguration. Fundamentally, he thundered, despite strenuous labour over the previous decade the amount of education taking place within the movement remained lamentable for an organisation ostensibly committed to it. For him, education meant the study of co-operative subjects in organised classes. The structures were there, and a great deal of effort had gone into the revision and development of syllabuses, textbooks and classes but, when, in the whole of Britain, only 1,200 adults were taking a course on co-operation, the movement could hardly congratulate itself on its educational ethos. He was scathing of the lack of serious commitment in local societies who preferred to spend their educational funds on 'tea, buns and the funny men'. Moreover, what funds were spent on educational activity were increasingly misdirected. There was no need any more for local societies to maintain libraries and reading rooms, which were now freely available. Nor was it the role of co-operators to supply evening, or science or art classes, which were properly the responsibility of local authorities. The real priority for the movement was classes in co-operation; 'Here there is no doubt – no hesitation. These deal with our very existence, and are as valuable to us as a knowledge of the principles of truth and honesty.' And the key to understanding the nature and importance of co-operation was to know more of the 'Story of the Past':

> We have been compelled to admit that co-operation has been more virile and valuable where its votaries have known most of the history of its founders ... surely there is nothing more inspiring than the lives of those who were faithful enough to struggle through a darkness we know nothing of, and to rejoice at a dawn which, in the brightness of today, seems to us dim. Co-operation will retain its coherence just so long as it is imbued by the spirit of the past.[23]

In the new context, the key was to provide for children, when minds were more readily formed. Junior classes were growing, but there was scope to do so much more. Rae thought that adult classes would only really succeed with a more receptive audience. Thus, it might be more effective simply to initiate discussions in ordinary social situations why (other than the dividend) people became co-operators before moving onto formal courses. Only after an initial course in co-operation should people be encouraged to pursue further study of industrial history, citizenship or economics.

From the late 1890s, a renewed impetus was given to education within the co-operative movement, especially formal classes. The educational committee put a great deal of effort into reorganising the programme, commissioning textbooks and promoting the place of education within the structure of the movement and among local societies. Although the committee continually bemoaned the lack of interest in 'solid educational food' (and the disappointment was never to go away), a great deal was achieved, to be built on in succeeding years. In part, and in particular, the initiative was a reaction to developments in state education; as local authorities did more, societies were doing less and there had to be a rethink about what co-operative education was about. The maturity of co-operation, the wider growth of the labour movement and debates about the relationships between labour, democracy and education also set changing and challenging opportunities. Initially, the tone was optimistic: co-operators should engage with debates about pressing social and economic issues, municipal development and the nature of citizenship. There was a need to train up people who could contribute to these discussions. The early twentieth century sounded a more defensive note: the movement's priority was to shore up its own identity and cohesiveness; to explain to its own members the proper basis and importance of co-operation. Most effectively, this was through reaching the children.

Co-operative history in the Edwardian period

During the first decade of the twentieth century, the Education Committee defined the key aims of co-operative education as:

> primarily, the formation of co-operative character and opinion by teaching the history, theory, and principles of the movement, with economics and industrial and constitutional history in so far as they have bearing on Co-operation; and secondarily, though not necessarily of less import, the training of men and women to take part in industrial and civic life generally.[24]

Although co-operative education ought to contribute to general civic life, the main aim was more insular, to form character and opinion within the movement. This was to be achieved largely through the study of history, and a broad and progressive range of courses was devised for both children and adults. How, then, was the programme organised and what kind of history was being taught? Historians of the Edwardian school curriculum have shown that it was suffused with narratives of the great and glorious progress of nation and empire through wise and benevolent leadership and heroic military exploits.[25] It was usually a homogenising story that glossed over social, political or religious conflict and enjoined working-class children dutifully to follow their leaders in supporting and sustaining nation and empire. For the most part, citizenship was conflated with patriotism; when many men, and all women, were still denied full political rights, citizenship was presented primarily as loyalty to the national/imperial state. Although sharing many of the prevailing pedagogical assumptions about the nature and purpose of historical teaching, unsurprisingly, co-operative education took a somewhat different tack.

To consider the nature of co-operative education in the Edwardian period, and the place of history within it, the 1910 Educational Programme will be used as an example, by which time there was already an extensive series of courses available.[26] For each one, there was a suggested syllabus, with supporting textbooks and an examination. Classes could be run locally using the recommended materials, and the education committee published a register of teachers if local societies felt they did not have sufficient expertise. Many of the courses could also be taken by correspondence. Courses on co-operation were divided into those for juniors and for adults, with each kind split into three sections – preliminary, elementary and advanced. There was also a small section of intermediate-level courses. For juniors, the three sections roughly corresponded to age groups of ten to twelve, twelve to fourteen, and fourteen to sixteen, although it was envisaged that they might subsequently be arranged more by ability. There was no set syllabus for the earlier sections, but some suggestions were made regarding the principal elements to be covered for those studying Junior Stage III. The syllabus was organised in an historical sequence from the social and industrial conditions of the eighteenth century through to the ideal of brotherhood still to be strived for in the future. There was no rosy nostalgia for a bucolic past. Pre-industrial life was presented as brutish and limited, with severe and unjust laws, widespread ignorance and no compassion between rich and poor. Although cottage industry had its freedoms, village life was very isolated and restricted. The factory system brought no respite, with further cruelty towards workers and children, stolen land and no unions. Against these conditions, however, reformers such as Robert Owen and Lord Shaftesbury made a stand and co-operation began to emerge. Cautiously, it was noted that the story of the French Revolution might be told at this point. The second half of the syllabus dealt more specifically with the emergence of co-operation. Pride of place went to the Rochdale Pioneers and their model of the distributive store. The contrast between these and private stores were highlighted as the Dividend, Source, and Purity of goods, but teachers were advised to '[k]eep "divi" in background, make "conditions" chief thought'.[27] Examples from the natural world would show how co-operation was a natural condition. Similarly, the Co-operative Wholesale Society (CWS) and productive co-operation were presented as natural developments from the distributive stores. The course concluded with an optimistic look to the future.

Admirable advice was given on how to engage youngsters in the lessons. They should not be more than an hour long, with the course spread over twelve weeks. It was emphasised that the method of teaching should not be to the textbook but 'should be rather that of picture making. The conditions of the industrial classes at the beginning of the last century, and the story of the Pioneers, should be made the subject of a series of graphic picture lessons' and classes should be livened with song, recitations and lantern slides.[28] Blackboards should be used and the children's illustrations and writings used to decorate the classroom. Marks should be awarded for contributions, suggestions and answering questions, and the mark list exhibited. Examinations were a prominent feature of co-operative education. For juniors, there were no papers for the first two sections, but there was for Stage III. It was a formal printed paper with strict instructions to do no more than eight of the twelve questions in the allotted two hours.[29] Sample questions covered the meanings of key terms, the lives of Owen and Shaftesbury, the opening of the Toad Lane store, and the differences between co-operative stores and private shops. Many of the questions were leading: for example, candidates were asked to define co-operation and competition, state which was better and to give reasons why. Papers done by juniors were marked locally, although a crib sheet was distributed to advise teachers on how to allocate marks.[30] To encourage participation, societies were invited to submit their best papers to the educational committee for re-marking, and awards were made for the best nationally. In 1910–11, 117 of the Stage III junior co-operation papers were submitted for central remarking.[31] The examiners were cautiously pleased with the standard although they complained that, despite all admonishments, there was still a heavy reliance on the textbook. In general, the children did best on the narrative questions on people and place, their own societies and memorising co-operative songs. The more conceptual questions on the differences between co-operative and private shops posed more difficulties and there was much misunderstanding over the nature of co-operative productive societies. Altogether, however, the examiner was quite pleased. There was 'abundant evidence that a good foundation in co-operative knowledge and principles has been laid by these young students – the co-operators of the future'.[32]

Through the first decades of the twentieth century, the standard text-book on co-operation for children was *Our Story* by Isa Nicholson.[33] Written at the request of the Education Committee and first published in 1903, it went through numerous editions, selling in huge numbers. By 1907 it had already sold 31,000 copies and been translated into six languages.[34] It was the principal resource for teachers and young co-operators alike, and so set the parameters for understanding the nature of co-operation. It was a mixture of history, moral story and basic guide to the main components of the movement. The first two-thirds of the book described a narrative arc from 'The Darkest Hour' to 'The Day of Success', very much underpinning the syllabus for junior co-operators. It was slightly more optimistic about pre-industrial times, when conditions for handloom weavers might not have been good, but they had some independence, could combine weaving with other occupations and, being not so far off a master workman, could hope to rise in the world. Factories, however, reduced men to hands, or undercut them with women, children or pauper apprentices, enriching the masters and impoverishing the workers. Light began dawning with Owen, who provided better conditions for his employees, especially children, but failed to establish co-operative ideas on a large scale. The other key figure was Shaftesbury, who strove for better conditions for children. Although he objected to the socialist basis of Owen's ideas, his commitment to peaceful change for the good of all classes demonstrated that he was effectively a comrade to Owen.

The pivotal point was the Rochdale Pioneers and the opening of the Toad Lane store. In the turmoil of the mid-1840s, the 'totally uneducated class' resorted to rioting and, while some masters were kind-hearted, there was always a gulf: 'The masters gave, but the workers wished to share! The rich believed in charity, the poor asked for justice.'[35] The Pioneers struggled to raise sufficient capital, supporters struggled to get to the store and pay the relatively higher prices, and the initial provisions were decidedly meagre, so the colourful account of the opening night highlighted the achievement. Contrary to the advice of the education committee, however, for Nicholson the 'Day of Success' was the first 'divi day', when supporters of the store were able to get new clothes, or new teeth or even a piano! The rest of the book provided an account of the main features of the modern movement. What was involved in establishing a distributive store was set out. Nicholson was critical of the trend towards imposing town edifices, arguing that a network of smaller, more modest stores was better. Stores, however, depended on customer loyalty, and healthy retail trade was the foundation of all the other worthy activities a society might sustain. Although logically prior, productive co-operatives came after the stores and an account of the emergence of the CWS and Scottish Co-operative Wholesale Society was given. The book concluded with a homily on the benefits of co-operation, materially and physically, but also the opportunity for self-improvement. This was not just an insular benefit, but the foundations of healthy citizenship, which prompted a greater interest in local society, welfare and governance. The book was romantic and heroic and progressive, but also described the hardship, struggle and achievements of working people.

For adults, there were further courses in co-operation, and more specific courses in industrial history, economics and citizenship, also available by correspondence. They were intended to be the 'training ground of a future generation of members, committeemen, officers and employees of the society'.[36] The syllabuses followed the concentric model of reprising the main elements of earlier courses in greater depth. This had the practical benefit that students in more than one stage could be taught together. Thus, the preliminary stage was largely a revision of the upper level of the junior classes, while the elementary and advanced stages each began with an historical section, but then moved onto more contemporary issues such as the differences between consumer and producer associations and the role of education and propaganda. At the highest level, there was greater depth on the economics of co-operation and a section on contemporary problems of co-operation, including relationships between the movement and trade unions or municipal authorities and the possible limitations of voluntary co-operation.

The course in industrial history had a much longer time span, beginning in Anglo-Saxon England and ending, somewhat paradoxically, in the early nineteenth century. In many respects it provided a chronological background to the emergence of factory industry. Study of the medieval period focused on economic aspects of towns and markets, the development of the woollen trade and social aspects such as the Black Death and the Peasant's Revolt. The social and economic upheavals of the Tudor period and the discovery of the New World were considered, before going on to the industrial and agrarian revolutions of the eighteenth century. The elementary course concluded with 'The Gloomy Opening of the 19th Century'. The advanced course covered much the same topics, but with additional material on the Roman and Danish invasions, the manorial system and the guilds, medieval commercial policy and mercantilism, the struggle for colonial supremacy, the Old and New Poor Laws, and Free Trade. For those more interested in contemporary economic problems there were specific courses on economics, including topics on the growth of free industry, the meaning of wealth, production, consumption, capital, labour and income, supply and demand, value, and trade unions. An alternative syllabus was based more on the study of classical authors such as Adam Smith, Malthus, Ricardo and Mill.

Although the educational programme was geared overwhelmingly towards enhancing the co-operative movement, the course on citizenship remained. Guiding the syllabus was an analysis of the meanings of 'Citizen', 'Nation' and 'State'.[37] For the most part, the course covered the principal components of national and local government – as elected and administrative bodies and the history and principles of their organisation, roles and responsibilities – from the nature of representative government to the arrangements for roads, streets and buildings. A section on the 'Duties of Citizens in Relation to Local and Central Government' confirmed the duty of voting and the importance of exercising independent judgement. There was also discussion of associations of workers, the struggle between capital and labour and the relationships between labour and the state. Given the context of our sample year of 1910, with the increasingly dangerous debates around unionisation, labour representation and female suffrage, discussions of governance and citizenship were potent and radical.[38] Less inflammatory and more personalised, a section on 'The Industrial and Social Duties of the Citizen' considered the physical and moral conditions of success in life, the importance of training and the uses of machinery. Equally, the extent and advantages of empire with the importance of the colonies and imperial defence were included. The recommended textbook, not written in house, was Oscar Browning's *The Citizen: His Rights and Responsibilities*.[39] The numbers studying in adult classes were not large, with approximately 400 taking examinations in co-operation and about fifty each in industrial history and citizenship.[40] They seemed to take it seriously and the examiners were largely content with the standard achieved and the levels of intelligent, independent thought displayed.

By the outbreak of the First World War, the basic structures of co-operative education were in place, centred on inculcating the principles and ethos of co-operation, especially to the young, primarily through the study of the history and development of the co-operative movement with supplementary adult courses specifically on history and citizenship. To a large extent this followed contemporary thinking about the nature and purpose of history and citizenship teaching. The Board of Education favoured an historical approach for teaching on moral principles, the development of personal character and the duties of citizenship. Similarly, co-operative history was progressive and drew on romantic stories of heroes to inspire the young. Although espousing the highest ideals of engaging teaching, all too often, the classes seem to have been wedded to the recommended textbooks, and the prominent place of examinations constantly undermined the exhortations not to see examination success as the key criterion. In content and context, however, co-operative history was wholly different from that peddled in the elementary schools. An emphasis on recent urban and industrial history was quite different from the medieval and early modern rural focus of most school readers. Character and citizenship were not expressed solely through patriotic duty to nation, empire and authority; there was conflict in modern society, and established leaders could be challenged. Most importantly, working people had historical agency, tackling the problems they faced and constructing a new form of industrial organisation.

The extent of co-operative history in the interwar period

In the aftermath of the First World War, the movement, once again, seemed to be under threat. As with almost every other aspect of national life, co-operatives were affected by the war, but the movement worked with the coalition government on food production, retailing and rationing. Relationships soured when the government chose to classify co-operative dividends as profits and imposed the swingeing excess profits tax. The response to sell at cost evaded the tax, but ate into societies' resources. A further, dramatic consequence was the formation of the co-operative political party to seek to defend the interests of co-operation in government.[41] The need for new initiatives and directions had been seen even before the war when a full-scale survey of the movement's activities had been put in train.[42] Playing a significant part in the review was the recently appointed Director of Education, Fred Hall. Echoing Rae's position a decade earlier, Hall felt that the response of ordinary co-operators to the serious forces affecting the movement was somewhat lacking, which he ascribed to a failure to appreciate sufficiently the core values and principles of the movement. Consequently, more education was required to create a better informed, and more committed, membership and workforce. Through the interwar period, then, Hall and his colleagues further expanded the co-operative curriculum.[43] Building on solid foundations, an ever wider range of syllabuses was devised to explore different aspects of co-operation, social and industrial history, citizenship and social sciences. Increasing numbers took up the opportunities, particularly of young people and especially adolescents. The main part of this section considers how the educational programme had developed by the middle of the interwar period. A speculative discussion then raises the possibility of making comparisons between the place of history in co-operative education and history in the schools.

By 1930, there were almost seventy separate courses listed in the programme.[44] Although often with only a handful of attendees, very few did not attract any students at all. Almost half were for the training of employees or society officials to meet the requirements of a growing and increasingly complex and professionalised organisation. Co-operation remained the chief subject, and the opening statement on the objects of co-operative education remained the same as in 1910, with the emphasis firmly on the formation of co-operative character and opinion through teaching the history, theory and principles of the movement. The syllabuses were also much the same, with a strong historical dimension, and it was affirmed that '[a] right understanding of the past and the present is necessary for those who would fit themselves for building a better future'.[45] Following new progressive educational ideas, there was more careful advice on how the junior classes should be run. A session of ninety minutes should open with a song or recitation, feature only about forty-five to fifty minutes of actual class time and finish with more games and social activity. Lesson evenings could be broken up with lighter weeks as well. Classes should not exceed thirty and the teacher should not talk down to the children. Adult classes in co-operation built a progressive understanding of the movement through three stages. Alongside the standard courses in co-operation, there was now a wide range of more specialised syllabuses on various aspects of the movement. Students could study current problems of co-operation, and the connections between co-operation and general social issues. The more outward looking could focus on the nature and development of co-operation in Ireland or Denmark. In the uncertain relationships between the Women's Co-operative Guild and other parts of the movement, a series of three courses on co-operation and citizenship was constructed specifically for women.[46] The courses were designed to be taken consecutively; the first dealt with women in relation to their own store, the second with the movement as a whole and the third with wider questions, thus gradually broadening their horizons. It was emphasised that there was no admission fee and no examinations, unless there was a demand for one. For those who successfully passed through the three basic courses, there were more advanced options including on social history, women in industry, hygiene and physiology, or women reformers.

History and economics as they related to co-operation was taught and an important, though still secondary function of co-operative education was to train men and women to take part in social reform and civic life more generally. To this end, there was a number of courses on history and social science subjects. History was central:

> To the student of social questions, or the member of a working-class organisation, few subjects of study are of more importance than history, particularly Industrial History and Constitutional History. A study of these subjects gives him knowledge of the past, power for the present, and hope for the future. It enables him to review and avoid the mistakes of his predecessors and it cultivates the power to take, and the habit of taking, the long view.[47]

Thus, there were three courses in industrial history, an elementary one and an advanced one split into two parts, Part I going from 1066 to 1760 and Part II from 1760 to 1930. A suite of more specialised courses dealt with the 'Industrial Revolution', the period in which 'most of our present day industrial and social problems had their birth' and the study of which was essential for a right understanding of these problems, 'Economic and Industrial History of the Nineteenth Century', 'Reform Movements of the Nineteenth Century' and 'Constitutional History'.[48] Alongside the historical courses was a series on economics including general economics and more specific courses on 'Money, Prices and Banking', 'Business Organisation' and 'Industry and Commerce'. For those interested in contemporary social and political issues, the courses in 'Citizenship' and in local and central government were offered, as well as more theoretical ones in 'Political Science' and in 'Sociology and Ethics'. As an alternative way into the subject a new course was devised on 'Civics', which looked at other forms of community life and organisation besides the more formal structures of local and central government.

A significant development was the emergence of intermediate grade classes in co-operation. These were intended for adolescents who had been through the junior course, but were not ready to join the adult classes. They were first formed before the war, but grew rapidly during the interwar years at a similar time to the emergence of the Woodcraft Folk and other co-operative youth organisations.[49] Four parallel courses were devised, all of which had an essentially historical basis. The 'A' course took a biographical approach through a study of the lives of social reformers from within the movement and wider socialist thinkers and campaigners such as Owen, Fry, Kingsley, Thomas Hughes, Ruskin, Morris, E. V. Neale and Holyoake. Course 'B' was an extension of the study of the history and principles of co-operation, covering much the same kind of syllabus in greater depth. A novel perspective was provided in course 'C', which took industrial history and co-operation as its subject, but which drew on Hall's textbook, *Sunnyside*.[50] This text included an account of the formation of a model co-operative community, so the course, while drawing on the facts of the past was also, in part, an imaginative exercise. It was noted that such an approach would require careful interpretation by the teacher. Finally, course 'D' treated co-operation through the ages, which ranged widely over time and geographical area and drew on examples and analogies from the natural world as well as human interaction. The numbers taking these courses were quite substantial. In 1930, a total of 5,252 were enrolled in 131 classes, with course 'A' the most popular.[51] It is unclear precisely what age these students were. Intermediate classes were described as for 'adolescents', and the previous Stage III of junior co-operation was designated as suitable for those aged fourteen to sixteen, which indicates an age group in their mid- to late- teens. To put these figures in context, we can try to relate them to their peer age group studying history in the schools.

State schooling had expanded considerably during the 1920s, with more opportunities for adolescents. In elementary schools, the compulsory leaving age was raised to fourteen and more children stayed on beyond that, with a variety of post-elementary possibilities developing alongside the growing secondary school sector.[52] History was a central feature of the school curriculum.[53] After the First World War, there were attempts to broaden the scope of school history, to move away from an insular national narrative and adopt a more internationalist perspective. Experiments in progressive pedagogy were also encouraged. The focus on key events in national political history, however, remained and, when school textbooks had a very long shelf life, most historians see few changes in the nature and content of school history before and after the war. Nevertheless, in secondary schools, history was a popular feature of the new examinations at sixteen and eighteen, the School and Higher School Certificates. This is approximately the same age group as those taking Junior Stage III and intermediate classes in co-operation and raises the possibility of making some comparisons. The figures in Table 5.1 are for the cohort examined in 1930.

There is no room here to examine properly which of these figures can be compared meaningfully with each other, or indeed whether it would be possible to do so. The point of the juxtaposition, then, is to raise the possibility that they could be compared; that the number of young people in their mid-teens studying the history of the co-operative movement might conceivably bear comparison with the numbers following the standard nationalistic political narrative of the schools.

Table 5.1: Co-operative Union examinations vs school certificates, 1930 cohort

Junior Co-operation	
Enrolled	Examined
26,571	9,053
Intermediate Co-operation	
Enrolled	Examined
5,252	2,017
School Certificate	
Numbers taking history	Passed examination
48,200	23,183
Higher School Certificate	
Numbers taking history	Passed examination
1,058	820

Sources: Figures for co-operative examinations from *Co-operative Classes Session 1930–31: Results of Examinations* (Manchester: Co-operative Union, 1931); for school history from D. Cannadine, J. Keating and N. Sheldon, *The Right Kind of History: Teaching the Past in Twentieth-Century England* (Basingstoke: Palgrave Macmillan, 2011).

Conclusions

At the end of the nineteenth century, the co-operative movement launched a major campaign in education, especially in organised courses and classes. Partly, it was to reposition the movement's educational endeavours against the changing national landscape, but there was also a perceived need to revivify grassroots effort which had, apparently, lapsed into torpor. To begin with, it seemed designed not just as an insular pre-occupation, but to engage with the wider contemporary debates about citizenship, democracy and the role of labour. Quickly, however, a more defensive aspect prevailed, with greater urgency to promote deeper understanding of co-operation within the movement against threatening manoeuvres. A very similar situation prevailed in the aftermath of the First World War when, once again, co-operators looked to their own resources to stabilise, enhance and promote the importance and value of their movement through reflexive educational engagement. Throughout, the approach taken was, substantially, an education in history – of the origins and emergence of the movement, its founding principles and pervasive ethos, of its struggles and triumphs, and the importance of its continuing task. This was not unusual in contemporary educational thinking; history was the favoured means of instilling moral messages, character development and citizenship training. Where it differed was in the content and context of the curriculum. Co-operative history was about modern urban, industrial times, active and participatory citizenship, and the agency of working people to make their own history.

The educational programmes put in place were a remarkable achievement of scale, scope and organisation, but advocates constantly bemoaned the lack of interest in serious education in the movement. Indeed, it would be fair to say that only a small fraction of adult co-operators pursued classes, and many fewer continued to successful examination. Nevertheless, those who persevered constituted an educated cadre of some hundreds a year, leavening the movement and perhaps entering onto larger stages. At the same time, considerable efforts went into capturing the young and, here, the numbers reached are not to be derided. By the 1930s, significant cohorts of young people were taking advantage of the opportunities to explore their own history, culture and ethos. Repeating the caveats of the previous section, we cannot, here, go into the potential implications of this; whether and how it may have had an impact on popular understandings of the past, or on ideas of citizenship, or the development of the co-operative movement, or engagement with politics and civic life. That the questions can even be asked, however, raises interesting possibilities. Although most did not, significant numbers did take advantage of the resources put in place for co-operators, and especially the next generation of co-operators, to appreciate the distinguished history of their movement, and how this equipped them for the challenges of their times both within co-operation and for its wider role in society.

Notes

1 See, for example, Polyp, *The Co-operative Revolution: A Graphic Novel* (Oxford: New Internationalist, 2012).

2 P. Gurney, *Co-operative Culture and the Politics of Consumption in England, 1870–1930* (Manchester: Manchester University Press, 1996); C. Wrigley, 'The commemorative urge: the co-operative movement's collective memory' in L. Black and N. Robertson, eds, *Consumerism and the Co-operative Movement in Modern British History: Taking Stock* (Manchester: Manchester University Press, 2009), pp. 157–73; I. MacPherson, 'Community, individuality and co-operation: the centrality of values' in A. Webster, L. Shaw, J. K. Walton, A. Brown and D. Stewart, eds, *The Hidden Alternative: Co-operative Values, Past, Present and Future* (Manchester: Manchester University Press, 2011), pp. 203–25.

3 T. Woodin, 'Co-operative education in Britain during the nineteenth and early twentieth centuries: context, identity and learning' in Webster et al., *Hidden Alternative*, pp. 78–95.

4 Gurney, *Co-operative Culture*; N. Robertson, *The Co-operative Movement and Communities in Britain, 1914–1960: Minding Their Own Business* (Farnham: Ashgate, 2010); Woodin, 'Co-operative education in Britain'; K. Vernon, 'Values and vocation: educating the co-operative workforce' in Webster et al., *Hidden Alternative*, pp. 37–58.

5 See the Educational Programmes published by the Co-operative Union, National Co-operative Archive.
6 This chapter does not consider the even more impressive range of vocational courses developed for employees of the co-operative movement. For this aspect, see Vernon, 'Values and vocation'.
7 V. E. Chancellor, *History for Their Masters: Opinion in the English History Textbook 1800–1914* (New York: Augustus Kelly, 1970); J. A. Mangan, ed., *'Benefits Bestowed'? Education and British Imperialism* (Manchester: Manchester University Press, 1988); S. Heathorn, *For Home, Country, and Race: Constructing Gender, Class and Englishness in the Elementary School, 1880–1914* (Toronto: University of Toronto Press, 2000); D. Cannadine, J. Keating and N. Sheldon, *The Right Kind of History: Teaching the Past in Twentieth-Century England* (Basingstoke: Palgrave Macmillan, 2011); J. Keating, 'Approaches to citizenship teaching in the first half of the twentieth century: the experience of the London County Council', *History of Education* 40 (2011), 761–78.
8 K. Vernon, 'Co-operative education and the state, c.1895–1935', *Forum* 55 (2013), 293–307.
9 'Report of the Committee on Education', *Co-operative Congress Report* (1895).
10 Gurney, *Co-operative Culture*.
11 Reported in the 'Report of the Committee on Education and Production', *Co-operative Congress Report* (1896).
12 *Co-operative Congress Report* (1896), p. 114.
13 'Report of Special Committee on Education', *Co-operative Congress Report* (1898).
14 Ibid., p. 12 (emphasis in original).
15 See, for example, *Co-operative Educational Programme 1910* (Manchester: Co-operative Union, 1910).
16 'Report of the Committee on Education', *Co-operative Congress Report* (1899).
17 'Report of the Committee on Education', *Co-operative Congress Report* (1902–04).
18 'Report of the Committee on Education', *Co-operative Congress Report* (1899).
19 'Educational Conference', *Co-operative Congress Report* (1901), p. 198.
20 Vernon, 'Co-operative education'.
21 N. Daglish, *Education Policy-making in England and Wales: The Crucible Years, 1895–1911* (London: Woburn Press, 1996).
22 'How best can Co-operative Societies utilise their educational funds in view of the educational facilities now provided by municipal and local authorities', *Co-operative Congress Report* (1904).
23 Ibid., p. 282.
24 *Co-operative Educational Programme 1910*, p. 7.
25 Chancellor, *History for Their Masters*; Heathorn, *For Home, Country, and Race*; Cannadine et al., *Right Kind of History*; Keating, 'Approaches to citizenship teaching'.
26 *Co-operative Educational Programme 1910*.
27 Ibid., p. 12.

28 Ibid., p. 11.
29 *Examination Papers 1910–11* (Manchester: Co-operative Union, 1911).
30 'Juniors' examination in "Co-operation": hints to local examiners on marking papers', *Examination Papers 1910–11.*
31 *Co-operative Classes Session 1910–11: Results of Examinations* (Manchester: Co-operative Union, 1911).
32 Ibid., p. 20.
33 I. Nicholson, *Our Story* (Manchester: Co-operative Union, 1903).
34 'Report of the Committee on Education', *Co-operative Congress Report* (1907).
35 Nicholson, *Our Story*, p. 40.
36 *Co-operative Educational Programme 1910*, p. 9.
37 Ibid., p. 23.
38 D. Powell, *British Politics and the Labour Question, 1868–1990* (London: Macmillan, 1992).
39 Oscar Browning, *The Citizen: His Rights and Responsibilities* (London: Blackie, n.d.).
40 *Results of Examinations, 1910–11.*
41 P. Maguire, 'Co-operation and crisis: government, co-operation and politics, 1917–22' in S. Yeo, ed., *New Views of Co-operation* (London: Routledge, 1988), pp. 187–206.
42 F. Hall, *A Review of the Education Report of the Survey Committee as presented to the Swansea Congress of 1917* (Manchester: Co-operative Union, 1919).
43 Vernon, 'Values and vocation'.
44 *Educational Programme: Session 1931–32* (Manchester: Co-operative Printing Society, 1931).
45 Ibid., p. 5.
46 G. Scott, *Feminism and the Politics of Working Women: The Women's Co-operative Guild, 1880s to the Second World War* (London: UCL Press, 1998).
47 *Educational Programme 1931–32*, p. 89.
48 Ibid., p. 95.
49 J. Attfield, *With Light of Knowledge: A Hundred Years of Education in the Royal Arsenal Co-operative Society, 1877–1977* (London: Royal Arsenal Co-operative Society and Journeyman Press, 1981).
50 F. Hall, *Sunnyside: A Story of Industrial History and Co-operation for Young People* (Manchester: Co-operative Union, 1919).
51 *Co-operative Classes Session 1930–31: Results of Examinations* (Manchester: Co-operative Union, 1931).
52 G. Bernbaum, *Social Change and the Schools 1918–1944* (London: RKP, 1967).
53 Cannadine et al., *Right Kind of History.*

6

'The unit of the co-operative movement … is a woman': gender and the development of the co-operative business model in Britain

Rachael Vorberg-Rugh

In her 1891 history of the British co-operative movement, Beatrice Potter (later Webb) made a simple statement: 'Taken as a general fact, the unit of the Co-operative movement – the customer – is a woman.'[1] In doing so, Potter neatly elided a central contradiction that shaped the development of Britain's consumer co-operative movement from the nineteenth century: whilst most co-operative *customers* were women, most of its *members* were men. As was widely acknowledged by contemporaries, co-operative businesses depended on their ability to attract predominantly female customers to purchase food and household goods. Women were the primary consumers[2] of working-class families, and the movement's ideology privileged consumption as the primary means of social and economic change. This chapter explores how both of these aspects of co-operation created space for women's involvement, but contemporary gender norms also created constraints to their participation, with significant consequences for co-operative development.

Historians interested in co-operation and gender have tended to focus on the Women's Co-operative Guild (WCG), formed in 1883, and its activities as a pressure group representing women's interests inside and outside the movement.[3] Whilst not seeking to minimise this scholarship, this chapter seeks to shift the focus. Although the WCG still features prominently in my analysis, the emphasis is on the ways in which contemporary perspectives on gender shaped, complicated and sometimes constrained co-operative development. By mainstreaming gender as a category of analysis, I argue, historians can not only better understand the role of women in co-operation, but also better understand the co-operative business model itself. The chapter draws upon research for the author's doctoral thesis, and shares its focus on British consumer co-operatives up to 1920.[4] It draws on the records of local co-operative societies, national co-operative organisations, WCG records and co-operative periodicals, many of which are held at the National Co-operative Archive in Manchester.

The chapter begins by describing the context in which the co-operative movement developed, noting the importance of the gendered division of labour in household economy. Next, it outlines the development of the Rochdale business model, briefly discussing its antecedents and the implications of the Rochdale system for women as household managers. Subsequent sections highlight the importance of women's consumption to the movement's economic growth, and demonstrate the barriers to women's participation as members and leaders. As this chapter argues, although women's economic importance to the movement as consumers was widely acknowledged, their consumer power did not translate to high levels of female membership and participation in co-operative leadership.

This chapter is primarily a historical study, rooted in a specific period and place. Yet the questions raised are relevant to current issues regarding the under-representation of women in co-operative leadership and management in many developed and developing countries, discussed in Rawlings and Shaw's chapter 7 here. In terms of the theme of this volume, one question this chapter investigates is the extent to which women were able to participate in shaping the co-operative mainstream. At the same time, this chapter illustrates that co-operatives are not separate from the societies in which they develop, and that co-operative members carry with them many values and prejudices common to the communities in which they live, with important implications for co-operative governance. The subject is a complex one, and it is hoped that contemporary co-operators will find this chapter useful in reflecting on the extent to which their democratic organisations represent the totality of their membership, what strategies may be useful in increasing the participation and agency of women and other disadvantaged groups, and the ways in which their organisations both reflect and challenge existing mainstream cultural, economic, political and social views in their specific settings.

Gender and the development of the Rochdale model

British consumer co-operatives developed primarily among the urban working classes, in response to the difficult conditions of life in the emerging industrial towns of the nineteenth century. In such communities, the essential economic unit was the household, and all family members contributed to the effort to ensure its survival. Co-operatives developed during a period when the concepts of 'producer' and 'consumer' were deeply gendered, and the normative model of the working-class family posited men as wage earners and women as wage spenders. At the same time, widely accepted notions of 'separate spheres' for male and female activity – public and civic versus private and domestic – shaped the environment in which co-operatives operated. While such ideals did not always match reality – men did shop, and women did work for wages – they were nonetheless widely shared norms.[5] What emerges from numerous studies of working-class family life across this period is a complex picture, marked by largely separate fields of endeavour for men and women coupled with a strong sense of interdependence.[6]

Whilst all family members contributed to the household economy, the roles of males and females were quite distinct. Broadly speaking, children of both genders entered the workforce after completing their schooling and contributed most or all of their wages to the household income. Whilst men expected to remain in formal employment, many working-class women tended to end waged work upon marriage or around the birth of their first child.[7] Husbands were the primary wage earners, and handed over some or all of their weekly wage packet to their wives, who held the responsibility for household management. Married women sometimes re-entered formal employment, but for the most part they undertook casual waged work that could be combined with their household duties.

Whether or not they were employed, wives were expected to handle all of the details of the domestic sphere, including housework, childrearing and managing the household finances. Women used numerous strategies to stretch their families' limited income and such prudent expenditure could mean the difference between mere survival and a reasonable level of comfort.[8] The extent to which shopping remained a gendered experience is suggested in co-operative records, as when a Bolton co-operator suggested in 1914 that his society should open a separate store for tobacco, 'as men did not like to go into a provision shop'.[9] The gendered division of labour within the family economy of the working classes continued well into the twentieth century, even as living standards rose and new types of goods became affordable. This was the context in which the Rochdale model of consumer co-operation developed.

Gender equality was not a stated aim of the Rochdale Society of Equitable Pioneers, as put forth in their 1844 objects; however, the language of the society's formative documents specified that both men and women could be members.[10] Given that most men and all women were denied the Parliamentary vote in this period, and that most trade unions and friendly societies were single-sex organisations,[11] the

Rochdale Pioneers' decision to include women as well as men among their membership seems unusual. However, as will be discussed below, in designing their co-operative the Rochdale Pioneers drew on an ideological and practical legacy of women's activism in working-class movements. Moreover, by emphasising association by consumers as their central means of achieving social change, they created space for women's involvement due to their pivotal role in household consumption.

The Rochdale Pioneers did not 'invent' co-operation, but rather synthesised the experiences of the many earlier co-operative experiments which developed in Britain in the late eighteenth and early nineteenth century. Such 'pre-Rochdale' co-operatives[12] developed alongside other social, economic and political efforts, particularly Owenism and Chartism. The Owenite[13] movement's concern with gender equality is one antecedent of the Rochdale model's inclusion of women. During a period in which male superiority was taken for granted by legal institutions and individuals alike, Owenites such as Anna Wheeler argued that the inequality of the sexes was not a natural state, but a social construction that could, and should, be altered. By changing the institutions and circumstances which shaped masculine and feminine development, some Owenites argued, gender equality would be achieved.[14] This radical approach was apparently taken to heart by some of the early co-operative experiments that developed in the pre-Rochdale period, which included women alongside men as members.[15]

A second precursor of the Rochdale Pioneers' model of consumer co-operation is the Chartist[16] practice of 'exclusive dealing'. The People's Charter sought to expand the political franchise only to men;[17] nonetheless, the movement welcomed women's activism in support of its cause and drew particularly on their traditional role as the household's primary consumer.[18] The tactic of exclusive dealing asked Chartists to refuse to purchase goods from shopkeepers who did not support their cause. Successful consumer organising led some Chartists to organise their own co-operative stores, and numerous historians have documented the significant involvement of female Chartists in exclusive dealing and early co-operative development.[19] However, as Taylor argues, many Chartists did not share the Owenite view of the need for a transformation of gender relations, contextualising women's Chartist activities as an extension of their domestic role.[20]

Several of the original Rochdale Pioneers had direct links with Owenism and Chartism, and drew upon these movements' publications and their own experiences in developing what would become the Rochdale model.[21] During the 1840s and 1850s a number of co-operative societies opened using the Rochdale system, spreading first in the industrial cities of northern England and Scotland and gradually expanding throughout the country. By 1880 the co-operative movement counted over 550,000 members in around 950 local co-operative societies, loosely connected through regional and national administrative bodies. By 1920, the movement had grown to over 4.5 million members in nearly 1,400 societies.[22]

During the same period, co-operatives were increasing their economic influence. The Co-operative Wholesale Society (CWS) – a secondary co-operative whose 'members' were the local societies – originated in the 1860s as a means of supplying and distributing goods to co-operative stores. The CWS and its Scottish counterpart[23] became manufacturers in the 1880s, opening factories that produced a wide array of co-operative branded goods. By 1900 the Wholesales had significantly expanded their operations and the co-operative movement accounted for approximately 8.5 per cent of Britain's trade in food and household stores, a percentage that would rise to around 12 per cent in 1920.[24]

Numerous scholars have addressed the reasons behind the economic success of the Rochdale model,[25] but few commentators have addressed the appeal of the Rochdale system to its predominantly female customer base. For instance, although Gurney notes that 'the choice between Sunlight Soap, Lipton's Teas, or the products of the Co-operative Wholesale Society, the choice between being a co-operator or a "mass consumer," was a cultural and political choice of major consequence', he gives little attention to the fact that such choices were made almost exclusively by women.[26] Whilst one can debate the extent to which the Rochdale Pioneers and other early co-operators were concerned with gender equality, the fact remains that in order to succeed financially, co-operatives needed women to purchase the food and household goods they stocked. The Rochdale model offered significant attractions to women consumers by addressing some of their greatest needs as keepers of the family finances. What follows is a brief description of the main elements of the Rochdale model[27] and their implications for women.

Open membership was the first pillar of the Rochdale system: anyone could join the co-operative on the same terms as existing members. Members joined by buying a £1 share in the society, which could be paid in instalments – a key provision at a time when few working-class families were able to save from their weekly incomes. Membership provided two significant benefits. Firstly, the co-operative acted as a small savings bank, since members received a fixed rate of interest (usually around 5 per cent) on their shares. The principle of fixed interest on capital served a key purpose: by limiting the amount of interest they paid out, the Pioneers could use their trading surplus for other aims, including social and educational facilities as well as a dividend on purchases. This vital benefit of membership meant that each member received a portion of the society's earnings, based on the amount they had purchased during the previous quarter. Because the 'divi' came at the end of each quarter, but was earned through everyday shopping, it served as a kind of automatic savings bank rather than a painful deduction from the weekly housekeeping money.[28] Dividends could be used to meet financial emergencies or fund larger household purchases, or, when times were good, could be reinvested in interest-earning co-operative shares. In this way, co-operators could 'eat their way to a nest egg'.[29] Thus, the dividend was an important incentive for women to shop at co-operative stores and offered a substantial advantage over other retailers. The co-operative commitment to pure foods was another inducement, at a time when at a time when food adulteration was particularly rife.[30] Nonetheless, as one female co-operator put it in 1883, 'in urging our neighbours and friends to become members of our stores, dividend is our chief argument'.[31]

Democratic control was another central tenet of the Rochdale model. Once fully paid up, each member was entitled to vote in the society's quarterly meetings. Members elected the committee of management that oversaw day-to-day operations, and society rules required that major policy decisions be approved by members' meetings. To ensure that those with a greater amount of capital invested could not dominate the organisation, co-operatives adhered to a 'one member, one vote' rule, a key difference from joint-stock companies where votes were based on the number of shares held. The specific inclusion of women as members in societies' rules thus offered at least the nominal opportunity for women to participate in directing the business of co-operative stores. However, as discussed below, the opportunity for women to become co-operative members was often restricted as co-operatives developed.

'Come and *buy*! That is all'

As co-operatives grew more numerous in the mid nineteenth century, it became common practice for many societies to institute rules that restricted membership to one person per family. In practice, the named member was most often the male head of household. Since only members could vote in quarterly meetings and stand for election, other family members (wives and adult children living at home) were effectively disenfranchised. Whilst no gender disaggregated membership records exist for this period, anecdotal evidence suggests that female co-operative membership in the mid nineteenth century was small, and restricted primarily to widows. Societies gave a variety of reasons for restricting membership, including the widely bemoaned problem of 'surplus capital',[32] but contemporary commentators also put forward the view that one member was all that was required to represent the household.[33] Intriguingly, whether or not a woman was the named member, in most societies co-operative dividends were assumed to be the wife's property, even before the Married Women's Property Acts of 1870 and 1882 clarified wives' legal right to savings.[34] As Blaszak notes, this was good business practice for co-operative managers, who 'knew that they depended on the custom of the wife and could not afford to alienate her'.[35]

Although few women were members of their societies, co-operators of both sexes were well aware of the need to convince women to make their purchases at co-operative stores, rather than private shops. For instance, in the December 1865 edition of *The Co-operator*, John Whyatt of Manchester wrote an appeal to co-operative women: 'It is said that (as regards many stores) you pass your own husband's and father's stores, and go to those in which you have no interest, for *poor*, *dear*, and *adulterated goods*.' Whyatt continued:

> The millions of money which those dear, hard-toiling men earn in the year, is given to you, the 'women of England', to provide for you and your little ones; and can you pass 'their own shop' – YOUR own shop – and gall and grieve them by passing through the tow with your open baskets full of things bought elsewhere, whilst their goods are spoiling, neglected in their stores? [36]

Wyatt's criticism would be echoed by many co-operative leaders in the decades to come, and such calls for customer loyalty were delivered in distinctly gendered terms. The comments of the Grays society's Mr Brown in 1890 sum up the flavour of many such critiques: 'they knew it was a terrible job sometimes to get their wives to spend their money at the right place'.[37]

However, appeals for the loyalty of women to co-operative stores did not go unchallenged by female co-operators. A few months after Whyatt's piece appeared, Alice Wilson of Manchester wrote an article of her own:

> Permit me to suggest to Mr Whyatt, and to the Co-operative men generally, that if they honestly and earnestly wish to induce the women to become Co-operators, they do not go the right way about it. When we want to make a man into a Co-operator, what do we do? Get him to join the society – to become a member, of course. Well, you know 'that which is good for the goose is also good for the gander;' so, if you wish to make a woman into a Co-operator, get her to join the society – to become a member, of course – and then expect her to take an interest in her own affairs.[38]

Referring specifically to the question of one per household membership restrictions, Wilson commented: 'If one will do, why should it not be the woman? – more particularly as she is supposed to be the most interested in groceries and drapery.'[39]

Wilson's article provides a rare insight into a female co-operator's views in the 1860s. As will be discussed below, few women were involved in local or national co-operative leadership in the mid nineteenth century, and even fewer wrote in the movement's publications. However, by the 1880s, as issues such as married women's property, access to higher education, and female suffrage brought the 'woman question' to the fore of public debate, some co-operators began to raise concerns about the lack of women's participation in the movement. In 1883 Samuel Bamford, the editor of the weekly *Co-operative News*, inaugurated a 'Woman's Corner' section. In her inaugural column as its editor, Mrs Alice Acland wrote with frustration:

> What are men always urged to do when there is a meeting held at any place to encourage or to start co-operative institutions? – come! help? vote! criticise! act! What are women encouraged to do? – come and *buy*! That is all.[40]

Acland proposed a women's organisation to rectify this problem, and received enthusiastic response. The Women's League for the Spread of Co-operation (renamed the WCG the following year) began with a membership of seven. Membership grew steadily, rising to nearly 13,000 by 1900 and reaching over 45,000 in 1920 in in England and Wales; a separate Scottish Guild was organised in 1892.[41] Whilst it is impossible to assess how representative the WCG was of the views of the larger body of female members, it nevertheless became the primary vehicle for articulating women's position in the movement.

Open to women who were co-operative members, or the wives and daughters of members, the Guild had a two-fold purpose: to spread understanding and knowledge of co-operation among women, and to improve the position of women generally. To Guild members, these goals were intrinsically linked. Co-operative shopping could help women improve their economic standing, but it could also connect them to the movement's educational resources and social vision. The savings a woman generated through careful shopping and exclusive dealing with the co-operative could become a source of pride and self-confidence, and connect her to the movement's economic, social and political aims.[42]

Early in its history, the Guild began to refer to women's role as the movement's main consumers as 'basket power'. 'The Woman with the Basket' became the Guild's most identifiable symbol, appearing on its membership card in 1908. As described by the WCG, the woman with the basket was the ideal co-operative consumer. She was the 'Chancellor of the Family Exchequer', whose role as the wage-spender was vital to family prosperity. This wise co-operative consumer understood that her purchases represented good value for money, as foods were pure and unadulterated with no short measures, while household items were of better quality than cheaper shoddy goods. By buying all her goods at the co-operative, she not only earned a dividend, she helped build up the movement. Through the Guild, its leaders argued, women were educated to be just such ideal consumers – both for their own benefit, and that of the wider movement.

It was apparent to co-operators of both sexes that the 'bread and butter' purchases of the co-operative movement were made by women. In 1912, for instance, grocery and household items made up nearly 81 per cent of CWS sales, followed by drapery (7.6 per cent), boots and shoes (3.6 per cent), furnishings (3.4 per cent), coal (2.5 per cent), and clothing (2.1 per cent).[43] Some of these items were purchased by the CWS and distributed to societies, while others were produced in CWS factories. The more co-operative stores could encourage women to buy exclusively from their co-operatives, and particularly buy CWS-made goods, the higher their earnings, and therefore the greater the dividends that could be passed on to members. Women's loyalty to the store, then, was a critical feature of co-operative success.

Some co-operative leaders welcomed the advent of the WCG in the 1880s precisely because it might bring more women into co-operative stores. In 1894, Newcastle co-operator Mr H. R. Bailey introduced a motion honouring the WCG as a valuable addition to the movement, commenting: 'If the women withheld their baskets from the stores on Friday and Saturday there would be an end of distributive co-operation. Better set the women to work, so that the co-operative movement might benefit by their influence.'[44] As the CWS expanded its productive enterprises, movement leaders became ever more interested in channelling 'basket power' into support for CWS products. By the latter part of the nineteenth century, co-operatives faced an increasingly competitive market in consumer goods, and CWS leaders began to reach out specifically to women, employing a language of ethical consumption. From the outset, CWS leaders had encouraged co-operative members of both sexes to feel a sense of ownership and pride in 'their' factories. The Wholesale consistently stressed that its workers benefited from better wages and working conditions than those in private employ, and articles appeared in the co-operative press with pictures of the latest architecture, finest machinery, and the best facilities for workers. By the 1890s, the CWS was appealing specifically to Guild members, encouraging them to use their basket power to support good working conditions. By the early twentieth century, the CWS began working with WCG branches and societies' education committees to reach more women customers. The CWS promoted special, women-only 'Ladies' Concerts', combining musical evenings with lectures about the Wholesale. In Bolton, a series of eight such concerts was held in the winter of 1913–14. Women who attended also received samples of CWS products, including soap, biscuits and cocoa.[45]

There is plenty of evidence that local WCG branches made extensive efforts to promote co-operative productions at their local societies, both through 'push the sales' campaigns and social gatherings and by taking their concerns to management committees. One woman wrote to the Woman's Corner:

> I should like to tell you about the little store at Ramsgate ... Inside I found there was hardly anything to be seen but C.W.S. productions, and the manager told me that since the guild had started he had been repeatedly asked for C.W.S. productions, when before no one seemed to trouble.[46]

National Guild leaders could be critical of local societies if they felt they were not doing enough to promote co-operative goods, as when Margaret Llewelyn Davies (WCG General Secretary, 1889–1921) used the Woman's Corner to 'name and shame' stores in Heckmondwike and Burnley for advertising Rowntree's cocoa instead of the CWS brand, and not stocking CWS soap.[47] Another Guild leader reflected that local efforts did not always sit well with local managers and shop assistants, who sometimes looked on WCG members as 'troublesome busy-bodies' who had 'better be at home minding their own business.'[48] The Guild could also be critical of CWS leaders, lamenting in 1911 that the CWS had been slow to take suggestions from the WCG on organising a national push for the sales campaigns.[49] Such comments suggest that women's involvement in co-operative business matters, even as customers, was not always welcomed.

Open membership

From the 1880s on, increasing numbers of co-operative leaders sought to harness women's basket power to support co-operative businesses, in word if not always in deed. However, such calls were often limited to seeking more female customers – not members. Before the 1880s it was rare for women to attend co-operative meetings, whether or not they were members, and the Guild's early advocacy of female participation in co-operative affairs was considered radical. In her study of the WCG,

Scott notes that 'the experience of the infant Guild provides plentiful evidence of the extent to which respectable working class culture was saturated with rigid assumptions about feminine identity'.[50] The move by some women to translate their role as consumers to more active participation in co-operative democracy involved their entry into public spaces and arenas of business where they had heretofore been absent, and this was unsettling to many.[51]

From its earliest years, the WCG lobbied for greater participation by women in co-operatives, encouraging them to attend members meetings and, where possible, become members in their own right. By 1890 this had coalesced into a WCG campaign for 'open membership' – which the Guild defined as the right of all adults to become members in their own names, regardless of marital status. Since each co-operative society was responsible for setting its own membership rules, WCG members had to propose changes at members' meetings in each society, where they were at a significant disadvantage because so few women were able to vote. The Guild conducted a survey of societies in 1893 to determine how many societies allowed married women to become members, which provides a glimpse into the state of membership at the time. Whilst the survey covered only 84 societies out of the 1,141 then existing in England and Wales, it demonstrated a wide variation in female membership, with women representing an average of 24.9 per cent of these societies' membership.[52] Reliable statistics on open membership are difficult to find, but the evidence suggests that the Guild's campaign was a long and arduous one. Another WCG survey in 1902 found that 153 societies had open membership, but only 218 of the approximately 1,300 societies in England and Wales had responded.[53]

Whilst some male co-operative leaders supported open membership, in many areas there was significant resistance. At the Oldham Industrial society, where only twenty members of the 224-strong WCG branch were eligible to vote in quarterly meetings in 1903, a resolution in favour of open membership 'was received with derisive laughter'.[54] One member, Mr J. T. Taylor, attempted to use the Guild's 'basket power' arguments against them: 'If "Open Membership" would increase the trade of the store, it only proves that the women are not doing all the trade they can with the store. To give them votes on that account solely would be to put a premium upon disloyalty.'[55]

Anecdotal evidence suggests that open membership gradually increased in the early twentieth century – in part influenced by the WCG campaign, and in part by changing business circumstances. Issues of 'surplus capital' receded as societies and the Wholesales expanded into more areas of manufacturing, offering ample opportunities for co-operative investment. Local variations, remained, however, and even in 1921 Sydney and Beatrice Webb commented that open membership was rare in some parts of the country. The Webbs went on to note:

> The Co-operative machine is usually started by men, and it continues for the most part to be controlled by men, though the actual customers are mainly the women of the families concerned. Many of the societies, especially the newer and smaller ones, have as members more men than women, sometimes, at the outset, three or four times as many ... It is said that in some districts as many as 90 per cent of the members are women.[56]

Gender and the business of co-operation

The WCG campaign for open membership was a crucial first step in its efforts to increase women's participation in co-operative societies. However, if the woman with the basket was to be able to shape co-operative policy and practice, she would need to get elected to co-operative committees.[57] The national WCG and its local branches were considered auxiliary bodies to the movement, with no representation on local educational and management committees. Female candidates faced an uphill battle in standing for election. Once they had gained access to membership, women had to earn the votes of a predominantly male electorate, at least some of whom were opposed to the concept of women in leadership positions that had historically been the province of men.[58] At the same time, many women were loath to put themselves forward in an atmosphere of public scrutiny, particularly since so few women had experience in public speaking or participation in organisational life. Given these impediments, it is remarkable that so many women put themselves forward as candidates.

Beginning in the mid-1880s WCG members began to stand for positions on local education committees. This was in some ways a natural first step for women candidates. Within the movement, 'education' was a broad term that encompassed a wide range of activities, from classes in co-operation for children and adults to concerts, picnics and propagandist activities designed to 'educate' the neighbourhood about the co-operative store. In these arenas, it was a relatively easy to argue that female committee members could offer special expertise, based on their domestic responsibilities in educating children as well as their experience as shoppers. In 1885 Mrs Mary Lawrenson, a founding Guild member who served as its General Secretary from 1885 to 1889, became the first woman elected to a local education committee, at the

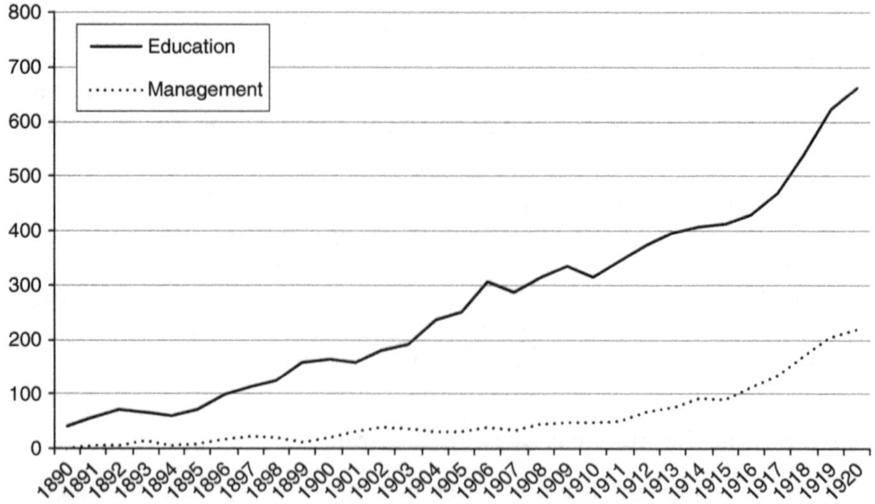

Figure 6.1: Female candidates elected to co-operative committees (England and Wales), 1890–1920

Source: Women's Co-operative Guild Annual Reports (1891–1921)

Royal Arsenal society.[59] By 1890, the WCG annual report noted that forty-two women sat on education committees in England and Wales, a figure that rose to 756 by 1921 (see Figure 6.1).[60] Guildswomen also gained influence on regional and national bodies. In 1897 Llewelyn Davies, the Guild's General Secretary, was appointed to the national education executive of the Co-operative Union (CU), and from that point on at least one woman, and sometimes two or three, served in this capacity.

In many societies, it was common for male co-operators to use election to the education committee as a stepping-stone to a position on their society's board of management. By and large, however, female candidates did not share this experience. Although women were able to achieve some success in the movement's educational organisations, access to positions on management committees proved much more difficult. The Guild's 1891 report is the first record of women on management committees – six women were elected, as compared with fifty-seven who were elected to education committees. By 1921, there were 241 female management committee members – over 500 less than their educational counterparts. The raw numbers suggest a number of possibilities, among them that fewer women came forward as candidates for business-oriented positions. However, because the Guild kept records of the number of candidates who stood for election between 1897 and

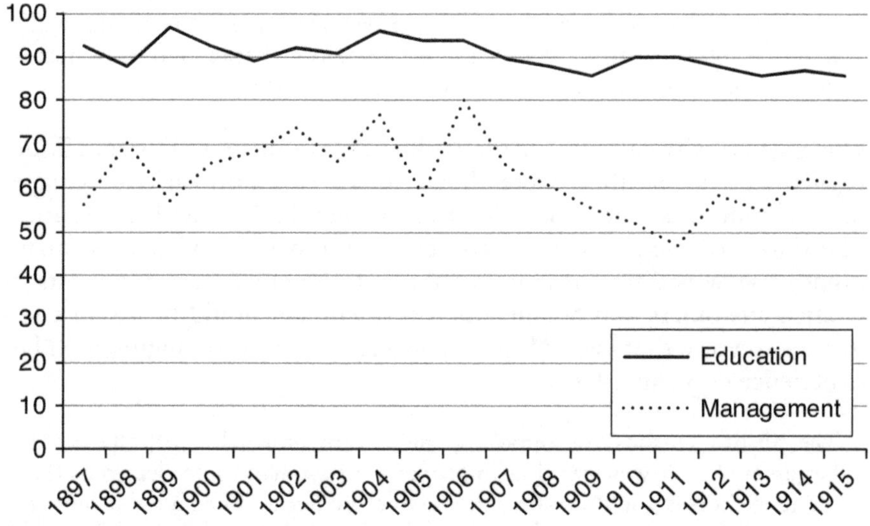

Figure 6.2: Success rate (percentage) of female candidates for co-operative committees (England and Wales), 1897–1915
Source: Women's Co-operative Guild Annual Reports (1898–1916)

1915, it is possible to determine the success rate for female candidates for both types of position (see Figure 6.2). In the case of education committees, female candidates were successful between 85.6 per cent and 96.9 per cent of the time, averaging 89.8 per cent over the nineteen-year period. By contrast, management committee candidates were successful between 46.7 per cent and 80 per cent of the time, with an average rate of 62.6 per cent.[61]

Despite these difficulties, Guild members continued to argue that women's basket power was a significant advantage to the movement, citing their expert knowledge of customer needs. One anonymous member wrote to the Woman's Corner that 'in all matters pertaining to the quality and price of goods a man has often even less knowledge to start with than a woman. For this reason her practical experience would be found specially useful on the "shop" and "drapery" sub-committees.'[62] An exchange of letters in the 1911 *Co-operative News* is illustrative of the arguments on either side. In the first, Mr C. E. Goodyear of Doncaster wrote that, whilst he was unaware of any women sitting on management committees:

> I feel sure that such experiments would not be successful. Large fields of usefulness are open to women in many directions in the co-operative

> movement. Women, however, cannot perform the duties of men, and will never be able to do so. ... It seems to me, therefore, that in matters of business women must be necessarily much inferior to men.[63]

One unsuccessful candidate from Woking, WCG member Florence Toon, replied, noting that there were already fifty women on various management committees. She responded that women had no wish to perform 'the duties of men', writing: 'The chief argument ... is that women's point of view is different from men's; and, therefore, in the interests of women customers and female employés, women should be on all committees to voice that view.'[64] In a subsequent letter, Toon highlighted her experience as a candidate:

> The absurd reasons for opposing me ... are unworthy [of] the word 'argument.' ... It was stated as improper for a woman to be elected as the merits of horses could not be discussed before her ... Then a great outcry was made against the store being ruled by a woman. How one woman was to do this against so many men I hardly know. The influence we are credited with is truly wonderful.[65]

It should be noted that not all men responded negatively to women candidates – Toon herself was nominated by two male co-operators, and there are many recorded instances of male support for female candidates. It is also true that some Guildswomen were able to gain election to regional and national offices beyond the educational sphere. The CU's Southern Section elected Lawrenson as its representative to the Central Board in 1893, and from that year on at least one WCG member represented the south on the movement's national body. Other sections were slower to elect female representatives – Mrs Mary Found was the first to represent the South-Western Section in 1917, and Mrs Mary Cottrell was elected by the Midlands Section in 1919.[66] In 1921, however, when Cottrell became the first woman elected to the board of the CWS, the largest co-operative business, many Guildswomen celebrated her victory as a major achievement.

Whilst women were able to make inroads onto management committees and in national administration, it is clear that women faced greater opposition when they tried to play a leadership role in the business side of the movement. While many co-operators saw educational, social and propagandist activities as consistent with women's domestic roles, female involvement in the day-to-day business of co-operative stores and factories was a greater stretch, and it is clear that many men and some women within the movement saw management positions as inappropriate for women.[67]

Conclusion

Although many co-operators were 'brought up to think that the co-operative movement recognised an absolute equality of sex',[68] in practice women who sought to expand their role beyond that of consumer faced significant opposition. Constraints on women's participation had a serious impact on the effectiveness of co-operative democracy, by restricting the voice of one of its dominant constituencies.

Much research remains to be done to investigate the impact of gender on co-operative business practices, to more fully analyse the extent to which women were able to shape co-operative policies and practices, particularly at the local level. The day-to-day operations of co-operative stores – determining what goods to produce and stock, the types of services co-operatives supplied, their employment practices, and the setting of prices and dividend rates – all of these decisions were made in a gendered context. The Guild certainly advocated for changes to a variety of business policies, from co-operative employees' wages and employment practices[69] to reduced dividend rates in order to reduce prices and encourage poorer consumers to shop at co-operative stores.[70] However, many women remained frustrated. In 1911, in a prize-winning essay reprinted in the Woman's Corner, Mrs Neal of the Bowes Park WCG branch gave her views on the consequences of women's limited role in co-operative leadership:

> If women had been equally trained in true co-operation, would stale goods and a slow sale have been the case in her store? Would unhygienic conditions have prevailed if woman's housewifely spirit had been allowed full play? Would women have been disloyal to the store if they had shared its responsibility? Would men have to be running about all over the country teaching women about their own cocoas and jellies – and actually how to make them! – if they had equally authorised their production? Would credit have got into the movement if women had known that co-operation had been originated as an escape from its misery and degradation? Would there have been the necessity for a minimum wage campaign for the women workers if co-operative women had shared the control of co-operative labour conditions? And would there have been such pressing need for children's guilds and circles had their mothers been imbued with co-operative principles?[71]

While it is impossible to know the answers to these questions, Neal nonetheless highlights the implications to co-operative business of constraints on women's participation. The WCG did much to create an alternative culture of co-operation in which women played a central part, shaping the movement as a whole by creating a new discourse around female consumption and opening new avenues for women to participate. Nonetheless, they could only act as a pressure group within the movement's mainstream, as long as women remained poorly represented among the membership and in local and national leadership. The ironic result was that a movement centred around consumer organising limited the participation of many of its customers, due to underlying tensions over gender roles.

While this study is historical in nature, it nonetheless offers insights into questions that remain problematic for co-operatives today. Despite the commitment to gender equality in the international movement's guiding principles,[72] research by Rawlings and Shaw (chapter 7, this volume) demonstrates that women's participation at all levels of the co-operative movement remains a problem in many developed and developing countries. Co-operative organisations reflect the norms and prejudices of their communities and members, even as they strive to change their societies for the better. Stated commitments to the values of equality and equity may create space for diverse members to participate, but structural and cultural barriers may nonetheless impede the progress of some unless co-operatives address them in practice.

Notes

1 B. Potter, *The Co-operative Movement in Great Britain* (London: Swan Sonnenschein, 1891), p. 191.

2 I use the term 'primary consumer' in recognition that men were also consumers, but were not generally responsible for procuring most household purchases. See M. Finn, 'Men's things: masculine possession in the consumer revolution', *Social History* 25:2 (May 2000), 133–55, and A. Vickery, 'His and hers: gender, consumption and household accounting in eighteenth century England', *Past & Present* Supplement 1 (2006), 12–38.

3 See for example N. Black, 'Part II: the Women's Co-operative Guild', *Social Feminism* (Ithaca, NY: Cornell University Press, 1989), 107–60; G. Scott, *Feminism and the Politics of Working Women* (Abingdon and New York: Routledge, 1998) and B. Blaszak, *The Matriarchs of England's Co-operative Movement* (Westport, CT: Greenwood Press, 2000).

4 R. Vorberg-Rugh, 'Co-operative contradictions: business, labour and gender in the British co-operative movement, 1880–1920' (DPhil thesis, University of Oxford, forthcoming).

5 F. Trentmann, 'Beyond consumerism,' *Journal of Contemporary History* 39:3 (July 2004), 373–401, p. 382.

6 There is a substantial secondary literature on working-class families in this period. See A. Clark, *The Struggle for the Breeches: Gender and the Making of the British Working Class* (Berkeley and Los Angeles: University of California

Press, 1995); L. Davidoff and B. Westover, eds, *Our Work, Our Lives, Our Words: Women's History and Women's Work* (Totowa: Barnes & Noble, 1986); J. Lewis, ed., *Labour and Love: Women's Experiences of Home & Family, 1850–1940* (London: Basil Blackwell, 1986); E. Roberts, *A Woman's Place: An Oral History of Working-Class Women, 1890–1940* (New York: Basil Blackwell, 1984) and L. Tilly and J. Scott, *Women Work and Family* (New York and London: Routledge, 1978, reprint 1987).

7 See N. Folbre, 'The unproductive housewife: her evolution in nineteenth-century thought', *Signs* 16:3 (Spring 1991), 463–84.

8 E. Ross, 'Fierce questions and taunts', *Feminist Studies* 8 (Fall 1982), 575–602, p. 576.

9 *Bolton Co-operative Record* (BCR) (April 1914), p. 3.

10 See National Co-operative Archive (NCA), *Laws and Objects of the Rochdale Society of Equitable Pioneers* (1844), p. 9; www. rochdalepioneersmuseum. coop/wp-content/uploads/2014/08/REPS-Laws-and-Objects-1844.pdf (accessed 4 February 2016). The first female member, a weaver named Eliza Brierley, joined the society in 1846. See Rochdale Equitable Pioneers Co-operative Society minute book (2 and 19 March 1846), NCA.

11 On trades unions, see B. Drake, *Women in Trade Unions* (London: Labour Research Department and George Allen & Unwin, 1920); S. Boston, *Women Workers and the Trade Union Movement* (London: Lawrence & Wishart, 1987); and D. Thom, *Nice Girls and Rude Girls: Women Workers in World War I* (London: I. B. Tauris, 2000), pp. 94–121. On friendly societies, see S. Cordery, *British Friendly Societies, 1750–1914* (Houndmills: Palgrave Macmillan, 2003) and N. Reader, 'Female friendly societies in industrialising England, 1780–1850' (unpublished PhD thesis, University of Leeds, 2005).

12 On pre-Rochdale co-operatives in England, see G. D. H. Cole, *A Century of Co-operation* (Manchester: Co-operative Union, 1944), pp. 12–38; M. Purvis, 'Co-operative retailing in England, 1835–1850: developments beyond Rochdale', *Northern History* 22 (1986), 198–215; and J. Bamfield, 'Consumer-owned flour and bread societies in the eighteenth and early nineteenth centuries', *Business History* 40:4 (1998), 16–36.

13 Owenism, a movement inspired by the writings of Robert Owen, which sought a social, educational and economic reordering of society on a more equitable basis, was fundamental to the ideological development of co-operation. See J. F. C. Harrison, *Quest for the New Moral World: Robert Owen and the Owenites in Britain and America* (London: Routledge and Kegan Paul, 1969) and S. Smith, *Robert Owen: Utopian Realist* (Manchester: Co-operative College, 2008).

14 B. Taylor, *Eve and the New Jerusalem: Socialism and Feminism in the Nineteenth Century* (New York: Pantheon, 1983), pp. 31–2.

15 For instance, a Ripponden society founded by Owenites in 1832 included seven women among its forty-five members by 1834. J. H. Priestley, *The History of the Ripponden Co-operative Society Limited* (Ripponden: Ripponden Co-operative Society, 1932), pp. 49–51.

16 Chartism was a working-class movement for political reform based around the 'People's Charter' of 1838. See A. Briggs, ed., *Chartist Studies* (London: Macmillan, 1959) and D. Thompson, *The Chartists: Popular Politics in the Industrial Revolution* (New York: Pantheon, 1985).
17 Taylor notes that the charter's first draft included extending the franchise to women, but this was withdrawn; see *Eve and the New Jerusalem*, pp. 270–1.
18 Chartists drew upon a long tradition of women's participation alongside men in protests over the availability and price of food and basic staples. See J. Bohstedt, *The Politics of Provisions: Food Riots, Moral Economy, and Market Transition in England, 1550–1850* (Farnham: Ashgate, 2010).
19 For examples, see Taylor, *Eve and the New Jerusalem*, pp. 265–75; N. Todd, 'The red herring war of 1872: women's rights, butchers and co-ops in the northern coalfield', in B. Lancaster and P. Maguire, eds, *Toward the Co-operative Commonwealth: Essays in the History of Co-operation* (Manchester: Co-operative College and History Workshop Trust, 1996), pp. 55–61, p. 55; M. Hilton, *Consumerism in 20th-Century Britain* (Cambridge: Cambridge University Press, 2003), p. 42; and P. Gurney, *Co-operative Culture and the Politics of Consumption in England, 1870–1930* (Manchester: Manchester University Press, 1996), pp. 14–15.
20 Taylor, *Eve and the New Jerusalem*, p. 267.
21 See NCA, '£28 that changed the world', www.archive.coop/hive/28-that-changed-the-world (accessed 4 February 2016).
22 Co-operative Union, *Co-operative Congress Report* (1881 and 1921).
23 A separate Scottish Co-operative Wholesale Society began in 1869. On the Wholesales, see J. Kinloch and J. Butt, *History of the Scottish Co-operative Wholesale Society Limited* (Glasgow: Co-operative Wholesale Society, 1981); and J. Wilson, A. Webster and R. Vorberg-Rugh, *Building Co-operation: A Business History of The Co-operative Group* (Oxford: Oxford University Press, 2013).
24 J. Jefferys, *Retail Trading in Britain 1850–1950* (Cambridge: Cambridge University Press, 1954), p. 19.
25 See Wilson et al., *Building Co-operation*, pp. 23–52.
26 Gurney, *Co-operative Culture*, p. 23. The WCG rates eight mentions in the book's 350 pages.
27 The central elements of the Rochdale model were: democratic structure based on one member, one vote; open membership; political and religious neutrality; fixed interest on share and loan capital; distribution of surplus on the basis of use (dividend); commitment to sell only pure and unadulterated goods; provision of education; cash-only trading. See Wilson et al., *Building Co-operation*, pp. 34–42.
28 P. Johnson, *Saving and Spending: The Working-class Economy in Britain, 1870–1939* (Oxford: Clarendon Press, 1985), p. 143.
29 G. J. Holyoake, *The History of Co-operation in England*, vol. 2, reprint edition (New York: AMS Press, 1971), pp. 111–12.
30 Gurney, *Co-operative Culture*, p. 14.
31 'A Lady Co-operator', *Co-operative News* Woman's Corner (WC) (17 February 1883), p. 144.

32 As co-operatives grew, so did their capital. If societies were unable to use their increased capital for internal business purposes or invest it profitably, they used various means to restrict member investment, including restricting the number of members per household. See F. Hall and W. P. Watkins, *Co-operation* (Manchester: Co-operative Union, 1937; reprint 1948), p. 142.
33 A. Wilson, 'A Word for Women', *The Co-operator* (1 March 1866), p. 218.
34 Potter, *Co-operative Movement*, p. 72.
35 Blaszak, *Matriarchs*, p. 50.
36 J. Whyatt, 'To the co-operative women of England', *The Co-operator* (1 December 1865), p. 172.
37 'Co-operative Education: The Ways and Means', *Co-operative News* (16 August 1890), p. 823.
38 Wilson, 'A Word for Women', p. 218.
39 Ibid.
40 *Co-operative News* WC (6 January 1883), p. 25.
41 Women's Co-operative Guild (WCG), *Annual Report* (1901 and 1921). On the Scottish Guild, see K. M. Callen, *History of the Scottish Women's Co-operative Women's Guild* (Glasgow: Scottish Co-operative Wholesale Society, 1952).
42 Gurney, *Co-operative Culture*, p. 62.
43 *Co-operative Wholesale Societies Annual* (Manchester: CWS, 1918), pp. 146–53.
44 *Co-operative News* (26 May 1894), p. 587.
45 Two 'Smoking Concerts' for men were also held, at which attendees received samples of CWS tobacco. *BCR* (November 1913), p. 13; (January 1914), p. 3; (April 1914), p. 3.
46 J. G., *Co-operative News* (3 March 1898), p. 251.
47 M. Llewelyn Davies, 'Un-co-operative practices', *Co-operative News* WC (12 February 1898), pp. 178–9.
48 C. Webb, *The Woman with the Basket* (Manchester: CWS, 1927), p. 82.
49 'The "Co-operative Shopping Week": what does it mean?', *Co-operative News* WC (11 February 1911), p. 298.
50 Scott, *Feminism*, p. 67.
51 Blaszak, *Matriarchs*, pp. 69–70.
52 A total of 137 WCG branches were attached to 121 societies, but several respondents did not include membership information. Complete data is available for 84 societies. The highest percentage of female members in the sample came from the Royal Arsenal society, where over 75 per cent of its 8,508 members were women. WCG, *Tenth Annual Report* (1893), pp. 56–70; Co-operative Union, *Co-operative Congress Report* (1893).
53 WCG, *Annual Report* (1901–02), p. 7.
54 'The closed door at Oldham', *Co-operative News* WC (2 May 1903), p. 520.
55 'A symposium on "open membership",' *Co-operative News* WC (30 May 1903), p. 652.
56 S. Webb and B. Webb, *The Consumers Co-operative Movement* (London: Longman's, 1921), p. 48.

57 This was apparent to many male co-operators. At the 1903 debate on open membership in Oldham, a management committee member spoke in opposition, commenting 'that if the main object of the Women's Guild was office seeking, the sooner it was ended the better'. This remark was 'met with very evident approval, being greeted with loud applause'. 'Closed door at Oldham', p. 520.

58 This was also true of women seeking election as their societies' representatives to CWS and SCWS delegates meetings and the annual Co-operative Congress.

59 *Co-operative News* WC (4 April 1885), pp. 306–7.

60 Unlike the WCG, the Scottish Guild did not keep statistics on women elected to leadership positions.

61 Blaszak uses these statistics as 'failure rates', in her chapter 'Gendered geography of the co-operative movement', *Matriarchs*, pp. 63–92. Her conclusions, particularly with regard to geographic differences in women's rates of election, are controversial. See J. Walton, 'Locality, gender and co-operation in England: a comment on Barbara J. Blaszak', *Women's Historical Review* 12:3 (2003), 477–88, and B. Blaszak, 'The hazards of localism: a reply to John K. Walton', *Women's Historical Review* 12:3 (2003), 489–98.

62 *Co-operative News* WC (4 January 1902), pp. 23–4.

63 *Co-operative News* (1 July 1911), p. 853.

64 *Co-operative News* (17 June 1911), p. 788.

65 *Co-operative News* (8 July 1911), p. 881.

66 Blaszak, *Matriarchs*, pp. 84–5.

67 Gurney, *Culture of Co-operation*, p. 65.

68 'The Guild Report', *Co-operative News* WC (30 May 1903), p. 653.

69 See R. Vorberg-Rugh, 'Employers *and* workers: conflicting identities over women's wages in the co-operative movement, 1906–18', in L. Black and N. Robertson, eds, *Consumerism and the Co-operative Movement in Modern British History: Taking Stock* (Manchester: Manchester University Press, 2009), pp. 121–37.

70 See for example, C. Webb, *High Dividends: What they Mean* (Kirkby Lonsdale: WCG, 1897) and WCG, *Co-operation in Poor Neighbourhoods* (Kirkby Lonsdale: WCG, 1899).

71 *Co-operative News* WC (23 September 1911), pp. 1232–3.

72 See ICA, 'Statement of co-operative identity, values and principles' (1995), http://ica.coop/en/whats-co-op/co-operative-identity-values-principles (accessed 4 February 2016).

7

A continuing challenge: women and leadership in co-operatives

Barbara Rawlings and Linda Shaw

> We all need to acknowledge that since its inception, co-operation has upheld equality between man and women as a key principle. And yet around the world that equality is still more noticeable in its omission than its commission.
>
> Dame Pauline Green, International Co-operative Alliance President[1]

On her 2009 election as the first women president of the International Co-operative Alliance (ICA), the apex body of global co-operation founded in 1895, Dame Pauline commented on the existence of persistent inequalities in the movement. This paper takes as a starting point the assertion that co-operatives still fail to put into practice gender equality despite the great potential that these member-based organisations have for promoting it. Our aim is to review the evidence for this statement with a primary focus on women's presence at leadership level in co-operatives around the world.[2] We were interested to see if, and how, this duality was reflected in the literature alongside a review of wider discussion of gender and leadership in co-operatives.

As we will show, the evidence turns out to be patchy, and much of it in the nature of reports and descriptive accounts. In terms of policies, whilst the authors take the view that gender mainstreaming would be an effective means for promoting gender equality, a finding from this review is that it is not at present widely used in practice in co-operative settings, or much discussed in the co-operative literature.

As is widely acknowledged in the literature, co-operatives are enterprises with management structures, and they are also member-based organisations that strive to achieve both economic and social outcomes.[3] Unlike 'conventional' business models, there are two paths to leadership: through the management of enterprise and the associative structures of membership. Co-operatives need to address gender equity in terms of leadership in both these aspects. We were interested to see if, and how, this was reflected in the literature.

This necessitated a review of the gender dimensions within the democratic aspects of co-operatives, including their elected boards, as well the situation within the operational management structures of co-operative businesses. A review and analysis of the growing literature on co-operative management and leadership were supplemented with some of the relevant research from the extensive literature on gender and wider business leadership. Collection and analysis of internally generated co-operative movement data on gender produced some useful, albeit limited, findings.[4] For example, in 2013 the International Co-operative and Mutual Insurance Federation (ICMIF) carried out a survey into women's leadership among its members. Of the 214 member organisations, ICMIF found that twenty (13.6 per cent) had women as CEOs. This is a significantly higher proportion than found in non-mutual insurance companies. At board level the picture further improved, with 25 per cent of ICMIF members surveyed having three or more women on their boards – again comparing favourably with the mainstream insurance sector.[5] As yet such findings have not resulted in further academic interest, as will become evident from discussion below. The ICA, however, has commissioned some research into gender and co-operatives which is still ongoing at the time of writing, but the first-stage report will be referred to.

The chapter is divided into four sections. The first two review the evidence, starting with a review of the literature on women and leadership in the developed world, and then the leadership situation in the context of co-operatives in developing countries. Section three discusses the lack of available data as identified in the review, and section four proposes changes to both operational co-operative practice and to research practice.

Women and co-operative leadership in the developed world

For the developed world, there is a large and growing literature on women and business leadership, especially at board level, within investor-owned companies.[6] Whilst there is an overall consensus on the benefits of having gender-equitable and more diverse boards generally, there is considerable debate and controversy over how best to achieve this. The implementation of a quota system reserving a minimum number of seats for women is now happening in several European countries, the first being Norway in 2004. In March 2015, the German parliament passed a law requiring a minimum of 30 per cent women on the non-executive boards of the country's largest companies with plans to increase the quota to 50 per cent by 2016. Smaller companies will be required to set binding targets for increasing the number of women on their boards.[7]

To date, the evidence on the impact of board quotas for women is mixed.[8] In a global study, Pande and Ford found that quotas have increased the numbers of female business leaders. However, there have been attempts to lessen the effectiveness of quota policies by various strategies, including increasing the size of the board so that existing male members would not need to be replaced, and recruiting the same woman to sit on multiple boards rather than allowing less experienced women opportunities to take on these new roles. The authors also found some negative short-run impact on economic returns, but speculated that this may be more a product of negative perceptions rather than women's behaviour.[9]

By contrast, the literature on women's leadership in democratic member-based organisations (MBOs), such as co-operatives and trade unions, is much smaller. There are some interesting historical examples but in the contemporary literature on co-operatives there has been more of a focus on the factors facilitating member participation and less of a focus on co-operative governance.[10] Of note are the studies by Cornforth,[11] who developed a typology of the differing roles adopted by co-operative boards in the context of wider debates over corporate governance, and, more recently, by Birchall, who discussed the governance of large co-operative organisations.[12] Unfortunately, none of these studies tackles gender issues in any depth, and Birchall specifically calls for further research into the lack of diversity on co-operative boards globally. Also relevant is a recent study about leadership in co-operatives in East Africa which poses the question as to what good leadership looks like in a democratic organisation. According to Bottelberge and Agevi, the distinctive success factors for MBOs are strong leadership and good management combined with a knowledgeable and empowered membership.[13]

Other MBOs, such as trade unions, have received more attention than co-operatives in terms of leadership and gender issues. A recent study of trade unions in the UK and in the USA, for example, revealed that women are still under-represented in leadership positions. However, although women have made gains within union leadership and decision-making structures, in none of the unions in the study did the female proportion of women at leadership level reflect the female proportion of members. Gaining leadership positions remains far from a smooth process and women face multiple barriers including the gendered division of domestic work, the organisation and nature of women's work, the organisation and nature of trade union work, and the masculine culture of trade unions.[14]

In developed countries, there is a greater wealth of studies of co-operative history, which not only remind us of the deep-seated nature of gender inequities but also of the ways in which they have been challenged. Here, the experience of the UK co-operative movement seems pertinent. The modern consumer co-operative movement began in 1844 when the Rochdale Equitable Pioneers Society opened their store. The founding documents referenced both men and women as members, and Eliza Brierley became their first woman member in 1846. This was very radical in the context of the times. From the beginning, women could become co-operative members in their own right and participate as members in the democratic life of their societies. This contrasts sharply with women's experience of parliamentary politics, as it was not until 1928 that women in the UK gained the right to vote on an equal basis with men. In the case of the consumer co-operatives, it is important to note that most of the shoppers were women, and most of the dividends were collected by women. However, despite the outward commitment to gender equality it should be noted that, until the First World War, most societies only allowed one member per household, and as this was usually the husband, very few women had voting rights or the opportunity to take on influential roles (see Vorberg-Rugh, chapter 6 this volume).[15] In response to this, in England and Wales, the Women's Co-operative Guild was set up in 1883 to encourage women to become members in their own right and to stand for election onto local and national committees. Though some progress was made, the rate of change remained slow.[16]

Turning to the contemporary literature specifically on co-operatives, there is a small but growing number of studies, some very recent, that tackle gender issues within co-operatives. Studies of the contemporary situation for women in the UK movement remain few in number. A 2007 UK study, which focused mainly on co-operative businesses in the north-west of England, found that smaller co-operatives tended to have greater gender equality but little opportunity for career advancement.[17] The larger co-operatives offered more opportunity. However, women reported that home responsibilities, part-time working and heavy workloads meant that in practice relatively few were able to advance far up the career ladder, and that the higher management levels were still largely composed of men. A review of UK co-operatives in 2014 reported that women's participation at board level was around twice the level that held for leading shareholder companies.[18]

A study of the situation in Norway found that women on co-operative boards often focused on 'quality' issues, such as employment policies and working procedures, whilst men focused on 'business' issues of finance and technology. The research found that the focus on quality issues led to business stability and argued that women were better at long-term planning and less interested in quick returns. Men, on the other hand, were interested in immediate effects, and more likely to take risks. Having more equal numbers of men and women on the board, meant decisions were more rounded and balanced.[19]

In Ireland, a study of credit unions carried out in 2001 found that men tended to predominate in the leadership roles of the larger organisations, and in the key roles of Chair and Vice Chair. The writers suggest that men see larger organisations and key positions as offering them more power, and this is what attracts them. They are less likely to compete for positions in smaller organisations and less influential roles on larger boards. At the same time, women reported that they feel uneasy about taking on important roles because of what they regard as their own lack of knowledge and, again, because of time commitments at home.[20]

In 2003, 800 women in Italian co-ops were surveyed. Again, the biggest barrier to more active participation was reported to be a lack of time. The women said that meetings were usually held in the evenings – a better time for men than for women – and that they were discouraged by the formalities and hierarchies involved. Nevertheless, the women tended to be better qualified and better trained than men, although in general they received less pay for their efforts. Because of the barriers imposed by the heavy domestic responsibilities of women, another Italian study looked at whether co-operatives encouraged a healthy work–life balance. It found that co-operatives which contained many women, or which had a woman manager, were more likely to adopt 'family friendly' approaches which offered members a better work–life balance, even though this could mean more cost to the organisation.[21] An ongoing study has looked at data from 440 member-owned enterprises across the USA, and has found that representation of women on boards is much lower in some sectors, particularly agriculture, and much higher in others such as education, arts and crafts, and grocery.[22]

Given the scale and scope of co-operatives in many developed countries, the lack of academic and research interest is disappointing. The studies that do exist have typically been supported or generated from within the movement and do not seem to have generated a wider level of academic debate. Perhaps unsurprisingly, they reveal considerable variations in the level and type of participation from country to country and sector to sector, with the US data reporting the least in agriculture and the greatest presence in handicrafts. The evidence remains fragmented and insufficient to provide much in the way of concrete explanations and establish patterns of engagement. These studies indicate the existence of a continuing and significant gender gap with a number of barriers still preventing women's participation at leadership levels. These barriers are not exclusive to the co-operative movement, and similar barriers – such as male attitudes, lack of opportunity and lack of encouragement, as well as time commitments and unsocial hours of boards – are also widespread in other forms of business.[23]

Women and co-operative leadership in the developing world

A second question addressed was whether the literature on women, co-operatives and leadership in developing countries pointed to a different picture. While recognising that this term covers many different areas and cultures, with different levels of wealth and poverty and special problems pertaining to each area, we investigate women and leadership in three main regions – sub-Saharan Africa, Latin America, and South Asia.

Currently, there is a growing literature on the benefits of collective action and collective entrepreneurship for women in both rural and urban areas. In a study of community forestry organisations in South Asia, for example, Agarwal explores how the proportion of women participating in an organisation impacts levels of effective participation. She found that a critical mass of a quarter to a third of women members helped ensure their effective participation, demonstrated by activities such as public speaking and holding office.[24] Unfortunately, although much of the literature on collective action includes co-operative examples, there is scant recognition of the specificities of the co-operative model and little which specifically addresses leadership issues.[25]

There has been a considerable focus on women in agriculture in development literature, since far more women are engaged in this work than in any other occupation. In developing countries, around 70 per cent of women work on the land. In Africa, they produce about 80 per cent of the food that is consumed locally, though women working in agriculture remain the poorest in the population.[26] Membership of a co-operative can offer enormous benefit in terms of training, resources and markets, and these benefits are cited in a number of studies which are discussed below. A recent survey of the literature on co-operatives in developing countries argues that there is mixed evidence for the empowering effect of participation in co-operatives on women. There is no inevitable connection between participation and empowerment for women, with co-operatives reflecting existing power relations within society as they do in the developed world as well. Nevertheless, there is some evidence that positive empowerment outcomes can occur for women.[27]

Sub-Saharan Africa

The benefits of co-operative membership for women are analysed in some recent work on East African co-operatives. In a study of Manyakabi Area Co-operative Enterprise in Uganda, Ferguson and Kepe show that benefits to women members are both monetary and intangible. The researchers found improved levels of confidence and negotiating skills among women members as well as the ability to take control of some household decisions.[28] Preliminary research findings from Hannan on dairy co-operatives in Kenya concur with this assessment of the importance of non-monetary as well as monetary benefits of co-operative membership for women. Hannan's research emphasises the important role of co-operatives in channelling and providing training and access to agricultural expertise.[29]

An International Labour Organization (ILO) study on women and co-operatives in East Africa – specifically in Kenya, Uganda and Tanzania – provides some much-needed and very timely information and is worthy of extended discussion here.[30] Its findings are largely in line with those from other regions. Women now constitute between a third to a half of the overall membership of co-operatives but there are large variations between sectors and localities. In particular, women are only marginally present in the membership of the co-operatives related to cash crop export such as those marketing coffee, cotton and tobacco. This is largely due to the continuing tradition of male ownership of land and crops. Typically, membership of a coffee co-operative has been limited to those who own the coffee bushes. Bylaws may allow only one member per household or require that a member should own property or resources. This means that the husband is often the member, not the wife. Since their businesses may be quite separate – the man often developing cash crops whilst the woman grows for local consumption – the woman may get no benefit whatever from the co-op whilst the man gets seeds, credit, training, advice and access to markets. All the decisions in the co-operative are made by men, because the women, not being members, are not eligible to join committees or participate in the decision-making processes.[31]

By contrast, women are more present in sectors such as dairy, poultry, fruit and spice production, where land ownership is less critical. In a study of dairy co-operatives in Kenya, Hannan identified clear financial benefits for the women members (Hannan, chapter 13 this volume). Women are also more present as members in savings and credit co-operatives (SACCOs) though again this does depend on the sector that the co-operative represents.[32] In addition, women are particularly vulnerable to the 'land grab' takeovers by states and multi-national corporations, since they have so little apparent right to their land. Tandon shows how the resulting loss of land, or of choice about what to cultivate, leads to a loss to the local community of their traditional subsistence crops as well as a loss of crucial plant and species diversity.[33]

Women are also under represented in leadership positions, especially in agricultural co-operatives. The ILO survey reported an average women's presence on boards of 17 per cent, though this masked considerable variation between countries ranging from 7 per cent in Tanzania to 34 per cent in Uganda. By contrast, there was a far better representation of women on the boards of the financial co-operatives surveyed, with women making up almost half of the membership of boards. Another study revealed that, in the coffee co-operatives of northern Tanzania: 'The co-operative business is a man's business in Tanzania. Both men and women participate from the beginning. But when it comes to reaping, it belongs to men.' Women made up a fifth of the membership but very few were in leadership positions.[34]

A number of barriers were identified in the Majurin study as contributing to this under representation including:

- traditional social and cultural beliefs about appropriate activities and behaviours for women;
- the workload of women encompassing both domestic and productive responsibilities;
- women's more limited access to assets and opportunities whether land, education, information or credit; and
- constraints especially in relation to co-operative by-laws but also the operation of customary law in relation to inheritance and land ownership.[35]

Findings from focus groups carried out by one of the authors in Kenya emphasised the importance of socio-cultural beliefs, held by both men and women, in limiting women's aspirations. Majurin points out that the persistence of negative cultural attitudes towards women's leadership can be seen clearly in the fact that women tend to be less well represented in elected positions such as members of the board than as members of staff in managerial positions.[36] Women may be reluctant to vote for other women. The activities of women board members are scrutinised even after election. It can be deemed inappropriate for lone women board members to attend meetings or training out of their locality: as one person put it, 'one woman and eight men in a hotel, that's mischief'.[37] Campaigning for boards can also take place in bars and hotels considered unsuitable for women to visit or to stay in for any length of time.[38]

Report after report has found that when women earn money they spend it on food, education and health – exactly the things which help to raise families out of poverty – whilst men tend to spend it on themselves.[39] None of this makes for a satisfactory state of affairs. The rules on membership and the opportunities for women to benefit from and contribute to co-operatives are slowly improving, but meanwhile women and girls who work in agriculture largely remain powerless and uneducated labourers, with the dual task of working the land and running the household.

In Kenya, a new state constitution came into effect in 2012. This requires women to make up one-third of all elected bodies. As there are about 10,000 co-operatives in Kenya, this will mean a minimum of 15,000 women joining co-operative boards for the first time. At first glance this sounds like a great improvement for women. However, given that women tend to be less well educated than men, and that culturally they are used to taking a subservient role, there are fears that women will not have the skills, knowledge and confidence to engage in board activities. They may obtain a board position, but be quite unable to fulfil its requirements. This could ultimately be disastrous, both for the women involved and for the reputation of women as leaders. If this move is to have a positive effect, it must be accompanied by widespread training.[40]

There are other changes happening – the Uganda Co-operative Alliance has been working hard to promote women's participation at board level among its members and this seems to be having an impact.[41] In Malawi, some co-operatives have been targeting women for membership as it is felt they make more reliable and committed members. Many have policies to encourage women to join boards and some preliminary findings indicate that co-operative unions have between 18 and 33 per cent female boards. The success of these women leaders is found to encourage further participation from women members.[42]

Latin America

There is a limited amount of literature in English on the situation of co-operatives in Latin America. However, an ILO study of Latin American co-operatives reveals a similar pattern to that seen in other regions. Women remain under-represented in the decision-making bodies of co-operatives despite constituting over half of the membership. Their presence at leadership level is not proportionate to their membership presence. For example, women make up only 16 per cent of the elected boards and only 8 per cent of the presidents while making up a majority of the lower-level administrative staff. A quarter of co-operatives did have gender committees charged with improving levels of women's participation.[43] To help tackle this imbalance, a Regional Gender Equality Committee (CREG) has been set up to help improve inequalities, which were highlighted in a 2010 study they commissioned.[44] The situation appears to be better with respect to financial co-operatives according to a recent ICMIF report. This found that half of ICMIF's members in Latin America were led by a woman CEO and almost a third of North American members were also headed by a woman.[45]

Other initiatives to improve women's involvement in Latin American co-operatives reveal some steady but slow progress towards gender equity. One example is FENACOOP, a co-operative federation in Nicaragua comprising forty-one village-level co-operatives which provide their farmer members with marketing, finance and training. Of their 41,000 farmer members at the village level, just under a half are women. Oxfam Canada has worked with FENACOOP since 1998 to help increase levels of women's participation. A gender audit was carried out in 2006 as a starting point for a gender mainstreaming programme, and the results were published in a booklet. Following the audit, a number of important changes have happened. Women are participating more and making their views heard. At the village level, land is increasingly being registered jointly in the names of both women and men, helping women gain access to credit. Women farmers also receive more technical training in farming and are participating in external leadership programmes. There is still a long way to go but the authors argue that there is now a 'critical mass' of women leaders which will continue to help drive further change. This is seen as crucial, allowing women to have their own spaces and resources to enable them to participate more effectively in decision-making processes.[46]

Other initiatives include Cafenica, an association of ten coffee-producing co-operatives in Nicaragua, which set up an alliance, 'Las Flores de Café', in 2006 to promote the participation and development of women in member organisations. An example of training in co-operative membership and leadership is found in COCLA, a co-operative union in Peru for small-scale farmers who produce mainly coffee. Through outreach work and training in co-operative principles, business, finance and personal development, women have been gradually encouraged to join co-operatives and later to stand for election to boards.[47] In a striking example, Vicari's study of a nut producers' co-operative in Brazil shows how co-operatives can assist with human development and crucially help to empower their women members through active participation within their co-operative. This was evident in women's participation both in the decision-making processes in the co-operative and also within the household.[48]

Asia Pacific

A 2006 study by the International Co-operative Alliance Regional Office for Asia and the Pacific (ICAAP) set out to collect gender disaggregated data, in order to map progress and gaps in participation of women in co-operative leadership and membership. The study aimed to establish a standard system for generating, analysing and using gender-disaggregated data, to assist co-ops in collecting this data and to publish regular reports. In this way benchmarking and progress would be charted.[49] Unfortunately the response to the survey was much less than hoped for and much of the data was of poor quality, but enough data was collected for the study to report with reasonable confidence on the following findings. They concluded that women were still heavily under-represented at leadership levels. Overall, Pakistan and Korea had the lowest overall status of women in co-operatives, while Singapore, the Philippines and Vietnam did better. Nepal came out very well, but, as the researchers pointed out, it has a high proportion of women-only co-operatives.

On average, women constituted around 31 per cent of total members in co-operatives, but this varied considerably across countries and sectors. For board members, there were three times as many men as women. The researchers concluded that 'in short, even though the representation of women in co-operatives does not seem to be very low, their representation in decision-making is extremely low'.[50] This gender gap was particularly marked in attendance at apex-level annual general meetings and board meetings, which was found to be much lower for women (4.9 per cent and 4.2 per cent for women as against 95.1 per cent and 93.1 per cent for men). At primary co-operative level, proportions of women attending annual general meetings are much greater, but this varies from country to country. In primary co-operatives, attendance of women at board meetings was also found to be very low.

One way of tackling this huge gender gap in South Asia has been the development of women's co-operatives. Perhaps the best-known example of this is the Self Employed Women's Association (SEWA). Based in western India, SEWA uses both trade-union and co-operative models for organising its women members, who now number over one million. Over one hundred SEWA women's co-operatives now exist and their activities include handicrafts production, childcare and health-care provision. There is also a women's co-operative bank which was set up in 1974 to provide otherwise unobtainable financial services for SEWA members. The bank has eight formal branches and a network of community *saathis* (companions), and counted 60,000 members in 2008. The majority of account holders are urban women (80 per cent), who are street vendors and home-based workers, to whom the bank offers savings, credit and insurance products.[51]

Although the achievements of SEWA have been very important in this regard, large-scale women's co-operatives have also been developed in other areas in India. Based in South India, the Indian Co-operative Network for Women provides micro-finance for women, skills training, and support for enterprise development, and is developing social protection schemes. A simple credit model has been developed based on local groups of ten women, which are then in turn members of the national women's co-operative network.[52] Women's dairy co-operatives are another widespread example. Nepal has seen an increase in formal women's credit unions for women as part of wider credit union network in the country, which has emerged despite (or perhaps because of) the absence of specific legislative framework for credit unions.[53]

In India, the National Dairy Development Board initiated the Women Dairy Co-operative Leadership Programme (WDCLP) on a pilot basis in Western India. The success of this programme has led to its replication in other regions throughout the country. Under this programme, dairy co-operatives are formed with the membership as well as the management entirely composed of women milk producers. As a result, there are now over 10,550 women's dairy co-operatives. An analysis of the impacts of this programme in fifty villages indicated that co-operative training improved the capacity of rural women in income generation and saving, while participation in the co-operative led to better health, hygiene, functional literacy and knowledge of legal rights.[54]

However, findings from a recent study into the impact of dairy co-operatives on the economic empowerment of rural women in Karnataka, India, provide a cautionary note. Dohmwirth argues that whilst there can be economic benefits for women participating in dairy co-operatives, these economic gains do not always lead to greater empowerment for women. Lower levels of empowerment are attributed to a number of factors, including the top-down implementation of the WDCLP programmes and the reality that women may be 'forced' by men to participate in an income-generating programme as the only way to access its benefits. Lack of adequate education and training also hampers effective participation by women, in some cases leaving the men in effective control with the women acting as shadow managers.[55] Women's co-operatives look to meet the income and livelihood needs of women in both urban and rural areas. In addition, many have an explicit empowerment agenda and also aim to provide a strong voice for women in civil society. However, they remain largely limited to South Asia, which underlines the influence of the specific socio-economic context there.

Across the developing world, it is clear that women gain great benefits from their membership in co-operatives but remain heavily under-represented in leadership roles. This is particularly the case for agriculture, a sector which employs the most women but has very few women in leadership roles and, in some cases, in membership. There are many political, cultural, domestic and organisational reasons for this gender gap. It is also important to note the existence of considerable country differences and large variations across sectors. Women's participation in co-operatives has been enhanced, for example, by the growth of very successful women's co-operatives in South Asia, though this model has not been replicated elsewhere. As we have seen, the evidence for wider empowerment of women through co-operative participation is mixed though there are clear financial benefits.

Generating more evidence

One of the most insistent findings from this research project is the lack of academic research into gender equality in co-operatives and the consequent lack of published papers, with the exception of the work of the ILO. At the global level, the co-operative movement has attempted to address this absence by carrying out some internal surveys which have begun to map the broad contours of women's presence in co-operative leadership, especially in the insurance sector. However, there are still major gaps in data collection by the movement and, as yet, initiatives such as the World Co-operative Monitor do not currently ask for gender-disaggregated information. Research typically does not track the dual nature of leadership in co-operatives and dual routes to such positions.

A recent ILO publication also points out the lack of evidence documenting women's empowerment in relation to co-operatives and gender equity. Based on a survey with over 500 respondents from within the co-operative movement, the paper argues there is increasing attention paid to gender roles but that progression is still slow for women's leadership with some significant sectoral variations in line with the findings of this paper.[56]

What evidence there is, as this paper demonstrates, indicates the existence of a rich and complex picture of gender and leadership within the co-operative movement globally. Apart from the need for more baseline data, this study has illustrated the need for a broad-based research agenda which needs to address a number of interrelated issues. These include gaining a better understanding of the barriers to women's leadership and what strategies have been successful in shifting the balance of power within co-operatives. Within the co-operatives with a better representation of women, are there different models of women's leadership emerging? In addition, many more case studies are needed to unpack the ways in which co-operatives do, and do not, empower their women members and the women in the wider communities in which they operate.

It is clear that to address such questions, and to monitor more adequately the numbers and roles of women in leadership positions in co-operatives, changes need to happen in the collection of appropriate data. Suggestions for these are outlined in the second part of the next section.

Strategies for change

Strategies for change in co-operatives need to be informed by much more research and debate both within and outside the movement. We suggest that change needs to happen in two areas. Firstly, there need to be operational changes in co-operatives and in the co-operative movement which actively encourage the development of women leaders. Secondly, there need to be changes in research practice in this area.

Operational changes

All the evidence underlines the importance of education and training for women. We have seen how quota systems for co-operative boards are now being adopted in several east African countries which in turn raise the challenge to ensure that sufficient support and training programmes are in place for the thousands of new women board members.

Mentoring and role models are particularly helpful. Notably, almost all the female CEOs interviewed for the ICMIF study found it helpful to have role models and mentoring where available. However, few of these role models had been women.[57] In rural communities, women teaching and advising other women can be a powerful trigger for change – women agricultural advisors show farmers by example that it is possible for women to take on influential roles, and when there are women in leadership roles on boards and committees, it becomes that bit more possible for other women to see themselves too in such roles. Women's committees provide valuable opportunities to gain experience of board behaviour and participation.

Women's organisations within the co-operative movement have a long history. They have been adopted in Latin America with some success. The ICA has a Gender Equality Committee, set up in 1995, which is one of the thematic committees and works to promote equality between men and women throughout the movement. In Asia, the Asia Co-operative Women's Forum (AWCF) has been working for many years as a resource and advocacy centre for women in co-operatives. It has members in six countries, has produced training manuals and distributes information about gender mainstreaming, which is described below. Training in gender issues for everyone has been shown to raise awareness and to change the behaviour of both men and women, and the AWCF offers gender training programmes in the Philippines.[58] Women-only co-operatives have been widely adopted in South Asia with mixed results and as yet have had only a limited presence in other regions.

Changes in research practice

The lack of useful evidence for this paper has suggested changes which can be, and to some extent are being, made which could ensure that future research programmes have more empirical evidence on which to base their discussions. For example, a gender-mainstreaming approach has been successfully used in some co-operative development projects to simultaneously improve both practice and data quality, as with the case of FENACOOP mentioned above. It seeks to integrate gender issues to all aspects of an organisation with an ultimate goal of achieving equality.[59] It draws attention to gender right from the start of any project or enterprise, so that it is fully integrated. Using gender audits at different stages of a project, it can identify any changes in the number, level and quality of contributions from both men and women, and can contrast the relative amounts of power and control that men and women hold. This information is used both as an evaluative tool, which has research potential, and to inform the development of further strategies to improve a gender balance.

When it comes to pure research and monitoring, a good starting point needs to be more and better gender-disaggregated data which is routinely collected by co-operatives at member and board level. At present it is far easier to access such information when it is about private companies. For example, Cranfield University School of Management produces the Female FTSE Report, an annual report on the numbers of women on boards in the top 100 companies listed on the London Stock Exchange.[60] There is a clearly a pressing need for real and major improvements in the way that gender disaggregated data is recorded, published and monitored for co-operatives. This also needs to take into account, if possible, the many variables that shape women's involvement both as members and as leaders in co-operatives such as sector, age, location and level of education as well as the dual nature of co-operatives recognising the potential for women's involvement both as active members and as employees.

An emerging policy agenda

In policy terms, therefore, much more can be done and a consensus is emerging on some of the key steps that could be taken.[61] Firstly, the co-operative movement can more effectively collect and track data on women's membership and leadership. More direct support for gender-equity training and related initiatives could also do much to facilitate the more equitable participation of women. Though there is a broad commitment to gender equity in the movement, more detailed strategies and policies also need to be developed and implemented. Secondly, working closely with external partners, including governments and the private sector, to share learning and good practice would also be valuable. Finally, more in-depth research is needed to inform policy development.

The recent ICMIF and ILO reports are helping to bridge the evidence gap. To conclude, we can only concur with the comments made in the introduction to the ICMIF report, which echo those of Dame Pauline Green:

> It would be expected that cooperatives and mutuals would be market-leaders in their HR practices and in particular would ensure that all their staff, women and men alike, were given the opportunities to realise their potential and advance their careers ... but even in the cooperative and mutual sector, men predominate at senior levels.[62]

On the evidence to date, despite some promising developments, there is still a long road to travel before women's leadership in co-operatives more accurately reflects women's membership. If they can achieve this balance, however, co-operatives can start to provide a real alternative to mainstream business. They can offer routes to leadership positions via their democratic membership structures as well as the internal management routes of 'mainstream' enterprises. Co-operatives are well positioned to contribute to the need for greater gender equity in business leadership: the challenge is to make it happen.

Notes

1 International Co-operative Alliance (ICA) President Dame Pauline Green, acceptance speech (20 November 2009), www.aciamericas.coop/IMG/pdf/ga2009-green-acceptanace.pdf (accessed 5 February 2016).
2 The authors are grateful to The Co-operative Group for supporting this research project.
3 H. Henry, *Guidelines for Cooperative Legislation*, 2nd edition (Geneva: International Labour Organization (ILO) 2005); S. Novkovic, 'Defining the co-operative difference', *The Journal of Socio-Economics* 37 (2008), 2168–177; H. H. Munckner, *Co-operation as a Remedy in Times of Crisis Agricultural Co-operatives in the World: Their Roles for Rural Development and Poverty Reduction*, Working Paper No. 41 (Trento: European Research Centre on Cooperatives and Social Enterprises, 2012).
4 A survey was sent out to ICA members but the responses were so small in number (less than five) that very little data was obtained.
5 International Cooperative and Mutual Insurance Federation (ICMIF), *Women in Leadership Positions* (Bowden: ICMIF, 2013).
6 S. Terjesen, R. Sealy and V. Singh, 'Women directors on corporate boards: a review and research agenda', *Corporate Governance: An International Review* 17:3 (2009), 320–37; C. Hoyt, 'Women and leadership' in P. Northouse, *Leadership: Theory and Practice* (Thousand Oaks: SAGE, 2010), pp. 301–33.
7 See CNN Money, 'Germany's new 30% rule for women boards' (8 March 2015), http://money.cnn.com/2015/03/06/news/women-boards-germany-30/index.html (accessed 5 February 2016).
8 European Commission, *Women in Economic Decision-making in the EU-Progress Report* (2012), http://ec.europa.eu/justice/gender-equality/files/women-on-boards_en.pdf (accessed 5 February 2016).
9 R. Pande and D. Ford, *Gender Quotas and Female Leadership: A Review*, Background Paper for the World Development Report on Gender Equality and Development (Washington, DC: World Bank, 2011).
10 J. Birchall, *People-centred Businesses: Co-operatives, Mutuals and the Idea of Membership* (London: Palgrave Macmillan, 2012); R. Hannan, 'Good co-operative governance: the elephant in the room with rural poverty reduction', *Journal of International Development* 26 (2014), 701–12.
11 C. Cornforth, 'The governance of co-operatives and mutual associations: a paradox perspective', *Annals of Public and Co-operative Economics*, 75:1 (2004), 11–32.
12 J. Birchall, *The Governance of Large Co-operative Businesses* (Manchester: Co-operatives UK, 2014).
13 P. Bottelberge and E. Agevi, *Leading Change in Cooperatives and Member Based Organisations in East Africa: Findings of a Study on Leadership and Leadership Development* (Nairobi: Swedish Cooperative Centre and Vi Agroforestry Regional Office for Eastern Africa, 2010).

14 G. Kirton and G. Healy, *Gender and Leadership in Trade Unions* (London: Routledge, 2012).
15 See National Co-operative Archive, 'Basket to Boardroom: Women in Co-operation', www.archive.coop/hive/basket-to-boardroom (accessed 5 February 2016).
16 G. Scott, *Feminism and the Politics of Working Women* (Abingdon and New York: Routledge, 1998); B. Blaszak, *The Matriarchs of England's Co-operative Movement* (Westport, CT: Greenwood Press, 2000); J. Wilson, A. Webster and R. Vorberg-Rugh, *Building Co-operation: A Business History of The Co-operative Group, 1863–2013* (Oxford: Oxford University Press, 2012).
17 B. Rawlings, *Third Sector Women in Management Project: Final Research Report* (Manchester: Inside Track and Co-operative College, 2007).
18 Birchall, *People-centred Businesses*.
19 D. Matsa and A. Miller, 'A female style in corporate leadership? Evidence from quotas', *American Economic Journal: Applied Economics* 5:3 (2013), 136–69.
20 D. G. McKillop, R. Briscoe, O. McCarthy, M. Ward and C. Ferguson, 'Irish credit unions: exploring the gender mix', *Voluntas: International Journal of Voluntary and Nonprofit Organisations* 14:3 (2003), 339–58.
21 B. Poggio, M. De Bon and S. Fedrizzi, 'Gli strumenti di conciliazione tra vita privata e lavorativa nella cooperazione Trentina' [Tools for balancing private life and work life in Trentino co-operatives], Association of Women in Cooperation with Trento Province and the University of Trento. Paper presented by the Federazione Trentina della Cooperazione at the conference 'Best co-operative practices for balancing work and life' held in Trento, Italy (10 June 2009).
22 B. Hueth and A. Reynolds, *The Cooperative Business Study, Summary Results*, Centre for Cooperatives (Madison: University of Wisconsin-Madison, 2014).
23 Ibid.
24 B. Agarwal, 'Does women's proportional strength affect their participation? Governing local forests in South Asia', *World Development* 38:1 (2010), 98–112.
25 E. Jones, S. Smith and C. Wills, 'Women producers and the benefits of the collective form of enterprise', *Gender and Development* 20:1 (2012), 13–32; H. Johnson and L. Shaw, 'Rethinking rural co-operatives in development: introduction to the policy arena', *Journal of International Development* 26 (2014), 668–82.
26 Swedish Cooperative Centre (SCC), *The Toughest Job in the World*, Facts from SCC No. 9 (Stockholm: Swedish Cooperative Centre, 2010). The SCC authors point out that whilst no one can identify the source of this last, much-quoted statistic, it is probably correct.
27 C. Dohmwirth, *The Impact of Dairy Co-operatives on the Economic Empowerment of Rural Women in Karnataka*, MS thesis (Ghent University, Waginengen University, University of Pisa, Agrocampus Ouest, Slovak University of Agriculture and Humboldt University of Berlin, 2014). http://lib.ugent.be/fulltxt/RUG01/002/166/755/RUG01-002166755_2014_0001_AC.pdf (accessed 5 February 2016).

28 H. Ferguson and T. Kepe, 'Agricultural cooperatives and the social empowerment of women: a Ugandan case study', *Development in Practice* 21:3 (2011), 421–9.
29 Hannan, 'Good co-operative governance'.
30 E. Majurin, *How Women Fare in East African Co-operatives: the Case of Kenya, Tanzania and Uganda* (Dar Es Salaam: ILO, 2012).
31 D. Prakash, 'Rural women, food security and agricultural co-operatives' (New Delhi, ICA, 2003), www.uwcc.wisc.edu/info/intl/rur_women.pdf (accessed 29 February 2016).
32 Majurin, *How Women Fare.*
33 N. Tandon, 'New agribusiness investments mean wholesale sell-out for women farmers', *Gender and Development* 18:3 (2010), 503–14.
34 S. Sutton, 'Voice and Choice, Collaborative Governance at Tanzanian Fairtrade Co-operatives', paper presented at Mainstreaming Co-operation conference, Manchester (3–5 July 2012).
35 Majurin, *How Women Fare.*
36 Ibid.
37 Findings from focus group discussion held in Nairobi, November 2011.
38 Personal communication from Dr Esther Gicheru, Principal, Co-operative University College of Kenya.
39 D. Elson, *Male Bias in the Development Process* (Manchester: Manchester University Press, 1995).
40 For discussion of this issue see ILO, 'Co-operative women's challenge in Kenya: strategies for encouraging women's participation on co-operative boards', www.ilo.org/public/english/employment/ent/coop/africa/download/womenschallenge workshop.pdf (accessed 5 February 2016).
41 A.-B. Nippierd, *Gender Issues in Cooperatives* (Geneva: ILO, 2003).
42 S. Vicari and A. Borda-Rodriguez, *Building Resilience in the Malawian Co-operative Movement* (Manchester: Co-operative College, 2014).
43 R. Mogrovejo, R. Mora and P. Vanhuynegem, *El cooperativismo en America Latina* (Cooperativism in Latin America) (La Paz: ILO, 2012).
44 'Gender equality and cooperatives in countries of Latin America' (21 July 2014), www.cicopa.coop/Gender-equality-and-cooperatives.html (accessed 5 February 2016).
45 ICMIF, *Women in Leadership Positions.*
46 B. Manchon and M. Macleod, 'Challenging gender inequality in farmers' organisations in Nicaragua', *Gender & Development* 18:3 (2010), 373–86.
47 COCLA and CAFENICA, unpublished case studies held by the Co-operative College, Manchester.
48 S. Vicari, 'The co-operative as an institution for human development: the case study of Coppalj, a primary co-operative in Brazil', *Journal of International Development* 26 (2014), 683–700.
49 I. Hirway and S. Lodhia, *Engendering Database in Cooperatives in Asia-Pacific Region* (Ahmedabad: Centre for Development Alternatives, 2007).
50 Ibid., p. 37.

51 See www.sewabank.com (accessed 5 February 2016).
52 See www.workingwomensforum.org (accessed 5 February 2016).
53 L. Shaw, *Co-operatives and Workers in the Informal Economy: Possibilities and Challenges* (Manchester and Cambridge: Wiego, 2014).
54 Overseas Cooperative Development Council (OCDC), *Co-operatives: Pathways to Economic, Democratic and Social Development in the Global Economy* (Washington, DC: OCDC, 2007).
55 Dohmwirth, *Impact of Dairy Co-operatives.*
56 ILO, *Advancing Gender Equality: The Co-operative Way* (Geneva: ILO, 2015).
57 ICMIF, *Women in Leadership Positions.*
58 See Asian Women in Co-operative Development Forum, 'AWCF conducts training for co-op', http://awcfcoopwomen.blogspot.co.uk (accessed 29 February 2016).
59 SCC, *Toughest Job.*
60 S. Vinnicombe, E. Doldor, R. Sealy, P. Pryce and C. Turner, *The Female FTSE Board Report: Putting the UK Progress into a Global Perspective* (Cranfield: Cranfield International Centre for Women Leaders, 2015).
61 ILO, *Advancing Gender Equality.*
62 ICMIF, *Women in Leadership Positions*, p. 6.

8

The wasted years? The Co-operative Party during the 1930s

Angela Whitecross

Introduction

The Co-operative Party was formed in 1917 to promote and protect co-operative interests by gaining direct parliamentary representation for the co-operative movement, a consequence of the political isolation felt by the UK co-operative movement during the First World War.[1] A department of the Co-operative Union, the Co-operative Party from the outset worked closely with local Labour Party organisations, although it remained unaffiliated to the Labour Party nationally. In 1927 what became known as the Cheltenham Agreement between the two parties outlined how they would work together to field candidates and in principle not contest each other at elections – and the essence of this agreement remains today.[2] In addition to a level of electoral expediency, this agreement reflected a common aim from both parties to replace capitalist modes of production. However the methods advocated to achieve the co-operative movement's vision of a 'Co-operative Commonwealth' were not identical to the Labour Party's interpretation of a 'Socialist Commonwealth', and this caused both real and potential divisions in the political relationship between the two movements.[3]

In recent years, the Co-operative Party has come in for renewed attention from historians; Robertson and Manton have addressed the nature of the tensions in the political relationship between the co-operative movement and the Labour Party more generally.[4] Despite the political relationship between the Co-operative Party and the Labour Party, these historians argue, the Labour Party did not take the political ambitions of the co-operative movement seriously, as was particularly evident during the Labour Government of 1945–51.[5] Similarly, scholars have argued that the Labour Party's apathy towards the co-operative movement created significant tensions in the relationship between the Labour Party and the co-operative movement, particularly when it began to directly undermine co-operative business interests.[6]

Moreover, interpretations as to why co-operative influence was minimal have focused on the perceived weakness of the co-operative movement from within the Labour Party. For example, Manton suggests that despite the co-operative movement representing the same working-class constituency, their ideas were not taken seriously by the Labour Party.[7] Manton cites three reasons for this: 'political friction' between the Co-operative Party and the Labour Party; ideological issues, notably the co-operative movement's opposition to state control as the only method of ownership; and the relatively poor performance of co-operatives as businesses in this period.[8] Although Manton raises some key points regarding the complex ideological and policy relationship between the Co-operative Party and the Labour Party, he is at times overly critical of the co-operative movement and underestimates the continued strength and relevance of co-operatives in working-class communities.[9] Furthermore, he does not explore in depth the 'problematic relationship' he described between the Co-operative Party and the Labour Party and thus his analysis of the political relationship remains somewhat underdeveloped.[10]

Integral to understanding the relationship between the Co-operative Party and the Labour Party, but co-operative politics more generally, is a greater appreciation of the structural relationship between the Co-operative Party and the wider co-operative movement.[11] This is an area often overlooked by historians – who have, as outlined above, tended to focus on the relationship with the Labour Party. Co-operative involvement in formal politics was, and remains today, a highly contested issue. In 2015 a vote at The Co-operative Group AGM on whether they should continue funding the Co-operative Party passed by a marginal 55 per cent to 45 per cent.[12] The impact of this division and uncertainty about the role, function and future of the Co-operative Party and the political culture in which it operated must be considered here in the context of the 1930s.

This chapter deepens the existing analysis by focusing on the development of Co-operative Party policy during the 1930s, a period which was also critical to Labour Party policy development. Francis argued that 'the content and character of the nationalisation programme of 1945 was very much a reflection of the socialist priorities and expectations of the 1930s'.[13] Similarly, Thompson suggested that the socialist thinking that took place following the collapse of the Labour Government in 1931 'had a profound impact on the evolution of socialist political economy in Britain in that decade'.[14] Consequently, it can be concluded that if the Co-operative Party was to have any influence on the postwar programme of the Labour Party, this would need to have been within the 1930s period of socialist rethinking and policy development.[15]

This chapter will consider the extent to which the co-operative movement, through the Co-operative Party, advocated co-operative forms of ownership in contrast to the Labour Party's focus on state solutions during this period of policy development. Carbery, in his 1969 study of the Co-operative Party, described the 1930s as 'the wasted years', in which he argued more time spent on policy had been necessary 'to argue the case for co-operative forms of social ownership to complement nationalisation'.[16] On one level, this chapter reaffirms Carbery's assessment, as during the 1930s the Co-operative Party did not succeed in its efforts to include co-operative ownership in Labour Party policy. However, progressing beyond this critical approach, it will demonstrate the various reasons why the policy development of the Co-operative Party was limited during this period – and thus also argue that the Labour Party's lack of engagement with co-operative political interests was not just a case of ignorance. By drawing on primary material from the Co-operative Party, the Co-operative Union and also the Labour Party archive, this analysis will broaden understanding of the political relationship between the Co-operative Party, the Labour Party and the co-operative movement, and will contextualise the tensions which emerged regarding the best route to socialism between the Labour Party and the co-operative movement during the 1945 period of Labour Government. Moreover, this illustrates the myriad of challenges the Co-operative Party faced in influencing the Labour Party mainstream and political mainstream as a whole in this period and beyond, despite the continued social, economic and cultural importance of the movement in Britain.

Britain Reborn: the building of the co-operative commonwealth?

Between 1931 and 1934 the Co-operative Party published a series of pamphlets outlining their political programme, entitled *Britain Reborn*. These pamphlets were arguably the first coherent political programme presented by the Co-operative Party. In 1930, at a joint meeting of the Executive Committee of the Co-operative Party and the Parliamentary Group, the Co-operative Union drafted a revised programme for the Party containing positive proposals for a practical solution for unemployment and reconstruction on co-operative lines.[17] This need for a greater co-operative identity in politics was emphasised again when the 1931 split of the Labour Government prompted not only the Labour

Party, but also the co-operative movement to reflect on their political direction.[18]

Carbery described the *Britain Reborn* series as so inconsistent and vague that they were 'embarrassing in their naivety', drawing on the pamphlets to argue that the 1930s represented a missed opportunity in developing a distinctly co-operative political policy.[19] However, the *Britain Reborn* pamphlets do provide clear evidence of the Co-operative Party's effort to define its policy agenda. Moreover, the content of these pamphlets formed the basis of the Co-operative Party's economic policies until after the 1945 General Election. This chapter will explore how their content reflects the extent to which the Co-operative Party was limited by various organisational factors in developing detailed policy statements, and how the policy espoused represented a practical level of consensus with the Labour Party regarding the first steps necessary to achieving a fairer and more equal society through socialist measures.

The *Britain Reborn* political programme was 'a series of pamphlets explaining the policy of the Co-operative Party for grappling with the unemployment evil and for starting the deliberate building of the Co-operative Commonwealth'.[20] Seven pamphlets were published between 1931 and 1934, concluding with a summary edition. The series was designed to be bright, colourful and appealing, and dealt with a range of subjects: *Power and Fuel*, *Transport*, *The Countryside*, *Buy British*, *Men and Money*, *Work for All* and *Civic Ideals*. Whilst the frontispiece of each pamphlet called for the 'building of the Co-operative Commonwealth', the content did not articulate distinctly co-operative methods of ownership. *Britain Reborn: No 1 Power and Fuel* advocated the 'establishment of a National Power Board to acquire all electricity and gas undertakings in Great Britain, and to organise, extend, and develop them into a unified and nationalised power and lighting authority with the primary object of providing the community with the cheapest and most efficient service that scientific knowledge and engineering can contrive'.[21] It also stated that coal was immediately ready for nationalisation, as 'systematic advanced planning can only come when the whole of the power and fuel resources of the nation are consolidated under national ownership and subject to unified administration'.[22] Similarly, *Britain Reborn: No 2 Transport* proposed a 'unified and nationalised transport authority' to acquire all railways, canals, air services and public road services'.[23] It stated that this was necessary as it was 'manifestly futile to rely on unification and co-ordination establishing themselves in the absence of public ownership'.[24] *Britain Reborn: No 5 Men and Money* also advocated the public ownership of the Bank of England.[25] There is nothing distinctly co-operative in terms of methods of ownership advocated in these three pamphlets, with all proposing that national boards be established to control these nationally owned services. Whilst this still represented collective ownership, none of the key principles of co-operation, such as voluntary association or consumer/worker/producer-controlled boards were proposed in these policies.

The consumer identity of the Co-operative Party was adhered to in *Britain Reborn: No 4 Buy British*, which outlined proposals for avoiding tariffs and consequently reducing prices for the consumer, reflecting the growing concern felt within the co-operative movement regarding the impact of tariffs and trade rings both on their trade and the consumer.[26] Intriguingly, however, the pamphlet seeks to promote the Co-operative Party as the embodiment of consumer protection, yet says little that is distinctly co-operative in method, focusing instead on their longstanding political support for free trade policies. *Buy British* did not offer a co-operative solution to the problems of wholesale, distribution and retail, despite these being key to the identity of the British co-operative movement.

The thwarting of voluntary co-operation? Co-operative responses to *Britain Reborn*

A detailed analysis of the Co-operative Party Conference Reports during the first half of the 1930s shows the content of the *Britain Reborn* pamphlets stimulated discussion amongst members of the Party, particularly regarding the type of nationalisation that these pamphlets espoused. Fred Longden, a parliamentary candidate for the Birmingham Co-operative Party, voiced his concern at the 1933 party conference that the methods suggested in *Britain Reborn* for the planning of public ownership and control may 'lead to the thwarting of voluntary co-operation and the founding of a new capitalism'.[27] Londgen clarified that he was not objecting to the Party's programme but just asking for 'a reconsideration of the methods implied'.[28] Likewise, another delegate wanted the Party to be more specific in regard to the constitution of 'National Boards'.[29] In response, Party Chairman Alfred Barnes stated that 'the whole conception and philosophy behind the Co-operative Party programme is that the boards should be controlled by democracies of consumers and producers through their representative bodies, like Parliament and local authorities'.[30] The *Britain Reborn* series had advocated that national boards would be created to manage the newly nationalised industries but had not outlined how these boards would be constituted, although

Barnes appeared to indicate here that this would be through state or municipal control – not though voluntary co-operation.

At conference the following year the subject of nationalisation and the *Britain Reborn* series was raised again by Mr Wheeldon from the Birmingham Co-operative Party, who stated he was aggrieved that the Executive Committee had not, as promised in the last Conference, discussed methods of ownership in *Britain Reborn* with them.[31] Wheeldon further added that he believed that Barnes' nationalisation was different from theirs.[32] Longden reiterated this point, stating that 'the party is demanding the old fashioned nationalisation', whereas he wanted something more inspiring for the youth, bigger and better than what the programme contained.[33] Barnes responded, stating that he had met with the Birmingham Party as agreed and had specifically outlined to them that public ownership meant 'full and complete nationalisation'.[34] This emphasis on nationalisation was resonant of the concurrent development of Labour Party policy under Clause 4 of its constitution, in which common ownership was interpreted as being achieved through state control and economic planning.

Longden stated that he was keen to ensure that Co-operative Party policy statements on nationalisation should not reflect the Morrisonian model epitomised in the London Transport Bill.[35] The model, which later formed the basis of the postwar nationalisation programme, did not embody worker or co-operative control but instead appointed specialist boards to the operation of nationalised industries. Clarifying why the Co-operative Party did not offer in its policy an alternative structure to this form of nationalisation and control, Barnes stated that he was keen to establish a measure of agreement on these political questions within the movement before the Party committed to a policy.[36] This exchange illustrates that although debates did occur over the policy outlined in *Britain Reborn*, particularly regarding co-operative methods, yet they were not progressed within the Co-operative Party. Barnes' point, that policy needed to come from within the movement, was crucial, and will be discussed further below.

On a more practical note, it is evident that these pamphlets were intended to be used to encourage policy discussion within the co-operative movement, as indicated by the report of the Co-operative Party to Co-operative Congress in 1932. It outlined how the pamphlets 'are excellently compiled, well-illustrated and have created a widespread impression', adding that they were 'invaluable to speakers, students and others who are anxious to secure the most up-to-date information upon the leading problems of the day'.[37] The General Election in November 1931 provided an opportunity for this newly written policy to be tested with the Co-operative Party manifesto of 1931 boldly stating 'Capitalism must give way to Co-operation'.[38] A speech by a Co-operative–Labour MP, A. V. Alexander, at Queen's Hall in London in October 1931 emphasised the distinct and practical contribution the co-operative movement offered through this new political programme.[39] This speech was one of many within a series of conferences organised by the Co-operative Party in the autumn of 1931 to promote and publicise their programme. Alexander's speech reflected the policy outlined in the *Britain Reborn* pamphlets, as he lobbied for state control of power, fuel and transport.[40] However, Alexander's speech, like the pamphlets, did not contain anything distinctly co-operative in terms of how co-operative methods should be used to reshape the economy. Instead it echoed the Labour Party's 1931 election manifesto, *Labour's Call to Action*, which also called for the national ownership and control of power, transport, and iron and steel.[41] However, Alexander was a dual Co-operative and Labour candidate and thus needed to represent both parties in his speeches. For practical electoral reasons, then, could the policy of the Co-operative Party be expected to offer a different message from that of the Labour Party? Did the *Britain Reborn* series therefore reflect not only a need for unity within the co-operative movement but also a need for unity across the wider labour movement?

Peter Shea, an active co-operator, commenting upon the *Britain Reborn* series in the 1950s remarked that 'more emphasis was laid upon the socialisation of nationalisation than upon the socialism inherent in the Co-operative Movement itself'. However, he added, this was 'of course necessary at this time'.[42] Therefore, although the *Britain Reborn* series of pamphlets can be criticised for not containing a clear co-operative message of ownership, Shea's writing only twenty years after their publication indicated that the content of these pamphlets reflected the political culture of the Co-operative Party of the early 1930s. In the seventh pamphlet, *Civic Ideals*, it stated that the national and municipal proposals framed in these pamphlets were designed to promote the maximum measure of unity between the co-operative, trade union and labour movements.[43] Furthermore, it outlined how 'it directs the right use of political power by indicating the type of services that first should be brought under public ownership' and 'describes the services that can be developed more rapidly and better on a Co-operative plan'.[44] Therefore, co-operative methods would be used in conjunction with public ownership (meaning state nationalisation) depending on the type of industry. However, *Civic Ideals* did not include a detailed list of which services would be developed on a co-operative plan. The 1934 summary pamphlet did outline how coal, oil, gas, electricity, railways, public road services, air services and waterways would all be brought under state and municipal control, while the Bank of England would be a publicly owned corporation. The only mention here of co-operative methods was a proposal for producer and consumer co-operative agencies in agriculture.[45]

Co-operative Party policy at the beginning of the 1930s echoed that of the Labour Party in advocating that key industries and services should be nationalised. Despite notional comments about the role of the co-operative movement in restructuring the agricultural sector, an area where the co-operative movement had significant vested interests, the pamphlets as a whole did not provide a clear blueprint for a society arranged on co-operative lines. This is reflected in a resolution at the 1933 Co-operative Party conference which outlined:

> The object of the Co-operative Party is the establishment of a co-operative commonwealth, wherein the means of production shall be collectively owned, and wherein the co-operative movement shall function as the medium for the provision of the personal and domestic requirements of the community.[46]

In moving this resolution, T. E. Williams of the Royal Arsenal Co-operative Society stated that its purpose was to focus attention on the role the movement could play in a collectivist state – hence the emphasis on 'personal and domestic'. Whilst this resolution was 'heartily accepted' by the whole conference, there was no discussion of its details or the distinctions between the various forms of collective ownership. Whilst calling for a co-operative commonwealth, the resolution did not argue for a radically alternative approach to that of the Labour Party in this period. This is perhaps unsurprising given that its mover, T. E. Williams, was part of the Royal Arsenal Co-operative Society, which affiliated directly to the national Labour Party. Williams himself was a member of the Labour Party's National Executive Committee. Again, this brings to the fore the issue of the dual identity within the Co-operative and Labour Parties.

Relationship with the Labour Party

Building on this issue of the potentially problematic dual identity of Labour and Co-operative, this section will consider to what extent the political relationship with the Labour Party impeded the Co-operative Party's policy development. At the 1932 Party Conference, Albert Ballard, a party organiser in Sheffield who would later become the party's Chairman, outlined the Co-operative Party's municipal policy.

Ballard stated that the 'programme was really getting down to the difference between the Co-operative Party and the Labour Party – not a difference in point of view, but a difference in contribution in the experience co-operators could make to the problem of municipal social problems'.[47] However, the first clause of this municipal policy, regarding democratic control, created discussion amongst delegates, with one Bristol delegate arguing that if the Labour Party brought a similar bill to the London Transport Bill (which had been based on expert board control) then the Co-operative Party and the movement must oppose it. In support of this, Mrs Ganley from the London Co-operative Society urged conference delegates that if they agreed with a principle then they should work for it'.[48] Yet delegates from the Royal Arsenal Co-operative Society and the Manchester and Salford Co-operative Society noted their concerns that this would put the co-operative movement at odds with the wider labour movement.[49]

Diplomatically, the Party Chairman Alfred Barnes advised that the adoption of this policy would not lead to differences with the Labour Party as, if a problem did arise, negotiations would take place and a friendly solution would be worked out.[50] As chairman, Barnes took on an intermediary role between the two parties and frequently underplayed these 'minor' differences regarding issues of control and ownership to facilitate a smoother relationship with the Labour Party. Moreover, Barnes' emphasis on 'nationalisation' over co-operative ownership was perhaps related to his personal commitment to this policy, epitomised during the 1945 Labour Government, when as Minister of Transport he drafted the Transport Bill which incorporated the board model of control.[51] Again, this suggests a blurring of identity between Co-operative and Labour politics throughout Party ranks. Although the Co-operative Party represented a movement based upon voluntary, democratic control, Barnes did not allow Conference to dwell on this crucial ideological point of difference between municipal and co-operative methods, arguably because dwelling on it represented the potential for division with the wider labour movement. Ballard retorted to Barnes that 'the folly of the Co-operative Party was that it was always apologising and wondering who they were going to offend'.[52] This observation from Ballard illuminates the inherent weakness of the Party, trying to please both the broader co-operative movement and the Labour Party, to the detriment of its own identity.

Nevertheless, this debate signals emerging differences between Co-operative and Labour ideology, particularly regarding the forms of ownership. It also reveals the diverse range of opinion within the Co-operative Party regarding policy, with some local Party organisations, notably the Manchester and Salford and Royal Arsenal, more closely identifying with the Labour Party than others.[53] This delicate balance between promoting co-operative ideology and maintaining a political relationship with the Labour Party was also evident at the 1935 Co-operative Party Conference. A resolution from the Co-operative Men's Guild advocated that the Party seek a scheme with the Labour Party in which only co-operative societies could import or distribute milk, and that this scheme be adopted into the Labour Party programme.[54] Moving this resolution Mr Holland stated 'we have to make it clear that the distributing structure under the socialist state was the one that the co-operative movement has built up' and argued that whatever happened to ownership, co-operatives must retain control.[55] This resolution indicates a clear awareness amongst some members of the Co-operative Party, and in this case also members of the Co-operative Men's Guild, that the unique control offered by the co-operative movement could be lost to state-controlled socialism. As Trentmann noted, 'milk served as the showcase for co-operative economics, and for many organised consumers offered practical proof that the movement could reform political economy without state assistance'.[56] Moreover, this resolution also reflected the need to both protect and promote co-operative business interests, due to the fact that by 1939 co-operatives had over a quarter of the national milk market.[57]

The advancement of this argument at Conference suggests that there was both a desire and expectation from co-operators to influence Labour Party policy, particularly regarding the control of industries in which the co-operative movement had significant business interests. However, the debate sought by the Men's Guild never materialised. Barnes, again acting as mediator, requested that the Guild not press the resolution at this stage. Barnes commented that the issue was already being discussed within the Labour Party and 'while our objective is yours, this type of resolution would cut across the procedure the National Co-operative Authority has arranged with the Labour Party'. He further added that 'it would not be fair to the Labour Party to ask them to incorporate a resolution of this kind into their Party programme at this stage'.[58] The Guild, upon an understanding that the Executive agreed in principle with the resolution, withdrew the resolution without further discussion.[59]

Organisation and political culture of the Co-operative Party

As described above, the political relationship with the Labour Party, both in terms of maintaining a focus on unity and in terms of the developing electoral relationship, had significant implications for Co-operative

Party policy development. Yet a sole focus on Co-operative and Labour Party interaction overlooks the impact of the Co-operative Party's relationship with the wider co-operative movement on its policies and strategies. The Co-operative Party was a department of the Co-operative Union and ultimately responsible to Co-operative Congress, which inhibited its ability to operate. In addition to the structural difficulties this imposed on the Co-operative Party's decision-making capacities, there were ideological and practical issues in play. As the political arm of a complex organisation, the Co-operative Party's political outlook had to contend with the breadth, diversity and size of the co-operative movement.

A 1944 pamphlet on the organisation of the Co-operative Party outlined its complicated structure. The Co-operative Union, the movement's central federal organisation for setting movement policy and practice, exercised significant control over the Co-operative Party. Firstly, the Union had direct representation on the Party's National Committee. Secondly, the Party was subject to the guidance of the Union's Executive Committee and Central Board. Thirdly, the Party was answerable to Co-operative Congress, the annual meeting of Co-operative Union member societies.[60] Consequently the Co-operative Party had limited authority over both its organisation and its policies. Decisions could be made within the Co-operative Party, but these decisions had to be ratified by the Co-operative Union. In essence, what this meant was that co-operative societies and individual co-operators who actively opposed or were indifferent to the Co-operative Party were able to influence the Party's direction and culture. In a 1960 study, Smith and Ostergaard outlined this paradox, stating: 'the Party's responsibility to Congress represents responsibility to a body composed of delegates with varied views on political action, including in some cases outright opposition to the idea of a Co-operative Party'.[61] Co-operative participation in politics was and remains a contentious issue which divided co-operators. Not all co-operative societies were supportive of the formation of the Co-operative Party and neither were all co-operators socialists and supporters of either the Co-operative Party or Labour Party. Recent work by Worley on the Labour Party has included the co-operative movement as just one influence in the 'Broad Church of Labour'.[62] However, the movement itself represented a 'broad church' of political opinion both beyond and within the labour movement.[63] Therefore, not only did the Co-operative Party conference have no final authority over the policies it put forward, it was also open to all within the movement, regardless of political inclination. Such circumstances stifled debate regarding potentially contentious policy issues.

As well as managing the relationship with the Labour Party, Barnes also made it clear to Co-operative Party conference delegates that he had to consider the structural factors of the co-operative movement when working out political forms, suggesting that it was the movement's control over Party policy which inhibited a more defined approach.[64] What emerges from an examination of Co-operative Party and Labour Party conference reports during the 1930s is that, although conference may not have publicly and democratically facilitated discussion regarding potential points of conflict over policy, discussions did take place elsewhere between the co-operative movement and the Labour Party regarding issues of political policy. As Barnes' response to the Men's Guild resolution in 1935 illustrates, one of the key reasons the milk supply and distribution resolution was blocked was that consultation with the Labour Party was already taking place – outside the scope of the Co-operative Party. An examination of Co-operative Congress reports reveals that negotiations were instead led by an Agricultural Policy sub-Committee of the National Co-operative Authority (NCA, described below).[65] Although the Co-operative Party was represented on the NCA, the grassroots activists represented at Co-operative Party conferences remained disengaged from discussions regarding the policy of the Party. Instead, decisions affecting policy, which Party members would be expected to promote and implement in their locality, were not always made openly and democratically but took place behind closed doors.

The formation of the NCA in 1932 significantly affected the direction and mechanism of policy-making within the Co-operative Party, as both organisations participated in co-operative politics and co-operative policy, creating competing roles. The NCA was created in response to a recommendation from the Special Committee of Enquiry on the Future Government of the Co-operative Union.[66] This enquiry recommended that a National Co-operative Authority be created to make 'authoritative pronouncements' reflecting the joint opinions of all national co-operative organisations and that it be empowered to make decisions on co-operative policy between Congresses, subject to a two-thirds majority agreement.[67] Therefore, in addition to taking over the organisational negotiations between the Co-operative Party and the Labour Party in 1938, the NCA because of its policy remit took over other functions that the Party expected to fulfil, in attempting to influence the Labour Party. For example, in 1939 the NCA reported to Co-operative Congress that 'we are endeavouring, and with some success, to impress upon the Labour Party the fact that the consumer is a factor in political philosophy that requires more consideration than so far they have been disposed to give him'.[68] The report added that they were still faced with the difficulty as to whether certain trades should be carried on by co-operative societies, municipalities or by joint arrangements between the two, and that this ultimately represented the vital difference in party ideologies.[69] Whilst this suggests that debates continued regarding the role of the co-operative movement in Labour Party policy, however, the focus of the NCA was on the short-term trade interests of the existing co-operative movement. The Labour Party and the NCA were not engaged in a broader debate about where co-operative ideas of ownership would fit into the Labour Party's broader vision of socialism at this point, suggesting significant inertia within the co-operative movement regarding ideological discussions beyond their immediate trading remit. It was not the Co-operative Party which acted as a broker for these negotiations; nor was their content discussed in any detail at Co-operative Party conferences. This illustrates the relative lack of influence the Co-operative Party had over its own policy development, but also the limits to its ability to promote a positive political vision for the co-operative movement with the Labour Party.

The inertia of the co-operative movement

In 1925 the Co-operative Union included a commitment to the 'Co-operative Commonwealth' in its aims, which Cole suggested emphasised the movement's hostility to capitalism.[70] However, this chapter has demonstrated the limited extent to which the Co-operative Party, as the political arm of the movement, actively promoted a 'Co-operative Commonwealth', particularly in contrast to the Labour Party's increasingly statist approach to socialism. As Bonner argued, during the 1930s the Co-operative Union was more concerned with immediate problems of finance, trade and systems of management than with creating a political programme for a co-operative commonwealth.[71] Similarly, Gurney has shown how co-operators suffered constant pressure from external threats during the interwar years, and it is likely that this environment affected the political culture in which the Co-operative Party developed their political programme.[72]

The inertia of the co-operative movement to involvement in politics outside their immediate business concerns is best illustrated by the Co-operative Union's decision in 1935 to reject an invitation from the Labour Party to join the National Council of Labour (NCL). Amidst negotiations regarding the organisational relationship between the two parties it was proposed that the Co-operative Union join the NCL to participate in wider discussions on economic policy and consequently protect the needs of co-operative businesses.[73] The NCL, initially known as the Joint Council, then comprised the Trade Union Congress and the Labour Party.[74] Although Brookshire notes that the influence of the NCL on the Labour Party varied over time, he does argue that during the 1930s it was an important arena for Labour Party policy discussion.[75]

The invitation was declined by the NCA on behalf of the Co-operative Union, on the grounds that many of the items discussed by the NCL were outside their scope of interest.[76] The rejection was reported with disappointment at the Labour Party's 1935 Conference by G. R. Shepherd, the National Agent. He stated that they had invited the Co-operative Party to appoint representatives to the NCL because they were anxious to create one channel of communication between the co-operative movement and the trade union movement regarding policy, adding that he hoped the decision to decline this invitation was only temporary.[77] Although the Co-operative Party Executive Committee members had secured this invitation through their negotiations with the Labour Party, the wider co-operative movement was still reluctant to commit to any overt political involvement outside the scope of the movement's immediate interests. Therefore, although the Co-operative Party was mindful of the need to be actively involved in broader policy discussions, particularly when its MPs were to be bound by the standing orders of the Parliamentary Labour Party, it had no authority to act upon this and consequently was inhibited by the insularity of the wider co-operative movement. On this occasion a closer policy relationship between the co-operative movement and the Labour Party had been brokered by the Co-operative Party, yet was undermined by the NCA, who, as the representative policy voice of the movement, did not consider the impact of future policy on their business and trade concerns.

Thus, both the political diversity of the co-operative movement and the apathy of its leadership towards promoting distinct co-operative methods beyond its immediate business interests meant that it was not easy to formulate a policy which would meet the expectations of the entire movement. A commitment to the advancement of the co-operative commonwealth was not evident throughout the 1930s in the wider co-operative movement and this is reflected in the deliberately vague, arguably safe policies on ownership and control that were taken forward by the Co-operative Party in the 1930s.

Conclusions

The inability of the Co-operative Party or the co-operative movement to mainstream co-operative methods of ownership during the 1930s period of socialist rethinking is evident in *Labour's Immediate Programme*, published in 1937, which outlined the socialist measures proposed by the Labour Party to be implemented within one term of government.[78] This represented the culmination of the Labour Party policy development process that had been developing from 1932 and advocated the nationalisation of the Bank of England, coal, gas, electricity, land and transport, and economic planning as well as a commitment to social reforms such as improving education, welfare and the health service.[79] Furthermore, it was this programme that formed the basis for the 1945 Labour Government manifesto and the subsequent direction for the newly elected Labour Government.

Commenting on *Labour's Immediate Programme*, at the Co-operative Party conference in 1937, Barnes stated how 'in its main principles of action it corresponds to the Co-operative Party's One Parliament Programme adopted in 1933 and published as the *Britain Reborn* set of pamphlets'.[80] Therefore, during the 1930s the Co-operative Party also promoted state ownership and control of key industries as the first steps necessary to achieving a fairer and equal society through socialism and did not offer a co-operative alternative. This partly reflects an emphasis on unity which was vital in term of grassroots electioneering – as this chapter has suggested, the dual identity of Co-operative and Labour candidates was a factor in the determination of Co-operative Party policy. This has been emphasised by Gurney, who suggested that one reason discussions over policy were purposefully avoided was to play down divisions in policy so as to avoid embarrassment to those local parties working together.[81] However, the consequence was that at this formative time in the development of the economic policies of the Labour Party, the Co-operative Party restricted open debate and curbed what potential they had to make a positive co-operative contribution to the Labour Party programme.

Yet, this inability to promote co-operative methods of ownership as an alternative to the Labour Party mainstream of state socialism reflects the lack of an alternative co-operative vision during the 1930s. This was due to both the structural limitations in which the Co-operative Party operated and the disinclination of the wider co-operative movement to get involved in politics beyond their immediate trading concerns. As this chapter has demonstrated, debates which the Co-operative Party stifled in their conferences during the 1930s did represent an alternative vision to the statist model closely associated with the postwar Labour Government. A pamphlet written by Fred Longden in 1935 illustrates his view on the relationship between co-operation and labour, demonstrating how his approach was at odds with Co-operative Party leadership during the 1930s.[82] Longden outlines the crucial differences between co-operation and labour but concludes that a 'formation of a grand Tripartite' would ensure that socialists, trade unionists and co-operators would all work together to promote their common ideal and individual needs.[83] Yet even if Longden's vision of a grand tripartite had been realised, the ideological limitations of the co-operative movement at this time would have proved problematic. Despite a proclaimed commitment to building a co-operative commonwealth, the political vision of the co-operative movement was blinkered during the 1930s as it focused more on immediate business interests and did not consider the broader political application of co-operative methods. This ultimately inhibited the potential of the Co-operative Party to effectively mainstream co-operative methods in the policies of the Labour Party and politics more generally during the 1930s and 1940s. Furthermore, the challenge from The Co-operative Group board in 2015 suggests that this inertia to direct co-operative involvement in politics remains an issue today and thus continues to inhibit the mainstreaming of co-operative methods in contemporary politics.

Notes

1 T. F. Carbery, *Consumers in Politics: A History and General Review of the Co-operative Party* (Manchester: Manchester University Press, 1969), pp. 16–17.

2 *Co-operative Congress Report* (1927), p. 94. At a national level, this agreement provided for the establishment of a joint subcommittee representative of both executives, an exchange of minutes of both national executives and that joint campaigns be undertaken on special subjects during elections. Locally, it provided for affiliation between local Co-operative Parties or Councils and Divisional Labour Parties which would give them similar rights and responsibilities as other affiliated organisations. Crucially, however, this agreement was optional and stated that it was 'not intended to interfere with existing arrangements where co-operative societies are already affiliated or an arrangement has been established'.

3 G. D. H. Cole, *A Century of Co-operation* (Manchester: Co-operative Union, 1944), p. 318.

4 Some examples include: M. Francis, *Ideas and Policies under Labour, 1945–1951* (Manchester: Manchester University Press, 1997), pp. 83–9; K. Manton, 'The Labour party and the Co-op, 1918–58', *Historical Research* 82:218 (2009), 756–78; N. Robertson, 'A union of forces marching in the same direction? The relationship between the Co-operative and Labour parties, 1918–39' in M. Worley, ed., *The Foundations of the British Labour Party: Identities, Cultures and Perspectives, 1900–1939* (Ashgate, Aldershot, 2009), p. 224.

5 Francis, *Ideas and Policies under Labour*, pp. 83–9; K. Manton, 'The Labour Party and retail distribution, 1919–1951', *Labour History Review* 73:3 (2008), 274.

6 N. Robertson, *The Co-operative Movement and Communities in Britain, 1914–1960: Minding their Own Business* (Farnham: Ashgate, 2010), p. 122; P. Gurney, 'The battle of the consumer in postwar Britain', *The Journal of Modern History* 77 (2005), 965. Gurney cites the Labour Party's proposal to nationalise industrial assurance (which would have included the Co-operative Insurance Society (CIS)) as evidence of Labour Party malaise towards the co-operative movement.
7 Manton, 'Labour party and retail distribution', 311–12.
8 Ibid.
9 In 1951 the co-operative movement comprised 1,006 retail distributive societies with a combined membership of almost 11 million. It was not an insignificant movement. *Co-operative Congress Report* (1952), Appendix, Co-operative Statistics (1951), p. 7.
10 Manton, 'Labour party and the Co-op', 767–74.
11 This was a focus of my thesis research. A. Whitecross, 'Co-operative commonwealth or new Jerusalem? The Co-operative Party and the Labour Party, c.1931–1951' (PhD thesis, University of Central Lancashire, 2015), pp. 36–74.
12 J. Treanor, 'Co-op Group to keep funding party aligned to Labour', *The Guardian* (16 May 2015), www.theguardian.com/business/2015/may/16/co-op-group-averts-legal-action-by-agreeing-to-change-composition-of-board (accessed 25 August 2015).
13 Francis, *Ideas and Policies*, p. 90.
14 N. Thompson, *Political Economy and the Labour Party: The Economics of Democratic Socialism 1884–2005*, 2nd edition (London: Routledge, 2006), p. 92.
15 *Labour's Immediate Programme*, published in 1937, is viewed as the Labour Party's first programme for government and reflects an emphasis on policy development in the period 1931–37. Furthermore, the policies outlined in this formed the basis for the Labour Party's 1945 Election Manifesto.
16 Carbery, *Consumers in Politics*, p. 37.
17 Co-operative Union Minutes/Co-operative Party (4 November 1930), National Co-operative Archive, Manchester.
18 Co-operative Union, *The Crisis of 1931: being a statement of policy adopted by the National Committee of the Co-operative Party during the financial and political crisis of August and October 1931* (Manchester: National Co-operative Publishing Society, 1931), p. 19.
19 Carbery, *Consumers in Politics*, p. 37.
20 This statement was on the frontispiece of each pamphlet.
21 Co-operative Party, *Britain Reborn: No 1 Power and Fuel* (Manchester: Co-operative Union, 1931), p. iii.
22 Ibid., p. 32.
23 Co-operative Party, *Britain Reborn: No 2 Transport* (Manchester: Co-operative Union, 1931), p. iii.
24 Ibid., p. 22.
25 Co-operative Party, *Britain Reborn: No 5 Men and Money* (Manchester: Co-operative Union, 1931) p. iii.

26 Co-operative Party, *Britain Reborn: No 4 Buy British* (Manchester: Co-operative Union, 1931).
27 *Co-operative Party Annual Conference Report* (1933), p. 30.
28 Ibid.
29 *Co-operative Congress Report* (1933), p. 453.
30 Ibid.
31 *Co-operative Party Annual Conference Report* (1934), p. 12.
32 Ibid.
33 Ibid., p. 11. He argued that enlightened capitalism was offering more to the workers of the time.
34 *Co-operative Party Annual Conference Report* (1934), p. 12.
35 Longden's concerns over *Britain Reborn* reflect his earlier criticism of the London Transport Bill. At the second reading on 23 March 1931, Longden (then a Co-operative MP) expressed the view that the measure, instead of leading to nationalisation, would lead away from it, criticising the measure on the grounds that it did not suggest any means of giving the workers the right to interfere when their labour conditions were affected. See Co-operative Party, *Work at Westminster: Activities of the Co-operative MPs during the sessions of 1931* (Manchester: Co-operative Union, 1932), p. 5.
36 *Co-operative Party Annual Conference Report* (1934), p. 12.
37 *Co-operative Congress Report* (1932), p. 100.
38 Co-operative Party Executive Committee minutes (16 June 1931); Co-operative Party, *The Crisis of 1931*, Appendix I, *Co-operative Party General Election Manifesto* (1931), p. 32, National Co-operative Archive.
39 CC/AVAR 12/4-Speeches/Queen's Hall, London, 2 October 1931, Churchill Archives Centre, Cambridge.
40 Speech by A. V. Alexander, Queen's Hall, London, 2 October 1931/CC/AVAR 12/4-Speeches, Churchill Archives Centre.
41 *Labour Party Manifesto 1931: Labour's Call to Action*, http://labourmanifesto.com/1931/1931-labour-manifesto.shtml (accessed 27 January 2016).
42 P. Shea, *'Times Past': Paragraphs on the History of the Co-operative Party* (Manchester: Co-operative Union, 1955), p. 26.
43 Co-operative Party, *Britain Reborn: No 7 Civic Ideals* (Manchester: Co-operative Union, 1932), p. 49.
44 Ibid.
45 *Co-operative Party, Britain Reborn: Work and Wealth for All – A Summary of the Britain Reborn Series* (Manchester: Co-operative Union, 1934), pp. 4–5.
46 *Co-operative Party Conference Report* (1933), p. 24.
47 *Co-operative Party Conference Report* (1932), p. 26.
48 Ibid.
49 Ibid., p. 29.
50 Ibid., p. 29.
51 Barnes as Minister of Transport was the architect of the Transport Act of 1947, which nationalised the railways using the board model.
52 *Co-operative Party Conference Report* (1932), p. 30.

53 The Manchester and Salford and the Royal Arsenal societies were notably in many party conference debates more pro Labour Party than other societies and were the societies which moved a resolution for direct affiliation to the Labour Party at the 1945 Co-operative Party Conference.
54 *Co-operative Party Conference Report* (1935), p. 41.
55 Ibid., p. 42.
56 F. Trentmann, 'Bread, milk and democracy: consumption and citizenship in twentieth-century Britain', in M. Daunton and M. Hilton, eds, *The Politics of Consumption: Material Culture and Citizenship in Europe and America* (Oxford: Berg, 2001), p. 152.
57 Ibid.
58 *Co-operative Party Conference Report* (1935), p. 42.
59 Ibid.
60 J. Bailey, *The Co-operative Party: An Outline of Organisation* (Manchester: Co-operative Party, 1944), p. 14.
61 B. Smith and G. Ostergaard, *Constitutional Relations between the Labour and Co-operative Parties: An Historical Review* (London: Hansard Society for Parliamentary Government, 1960), p. 2.
62 Worley, ed., *Foundations of the British Labour Party.*
63 D. Stewart, '"A party within a party?" The Co-operative Party–Labour Party alliance and the formation of the Social Democratic Party, 1974–81', in A. Webster, L. Shaw, J. K. Walton, A. Brown and D. Stewart, eds, *The Hidden Alternative: Co-operative Values, Past, Present and Future* (Manchester: Manchester University Press, 2011), pp. 137–56, p. 137.
64 *Co-operative Party Annual Conference Report* (1934), p. 12. This discussion was on finance.
65 The National Co-operative Authority's report to Congress in 1935 outlined these discussions. *Co-operative Congress Report* (1935), p. 74.
66 *Co-operative Congress Report* (1932), Appendix: Report of the Special Committee of Enquiry on the Future Government of the Co-operative Union, p. 431.
67 Ibid. The National Co-operative Authority (NCA) comprised the Executive Committee of the Co-operative Union, four representatives from the Co-operative Wholesale Society, two from the Scottish Co-operative Wholesale Society, two from the Co-operative Party, one from the Co-operative Press and one from the Co-operative Productive Federation.
68 *Co-operative Congress Report* (1939), p. 463.
69 Ibid.
70 Ibid., p. 303.
71 A. Bonner, *British Co-operation* (Manchester: Co-operative Union, 1961), p. 206.
72 P. Gurney, 'Co-operation and the "new consumerism" in interwar England', *Business History* 54:6 (2012), 905–24, p. 907.
73 Joint Committee of Labour Party and Co-operative Party/Minutes, 30 May 1935, LPA. Co-operative Party candidates were being requested to sign the

Standing Orders of the Labour Party and this was offered as a concession for doing so.

74 See Jerry H. Brookshire, 'The National Council of Labour, 1921–1946', *Albion: A Quarterly Journal Concerned with British Studies* 18:1 (1986), 43–69, for further details on this body.

75 Brookshire, 'The National Council of Labour', p. 45.

76 *Co-operative Congress Report* (1936), p. 71.

77 *Labour Party Conference Report* (1935), p. 141.

78 M. Worley, *Labour Inside the Gate: A History of the British Labour Party between the Wars* (London: I. B. Tauris, 2005), p. 194.

79 Ibid.

80 *Co-operative Party Annual Conference Report* (1937), p. 10.

81 P. Gurney, 'Labor's great arch: co-operation and cultural revolution in Britain 1795–1926' in E. Furlough and C. Strikwerda eds, *Consumers against Capitalism: Consumer Co-operation in Europe, North America and Japan, 1840–1990* (Oxford: Rowman & Littlefield, 1999), p. 156.

82 F. Longden, *Why a Feud between Co-operation and Labour?* (Stafford: Staffordshire Area Co-operative Party, 1935), U/GPI/11/40, Teesside Archives.

83 Ibid., p. 23.

9

New models of ownership and governance

Cliff Mills and Ruth Yeoman

Two hundred years ago in the United Kingdom, the concept of mutual enterprise was little known and still in its infancy. However, from the basis of its friendly society roots the concept of mutuality was developing rapidly in the face of increasingly harsh living conditions and the challenges of industrialisation. One hundred years later, mutuality was not just mainstream. Co-operative societies, friendly societies, building societies and a range of other primary citizen-based enterprises and secondary societies were an established part of the economy and played a significant part in shaping British society. By the end of the twentieth century, however, co-operation and mutuality seemed to have become irrelevant. Much of the building society movement had demutualised, and co-operative retailing was in rapid decline. Friendly societies and other mutual initiatives to support citizens in times of hardship were marginalised by the creation of a welfare state and National Health Service (NHS). Self-help rooted in mutual and community-based relationships simply did not fit the culture and ethos of the day, which was more characterised by individualism, widespread faith in a market-based approach, and a neoliberal obsession with investor ownership.

The first decade and a half of the twenty-first century have witnessed an extraordinary desire to recapture the essence of mutual enterprise, and to make it work as an alternative option to both investor ownership and state or municipal provision. Co-operation and mutuality are becoming mainstream again – or, at least, many want or are seeking to make that happen. 'Roller-coaster' might be something of a misnomer to apply to a process straddling two centuries, but it does seem to reflect the widely changing significance of a set of ideas, operational practices and organisational structures which are today right at the heart of developing ideas about not just how to deliver services and run businesses, but how to build healthy and sustainable links between community and enterprise, how to share power, how to address the challenge of increasing inequality, and how to live our lives in a way which does not diminish the opportunities for future generations.

This chapter will not seek to explain the reasons behind the rising and falling significance of co-operation and mutuality in the UK over its lifetime so far. What it will seek to do is to identify and explore some of the new ideas connected with co-operation and mutuality that are emerging at this particular time in the context of public sector reform; to understand them in their historical context and in what ways they are cutting new ground, particularly in redistributing power; to consider how they are capable of a much wider transformative effect; and finally to comment on the thorny question about development: if these really are good ideas at a number of levels, what can be done to enable them to take root and bloom on a much wider scale? In passing, some reflections will be offered which compare these developments with some of the current problems in the continuing evolution of mainstream co-operation, illustrated by the recent problems of The Co-operative Group (see also chapter 16 in this volume).

Multi-constituency rather than single-constituency mutuals

The first and most obvious change being introduced through what are termed 'new mutuals' appearing in the public sector in the UK is the widening of ownership to a variety of constituencies including customers and producers, and sometimes others. This is not to say that the concept was unknown in previous times, but the mutual traditions which have survived into the current century are largely customer-based mutuals which are owned by their customers: co-operative retail societies, building societies, friendly societies and mutual insurers. This can be illustrated by the case of the co-operative shops which were started as a way of enabling people living in highly straightened circumstances to gain access to uncontaminated food at a fair price. The Rochdale Pioneers brought together potential customers to provide funding to open a shop which they would own and control. The owners or members *were* the customers; and when hundreds of other communities followed suit and established their own co-operative stores, this resulted in a large movement of what became known as 'distributive societies'.

Needless to say, there were many other co-operative initiatives, including groups of workers or artisans who got together to establish 'productive societies' which were owned and controlled by the producers themselves. This included such trades as the production of clothing, boots and shoes, as well as some of the traditional building trades. Others went further and established jointly-owned societies owned by both customers and producers, between whom any trading surplus was shared in order to ensure not just a fair price for customers, but a fair wage for producers.[1] Both such models survived into the twentieth century, but by 1900 there more than ten times as many distributive as productive societies and their respective size in terms of capital was twenty-five times as big (distributive societies £20.6 million; productive societies £0.8 million).[2] Consumer societies continued to dominate the UK co-operative movement, and although there have been various times at which new worker-based or co-partnership societies have emerged in significant numbers, they tend to be small businesses.

During the late nineteenth century, there was much debate about whether or not workers should be entitled to a share of any surplus in the form of a bonus. This was powerfully opposed by Beatrice Potter (later Webb), including in her book *The Co-operative Movement in Great Britain*,[3] and the eventual outcome was that through the twentieth century, employees of the retail societies were generally not entitled to receive a share of the surplus. As a result, there was no separate 'employee constituency' of members. To this day, although many employees of the large retail societies are members of their employing society, they are part of a single constituency of members. Rules generally ensure that at each tier of governance, employees are always in the minority, to ensure that societies remain consumer controlled.

In the context of public sector reform in the current century, as in a number of other areas, a strikingly different approach was given prominence by legislation when a new type of corporate entity – the public benefit corporation – was created for the National Health Service. Health legislation in 2003[4] introduced what are more commonly known as NHS Foundation Trusts, and now such organisations account for the bulk of the acute (hospital), mental health and specialist secondary care services in England.

Foundation Trusts are required to have a minimum of two constituencies: public, and staff. The legislation allows them, if they wish to do so, to have further constituencies of patients and carers, though to date the majority have chosen to have just public and staff constituencies. Because these organisations are created for a public purpose, the legislation requires them to be democratically controlled by public members. Whilst staff must have a minimum level of representation within the governance (see further below), it is always less than that of the public.

This introduction of staff as a constituency breaks the mould of traditional mutuality, for the reasons explained above. But it is in a very different context for two key reasons: (a) NHS Foundation Trusts, and other organisational models which have followed their lead, do not make any distribution of surplus to their members (all profits are retained for inward investment); and (b) these organisations are providers of public services which are generally publicly funded. This means that there is no real economic relationship between the member and their society. For many in the traditional mutual sector, this results in such organisations being a very limited form of mutuality. It has to be recognised, however, that this new form of ownership where individuals replace the state as the underlying owners, and the introduction of a form of democratic governance giving voice to users and producers, is a very significant development in public services.

Other examples of where this multi-constituency model has been introduced are Rochdale Boroughwide Housing (RBH), a registered provider of social housing running 13,500 homes in Rochdale, Heywood and Middleton; Salford Community Leisure, a provider of leisure services, community centres, libraries and museums; Knowsley Youth Mutual, a new provider which has taken over the provision of youth services in that area from the local authority; and Care Plus Group, a provider of community health and social care services in North East Lincolnshire. These organisations all represent a significant new departure in terms of organisational design, but they also represent a different approach to power sharing.

A power-sharing model for public service transformation

The multi-constituency approach is a power-sharing arrangement which reconfigures the relationship between staff and service users. In essence, the multi-constituency mutual is a response to a contemporary crisis of organisational power which afflicts both private and public organisations. This crisis is characterised by loss of diversity in power sources as a consequence of power consolidation by hierarchical elites. This gives rise not only to alienation in our working together as producers and living together as citizens, but also to brittle organisations which are vulnerable to external shocks and internal de-legitimisation. Clegg, Courpasson and Phillips comment that 'power without morality is despotism, while morality without power is sterile'. They argue that this demands attentiveness to 'the combination of democracy, power and morality'[5] to create more power-full organisations characterised by heterarchy and responsible autonomy which

> means the separation of powers; it builds sovereignty into practice rather than the precedent of domination. It sets up, at best, internal systems for

> the exercise of voice, the calling to account, and the checking of power, and encourages coevolutionary learning.[6]

An organisation lacking in power diversity is a monovocal organisation. Such organisations are less responsive to staff, customers and service users, and are therefore less likely to foster the information flows and expanded perspective upon which good decision-making depends. Conversely, polyvocal organisations support difference, conflict and disagreement, making these productive through the control mechanisms of representation-based governance and the participatory mechanisms of direct democracy at the level of the task. Practices of polyvocality combined with organisational power diversity are the basis for the co-design and co-production of new public services.

Sherman argues that one of the reasons we engage with others in common pursuit is 'we simply value doing things for their own sake'. This is because 'we value creating a shared world and the mutuality that is defined by our interactions. The pleasure of mutuality at the expansion of self that comes with it is part of human flourishing.'[7] Creating mutual organisations requires us to participate with others in joint sense-making, out of which emerge the norms, behaviours, systems and processes that construct the common life. Through processes of interrelating through shared endeavour, we create 'a sense of tracking something with one another, of creating a sense of unity through attunement to each other other's moves'.[8] This mutual joining of mind, feeling and effort is not fully described by fairness or even care; rather, it is a dynamic interaction which creates a temporary sense of unity between two or more individuals engaged in a common purpose. Mary Parker Follett describes the experience of community group work as one which aims at neither compromise nor consensus, but at an integration of the differences which individuals bring to their interrelatedness. Power in moments of genuine integration is not coercion or a balance of power, but is coactive power (power with) in which all share in the production and the enjoyment of the outcome.[9]

How does the conflict of interest between customers and staff work itself out in practice? Customers always want better and cheaper services, and staff always want improved terms and conditions and better pay; these economic interests are opposed to each other. The reality, of course, is that this 'conflict of interest' (perhaps better referred to as a tension) exists for any business, whatever its form of ownership. It is the function of the business itself, whatever form it takes, to find a resolution to this tension in the day-to-day operation and long-term strategy. Where those interests have a voice within the business, that tension can be resolved through listening to that voice. But where such interests have no such voice, they will still fight to be heard – through a trade union, the press, pressure groups and so on – though their likelihood of being heard is limited.

Most businesses are owned by the providers of capital (the investor-owned company), which is a third competing interest in addition to labour and custom. Such businesses are ultimately run for the benefit of their shareholders, and structurally the company model provides no voice within the formal governance for customers or staff: that is the basic design of the investor-owned company model. So customers and staff are always seeking to be heard 'from the outside', because they have no embedded voice in the design of the model. The mutual approach has always challenged the dominant model of investor ownership, initially by customers establishing and funding their own businesses in competition (co-operative stores), which operate for the benefit of customers and the wider community. But the new mutual organisations emerging from public sector reform represent a more radical challenge to monovocal businesses.

Voice

Voice is key to heterarchy or organisational power diversity.[10] Hirschman describes voice as 'any attempt at all to change rather than to escape from an objectionable state of affairs'.[11] In more conventional terms, Lavelle, Gunnigle and McDonnell define voice as 'any type of mechanism, structure or practice which provides employees with an opportunity to express an opinion or participate in decision-making within their organisation'.[12] Conceptually, voice goes beyond having a say, since having a say does not automatically imply influence. For example, Heller distinguishes between having a share in participation (as taking part in an activity) and having a share in power (as having a degree of influence over an activity).[13] If voice means to actually experience having a share of power, then voice is not realised by a purely structural or procedural approach. Simply setting up structures will not guarantee that each individual worker or stakeholder will actually experience voice as influence-sharing, because many voice systems have 'deaf ears'. Having a voice is the social and interactive experience of being listened to by others, and being treated as an equally worthy person with an equally valid point of view – it is not the experience of simply knowing structures are in place. Wilkinson and Fay suggest that 'voice may need to be bundled, and then embedded. Once implemented, voice can shrivel. There seems to be a life cycle in relation to specific schemes.'[14] In particular, a voice system can be kept alive by ensuring there are multiple channels for voice to be expressed, including direct individual participation, such as team meetings and strategy days, and indirect collective representation, such as employee representatives on the board and a strong union presence.[15]

Wegge, Jeppesen and Weber identify the importance of 'structurally anchored organisational democracy' including 'broad-based and institutionalised employee influence processes that are not ad hoc or occasional in nature'.[16] This involves moving away from the leader–subordinate dyad to 'the constructive participation of all organisational members in the creation and implementation of organisational values, norms and rules'.[17] This implies a system of democratic authorisation at the level of the organisation,[18] as well as participatory practices at the level of the individual.[19]

So although the multi-constituency approach is not unknown within the co-operative heritage as explained above, it is a real novelty at the scale of organisations in which it is now being introduced, and in terms of its potential impact as a model of power sharing. By building into the very design of the model an embedded voice for customers and employees, it deliberately seeks to use the mechanism of the organisation itself both to resolve tensions between the two constituencies, and more importantly to bring the two constituencies together so that they can work collaboratively together for the wider benefit of the organisation and the community which it serves. We will return to this again later.

Governance design

The introduction of different constituencies of owners creates a number of generic issues for the design of governance, and further specific issues in certain regulated sectors. The first and most obvious generic issue concerns governance: if there are two or more constituencies of owners, what are the arrangements to give an effective voice to such constituencies in a way which is both supportive and beneficial to the delivery of the business? In particular, with two or more constituencies there needs to be a forum through which dialogue between them can develop and a relationship be developed.

Whilst it is possible to address this simply by enabling the different constituencies to be represented on a multi-constituency board, this can pose challenges. For smaller businesses operating in unregulated sectors, such challenges may not be insuperable. So, for example, when Salford Community Leisure first established its own independent existence to take over the provision of leisure services from Salford City Council, it adopted this approach. However, once it had taken over community centres, libraries and museums, it found that it was difficult for the breadth and scale of businesses to be effectively governed using a multi-constituency board without it becoming large and therefore unwieldy. In social housing, which is a regulated sector, there are statutory issues which impede the inclusion of employee representatives as board members. There may be other specific situations where the inclusion of employee representatives on a board sits uncomfortably alongside the board's role of overseeing a chief executive in the discharge of their functions.

There is a further generic problem which arises in the context of very large businesses, or where the sector they are operating in involves substantial technical expertise. This is at the heart of problems recently encountered by The Co-operative Group, and the issue is relatively simple. When the Rochdale Pioneers opened their store in 1844, the idea of elected representatives of members acting as a committee or board did not seem far-fetched. The business of running a small retail business did not require special training or expertise which could not be provided by individuals who were competent at managing a modest household budget. It required common sense about issues that might arise at some point, an understanding of the need for income to exceed expenditure, and an openness to discuss and find resolution to issues which might be addressed by more than one solution. Once the business needed a shop-keeper or store manager to be employed, this itself could start to provide an opportunity to introduce particular skills or knowledge (how to store food, buying skills etc.). But the elected board remained in charge and in control.

This 'traditional Rochdale model', which operates in most UK retail societies to this day, is based upon the members electing a board of directors from amongst their number. Those board members are then responsible for overseeing a chief executive whom they appoint and can remove. That chief executive is in charge of running the business, including appointing other specialist executives as the business requires – finance, human resources and so forth. But that chief executive is not a member of the board, nor are any of the other executives. The board, composed as it is of individuals elected by the members who may have no experience of running a business and are not even elected on that basis, may (and probably will not) have the skills and experience needed to run the business, so they must employ people who do have such skills. This is the role of the executives, to whom the day-to-day running of the business is entrusted.

This now raises a significant legal problem. The UK law about directors, which has developed over the last hundred years or so and has now been codified in recent legislation,[20] requires a director of a company 'to exercise reasonable care, skill and diligence' in carrying out their function, and that level of knowledge skill and care includes an objective element – namely 'the care, skill and diligence that would be exercised by a reasonably diligent person with the general knowledge, skill and experience that may reasonably be expected of a person carrying out the functions carried out by the director in relation to the company'. In other words, the law expects a person who is a director of a company to have a level of general knowledge, skill and experience appropriate to the business of the company. An individual elected to office through a democratic process may not have such knowledge, skill and experience. Whilst training and development can be helpful, at some point in terms of the scale and complexity of the business it becomes questionable whether democratically-elected individuals, even with the help of training, are appropriate to carry the directorial responsibilities for the business.

Co-operative societies operate under the statutory regime established now by the Co-operative and Community Benefit Societies Act 2014, and not under the Companies Act. This means that the Companies Act codification of directors' duties does not strictly apply to directors of a co-operative society. However, the codification of directors' duties in the Companies Act 2006 was intended to put into statutory form the existing law about directors' duties of corporations which had been developed by the courts through decided cases (the common law). So the starting common law position for analysing the law about directors of co-operative societies is unlikely to be very different. Furthermore, although a court looking at a co-operative society would recognise that it was not a company and needed to take into account the governance design based on elected representatives, it would still be likely to come to the view that there was some objective standard that must be applied to co-operative directors, simply because they are in a fiduciary role with quasi-trustee responsibilities in relation to assets which belong to the society rather than to themselves personally.

In other words, not only does any business require those in charge to have a level of competence appropriate to the business if it is to survive and succeed, so does the law. So a governance model based on entirely elected directors, overseeing an executive who most likely does have the necessary skills and expertise to hold a position of such authority but constitutionally does not sit on the board, at best sits uncomfortably with the law. Most probably the law would treat such executives as directors, notwithstanding the constitutional provisions.

During the 2013 crisis at The Co-operative Group, the Myners Review[21] focused on this issue of board competence, arguing that the elected board lacked the necessary skills to have strategic leadership, with the result that the board made decisions promoted by the chief executive which they should not have made. As a result of this analysis and heavy criticism by the Myners Review of some key strategic board decisions, very substantial changes were made to the governance structure of The Co-operative Group. These changes, which will not be explored further here, have been subject to much debate and criticism from within the movement and it seems improbable at this stage that the solution applied will find favour with any of the other large UK retail societies.

So the fundamental question for large and potentially complex mutual and co-operative organisations is this: how can they have what might be termed 'competent governance' whilst maintaining member control? The co-operative movement needs to find its own answer to that question. Meanwhile, however, an entirely different approach to governance has been emerging in the public sector. Whilst this will not find favour with some co-operators, it nevertheless provides a template for an alternative option. This alternative approach was also introduced by the creation of NHS Foundation Trusts in 2003.

Essentially, this alternative approach addresses governance of large and complex organisations in a different way.

- It recognises that (a) competence and (b) 'democratic representativeness' are both essential ingredients of the governance of a large mutual organisation.
- It splits these two required ingredients between two different parts of the organisation:
  - It seeks to construct a board designed to assure competence, by requiring that all the members of the board must have the necessary knowledge, skill and experience to do their job, and that they are all appointed in order to secure the best candidate.
  - It constructs a separate democratic body which is designed to be representative, comprising elected representatives of the various constituencies of members, with the opportunity for external bodies to be invited to send representatives as well.
- The role of the board is to run the business, but subject to certain constraints which do not apply to the directors of a company.
- The role of the democratic body is to provide a voice for the different membership constituencies and the community served by the organisation, and it has the power:
  - to influence the forward plans by working with the board in setting them; and
  - to monitor and hold the board to account in delivering the plans.

- The democratic body has the power to enforce its role because it both appoints and can remove the nonexecutive directors who are a majority of the board and include its chair.
- The board comprises a minority of executive directors, appointed by the nonexecutive directors who constitute the majority and include the chair. The nonexecutive directors' role is to be independent and objective and to provide an ongoing scrutiny role of the executives on behalf of the democratic body.

This is a radically different approach. Its success ultimately turns on the relationship between the democratic body and the board. The board needs to be open to the influence of the members' representatives, and to learn to work collaboratively within them. It requires a different style of management which is listening, willing to be influenced, and fundamentally collaborative. It requires a style of leadership which is consensus building and empowering, and where management control is held in tension with the empowerment of the constituencies of interest.

Leadership

Processes of bargaining to establish social co-operation require a particular kind of leadership work – one which aims to create and maintain the deliberative space for dialogic conversation between constituencies. Mutual organisations require an appropriate leadership model, combining leadership behaviours in mutual values and principles, and managerial competence in creating and sustaining the policies, practices and procedures relevant to enacting the mutual organisational form. This demands attention to the content, mode and basis of leadership. With respect to the content of leadership, responsible or virtuous leadership provides the behaviours and orientations that he or she who leads is expected to model. Furthermore, in a mutual organisation where organisational practices are designed to integrate multiple constituencies and conciliate diverse perspectives, leaders need to exercise wisdom and judgement,[22] in additional to possessing the relevant skills and competences.

In a fully realised mutual organisation, the mode of leadership is based upon distributed leadership[23] rather than the singular, heroic leader.[24] The exercise of voice requires leadership capabilities to be widely disseminated through the organisation with the result that leaders emerge and are appointed not just according to formal status but also according to the needs of the situation. In their study of OP-Pohjola Group, a Finnish financial group containing 198 local member co-operative banks, Saila, Iiro and Pasi identified the following characteristics of shared leadership:

- recognised in the quality of interactions;
- evaluated by how well the problem was solved together;
- enacted in how all individuals contributed to the process of leadership;
- understood as a joint effort of interdependent individuals, including high levels of communication; and
- aimed at mutual benefit and the common good.[25]

Finally, the basis of leadership is deliberated authority,[26] where co-ordinative power is legitimated through democratic representation. Consequently, where there is extensive employee, and even member, involvement in organisational leadership (EIOL), the 'division of leadership tasks between different people at several levels of the organization' becomes a high-performance work practice.[27]

Learning from new mutual organisations

There is a wide range of experiences which have emerged from new mutual organisations, including the 147 NHS Foundation Trusts that have been created so far. Conclusions must be drawn cautiously from Foundation Trusts because, although they are now member based and owned independently from the state, their independence is substantially constrained. This is because of their regulatory framework, the economic regime under which they operate and through which they are unable to set their own selling prices, and a number of other factors which are due to the fact that the Secretary of State for Health still owes statutory duties in relation to the provision of a national health service, which effectively prevents complete independence. Having said that, the learning from this new approach to governance, and the way it has been voluntarily implemented in the other examples given (RBH, Salford Community Leisure, Knowsley Youth Mutual and Care Plus Group), is introducing a credible modern approach to mutuality and opening up opportunities elsewhere in the public sector.

This is important, because although 'mutuality' is back on the table in the context of public sector reform, traditional single constituency mutuality does not provide a particularly attractive starting point; traditional co-operative governance based on fully elected boards is treated with considerable suspicion by many professionals and managers, and this suspicion has now been reinforced by the unfolding events at The Co-operative Group. So this new design of ownership and governance not only meets those criticisms head on through its competence-based board, which is democratically accountable to grassroots members, but it is actually a significant improvement on existing governance mechanisms in the public sector which also suffer from the competence problem: for example, traditional boards for housing associations on a large-scale transfer of housing stock, based on one-third tenants, one-third councillors and one-third independents.

How the ownership and governance model affects delivery

The development of a co-operative way of trading in the mid nineteenth century did much more than introduce an alternative ownership and governance model. It introduced a wholly different way of trading. Through ownership by customers and the empowerment (as we would say today) of people, particularly women, who previously had little if any voice in society, a range of other consequences followed (see also chapter 6 in this volume).

In relation to the day-to-day business itself, a highly customer-focused culture became established. It was not just that members had access to their elected representatives and members' meetings to ensure that the business evolved to meet their needs, but wider customer-focused reforms evolved over time based on the underlying commitment to meeting the needs of members: weights and measures to ensure that customers were treated fairly, and the right for women to become members, vote, and access funds through their society. Other developments took account of the needs of employees, including limitations on their working hours, effectively a minimum wage and other benefits.

These were simply manifestations of a business which had a different purpose and outlook from traditional businesses. Whereas the focus of the latter was on optimising profits and delivering economic value to their investor owners, co-operatives in reality existed for an underlying social purpose. This is illustrated by the objects of the Rochdale Equitable Pioneers, which expressly set out to provide (as well as a store for the sale of provisions) housing, employment, education, the encouragement of sobriety and the development of a new type of society. Through the provision of education, access to books and newspapers, and leisure and cultural activities, societies were the early providers of public services. We would say today that such societies were operating for a 'social purpose', rather than for the private benefit of their owners. This was both an intentional and a natural consequence of their form of ownership and governance.

The contrasting, traditional model of trading which was dominant then and remains dominant today not only focuses on the private benefit of investors as the reason for businesses' existence, but in order to optimise profitability by beating their competitors it inevitably leads them to minimise the expense of employees, to secure the lowest possible prices from suppliers whatever the impact it may have on them, and to sell products and services designed to optimise margin rather than to meet the best interests of customers (the 'negative externalities', as they are known to economists). Parliament has frequently had to intervene to protect the interests of, for example:

- employees, through legislation about a safe place of work and a fair approach to employment;
- customers, through food and hygiene standards, weights and measures, and outlawing misrepresentation; and
- the environment, to prevent businesses from saving money by dealing with waste inappropriately.

The extensive programme of privatisation of former public services, which has been ongoing since the 1980s, has resulted in this highly commercial and profit-focused business approach being introduced into a whole range of services where it runs counter to the nature of the service being delivered – such as personal care. Concepts developed to deliver efficiency in manufacturing are being applied (because they are perceived to deliver economic benefit) to health, social care, and offender management, for example; and legal mechanisms such as contractual arrangements developed, for example, for the construction industry are used (for similar reasons) to commission personal services.

Whilst in the private sector this results in narrowly focused businesses with a highly commercial relationship, who have customers or consumers, we see similar impacts in relation to those services which have remained under state or municipal ownership. In the interests of achieving efficiency, they increasingly tend towards a centralised, command-and-control approach, leaving little if any scope for local adaptation to meet differing needs; and because of the perception that the private sector knows best about economic efficiency, the public sector is under pressure to emulate its processes and practices to deliver comparable efficiency. The result is a service delivery model in many areas of public service which reverts to a binary, us and them, 'done-to' approach, and citizens who become dependent on services which they are encouraged to access as consumers. A further result is the loss, amongst citizens, of any sense of the real cost of what they are receiving (or the fact that its availability is in practice limited), or any sense of responsibility for seeking to minimise their cost to the public purse through self-limiting draw-down of services, or taking steps to minimise their need for services – for example, through adopting a healthier style of living.

It is against this background, which is inevitably leading to a constantly increasing demand for services by an ageing population that the state can no longer afford, that a fundamental change is now seen as essential from a public policy point of view. For example, a recent high-level policy statement from the NHS[28] called for

- a more engaged relationship with patients, carers and citizens;
- a radical upgrade in prevention and public health;
- ensuring that when people do need health services, they gain far greater control over their own care; and
- decisive steps to break down the barriers in how care is currently provided.

This implies a radically different approach to power sharing.

It is hardly surprising, therefore, that in the current context co-operative and mutual forms of ownership and governance appear to be highly attractive. Through multi-constituency membership, they can obviously provide the basis for that different relationship with users and citizens; through employee participation in ownership, they can secure that much-desired buy-in and support from staff who can make such a difference if and when they want to; and through bringing users and producers together within the organisation, they can start to move forward with provision on the basis of co-design, co-production, and ultimately co-ownership of the underlying problem which needs to be solved.

So co-operation and mutuality are becoming mainstream in terms of popularity: citizens, government and many employees like the social purpose; many find the idea of mutualisation more attractive than privatisation because of their experience of privatised utilities in terms of service quality and cost; for government, transferring ownership away from the state without it being seen as privatisation is clearly beneficial; and for those who are genuinely interested in moving to a radically different model of service delivery, co-operation and mutuality offer a platform from which to imagine a whole range of different and often rather more appropriate approaches.

Supporting the advance of modern co-operation and mutuality

But delivering this, and enabling mutuality to have the transformative effect that is needed, is in practice much more difficult. The first reason is that the current agenda is mainly driven by a political timetable based around electoral cycles at national and local level. The development of sustainable mutual service providers is not amenable to imposed timescales – particularly very short timescales measured in months or even weeks. The second reason is that mutuality cannot be imposed. Whilst those in senior positions need to take the lead, mutuals need to emerge from the bottom up: they cannot be 'created' from above. Unless individuals at the grass roots embrace the idea, engage with it, take ownership and take it forwards, then what will emerge will probably not be much different from what was there before. The third reason is the current approach being followed to 'mutualise public services' (the very idea of referring to it as 'mutualising' being unhelpful for the reason just given), which sees the process as a transactional one, based on a transfer of ownership from the state, and the creation of a new corporate entity to assume responsibility for delivery. There does need to be a transfer, as well as the establishment of a new organisation, but these are not what create the change. Change occurs when people – those who use services and those who provide them – start to behave differently and adopt a mutual approach. Cultural change requires vision, the development of values that people will sign up to, and the willingness to allow those values to change their behaviour. A new ownership and governance structure can help to support and encourage that, and make it longer lasting, but on their own they will not deliver it.

So the starting point is not a transaction involving the transfer of business and assets. The starting point is the development of a new vision for a service, based upon a contemporary approach to the relationships and power sharing in the context of that service, which can enable a different delivery approach to emerge. A mutual or co-operative approach to health and care, or rehabilitation of offenders, or education are achievable, but they require those currently providing and receiving such services to envision the new possibilities first. So if the desire to move towards a co-operative or mutual approach in public services is to be fulfilled in the coming years, the vision needs to come first. The structural solutions, including some of those articulated here, should follow.

Notes

1 See for example the Barwell Boot and Shoe Manufacturing Society, in National Co-operative Archive, 'Acting on principle: how co-operatives became legal', www.archive.coop/wp-content/uploads/2014/10/acting-on-principle-NOV1402.pdf (accessed 9 February 2016).

2 Ibid.

3 B. Potter, *The Co-operative Movement in Great Britain* (London: Swan Sonnenschein, 1891).
4 *Health and Social Care (Community Health and Standards) Act 2003*, www.legislation.gov.uk/ukpga/2003/43/contents (accessed 9 February 2016).
5 S. R. Clegg, D. Courpasson and N. Phillips, *Power and Organizations* (London: Sage, 2006), p. 384.
6 Ibid., p. 137.
7 N. Sherman, 'The virtues of common pursuit', *Philosophical and Phenomenological Research* 53:2 (1993), 277–99, p. 278.
8 Ibid.
9 M. Parker Follett, *The New State: Group Organization the Solution of Popular Government* (London: Longman's, 1918).
10 R. Yeoman, 'From traditional to innovative multi-stakeholder mutuals: the case of Rochdale Boroughwide Housing', in J. Blasi, C. Borzaga and J. Michie, eds, *The Oxford Handbook for Co-operative and Mutual Business* (Oxford: Oxford University Press (forthcoming 2016)).
11 A. Hirschman, *Exit, Voice and Loyalty* (Cambridge, MA: Harvard University Press, 1970), p. 30.
12 J. Lavelle, P. Gunnigle and A. McDonnell, 'Patterning employee voice in multinational companies', *Human Relations* 63:3 (2010), 395–418, p. 396.
13 F. Heller, 'Participation and power: a critical assessment', *Applied Psychology: An International Review*, 52:1 (2003), 144–63.
14 A. Wilkinson and C. Fay, 'New times for employee voice?', *Human Resource Management* 50:1, 65–74, p. 72.
15 A. Pyman, B. Cooper, J. Teicher and P. Holland, 'A comparison of the effectiveness of employee voice arrangements in Australia', *Industrial Relations Journal* 37:5 (2006), 543–59.
16 J. Wegge, H. J. Jeppesen and W. G. Weber, 'Promoting work motivation in organisations: should employee involvement in organisational leadership become a new tool in the organisational psychologist's kit?', *Journal of Personnel Psychology* 9:4 (2010), 154–71, p. 162.
17 A. P. Verdofer, W. G. Weber, C. Unterrainer and S. Seyr, 'The relationship between organizational democracy and socio-moral climate: exploring effects of the ethical context in organizations', *Economic and Industrial Democracy* 34:3 (2013), 423–49.
18 C. McMahon, *Authority and Democracy: A General Theory of Government and Management* (Princeton: Princeton University Press, 1994).
19 See R. Yeoman, *Meaningful Work and Workplace Democracy: A Philosophy of Work and a Politics of Meaningfulness* (Houndmills: Palgrave Macmillan, 2014).
20 *Companies Act 2006*, section 170 and following, www.legislation.gov.uk/ukpga/2006/46/contents (accessed 9 February 2016).
21 P. Myners, 'The Co-operative Group Report of the Independent Governance Review' (2014), www.co-operative.coop/corporate/lord-myners-review (accessed 22 February 2016).

22 S. S. Taylor, D. Ladkin and M. Statler, 'Caring orientations: the normative foundations of the craft of management', *Journal of Business Ethics* 120:3 (2014), n.p.
23 D. Fitzsimons, K. Turnbull James and D. Denyer, 'Alternative approaches for studying shared and distributed leadership', *International Journal of Management Reviews* 13:3 (2011), 313–28.
24 C. L. Pearce and J. A. Conger, 'A landscape of opportunities: future research in shared leadership', in Pearce and Conger, eds, *Shared Leadership* (Thousand Oaks: Sage, 2003), pp. 285–303.
25 R. Saila, J. Iiro and T. Pasi, 'Diversification through acquisition: co-operative banks as dynamic players in competitive markets', *International Journal of Cooperative Studies* 1:2 (2012), 37–46.
26 M. Alvesson and A. Spicer, 'A stupidity-based theory of organizations', *Journal of Management Studies* 49:7 (2013), 1194–220.
27 Wegge et al., 'Promoting work motivation', p. 154.
28 National Health Service, 'Five year forward view' (October 2014), www.england.nhs.uk/wp-content/uploads/2014/10/5yfv-web.pdf (accessed 9 February 2016).

10

Co-operatives in health care: global prospects for the development of co-operatives as instruments of consumer-centred health care

Vern Hughes

There is growing international interest in consumer co-operatives in health care, driven by recognition of continuing state and market failure in the provision of health services: both the public sector and the private sector have been unable to contain health costs and integrate care to meet the personalised needs of consumers.[1] Health reform is arguably the most difficult area of social innovation and policy reform for communities and governments around the world. Highly fragmented service systems built around complex disciplinary boundaries, strong professional guilds, residual cottage-industry modes of service delivery alongside large-scale state-run systems, and dual public and private financing systems make the task for reformers and innovators daunting to say the least. Medical provider interests are amongst the most powerful of industry interests. Health consumers are amongst the weakest and least organised categories of consumers. In most societies, health-provider interests have managed to thwart efforts to restrict their market power and promote greater competition. Perhaps more than any other, health is an industry built upon provider capture, entrenched silos, and a dealignment of supply and demand.

Yet in every society, the imperative for major structural reform in health care is undeniable. As societies develop, the costs of health care increase and the gap widens between consumer expectations of quality care and the capacity of systems to deliver it. In Western societies, health costs are the fastest-growing component of national budgets. In developing countries, expectations of improvements in health systems remain thwarted by inadequate system capacity and dependence on external silo-specific aid. The health budgets of all governments are constantly strained and cannot stretch to accommodate uncapped growth in consumer demand.

The international co-operative movement has acknowledged the potential for co-operation in health care in the twenty-first century, but has been daunted by the complexity and scale of health systems and the highly politicised nature of public debate about health-care provision.[2] In societies with well-developed state-run health systems, co-operative movements which are actively seeking entry into industries such as energy, information technology, and new media have baulked at entry into health care on the grounds that public sector provision is well established. In countries where poor public policy has created artificial scarcities of health professionals, co-operators have sometimes worried about their capacity to recruit professionals to non-traditional settings. In most countries, public policy tends to privilege health professionals over consumers in the design of systems, and co-operators have hesitated over their ability to influence policymakers. A curious exception prevails in Western aid to health projects in developing countries, where governments and non-governmental organisations (NGOs) both prefer community-based models of health-care delivery in the developing world, but not in their own countries!

This chapter makes a case for consumer co-operation in health care as the most effective instrument available to us for integrating care and containing costs. Neither public sector nor private sector provision has been able to serve as an effective instrument for the development of consumer-centred health care. A stated goal of 'consumer-centred' or 'consumer-directed' health care is now favoured by policymakers in most western societies.[3] It reflects the consumer-centric culture of the twenty-first century. While definitions of 'consumer-centred' vary – from a focus on the exercise of consumer 'choice' and 'preference' to a focus on consumer-centred information systems and financing – the framework is here to stay. The struggle for policymakers has been how to apply this framework to systems that remain provider-centric in structure. This tension between consumer-centred goals for health care, and provider-centric delivery systems creates space for consumer co-operation to be explored. The co-operative model of enterprise (member ownership with democratic governance) has a long history, and member-owned frameworks for the provision of health care have an even longer lineage. It is my contention that this model is not only well suited to twenty-first-century consumer-centred health care, it is the only framework that can enable a transition in health care from provider-centred systems to the new century's consumer-centric paradigm.

Consumer intermediaries

The beginning point in appreciating the necessity for consumer co-operation in health care lies in understanding what economists call 'information asymmetries' between doctor and patient. Consumers on their own cannot possibly acquire sufficient knowledge about health-care interventions and strategies – their effectiveness, risks and costs – without the assistance of an intermediary who can acquire this knowledge on their behalf. Without a consumer intermediary, the information asymmetry between doctor and patient is so great that it renders a functioning market in health care impossible. The intervention of consumer intermediaries, however, makes a functioning market viable.

The framework put forward by A. C. Enthoven of 'managed competition' in health care based on consumer intermediaries is useful for examining the potential of consumer co-operation.[4] Its features are the following:

- Information asymmetries between doctor and patient require the intervention of intermediaries or agents, which make available comparative price and service-quality data to patients, and enable patients as consumers to purchase (individually or collectively) their preferred services.
- The purchases facilitated by consumer intermediaries must be fully costed. Costs for episodes of treatment or care must be specified and transparent so that intermediaries may substitute lower-cost for higher-cost purchases.
- To offer integrated and cost-effective care, consumer intermediaries must be able to package a mix of services and insurance products to meet a variety of consumer preferences.
- Consumer intermediaries must be able to compete with each other for subscribers or enrolees (members) on the basis of package price and service quality.
- Consumer intermediaries require a framework of internal and external regulation to limit the impact of adverse selection and moral hazard.

These elements constitute the core functions of consumer co-operatives in health care. To operate effectively, consumer intermediaries of this kind require the operation of two co-incidental markets – one to create competition amongst consumer intermediaries for the allegiance of consumers, and the other to create competition amongst providers in supplying services to intermediaries. Agents or brokers like this operate in almost all other industries – agriculture, finance, real estate, insurance, disability, the law – and co-operatives have emerged to undertake these agency and brokerage functions in most societies. Historically, they emerged in health care, too, from the early 1800s onwards, but took a battering from both providers and states during the twentieth century.

In the English-speaking world, consumer intermediaries in health care were remarkably well developed in the nineteenth century. They spread throughout the English-speaking settler societies, usually under the name of 'friendly societies' or 'mutual provident societies'. In Australia, for example, friendly societies were consumer-governed associations which contracted with medical providers for capitation-based payments for medical services (capitation means a per-person payment or subscription rather than a fee for service). For a (usually) quarterly subscription, doctors were contracted by lodges (local branches) of the friendly society to provide general practitioner services to a pool of members. Contracted doctors were obliged to attend to the health needs of this pool of members, and had a strong incentive to keep them healthy. Networks of bush and community hospitals were established and financed on a similar subscription basis, with visiting doctors engaged on a mix of capitation-based contracts and fee for service. Infrastructure financing for clinics and community hospitals was built into the subscription-financing model. Subscription systems of financing also formed the basis of pharmacy-service provision through friendly society dispensaries. Between 1860 and 1900, most pharmacists and a large proportion of doctors in Australia were employed by their patients through these forms of what health economists now call 'prepaid' health care. Fee for service was not the principal form of health-care financing.

These consumer-based innovations in health-care financing and provision are largely unknown to today's health policymakers. Between the beginning and middle years of the twentieth century, medical and pharmacy professional guilds fought a long battle to free themselves from the contractual and regulatory relationships initiated by these consumer societies. By the late 1940s this battle had been largely won by the professional guilds in the English-speaking world, when state-run systems of insurance effectively removed consumer intermediaries from the health-care landscape. The British and Australian Labour governments of the 1940s wanted the function and power of consumer intermediaries removed, because of a political conviction that state-run systems of insurance were preferable to those that were voluntary, community based and independent of government. To install such systems, it was necessary to dissolve consumer-based subscription systems.

This dissolution simultaneously increased the power of the health professions and weakened the power of health consumers.

Consumer governance

It is worth highlighting three features of the consumer governance that emerged in these settings that are of critical importance for the future of co-operation in health care: consumer ownership, self-help and self-regulation. The pool of members created by consumer intermediaries in the nineteenth century provided an integrative structure through which disparate components of health care (medical practitioner services, pharmacy services, nursing care and community hospitals) could be pulled together to serve a fixed cohort of consumers. It was the consumer intermediaries – the societies – that owned the provision of services, financed it, constructed the infrastructure for it and regulated it. Disciplinary boundaries between professions and functions existed but did not define the structure of health-care provision or its ownership.

From the vantage point of the early twenty-first century, it is difficult to comprehend the scope and scale of consumer sovereignty in health care that these structures represented. The contemporary fragmentation in health delivery by professional discipline now runs very deep, and is buttressed by practitioner-controlled accreditation and regulatory regimes (oriented to restricting supply), often with legislative protection for the market sovereignty of practitioner and provider. For most of the twentieth century Australian legislation, for instance, permitted only peer-accredited practitioners to own private medical and pharmacy practices, and prohibited their advertising on price.[5] A former Secretary of the Department of Health in the Australian State of Victoria has described this terrain as the 'East Berlin circa 1989 model of health care in which providers intimidate patients, terrorise governments and steal all the money'.[6] If this Berlin Wall is to be torn down, it is difficult to imagine any force other than consumer co-operation having either the will or structural capacity to do it. In this sense, consumer governance generated by a fixed membership pool of consumers is an essential structural requirement for transitioning away from the systemic fragmentation wrought by provider and practitioner sovereignty towards consumer sovereignty in health care.

Secondly, consumer governance is also the only governance structure in health-care provision that is fully compatible with an 'active agency' model of health maintenance and self-care. This model, whereby individuals as consumers are engaged as active agents in modifying their behaviour to manage their own health risks, is counterposed to the 'casuality' model of health care, in which illness is viewed essentially as an act of God.[7] Active agency implies the facilitation of self-direction in health maintenance and illness prevention, not passivity. It implies a culture of self-help. Private sector providers and practitioners in fee for service have no incentive to encourage self-help, while those in private insurance settings have the incentive but not the capacity to encourage it. Self-help in health care requires social reinforcement to be effective; solitary efforts to eat well and minimise health risks are difficult to sustain without peer support. An association of health consumers is a self-help association, conferring the status of *member*, not *client*.

Social connectivity is essential for good health maintenance. Social isolation compounds health risks. The early friendly societies conducted their health-care provision in a context of sociality, combining social functions, adult education, sport and recreation, with contributory financing towards the collective well-being. Lodges provided a small enough scale for these activities to enable effective sociality and not impersonal service provision. All contemporary literature on active health maintenance contains an emphasis on sociality that the early friendly societies embodied instinctively in their social and co-operative practice. If 'takeaway' medicine has limited impact in the absence of social bonds, the question for health reformers is how these social bonds might now be reconstituted in health-care settings for the chronically ill, the aged, the mentally ill, the disabled and the socially isolated.

Thirdly, if associations of consumers are self-help organisations, they must also be self-regulating within a context of appropriate but minimal external regulation. Consumer preferences in health care are increasingly diverse, and associations of consumers will adopt various philosophies of care. Some of the early friendly societies were based on religious cultures, some on secular societies of brotherhood, some on the labour movement and some on ethnicity. The selected bond of friendship need not concern us. What is important is the freedom of consumer intermediaries to determine their own values and philosophy of health care. Many consumer intermediaries today will be based on communities of interest such as sporting and outdoor physicality, or New Age naturalism, or indigenous people's well-being, and will seek to integrate the provision of health care with the strengthening of these communities. They will harness the community resources, infrastructure and volunteer networks of their communities for this purpose. As consumer-governed, self-regulating entities, associations of consumers will wish to make their own judgements about which practices enhance good health, and which practices are injurious to good health. They would have low tolerance levels for lifestyle preferences that are injurious to good health, and would self-regulate accordingly. They would also have low tolerance levels for incompetent or lazy practitioners or poorly performing programmes. The ability to self-regulate on these matters, in a context of appropriate external regulation, is critical for consumer co-operation in health care.

Two case studies

Seattle's Group Health Cooperative

Group Health Cooperative in Seattle is a consumer-governed health-maintenance organisation formed in 1947.[8] It began as a community coalition dedicated to making quality health care available and affordable. Its initial pool of medical staff was drawn from a group practice whose members were blacklisted by the American Medical Association for contracting medical services to industrial plants during the Second World War. Today Group Health operates twenty-five primary care centres, two hospitals, an inpatient centre, a skilled nursing facility, and five speciality medical centres within a culture of consumer governance. It contracts with forty other health institutions for selected speciality services.

Group Health has 600,000 members and 7,000 staff (full-time employment), including 1,000 physicians and other medical staff and 1,500 staff nurses. It contracts with a further 2,000 non-staff medical practitioners. Medical staff form a self-managing group which contracts directly with the co-operative for remuneration for services. The contract determines the size of the medical salary pool, which is calculated as a fixed payment per member. The medical group works with its own capitated budget (also a fixed payment per member). The co-operative is governed by an elected eleven-member board of trustees. All are consumers and all are volunteers. There are twenty-three local advisory councils that advise the co-operative on various matters: a majority of council members are elected consumers.[9]

As a health-maintenance organisation, Group Health describes itself as a provider of 'comprehensive, co-ordinated medical care for a fixed, pre-paid fee with minimal co-payments'. As a managed-care organisation, it describes its purpose as 'the full integration of healthcare delivery and healthcare financing' with five characteristics: 'comprehensive coverage, co-ordinated services, strict performance standards, consumer involvement, and pre-determined payment'.[10]

Group Health's consumer governance is the principal generator of its success. Its consumer ownership model provides a winning point of market differentiation from investor-owned managed-care businesses in the cut-throat US health-care market. Its 'active agency' model of care is integrated with co-operative 'membership'. Membership entails access to an online portal which provides each member's health record, health maintenance plan, dietary and exercise schedule, medication record and health goals. The co-operative's capacity to self-regulate allows it to implement behaviour-modification plans with consumers, and build incentives and penalties into these plans with consumer consent.

A compatible public policy and regulatory environment has enabled Group Health Cooperative to develop since 1947. In other countries, less-compatible policy and regulatory environments can undermine consumer co-operation.

Yallourn Hospital and Medical Society

The Yallourn Hospital and Medical Society was formed in the coal-mining communities of the Latrobe Valley east of Melbourne, Australia, in 1924.[11] It was established as a friendly society to provide medical and hospital services to these communities on a subscription basis, combining an insurance function with provision of medical clinics, pharmacies and hospital services. At the end of the twentieth century, the Society provided health-insurance products, ran two medical clinics and seven pharmacies, and owned a half share in a private hospital situated among working-class communities with a population of 150,000.

The Society was based on consumer governance. Consumer ownership allowed it to develop several different components of health care under the sovereignty of members. Social connectivity was encouraged, with active roles for member volunteers in supporting ill and infirm members, assisting in transport for the immobile, and assisting in home-care supports. The Society's desire to self-regulate in developing consumer well-being was constrained, however, by inappropriate external regulators.

For eighty years, the Society combined a general membership subscription covering medical and pharmacy services, and an insurance membership subscription covering hospital services. The two functions could never be fully integrated because of external regulatory impediments. The Australian health insurance regulator from the 1940s insisted upon a splitting of health insurance and health-care provision, despite the Society's desire for integration. After a half-century of dispute and struggle, the regulator intervened in 2007 to close the Society, transferring the insurance business to a for-profit insurer, and the medical clinics and pharmacies to for-profit, practitioner-owned chains. Eighty years of consumer-governed self-help thus ended abruptly and ignominiously.

Transitional strategy

Despite their divergent fates, Group Health and Yallourn provide a clear enough snapshot, for our purposes, of the structure of consumer intermediaries and their potential shape in health-care provision. Consumer intermediaries of this kind can be initiated on a large scale in the twenty-first century, using the organising and marketing platforms of the digital era. The following is a suggested five-point transitional strategy involving immediate member aggregation and enterprise activity on the part of a wide variety of existing associations in both developed and developing countries:

1. Organisations which have enrolled memberships (voluntary associations, clubs, business associations, faith groups) can act on behalf of their members in exploring the provision of health care. An initial educative focus would examine the potential of enhanced market power for consumers of health care through the intervention of consumer intermediaries.

   There need be no prescribed structural form for consumer intermediaries in these early stages: the function may be performed by any entity with a capacity to aggregate member enrolments, manage their financial entitlements and enter contractual arrangements on their behalf, and manage member relationships to the mutual satisfaction of the intermediary and member. Through a process of alliance forming, new entities comprising sizeable aggregates of health consumers could be assembled with significant market purchasing power.
2. Intermediaries would aim to make available to their members comparative price and service quality data on available services and insurance options. The intermediaries would package these arrangements in various formats.
3. Intermediaries would acquire suitable information and health record systems (templates and system options are available from existing co-operatives in health care), which intermediaries would make available to their consumers for use in consolidating information from diverse practitioner and service-delivery types in one platform. Intermediaries would favour practitioners and providers who voluntarily agree to enter records of consultations, treatments and appointment schedules in their member health record. The record would not be a substitute for practitioner records: it would be a consumer-held record issued by the intermediary and would serve as a *de facto* membership card of the embryonic co-operative. Use of the record by provider and practitioner

organisations would subsequently form the basis for preferred provider arrangements.

4. With an information system transferable across service-delivery types, intermediaries can then proceed to develop new service-delivery systems. Even within existing systems of payment for health services, intermediaries could introduce new models of primary care. These could take the form of contracts with, or direct employment of, primary-care teams comprising general practitioners as well as nursing, allied-health and domiciliary-care providers. As an intermediary acquires the capacity to assemble episodes of care in integrated formats, and price these accordingly, it can then proceed to develop shared arrangements between its primary-care teams and other providers, including hospitals, in relation to components of care such as pre-admission and post-discharge care.
5. Intermediaries which develop some degree of integration of information and service delivery systems will also introduce billing and payment systems for episodes of treatment or care which are inclusive of various practitioner and service types. These systems may entail a single billing and transaction payment for members, with the co-operative allocating payments to providers for the component parts of an episode of care.

These five functions can be developed incrementally by intermediaries based on existing membership organisations. They do not require all components to be assembled at once. This incremental strategy allows consumer co-operatives in health care to be assembled over time, using online platforms and communication tools that were unavailable to the founders of Group Health or Yallourn, which can be built to accommodate a growing number of functions and increasing levels of complexity.

Four entry points

Within this five-point development strategy, emerging co-operatives in health care will nevertheless tend to adopt one of the following four entry points into health-care markets:

- locality-based primary care;
- conversions of public sector services;
- consumer health-insurance plans; or
- co-operative managed care.

Locality-based primary care

Locality-based initiatives in primary care established with a co-operative governance structure are well developed in Canada,[12] Spain, Central America and India. Their potential for development as consumer intermediaries in the purchase and co-ordination of additional health services is high. Most of the Canadian and Indian primary-care co-operatives are publicly funded from primary health-care budgets.

South Kingsville Health Services Co-operative in the disadvantaged western suburbs of Melbourne, Australia, is a self-funding variation on this pattern. Formed in 1980, South Kingsville is a co-operative of 10,000 members who elect a governing board which engages twenty general practitioners, several dentists, and a team of allied-health practitioners and educators.[13] It operates two clinics in low-income suburbs, and since its formation has received no grant funding from any tier of government. It is a self-sustaining not-for-profit business through its fees for services. From its establishment, it has sought to integrate health care with social supports for the sick and elderly, and has extensive teams of volunteer home visitors working in partnership with its primary-care practitioners. It bases its structure and operations on the truism that socially connected people live healthier lives. For many years, it has sought unsuccessfully to entice health policymakers to support it to trial capitation-based payment systems rather than fee-for-service arrangements, so that it might more adequately fulfil its mission of keeping its pool of consumer members healthy and out of surgeries and hospitals. It has, however, yet to persuade policymakers to commit to this course.

Because it is a product of grassroots community innovation and is self-funding, South Kingsville occupies an unusual space. Because it is a self-funding business, it is not regarded as a public sector community health centre. Because it is owned by its consumers, it is not part of any health provider association. And because it actually contracts with practitioners, pathology companies and general-practice training authorities, it is not regarded by the so called 'consumer-health' networks as a lobbyist for the consumer viewpoint. In the nineteenth century, South Kingsville would have been regarded as unremarkable. In a century dominated by politicians and provider guilds, it has been difficult to pigeonhole. It does, however, serve to illustrate one possible model of intermediary between doctor and patient of the many that might be devised.

Conversion of public sector services

A second possible point of entry for co-operatives lies in the conversion of public sector services. In several countries, an agenda of 'mutualisation' of public services is being developed, with the aim of developing a greater responsiveness on the part of services to local needs. This agenda is well developed in the UK, where the process in health care is best exemplified by Your Healthcare Community Interest Company in Kingston upon Thames.

Your Healthcare began trading as a social enterprise in 2010 after separating from the Kingston National Health Service (NHS). It remains funded by the NHS, with 607 staff providing twenty-three distinct services including school health and health visiting, rehabilitation, community and specialist nursing, allied-health therapies, and learning-disability services to a registered GP population of 187,000.[14] Since separating from NHS, Your Healthcare has established a membership-based governance structure, with membership open to staff, service users, carers and registered volunteers (community members), and those employed on a permanent or fixed-term basis (staff members). Members appoint a Council of Governors and Board of Directors. The Council of Governors comprises nine community governors elected by community members, four staff governors elected by the staff members, and up to four appointed governors. The Council of Governors, amongst other things, appoints and removes the chair and other nonexecutive members of a Board of Directors, and works with the Board in preparing and approving the company's mission, strategy and forward plans. The Board of Directors manages the affairs of the company. Variations on this theme have been developed in several 'mutualised' segments of the British NHS.[15]

Consumer health-insurance plans

A third possible point of entry for emerging co-operatives is in the construction of consumer health-insurance plans without direct health-care provision. This course will typically follow a process of alliance-forming between several membership-based entities as outlined previously, in countries with well-established health insurance systems. In the USA the process developed in North Dakota in recent years in constructing a health-insurance plan for a statewide community on an opt-in co-operative basis is a good example. An outline of the process is available through the office of Democratic Senator Kent Conrad (North Dakota).[16]

Co-operative managed care

The co-operative managed care option is available for members of established health-insurance plans who wish to add health-service provision to an existing health-insurance function. The success of Group Health Cooperative is increasingly serving as a beacon that draws global interest in this option.

Conclusion

Consumer co-operatives in health care have evolved around the world without a common template, and without co-ordinated development. If the co-operative movement is to realise the potential for co-operative development in health care, a guided and intentional process of development will be needed, flexible enough to allow consumers to improvise in response to their unique circumstances, but supported enough with external assistance to allow the expertise developed by other consumer co-operatives to be shared.[17]

To this end, an International Working Group on Consumer Co-operatives and Social Enterprise in Health Care has been established to co-ordinate this work. Its convenor is Vern Hughes. It welcomes enquiries from existing and prospective consumer co-operatives and social enterprises around the world.

Notes

1 International Health Co-operatives Organisation (IHCO), *Better Health and Social Care* (Geneva: IHCO, 2014).

2 See, for instance, United Nations (UN) Department for Policy Coordination and Sustainable Development/International Co-operative Alliance (ICA), *Co-operative Enterprise in the Health and Social Care Sectors: A Global Review and Proposals for Policy Coordination* (Geneva and New York: UN, 1995).

3 National Council on Disability (NCO), *Consumer-Directed Health Care: How Well Does It Work?* (Washington, DC: NCO, 2004).

4 A. Enthoven, 'Consumer-choice health plan', *New England Journal of Medicine* 28 (1978), 650–8, 709–20; Enthoven, 'The effects of managed competition', in R. Helms, ed., *Health Policy Reform: Competition and Controls* (Washington, DC: American Enterprise Institute, 1993), pp. 218–27.

5 For more on Australian health care, see R. Scotton, *National Health Insurance in Australia: New Concepts and New Applications*, Working Paper No. 11 (West Heidelberg: Centre for Health Program Evaluation, 1991) and R. Scotton, 'Managed competition: issues for Australia', *Australian Health Review* 18 (1995), 82–104.

6 J. Paterson, *National Healthcare Reform: The Last Picture Show* (Melbourne: Department of Human Services, Government of Victoria, 1996).
7 J. Goldsmith, M. Goran and J. Nackel, 'Managed care comes of age', *Healthcare Forum Journal* (September/October 1995), 14–24.
8 A. Davis and L. Andrews, 'Group Health Cooperative: how the system works', *Journal of Health Care Benefits* 2:1 (1992), 59–64.
9 Group Health, *Group Health News* (21 May 1993).
10 Ibid., pp. 3–4.
11 V. Hughes, *Co-operative Health*, Paper No. 3, Co-operative Opportunities Project (Melbourne: Co-operative Federation of Victoria, 1996).
12 See Canadian Co-operative Association (CCA), *Health Care Co-operatives* (Toronto: CCA, 1995) and CCA, *Facing the Future: A Symposium on Co-operative Alternatives for Public Sector Restructuring* (Toronto: CCA, 1996).
13 Hughes, *Co-operative Health*.
14 C. Mills and C. Brophy, *Community Health Services: Made Mutual* (London: Mutuo, 2011), pp. 30–2.
15 Ibid.
16 Senator D. Conrad, *Consumer Health Plan* (Washington DC: United States Senate, 2012).
17 See M. Ohya, 'The role of medical-health co-operatives in Japan', pp. 95–100, and J. Olsson, 'Co-operatives in health care and social services: a new task for the ICA', pp. 69–76, both in *The World of Co-operative Enterprise* (Oxford: Plunkett Foundation, 1996).

11

The re-emergence of the co-operative model for architects

Stephen McCusker

Introduction

The roots of some existing architectural co-operatives can be traced back to the 1960s. Many have come and gone but in recent years there has been a marked interest and enquiries from architectural practitioners about the application of the co-operative model.[1] The use of architectural practices serves as a case study of a particular profession both within the much larger construction industry, and the co-operative movement generally, during an uncertain economic climate. This chapter is not intended to be a statistical analysis of architectural co-operatives, but more an acknowledgement of overlapping trends within both the co-operative movement and the architectural profession that, when combined, appear to encourage the co-operative model within the profession. The ensuing discussion explores both the economic and professional contexts before considering timing and other factors that may influence this, drawing from past and present architectural co-operators alongside the personal reflections of the author, a practising architect and co-operator. Figures and statements that are not attributed to a specific publication were sourced by the author directly at the time of investigation.[2] Co-operatives of professionals working in architectural design are not new. One of the most famous was the CAIRE co-operative set up in northern Italy in the decade after the Second World War, a co-operative of architects and town planners which made a major impact in the postwar reconstruction of several major Italian cities.[3] This chapter demonstrates that this tradition is not only alive and well, but appears to be having something of a renaissance and has a promising future.

Economic context

Building and development are inextricably linked to the current global financial situation. In 2009, following a large number of redundancies at his practice, Richard Rogers, a renowned architect recognised by the general public, described the economic downturn as the most ruthless and wide ranging he can remember – particularly in the architectural sector.[4] With a 40 per cent reduction in demand for architects' services in the UK between 2008 and 2009 and the significant rise in the number of architects claiming Jobseeker's Allowance (JSA), reports claimed that architects were 'joining the ranks of benefit claimants at a faster rate than any other profession'.[5] In March 2009 Sunand Prasad, president of the Royal Institute of British Architects (RIBA), estimated that 30 per cent of architects were unemployed or underemployed.[6] Although the number of architects underemployed is difficult to ascertain – we will return to this – official figures suggest that the number of unemployed architects claiming benefits peaked in August 2009 at approximately 7 per cent of the profession.[7] While similar to unemployment rates generally for a time, the official unemployment figures for architects decreased after this point, stabilising at approximately 3.5 per cent of the profession in 2011.[8] In a review of survey data in the *RIBA Journal* in 2012, Vince Nacey, director of the Fees Bureau, commented that the growth of small architecture practices, such as sole traders, being set up by previously unemployed architects might partly explain falling unemployment figures. However, Nacey cautioned that since such firms were young they may not yet be well enough established to find sufficient work and, consequently, incomes may be low.[9] Thus it does not necessarily follow that those architects who have stopped claiming benefits are now gainfully or re-employed. In addition, the Office for National Statistics' reports make it clear that the claimant count measures the number of people claiming JSA, and this differs from unemployment figures as some unemployed persons are not eligible.

While based on only a sample of UK architects, a RIBA survey in July 2011 recorded that as many as 27 per cent of architects who had responded reported that they had personally been underemployed.[10] This is a trend that continues within the profession and has recently been acknowledged in the general economy by the Office for National Statistics when they highlighted the number of underemployed workers had risen by 980,000 since the start of the economic downturn in 2008 to stand at 3.05 million in 2012.[11] It asserted that some of these are self-employed workers who may have low hours of work as a result of low demand for their services or may be settling for a part-time role when they would prefer a full-time one. This perhaps reflects those described by Nacey who declared a fall in full-time activity and a record rise in underemployment.[12] Of responding architects working in two-person firms, 48 per cent reported being underemployed, closely followed by sole principals at 29 per cent and principals in partnership at 22 per cent.[13] These percentages seem comparatively high next to the underemployment rate amongst salaried architects in private practice and public sector positions, which came in at 10 per cent and 5 per cent respectively. It has been suggested in the past that co-operative communities are the resort of the unemployed,[14] and certainly this seems to be a contributing factor to the recent establishment of some architectural co-operatives. A fall in demand for architectural services and the flexibility offered by some co-operative structures may also be contributing to the rise in numbers of architects choosing to investigate or set up practice in this way. It is difficult to ascertain precise numbers as enquiries with Co-operatives UK, and respective approaches, do not always result in a registered co-operative, but what has been highlighted is a renewed interest in the model for architectural professionals. Before we come to that, let us consider the profession of architecture and the relevance of the co-operative model.

Professional context

In accordance with the Architects Act 1997, and subsequent amendments, only those individuals entitled or appropriately registered with the Architects Registration Board may refer to themselves using the title 'architect'. Within the UK, there were approximately 30,000 registered architects in 2000–01.[15] When the recession was officially reported in 2009, membership had risen to approximately 33,000 and at time of writing (in 2012) the figure is approximately 34,000. The number of new admissions peaked in 2008 at the height of the building boom and only regained a similar level in 2012.[16] While this chapter originally intended to consider architects as a specific profession, it became apparent that it would be an unfair reflection if restricted solely to registered architects. In the first instance, the term 'architect' and associated reports may not always refer to the same subset of the industry. For example, some data refers to the UK government's skilled labour definition 2413 which may include registered and partly qualified architects alongside architectural consultants and landscape architects.[17] Similarly, although RIBA surveys, such as the annual RIBA/The Fees Bureau Architects Employment & Earnings Survey cited in note 10 are useful sources and help to identify trends, they are not necessarily reflective of the UK profession as a whole.

Architects are not required to become RIBA chartered members, though many do, and such surveys are often conducted amongst RIBA members exclusively. For the purposes of this discussion we are therefore referring to the profession of architecture rather than registered architects, but, as will become apparent, this also extends to associated professionals within the fields of landscape architecture and engineering.

Consequently, it is difficult to distil exactly what defines an 'architectural co-operative' and there is no single register of practices that identify them as such. In their 2011 book, Awan, Schneider and Till provide a useful introduction to these, perhaps providing what most closely resembles a definitive list of architectural co-operatives.[18] Their list refers to established architectural practices such as Edward Cullinan Architects, City Design Co-operative, Collective Architecture, Matrix Feminist Design Co-operative and Urban Environment Design (URBED) as well as more theoretical organisations such as GLAS (Glasgow Letters on Architecture & Space). However, the list of architectural co-operatives seems to be ever changing and the published list does not refer to other co-operatives such as the Cave Co-operative, Leeds Environmental Design Associates (LEDA) and Loop Systems.

Referring to Edward Cullinan Architects (recently renamed Cullinan Studio), Awan, Schneider and Till suggest their structure has become the accepted model for operating as a co-operative within the architectural profession. Cullinan Studio is well regarded within the profession, with roots dating back to the 1960s and a plethora of awards and peer acknowledgement since (including the award of the RIBA's Gold Medal to Edward Cullinan in 2008). Within this field Cullinan's have a long-established reputation for practising co-operatively. Although they described themselves as a co-operative prior to 1989, they were unable to establish themselves legally as such (due to professional restrictions which are discussed later) and developed their own ratio system of profit share.[19] Edward Cullinan owned the assets until he settled these with an employee benefit trust in 1990, and in 2010 they joined the Employee Ownership Association, affirming their core values about how the business is run.

This is different to the arrangement at Loop Systems, a limited company established in 2002 that became a formal workers' co-operative in 2009. It has a collective management structure where full-time employees are both directors and co-operative members, each receiving the same rate of pay. This is similar to the structure at the Cave co-operative. Both companies have contracted other staff and/or assistants who are not members of the co-operative. LEDA uses a co-ownership structure with salaries based on market rates and a directorship that does not match membership, whereas Glasgow's Collective Architecture is, as the name suggests, a collective, not a co-operative, operating a shared-ownership scheme via an employee benefit trust. Whatever the form, membership is always voluntary and some employees choose not to partake. Indeed, an employee at a practice no longer in existence indicated that only around 60 per cent of staff ever took up membership in their co-operative, and consequently, it didn't take off in the same way. A deeper review[20] therefore indicates that there are perhaps two models for architectural co-operatives: a worker co-operative with a flat structure and equal membership with equal remuneration, or an employee-ownership structure with co-operative principles where remuneration is based on market-recognised salaries and/or a scaled distribution of profits.

So, there is no formula or best-practice model for an architectural co-operative – although, as discussed later, size clearly influences the structure – and it is the practice's association with co-operative terms that identifies them. Similarly, architecture is a very broad umbrella for the services these practices provide. Although there is clear representation from architects as more traditionally defined, it also encompasses the landscape architecture of City Design Co-operative and LEDA's environmental engineering.

Within this paper I therefore consider a sample of UK co-operatives, collectives and employee-owned enterprises that provide architectural services.

Timing

There may currently be as many as fourteen active architectural co-operatives/collectives in the UK, of which eight were successfully contacted during the preparation of this chapter. Architecture does not therefore represent a significant portion of the 6,169 registered UK co-operatives existing in 2013.[21] It does not feature in the UK co-operative 'top 100', whereas renewables, energy and housing co-operatives do. Nor does architecture come near the number of registered media/communications or food retail/wholesale co-operatives. However, prior to the economic downturn of 2008 and the official recession that followed, there were perhaps only ten active architectural co-operatives/collectives, with a further seven established thereafter.

Timing, as they say, is everything and it became apparent during the course of this study that there are undoubtedly parallels to be drawn from previous UK recessions. Webster has compared the regrouping and revival of co-operatives in the 1980s and 1990s to the contemporary resurgence as a reaction to the gross excesses of greedy bankers, and it is certainly worth looking at previous recessions to establish if this is a contributing factor.[22] Indeed, at least six architectural co-operatives appear to have been set up or converted from another form of practice in the early 1980s, when the UK was feeling the effect of another recession; perhaps a further six were successfully established by the mid-1990s.[23] At their 1981 conference, RIBA ran two seminars entitled 'Democracy in Practice', developing sufficient interest for the Salaried Architects Group (SAG) to follow this up with a publication intended as 'an appetiser rather than a handbook' for those eager to learn about running a practice on co-operative principles.[24] Coincidentally, this seems to have occurred just as the Co-operative Wholesale Society's own architects department started to disappear. Of course, Cullinan had already established his practice in 1965 with co-operative principles rising to the surface in 1969, though no written constitution existed for some time after that.[25]

However, co-operative popularity is not just down to economics. The introduction to the SAG publication highlights that it had not been possible for RIBA members to set up a co-operative until a change in the Code of Professional Conduct permitted them to limit their legal liability.[26] It just so happens that this professional freedom occurred at the same time. Only a few years before, Wooley had discussed these problems of common ownership in practice when he championed the need for more co-operatives but consequently feared it was unlikely to happen.[27] This is perhaps analogous to how the evolution of the Industrial & Provident Societies (IPS) Act influenced the modern co-operative movement in the 1800s. Within five years of the 1862 IPS Act, which allowed co-operatives corporate status, 1,052 societies were certified by the registrar.[28] At least 286 of those were dissolved within a few years, but 190 new societies were registered in 1868.[29] However, recent growth in the co-operative movement is probably not attributable to improvements in co-operative law, and the renewed interest for architects is certainly not due to changes in their legal structures.

Recently, the co-operative model has received a certain visibility, marked by increased public awareness and appearances in popular culture. When discussing this resurgence it has been suggested that the cause may simply be that 'co-operatives are cool again'.[30] Some, however, remain of the opinion that worker co-operatives belong to another culture or place. For example, during a radio interview regarding the proposal to have worker representation influencing the income of their respective company executives, Dr Heather McGregor, a business executive and national columnist, responded: 'We do not operate worker's co-operatives; if they all want to work in a workers' co-operative, everybody can move to Cuba.'[31] And yet, Co-operatives UK reported that the number of co-operatives grew by 23 per cent between 2008 and 2011, with a surge in co-operative establishments in 2010 and 2011.[32] This could be linked to general co-operative campaigns, including the United Nations' designation of 2012 as the International Year of Co-operatives, but may also be related to government campaigns encouraging employee ownership, culminating in the then Deputy Prime Minister Nick Clegg's vision of a 'John Lewis economy'.[33] This formed part of the coalition government's wider policy of promoting a 'Big Society', in which co-operatives, mutuals and social enterprises were intended to play a much more prominent role in society and the economy, as the state retreated in the wake of unprecedented cuts in public expenditure.

Looking back to the 1980s, it would appear that at least one architectural practice was established with the support of similar promotions in the shape of the Co-operative Development Agency (CDA).[34] Having emerged during another period of economic turmoil, the CDA was active from 1978 until 1990 and, financed by government grants from sources such as the Secretary of State for Employment, it promoted the development of the co-operative sector of the economy in an advisory, promotional, representational and educational capacity.[35] Coates and Hillard place this in its political context, also attributing the contemporaneous rise in co-operative establishments to the Manpower Services Commission job creation programmes and the activities of radical Labour local councils.[36] Perhaps even more interesting is their discussion of the Thatcher government's proposal to spread capitalist ownership via Employee Share Ownership Plans, and the parallels that might be drawn between that and the recommendations of Nuttal's *Sharing Success*, which consulted employee-owned practices such as Make Architects and the Arup Group, both of which are well known within the architectural profession, though not necessarily as employee-owned businesses.[37]

There have also been sector-specific campaigns and so it may be that a general shift in awareness and attitude towards co-operatives has become visible in the architectural profession too. Launched in 2010, the Creative Co-operatives initiative targeted, among others, freelancers and newly self-employed people looking for innovative ways to work.[38] It strongly recommended co-operatives as an alternative to working alone, sharing resources and overheads to reduce both risk and costs – all matters relevant to the rising number of small architectural practices and sole traders mentioned before who might struggle to make sufficient profit to generate a decent income. Nacey reported in 2012 that since 2008 sole traders surveyed had seen income drop 28 per cent and were earning 20 per cent less than the average architect.[39] Sharing resources and searching for work together can assist in addressing this but may not necessarily result in matching average salaries. Consequently, though not part of this chapter, it may be worth accurately comparing incomes of architectural co-operative members with those of sole traders or other company structures to test this assertion. The UK worker co-operatives blog has attempted to identify turnover figures for architect co-operatives but only obtained figures for three practices, compared to the nine they listed at the time.[40] In any event, co-operative businesses exist to serve their members and although sharing the profit is part of that, work–life balance seems to play a part too.[41] This seems particularly relevant to the recently established or start-up architecture co-operatives that can't always live up to market salaries but do tend to favour alternative rewards.

Structural support

A two-year study that finished in 2010 revealed that graduates in art, design, crafts and media subjects placed a high value on opportunities to make full use of their knowledge and skills, earn a stable income, pursue or maintain creative practice and have time with family and friends. It suggested that creative industry graduates may be trading off higher earnings in their career choices to achieve more satisfaction in terms of work–life balance, personal development and independence, and this was influencing their decision process.[42] This was something that most architectural co-operators thought was the strongest benefit of the model but it does not have to be at the expense of profitability. While Cullinan's do not consider themselves to be commercially driven, they have been in business for nearly fifty years – surely an indication of commercial success, if not drive – and they also take pride in a relatively low staff turnover and fantastic employee engagement. Loop Systems discuss the personal benefits of their structure in their contribution to the Creative Co-operatives campaign, citing flexibility and making decisions together on the ground as some of the benefits of working together in a co-operative.[43] Similarly, LEDA also identified with the work–life balance aspect of the model, and both Collective Architecture and Cave recommended it in terms of structured, but flexible, working hours that can support one's personal life. With this comes the possibility of individuals developing their own interests. Research and teaching at academic institutions, such as architecture schools, seem to play a part in Collective Architecture, Loop Systems and URBED. While, once again, this is not exclusive to co-operatives, it can assist in diversifying income streams, reducing reliance on design commissions and was acknowledged as beneficial to practices in terms of networking, additional income, finding new employees and developing the visionary mantra that underpins boutique practices by testing it against the rigours that teaching provides.[44]

The features current architectural co-operators frequently suggested as important were: a common purpose, transparency, contributing to decision-making, better treatment of people (when compared with some experiences in other practices) and design team collaboration. The most repeated benefit was working in practice as a team with the same aims and objectives, but this is not the preserve of today's co-operatives. Describing the Design Co-operative in 1982, Ian Finlay said: 'uniting the group from its earliest days was a mutually felt dislike for working within a rigid hierarchical structure'.[45] This echoes some of the comments by current practices, which expressed their preference for a collective or 'flat' management approach which differs widely from general practice where the principals/directors have a hierarchical approach. However, that does seem to be more a choice than a requirement since even the employee-ownership models, which usually feature some degree of hierarchy, provide an opportunity to have a greater say without having to buy in to a partnership. Oliver James, a popular psychologist who contributed to recent co-operative publications, might say that because this approach works with rather than against people, we might end up leading saner, more fruitful lives and it is for this reason that we prefer the co-operative or collective model at work.[46] One architect said that, without a doubt, quality of life was top of the list: 'we are in control'.

This is not to say that membership of an architectural co-operative removes all the stress associated with running more traditional forms of practice but it can help with alleviating pressure. When it does occur, the members spread the weight by addressing issues together. Even the success of Cullinan's had difficult days in the past when no fees were coming in, but they would address this together by everyone going without pay.[47] The common ownership of the entity under threat helps the practice respond as that entity rather than an individual, a form of alliance that is perhaps invaluable in the turmoil of the current construction climate and something that was also expressed in the past: 'A Co-operative enhances your responsibility yet lets you share it with others – we're jointly responsible for this thing we've set up. We pool our Strengths.'[48]

Size matters

Some members belonging to larger practices mentioned that the process of making decisions together could be cumbersome in bigger co-ops, something that seemed to be a relatively straightforward process for the nimble little practices. Although they have been as many as forty-five strong, while this chapter was being investigated Cullinan's had approximately thirty-five staff, of which twenty-five were members; Collective Architecture had a similar number of staff and were delighted to be growing.[49] These are considered to be 'large–medium' practices within the profession and are, in architectural practice terms, comparatively huge next to the small, two-to-three person co-operatives that have emerged recently – referred to as 'micro practices'.[50] Historically, there was a view that the maximum number of members should be about fifteen, and that above twenty it became difficult to effectively involve everyone.[51] This may be a reference to one of Parkinson's laws[52] but actually used to concern Cullinan's. Although they used to think twenty-five was the optimum, they have found that they can shrink or grow and their system, based on their early model, still works. Perhaps one of the reasons this is so successful is due to the internal structure that allocates staff across eight distinct management teams. In parallel to this, the architectural services are delivered through five project groups. Members therefore may be part of the same project group but reside in different management teams, or vice versa. Hence, while there is potentially a relationship between the size of the practice and its form (the larger practices seem to lean towards collective/co-ownership models compared to the worker co-ops of the micros) they may all function on a similar basis with internal teams being of a similar size to the micro practices. This permits the quick-thinking agility that the smaller practices benefited from. Certainly, Loop Systems traded for nearly seven years with three, equal, architect–directors. Decisions were quick and there was always the benefit that no votes were hung. (However, this did not seem to have been affected when the practice membership reduced to two.) The growing polarisation in the size of practices featured among trends noted by RIBA perhaps reflects the two types and size of practice trending within architectural co-operatives. Approximately 10 per cent of 1,836 UK practices they surveyed in 2011–12 were in the same range as Cullinan's. Micro practices accounted for nearly 36 per cent, but if they also admitted practices with a headcount of less than ten, this would have accounted for nearly 66 per cent of all practices surveyed.[53] In fact, a few years later the RIBA Business Benchmarking Report found that 40 per cent of Britain's architects are employed by just 3 per cent of practices with the majority of firms employing fewer than six members of staff. In an associated statement about this polarisation, Richard Brindley, RIBA's executive director of membership and profession, described this majority as being focused on self-managing very small, locally based and often 'hand to mouth', operations.[54] This description seems applicable to some of the small architectural co-operatives and echoed the findings and predictions of the RIBA's Building Futures think tank in 2010, which indicated a growing need for small, local practices and the unprecedented growth of global, integrated consultancies.[55]

Such integrated or interdisciplinary practice, however, is not restricted to the giants. As the role of the architect becomes diluted and distributed between other professions (e.g. engineers, project managers, surveyors), they have begun to see a future where they apply the same skills to an array of physical and/or design problems. This new era of transdisciplinary creative consultants or 'design houses' is something that younger members of the profession are keen on and it suits the flexibility of the small co-operative model particularly well.[56] For instance, LEDA, which positively describes itself as an integrated design practice (rather than an architectural practice), started as a partnership between two engineers and one architect in 1997. They confirmed in discussion with the author that this bias had continued with five engineers and only two architects within a staff totalling nine, and firmly believed that the business model they have supports their in-house collaborative design dialogue across the disciplines rather than separate processes for different professions. Focusing on design education, the Multi-disciplinary Design Network highlights pertinent points about teamwork and collaboration in design industries. Solving the problems of the future in an economically sustainable way 'will demand new approaches to innovation, new combinations of skills, and teams of people who can combine their disciplines and expertise in new ways'.[57] What's more, the Network found that companies that invest in their design capability and develop a reputation for innovation can avoid competing on price alone.[58] Surely this is music to the ears of any business, but also supports the Building Futures forecast that small, local practices (such as those being set up as co-operatives) will be judged on their ability to produce a personal service, clearly differentiated from their competitors in terms of the value added – a value that can be enhanced by a transdisciplinary approach. And was this not the making of the original Rochdale Pioneers, who supplied better-quality goods at the same price?

Service provision

The aim to provide this 'value-added', quality service also seems to influence the emergence of architectural co-operatives in two ways: their approach, and their sector or client base. While these can be separated, the co-operative model offers an opportunity to blend them to inform the ethos of the co-operative practitioner in the architectural profession.

Regarding approach, one of the most striking quotes from the recent

Building Futures report was the statement that architects are so preoccupied with their 'vocation' that they do not consider that practice is a business and consequently become 'arrogant and focused on embodying their own ideologies rather than providing a service to clients'.[59] But what if they were able to embody an ideology *and* provide a satisfying service to clients? Setting the headlines of 2013 aside, The Co-operative Bank has benefited from positive press in recent years as an alternative to the banker bonuses and trading that contributed to the current economic downturn.[60] But, this effect has not been restricted to banking and has rippled across the surface of many sectors, including architecture, where some have commented on the growth of larger conglomerates that turn attention from design-led practice towards cost-driven consultancy.[61] Others believe that clients (many of whom are domestic consumers with projects for their own homes) increasingly want to see personal commitment to their building project and build a relationship with the people that are going to support them through the process.[62] Many architectural co-operators identify with these issues and consider themselves to be a part of design-led practices with client relationships that reflect their co-operative approach to the work.

Once again, we find that this is not a recent development within the architectural profession. In 1975 the Architects Revolutionary Council (ARC) initiated a campaign for a New Architecture Movement (NAM) aiming to capitalise on the altruistic instincts of architects and hoping to bring a moral and social conscience to the profession by emphasising social responsibility and the need to relate directly to people at the grass-roots level.[63] The NAM campaign seems to have resonated with many at the time and certainly informed both Matrix Feminist Architectural Co-operative, established in 1981, and The Design Co-operative, not only in the establishment of their co-operatives but also in the type of work they undertook and how they approached it.

Wooley, who wrote extensively about it at the time and was an active participant, is careful to highlight that this 'community architecture' cannot be reduced to a simple formula and that those involved in it should not be considered on the fringes of the profession, but rather as using their approach to improve their service and the public image of the architect.[64] User-centric design, for instance, can be applied to home-owners or factory workers just as easily as it can to community groups. The community architecture theme does seem to thread its way through architectural co-operatives to the recent renaissance too, whether it's URBED undertaking training events for tenants to empower them to make informed decisions, or Loop Systems, whose members have all worked in at least one Community Technical Aid Centre supporting a variety of community-led projects.[65] Both organisations continue to work with community and voluntary sector groups from their bases in Manchester, just as the Design Co-operative did in the 1980s.

The Design Co-operative was of the first true architectural co-operatives to be established. Emerging from the Manchester Community Architecture Group, it set out to use their combined experience and skills in working with and assisting others in a socially responsible way.[66] Matrix also manifested their work with a variety of groups alongside a commitment to mobility and accessibility within the built environment.[67] Referring to the 2011 Localism Act, intended to decentralise government bureaucracy and replace it with local democracy and individual responsibility, RIBA highlighted the significant role that architects could play in assisting neighbourhood planning to realise quality development. While RIBA champion the architect's specific skills of analysis, interpretation and visioning of place, they also warn that the success of this will be dependent on the professional's ability to appropriately engage with local people and local issues – designing 'with' rather than 'for' communities.[68] Given their internal structures and approach it is therefore clear why those interested in this work might opt for co-operative structures and their tailored, personal service.[69] And so, this trend continues within architectural co-operatives, a fitting response to the International Co-operative Alliance's seventh principle: concern for community. This social responsibility also extends to sustainable development and an environmental approach to design that was voiced by architectural co-operators. The Cave Co-operative, who found out about co-operatives through their third-sector work, set themselves up after winning a commission for a sustainable city farm and continue that type of work, considering materials such as straw bales for their projects. While LEDA do have links with community practice, they didn't feel that their co-operative model influenced the type of projects they worked on but they do have a focus on environmental design and, along with other architectural co-operatives, are members of the Association for Environment Conscious Building (AECB). Indeed, an architect from one of these co-operatives was very clear that although they majored in 'green' projects and were AECB members, this is just a trend and not an explicit part of their service to the exclusion of other types of work.

Reflecting on my own practice, the reputation of Loop Systems seems to be building on our approach and service with a strong client base that shares and generally appreciates our values. Clients range from commercial co-operatives to domestic customers intent on retrofitting their homes to improve both functional and environmental performance. While there are trends regarding the types of projects within co-operatives such as ours and others, to think of architectural co-operatives in this way may prevent us from seeing the opportunity that these practice models offer to the profession, just as Wooley highlighted when he resented that a participatory approach should be interpreted as belonging to community architecture or its like.[70]

Conclusion

With a growing number of small practices, it could be said that the interest in co-operative structures is perhaps more about convenience of form rather than ethics, for example as an alternative to partnership, but even so there is no single, successful formula for working as an architectural co-operative. Whether it's an employee-ownership model or a worker co-operative they are all part of a wider co-ownership set of associated businesses that share values. Nonetheless, one wonders if there is a tipping point when worker co-operatives no longer satisfy as the model for a growing architectural practice. While it was clear that all the practices support collaboration and participation, this does not mean that design is undertaken in a consensual way. Design needs strong leadership and perhaps employee-ownership models are more commercially successful because they have team leaders, senior levels and a hierarchy within them rather than a fully equitable system. Equally, this does not necessarily require the sacrifice of individuality – as we have seen, they may still flourish and their own interests can be an asset to practice.

This chapter set out to explore possible reasons behind the rise in interest in, if not the establishment of, architectural co-operatives. It is as much a discussion of parallels between current interest in the model and that of the past but the causes of chronological spikes in these architectural co-operatives can be attributed to the confluence of:

- economic recessions;
- promotion of the co-operative model; and
- a principled paradigm shift in approach to architectural practice.

There is a clearly a link between economic climate and co-operative formation, but this does not preclude the establishment of them outside recessions. While one practitioner said their decision to set up as a co-operative in the 1980s was semi-political, and an alternative to the Thatcherite culture of the time, they stressed that the basis of their co-operative practice concerned quality and it was not necessarily a political movement. They were not alone in this assertion, with other architects emphasising that it was about quality versus slave labour, both in terms of internal employer–employee relations and external service and/or products. Once again, this attitude to architectural practice motivated by ethics and principles is not limited to either architectural co-operatives or a particular point in time.

While some are perhaps of the view that architects co-operatives are breaking new ground, it is clear that we are only renewing interest at a time when some are reconsidering their professional vows and what they stand for in the wake of consumers demanding satisfaction. One architect suggested there had been a shift in attitude from the belief that co-operatives 'used to be all about sandals' to understanding it more as a way of working. While market research indicated that the majority of people know what a co-operative is, despite recent campaigns it appears that 43 per cent could not think of any co-operatives, and 40 per cent thought it was old-fashioned term.[71] This is something that has perhaps already been addressed in the public realm but could benefit from further promotion within the architectural profession to demonstrate the value of architectural co-operatives as a value-based, democratic alternative and viable commercial model where architects can share skills and resources. As political cartoonist Polyp put it at the Creative Co-operatives launch in Manchester: 'We need to get people to start seeing co-operatives as a democratic business model, and not a bunch of hippies in rainbow jumpers and dungarees talking about their feelings at the morning planning meeting.'[72]

Notes

1 Enquiries noted by Co-operatives UK, personal communication with John Atherton.
2 The primary investigation and interviews took place in 2010–11 and were compiled in 2012.
3 M. Maccaferri, '"A co-operative of intellectuals": the encounter between co-operative values and urban planning. An Italian case study' in A. Webster, L. Shaw, J. K. Walton, A. Brown and D. Stewart, eds, *The Hidden Alternative: Co-operative Values, Past, Present and Future* (Manchester: Manchester University Press, 2011), pp. 251–65.
4 A. Winston, 'Rogers Stirk Harbour to make 35 redundancies', *Building Design* (2 March 2009).
5 Construction Products Association/Experian Construction Industry Economic Forecast, July 2009 in C. Jamieson, *The Future for Architects?* (London: Royal Institute of British Architects, 2010), p. 33; J. Percival, 'Architect job losses soar as crunch hits construction', *The Guardian* (20 March 2009).
6 Percival, 'Architect job losses'.
7 M. Fulcher, 'Number of unemployed architects rises for 16th month in a row', *Architect's Journal* (17 September 2009).
8 M. Wilding, 'Architects remain uncertain while unemployment continues to

fall', *Architect's Journal* (21 April 2011). The annual report figures from the Architects Registration Board (ARB) suggest approximately 33,000 architects were registered at the time. This has been compared to a figure of 1,175 unemployed architects, as quoted by R. Waite, 'Confidence drops as unemployment rises', in *Architect's Journal* (26 September 2011).

9 V. Nacey, 'Going steady?', *RIBA Journal* (2012), www.ribaj.com/culture/going-steady (accessed 20 January 2016).

10 The RIBA's monthly Future Trends Survey was launched in January 2009 to monitor business and employment trends affecting the architects' profession. See www.architecture.com/RIBA/Professionalsupport/FutureTrendsSurvey.aspx (accessed 29 February 2016).

11 In June 2013, 21 per cent of respondents to a RIBA survey reported that they had personally been underemployed in the preceding month; *RIBA Future Trends Survey* (July 2013). See also Office for National Statistics, 'Underemployment up 1 million since 2008' (9 February 2013), www.ons.gov.uk/ons/rel/lmac/underemployed-workers-in-the-uk/2012/sty-underemployed-workers-in-the-uk.html (accessed 10 February 2016).

12 Nacey, 'Going steady?'

13 Ibid.

14 B. [Potter] Webb, *The Co-operative Movement in Great Britain* (Aldershot: Gower Books, 1891, reprint 1987), p. 29.

15 ARB, *Annual Report* (2012).

16 Ibid.

17 *Codes of Practice for Skilled Workers, Standard Occupational Classification (SOC) Codes Version 07/13* (London: Home Office, July 2013).

18 N. Awan, T. Schneider and J. Till, *The Spatial Agency: Other Ways of Doing Architecture* (Abingdon: Routledge, 2011), pp. 130–2.

19 T. Wooley, 'Cullinan's co-op', *Architects Journal* 166 (1977), 741–2.

20 By S. McCusker.

21 *The Co-operative Economy* (Manchester: Co-operatives UK, 2013), p. 12.

22 T. Webster, 'Can values make a difference? Co-operatives: moving from the Rochdale Pioneers to the 21st Century', *Journal of Co-operative Studies* 42:3 (December 2009), 46.

23 Established through the author's research, with the assistance of John Atherton at Co-operatives UK.

24 Salaried Architects Group (SAG), *Architects Co-operatives: An Introduction* (London: RIBA, 1982), p. 3.

25 Wooley, 'Cullinan's co-op'.

26 It appears from the documents reviewed that this change to the Code of Professional Conduct occurred around 1981.

27 T. Wooley, 'Alternative practice', *Architects Journal* 166 (1977), 735–41, p. 736.

28 I. Snaith, *Handbook of Industrial & Provident Society Law* (Manchester: Holyoake Books, 1993, revised 2005), p. 3.

29 E. W. Brabrook, *The Law Relating to Industrial & Provident Societies* (London: Butterworths, 1869), p. xxv.

30 L. Bachelor, 'Why co-operatives are cool again', *The Guardian* (1 May 2010).
31 Today programme, BBC Radio 4 (22 November 2011).
32 Co-operatives UK, *The UK Co-operative Economy: Alternatives to Austerity* (Manchester: Co-operatives UK, 2012), p. 12.
33 The term was adopted widely in the media after Nick Clegg used it on 16 January 2012, saying 'We need more individuals to have a real stake in their firms. More of a John Lewis economy, if you like.' Excerpts from his speech and an associated report were reported in 'Nick Clegg unveils plans for "John Lewis economy"', *The Guardian* (16 January 2012), www.theguardian.com/politics/2012/jan/16/nick-clegg-unveils-plans-john-lewis-economy (accessed 10 February 2016).
34 SAG, *Architects Co-operatives*, p. 14.
35 See 'Records of the Co-operative Development Agency', http://discovery.nationalarchives.gov.uk/details/r/C747 (accessed 10 February 2016).
36 D. Coates and J. Hillard, 'The challenge to industrial democracy in Britain' in M. D. Hancock, J. Logue and B. Schiller, eds, *Managing Modern Capitalism: Industrial Renewal and Workplace Democracy in the United States and Western Europe* (New York: Praeger, 1991), pp. 138–40.
37 G. Nuttal, *Sharing Success: The Nuttal Review of Employee Ownership* (London: Department for Business Innovation & Skills, 2012).
38 Co-operatives UK, *Creative Co-operatives: A Guide to Starting a Co-operative in the Creative Industries* (Manchester: Co-operatives UK, 2010).
39 Nacey, 'Going steady?'
40 See Co-operatives UK, 'Size of worker co-op sector' (3 February 2012), http://workerco-operatives.blogspot.no/2012/02/size-of-worker-co-op-sector.html (accessed 10 February 2016).
41 Co-operatives UK, *Creative Co-operatives*.
42 L. Ball, E. Pollard and N. Stanley, *Creative Graduates, Creative Futures* (London: Council for Higher Education in Art and Design and University of the Arts London, 2010), p. xxiv.
43 Co-operatives UK, 'Neil and Stephen: Loop Systems', www.creatives.uk.coop/neil-and-stephen-loop-systems (accessed 3 July 2012).
44 Jamieson, *Future for Architects?*, p. 36.
45 'Democracy in Manchester co-op practice', *RIBA Journal* 89:8 (August 1982), 4–5.
46 O. James, *The Psychology of Co-operation: The Benefits of Co-operating for your Psyche and Society* (Manchester: Co-operatives UK, 2010).
47 Wooley, 'Cullinan's co-op'.
48 SAG, *Architects Co-operatives*, p. 16.
49 Their representative did mention that the percentage of members was usually much higher, but of those members, twenty-one were architects.
50 RIBA definitions state that a large–medium practice includes twenty to forty-nine, while a micro practice includes from zero to four.
51 SAG, *Architects Co-operatives*, p. 10.
52 With reference to government cabinets, Parkinson suggested that they may become inefficient if they grow bigger than twenty or twenty-one; C. N. Parkinson,

Parkinson's Law (and Other Studies in Administration) (Cambridge, MA: Riverside Press, 1957).

53 RIBA, *Business Benchmarking Survey for Chartered Practices* (London: RIBA, 2010–11).

54 E. Hopkirk, 'RIBA survey finds "split profession"', *Building Design* (18 April 2013).

55 Jamieson, *Future for Architects?*

56 Ibid.

57 Multi-disciplinary Design Network, *Multi-disciplinary Design Education in the UK* (London: Design Council, 2010), p. 9.

58 Ibid., p. 10.

59 Ibid., p. 14.

60 P. Collinson and R. Jones, 'Unhappy with big banks? You could move your money', *The Guardian* (10 February 2012).

61 Jamieson, *Future for Architects?*, p. 22.

62 Over the years Cullinan's have often debated what term to use when describing their 'share-owning' staff. Suggestions have been 'joiners' or 'partners', much like John Lewis. The important point is that each instance the title confers a status to employees that lets clients know whom they are working with, and Cullinan's feel this is an important feature of their service. Similarly, Loop Systems discuss how they opted for a collective management where all members are directors of the company and how important this is: 'I think from a client point of view, even before we signed up to be a formal co-operative, we were always clear that any architect they were talking to also had a share in the company, so there's a long-term interest. They're not getting an employee who might go to another company tomorrow, there will be continuity of the key persons.' See Co-operatives UK, 'Neil and Stephen'.

63 'Towards a new architecture movement', *Architects Journal* 162 (1975), p. 885.

64 Wooley, 'Alternative practice', p. 737.

65 Awan et al., *Spatial Agency*, p. 132. Community Technical Aid Centres were the fulfilment of another point raised by Wooley in 'Alternative practice', when he discussed the promise of these but raised concern regarding whether or not the funding necessary to establish them would materialise.

66 'Democracy in Manchester co-op practice'.

67 Matrix Feminist Architectural Co-operative, *Making Space: Women and the Man Made Environment* (London: Pluto Press, 1984).

68 RIBA, *Guide to Localism: Opportunities for Architects – Part One: Neighbourhood Planning and Getting Community Engagement Right* (London: RIBA, 2011), pp. 4 and 8.

69 Jamieson, *Future for Architects?*, p. 18.

70 Wooley, 'Alternative practice'.

71 E. Mayo and G. Simon, *Good Business: Public Perceptions of Co-operatives* (Manchester: Co-operatives UK, 2010).

72 Polyp, quoted in an email to the author to confirm his statement from 2010; see www.polyp.org.uk (accessed 10 February 2016).

12

Co-operatives and climate protection: housing co-operatives in Germany

Carolin Schröder and Heike Walk

Introduction

After the Fifth Assessment Report of the Intergovernmental Panel on Climate Change (IPCC) it became clear that global climate change was progressing much more rapidly than assumed a few years before.[1] The need for action is therefore all the more urgent – and we need to turn our attention above all to the collective activities and social dimensions of climate change and climate protection. In Germany, through the adopted Integrated Energy and Climate Programme of the Federal German government and the legal framework for action on climate change in 2007, municipal climate protection experienced a further increase. There are hardly any communities or towns that have not committed themselves to this issue. However, we are still observing a strong east–west and north–south divide, with the degree of commitment being much higher in the south and in the west. While in the 1990s municipal climate policies concentrated exclusively on climate protection,[2] in 2008 the Federal Cabinet adopted the German Strategy for Adaptation to Climate Change. This created a framework for adapting to the impact of climate change in Germany.

This chapter argues that great potential for climate protection activities can be found precisely in co-operatives and that co-operatives will become increasingly important for local sustainable solutions because of their capacity for participation and solidarity. The chapter starts with a short description of the need for climate protection at the local level, followed by an outline on co-operatives as collective actors for climate protection – with emphasis on their democratic and solidary capacity. Further, an introduction to the German co-operative sector is supplemented by research results on three different housing co-operatives and their climate-related activities, which provide insight into their participatory and solidary capacity, since these attributes can promote climate protection and sustainability projects and efforts. Finally, the concluding section addresses crucial aspects that facilitate participatory and solidary structures.

The need for climate protection at the local level

Climate change is a major challenge affecting most global, national and local economies, societies and natural resources in various ways: extreme weather events (storms, floodings, heat waves or droughts), rising sea levels, changes in precipitation rates (rainfall/snow, droughts etc.) and temperature averages. These events will affect people directly (in particular, the poorest), as they make livelihoods and living conditions more vulnerable. While climate change has quite diverse effects in different parts of the world and different impacts on population groups (women and men, rich and poor, old and young, urban and rural population etc.), areas of close geographical proximity may face very different challenges and thus require very different, location-specific approaches.

As a result, global climate change and its consequences have led to wide-ranging re-evaluation processes in both political and business circles: for a considerable time, climate protection activities on the global and national levels focused on technical solutions and legally binding agreements, but these have achieved rather poor results so far.[3] In consequence, municipalities developed and implemented regional and local climate protection activities from the mid-1990s onwards which combined technical and social aspects of climate protection and aimed at including a variety of participation by civil society actors, businesses and institutions. This approach is based on the insights

- that climate-protective technologies need to be adapted to their uses and users in order to be successful;
- that climate policies can be influenced at the local and regional level; and
- that the co-operation and participation of large parts of the society are crucial.[4]

Although action is still voluntary, at time of writing in 2014 many municipalities in Western Europe and in Germany have already presented more or less comprehensive climate protection concepts which are aimed at transforming municipal production and consumption patterns in order to move towards more sustainable societies. Obviously, the scope of action for local climate protection is limited to measures within municipal legal and socio-political capacities. This ranges from adapting technical solutions to local conditions, to supporting more vulnerable population groups, and to promoting changes of individual climate-relevant behaviour and investment decisions.

Co-operatives as collective actors for climate protection

Co-operatives are of specific interest when it comes to collective action for climate protection. They represent a well-established and institutionalised form of civil organisation with a diverse presence worldwide. The specific qualities of co-operatives – in particular their interconnected economic and social sustainability in times of rapid economic, social and technical changes[5] – prompted us to consider their potential ecological sustainability too. In the context of climate change, this raised the question to what extent co-operatives – or, to be more precise, the co-operative movement – could contribute to climate protection at the local and the global levels.

While they address various social, cultural, ecological and economic everyday needs co-operatives 'are based on the values of self-help, self-responsibility, democracy, equality, equity and solidarity' while their 'members believe in the ethical values of honesty, openness, social responsibility and caring for others'.[6] Their specific logic of collective action is characterised by an appreciation of local democracy and solidarity,[7] as co-operatives are inextricably linked to the sustainable functioning of local communities and markets.[8] Patera even describes co-operatives as an 'emancipatory social system'.[9]

Regarding co-operatives' capacities for climate protection, such an emancipatory social system can be considered as a solid base for designing and implementing local policies and strategies in, for example, housing, consumption, mobility and health that are related to the socio-economic characteristics (income, gender, age and health) of their members. Co-operatives networking with other groups and institutions may even have greater effects on local climate protection than individual activities. Quite obviously, this cannot be generalised as co-operatives vary in size and engagement, and in resources available. But at their best, they may develop and implement individual and collective strategies of dealing with, adapting or rather escaping the effects of climate change in the short, medium and long run.[10]

In the following section, we focus on the co-operative capacities of democracy and solidarity and their relevance, arguing that the principles of self-help and shared responsibility can trigger considerable bursts of motivation, specifically with regard to climate protection.

Democratic capacities

The participatory rights of co-operators differ fundamentally from the influential power of shareholders in other business forms: co-operatives as interest groups formed by individuals take their decisions democratically, transparently and based on equal rights,[11] with value creation remaining member oriented and collectively available. Indeed, the participatory rights are appreciated by most members and considered a great advantage.[12] But the level and number of participatory activities vary from attending an annual assembly to delegates and work groups entitled to prepare or take decisions on specific topics.[13] On the one hand, we find co-operatives where only a minority of members exercise their democratic rights via attending the annual assembly. Lack of time is the most prominent reason given that prevents members from participating. Thus, in consequence, the formation of will and the making of decisions, the two core elements of participation, are frequently concentrated in the board of directors,[14] not to mention the implementation of decisions. On the other hand, we find a considerable number of new, small co-operatives where members are actively participating in shaping objectives and services for a sustainable and climate-friendly future. The latter conceive involvement in collective structures as a practical opportunity to become informed and involved, to meet people, to support each other within a self-chosen community, to break down global problems into collective and local ones, to counteract feelings of powerlessness, and to collectively implement local solutions to specific problems.[15]

Co-operatives as organisations based on the notion of solidarity

The literature on co-operatives describes solidarity as one of their central values. Many authors argue that the idea of solidarity between people with similar interests stabilises the group,[16] and contributes to population groups' coping with several societal deficits.[17] However, only a few studies explicitly examine the notion and goals of solidarity in the co-operative context. This may be due to the general difficulty of capturing this concept. In the 1990s a couple of studies were conducted which identified trust as a key prerequisite for co-operative solidarity: Gherardi and Masiero describe solidarity in co-operatives as a relational pattern, as a form of collective action or network activity that builds on trust and can therefore also be understood as a competitive factor that makes co-operatives stand out from the private economy.[18] The recent trend to establish new, small co-operatives may be a consequence of this.

One challenge in the context of sustainable development would be to relate solidarity to climate protection. While there might be a diffuse consensus that global effects of climate change can only be dealt with via international solidarity between people and nations, it is worthwhile looking at potential contributions of co-operatives at the local level. Solidarity-based climate protection activities could be promoted by co-operatives via their members' and staff's daily routines, guidelines and rules as well as via political lobbying. In addition, solidarity-based solutions could be developed which provide access to more sustainable lifestyles for people with less money. Or, vice versa, it could be the case that collective climate protection measures might promote co-operative solidarity.[19]

The current situation of German co-operatives

In a similar way to other countries, the first co-operative-like structures in Germany evolved within the agrarian and food sector. But unlike in England and France, where early socialists such as Robert Owen and Charles Fourier were instrumental in the development of the co-operative sector, the co-operative movement in Germany in the early twentieth century grew apart from the worker's movement – except for the housing and consumer co-operative sectors.[20] Consequently, the most important spokespeople in Germany were neither peasants nor workers, but members of the middle class. Two particularly important spokesmen spread their Christian conservative and liberal ideas: Friedrich Wilhelm Raiffeisen and Hermann Schulze-Delitzsch. Raiffeisen, the founder of agricultural co-operation, was a young mayor in the slum areas of the Eifel. He acted within a framework of Christian conservative care. Schulze-Delitzsch, in turn, was a leftist politician and co-founder of the German Progress Party.[21] Along with the political ideas of these two leading German figures, the socialist and social reformist approach that characterised the co-operatives of the early twentieth century largely disappeared. Instead, economic benefits have gained more importance in large parts of today's German market-based co-operative model than aspects of solidarity.

Between 1950 and 1970, the number of registered co-operatives declined by almost a third (from more than 26,000 down to about 18,500), and in the three subsequent decades by another half (with only 9,500 registered co-operatives by the end of 1999, and a mere

Table 12.1: Number of co-operatives in Germany, 1980–2011

	1980	1990	2000	2010	2011
Co-operative banks	4,267	3,055	1,813	1,156	1,139
Credit co-operatives	4,246	3,037	1,794	1,138	1,121
Co-operative central banks	10	4	4	2	2
Special affiliated co-operatives	11	14	15	16	16
Rural co-operatives	5,228	3,725	3,815	2,480	2,413
Primary co-operatives[a, b]	5,168	3,672	3,780	2,474	2,407
Head offices[c]	60	53	35	6	6
Industrial co-operatives[a]	875	787	1,422	2,018	2,338
Primary co-operatives	856	772	1,410	2,009	2,329
Head offices	19	15	12	9	9
Consumer co-operatives	94	30	53	33	31
Primary co-operatives	55	28	51	32	30
Head offices	39	2	2	1	1
Housing co-operatives	1,217	1,172	1,991	1,931	1,921
Primary co-operatives	1,217	1,172	1,991	1,931	1,921
Head offices	–	–	–	–	–
Total	**11,681**	**8,769**	**9,094**	**7,618**	**7,842**

[a] Water, electricity and refrigerated glasshouse co-operatives, listed as rural co-operatives until 2008, have been listed as industrial co-operatives since 2009. The bioenergy, forestry and timber co-operatives that were in part listed as industrial co-operatives until 2008 have been listed as rural co-operatives since 2009.
[b] Excluding credit co-operatives with transactions in commodities. Including agricultural co-operatives.
[c] Since 2006, only main co-operatives have been listed.
Note: Up to 1990, data includes only federal states in West Germany, using Deutsche Mark.
Source: DZ Research, 'Die deutschen Genossenschaften 2012. Entwicklungen – Meinungen – Zahlen' (Wiesbaden: Deutscher Genossenschafts-Verlag eG, 2012), p. 40.

7,500 by 2006)[22] (Table 12.1). This can be explained by concentration in the financial co-operative sector and demutualisation in other sectors. Despite declining absolute figures, co-operatives still have more members than any other type of organisation, with some 20.5 million out of 80 million inhabitants Almost every German farmer is still a member of at least one co-operative, while more than 90 per cent of all bakers and butchers, an average of 60 per cent of craftsmen and an average 75 per cent of retailers are still organised in co-operatives. However, an ongoing concentration among credit and savings co-operatives can be observed. Nonetheless, there is a considerable number, especially of housing and producer co-operatives, to be found both in east and west Germany that date back well into the nineteenth century. The number of new co-operatives remains small, with just sixty newly registered co-operatives in 2003 in Germany (seventy-four in 2006), compared to more than 500,000 new registered businesses.[23]

Three current trends

The number of co-operatives is growing in certain sectors of the German economy, but declining in others. On the one hand, there have been constant merging and consolidation processes, especially in the credit sector, which have reduced the number of co-operatives from initially 27,000 to 7,619 in 2011.[24] On the other hand, there are growing numbers of new co-operatives, especially in the housing, energy and social sectors. There are three reasons for this.

Firstly, in a time of economic and social crisis the co-operative model is proving attractive in Germany. The consequences of decade-long privatisations and a growing mistrust in the established forms of (capitalist) economy have led to widespread discussions on the role of civil society in societal transformation processes. Examples of such discourses are the solidarity economy or 'post-growth society', which emphasises fundamentally different ideas of quality of life, access to resources, and civil society, economy and politics.[25] The recent co-operative boom in Germany, especially in the energy and housing sectors, may be interpreted as a first reaction to this. To what extent the 2006 amendments to the German Co-operative Act[26] have contributed or will contribute to this is disputed among experts, and will surely differ from sector to sector. One significant amendment to the Act was that the corporate purpose of the co-operative can now include social and cultural concerns, in addition to promoting the economic benefit of its members. Another change made the audit requirements easier for smaller organisations.[27]

A second impulse that boosted the growth of co-operatives at approximately the same time was triggered by a larger trend towards economically and socially sustainable organisations, alongside a general transformation of the energy system. An important reason for this rapid growth in this area – apart from the economic crisis – is that a law on renewable energies was introduced in 2000 that made it much easier for small organisations to produce renewables.[28] In consequence, and along with associations and private partnerships (*Gesellschaft bürgerlichen Rechts*), it was primarily the co-operatives that conceived different business models in this sector, for instance by taking over electricity grids, and creating systems of community self-sufficiency and bioenergy villages. Between 2007 and 2014, the total number of registered energy co-operatives in Germany grew to 973,[29] investing around 800 million euros into local or regional solar plants, wind farms and bioenergy plants by the time of writing.[30]

Thirdly, the United Nations (UN) International Year of Co-operatives in 2012 and the UN decade of co-operatives (2011–20) have significantly

Table 12.2: Co-operative members in Germany, by sector, 1980–2011

	1980	1990	2000	2010	2011
Members (in thousands)	**13,275**	**15,207**	**20,074**	**20,744**	**21,155**
Credit co-operatives	9,105	11,421	15,039	16,689	17,002
Rural co-operatives[a, b]	1,555	1,205	922	563	550
Industrial co-operatives[a]	337	257	255	315	407
Consumer co-operatives	665	600	825	355	350
Housing co-operatives	1,613	1,724	3,033	2,822	2,846

[a] Water, electricity and refrigerated glasshouse co-operatives, listed as rural co-operatives until 2008, have been listed as industrial co-operatives since 2009. The bioenergy, forestry and timber co-operatives that were in part listed as industrial co-operatives until 2008 have been listed as rural co-operatives since 2009.
[b] Excluding credit co-operatives with transactions in commodities. Including agricultural co-operatives.
Note: Up to 1990, data includes only federal states in West Germany, using Deutsche Mark.
Source: DZ Research, 'Die deutschen Genossenschaften 2012. Entwicklungen – Meinungen – Zahlen' (Wiesbaden: Deutscher Genossenschafts-Verlag eG, 2012), p. 40.

added to the publicity of co-operatives worldwide. The boom reflects both an increasing number of scientific articles and media reports as well as in the above outlined growth developments in various sectors (Table 12.2). But interestingly, most data available on co-operatives refers to their economic and legal aspects. German social sciences and interdisciplinary studies, in contrast, have largely neglected co-operatives. In consequence, there are hardly any qualitative studies concerned with co-operatives or their activities, specifically the solidarity-oriented and participative structures of this form of organisation. Recent publications by Zimmer and by Münkner and Ringle, analysing co-operatives as actors of civic society, are exceptions.[31]

Three housing co-operatives

One of the many types of co-operatives aimed at actively supporting solidarity and sustainable structures is the housing co-operative. With 3 million members (out of 20 million co-op members altogether) and 2.2 million units to take care of, these co-operatives provide 10 per cent of Germany's total housing stock. As most of this housing was built either between 1880 and 1930 or between 1950 and 1970, the need for renovation is significant. In combination with comparatively high standards for energy efficiency and rising energy costs, this has the effect that housing co-operatives implement more measures to increase energy efficiency than any other public housing organisation, not to mention private households.[32] There is a general interest among housing co-op members in investing money in their flats, because this has a dual function – members are both owners and users of the flats, creating a 'harmony of interests'.[33] This increased interest in additional functions, which often include also participatory and solidary aspects, goes along with the observation that German housing co-operatives are most active when it comes to environment and climate protection.[34] Below, we will present case studies of three German housing co-operatives and provide findings from our research regarding their specific participatory and solidary capacities.

Spar- und Bauverein Hannover eG

The housing co-operative Spar- und Bauverein Hannover, was established in 1885. It offers more than 8,000 apartments all over the northern German town of Hanover, as well as several financial services to its 23,000 members, of which senior citizens constitute the majority. Since the mid-2000s, many buildings from the 1890s and 1950s have been renovated with energy-efficient insulation and new heating systems. In addition, the co-operative was also one of the first in Germany to build new co-operative housing, in the mid-2000s, starting a small wave of co-operative building in Germany. From the 1960s until the mid-2000s, German housing co-operatives either reduced their housing stock or took over existing buildings. The co-operative has introduced a specific recycling system to their members, and conducts a yearly monitoring of its climate protection activities. Plans for the future include the installation of photovoltaic systems on rooftops, individual water meters and triple-glazed windows, and the introduction of incentives for using public transportation and the co-operative's transport services.

Participatory capacities

The annual assembly is organised as an elected delegates meeting. As in many co-operatives, attendance rates are very low; approximately fifty people attend. This may be because this assembly's function is merely to approve the annual report and the activities of the board. Nonetheless, and in order to integrate a variety of members' needs, the management board set up a range of services such as neighbourhood meetings, tenant group holidays and daily assistance services for senior citizens. After the board of directors decided to establish new meeting spaces in three Hanover neighbourhoods, all members were invited in 2012 to collectively develop ideas for using those spaces. Again, around fifty people participated.

Climate protection has become a crucial issue for the board of directors, for reasons of social responsibility as well as economic efficiency.

To underline this, the co-operative is a member of the municipal climate alliance, sent a team of young members to the municipal solar mobile race in 2011 and offers consultation and workshops on practical energy efficiency (such as how to properly use the new heating systems) to their members. In 2013, two workshops (called world cafés) on 'climate protection and our co-op' took place, organised by the co-operative and our research team. Roughly one hundred members attended out of curiosity, as they admitted that they are interested in the topic but feel that they do not have enough economic and professional knowledge to discuss or vote on major investments for climate protection that do not relate to their daily experiences. Nevertheless, many new ideas for climate-related measures were suggested. Of course, some voiced scepticism about benefits of more participation in the co-operative's decisions.

Solidary capacities

Members describe solidarity as collective action that creates shared values and, in consequence, allows for joint investment, for example in renovating flats or neighbourhood meeting spaces. According to their views, solidarity should be expressed by mutual respect, and by using personal, barrier-free forms of communication. Interestingly, members express their trust in the executive board and the co-operative structure as such by agreeing to decisions and by *not* showing up at the annual meeting – instead of legitimising the executive board or introducing topics they are interested in.

The aspect of solidarity within the co-operative can be seen, for example, in the realising of equal rises in rent for old and new buildings and in a special interest in joint events that deal with future issues. For example, in 2012 a world café on communication, climate change and neighbourhood was carried out with the members. The number of participants was encouragingly high and the feedback from the participants on improving the living environment was very positive. Proposals have been developed, for example, on urban gardening, vegetable crates and energy conservation.

Weiberwirtschaft eG

The women's co-operative WeiberWirtschaft eG in central Berlin was established in 1992 to support women in green businesses. After renovating a former industrial site, they provide approximately 7,100 square metres of office space for some seventy businesses of different sizes, including a children's daycare facility, conference rooms, restaurants, a start-up service for women in green businesses, a meeting space for networking activities, and thirteen flats. The majority of the members are based in Berlin but others live in a variety of locations all over Germany and Europe.

The ecofriendly renovation of the site, financially supported by public funds from the Berlin state, concentrated on reducing energy consumption and harmful emissions. Due to their ecologically responsible overall concept, the co-operative won several national and European awards for their ecological concept (e.g. Naturschutzbund Germany 2004) and innovation (Prize of the Regions, Council of Europe, 2008). Up to the present day, international delegations come to visit this 'biggest start-up for women in green businesses in Europe'. In addition, bike parking, unsealed yards, green roofs and façades were realised, and nesting boxes and bee stocks were added in 2014.

Participatory capacities

This co-operative is characterised by a heterogeneous member structure, as the interests of women renting the flats are somewhat different from those renting business spaces, those running the co-operative, and those living in Berlin, other parts of Germany or in Europe. In consequence, it is difficult for some women to attend the annual assembly, and personal communication between the residents and the business owners is more frequent than between other members.

Beyond annual meetings with comparatively low attendance rates, several work groups have existed over the years. Career counselling, networking and raising political awareness for women in green businesses constitute one major aim of the co-operative. It also has also become a European and global role model as many international visitors come to learn about environmentally friendly renovation and women-run green businesses. To its members, it also offers consultation on green investments, on recycling and on waste disposal. In practice, the decisions of the executive and the supervisory board are usually ratified by the members.

Solidary capacities

Supporting women in green businesses and collectively solving individual problems of women in business are the shared objectives of the members. Unlike with many other co-operatives, knowledge exchange on solidarity and its practical implementation are a regular topic at meetings and in the newsletter. As one member of the managing board stated, this is 'part of the overall business strategy'. In consequence, a significant rent reduction for office and business spaces during the start-up phase was implemented. Some women even feel that this co-operative is less profit-oriented than others, as the members are economically independent from the co-operative.

Solidarity among members is shown by their investing collectively in printers, internet provision, counselling services and recycling systems. Similar to the Spar- and Bauverein Hannover, members argue that solidarity is also apparent in personal forms of communication, in mutual support in daily matters such as swapping flats according to changing needs, in sharing rent for collectively-used office spaces or in lending money for the membership fee.

Möckernkiez eG

Another housing co-operative is the Möckernkiez Initiative in Berlin, registered as a co-operative in 2009. Its 1,500 members (in 2014) plan to build and inhabit a new neighbourhood in the inner city with ten to twelve apartment blocks, creating 460 flats and nineteen business units by 2017.

Members aim to relate eco-friendliness to business and argue that (socially) sustainable urban development can only be based on a more systematic use of ecologic building materials while making living conditions more sustainable. Some of the business units will be used for public children's and youth clubs open to all, a kindergarten, an accessible hotel and an organic supermarket. It explicitly targets the ecological dimension of sustainability by constructing passive houses with ecological building materials (including rooftop and wall greening), by raising awareness of natural resources and by introducing new technologies such as wastewater heat usage, block heating stations, photovoltaic rooftop systems and smart energy grids. In addition, the members share a vision of affordable housing that is intergenerational, barrier free, multicultural and socially inclusive.

Participatory capacities

During planning stages, bimonthly members' meetings with discussions on various topics took place that were each attended by more than 200 members. In addition, various groups worked on concepts and strategies (mobility, barrier-free structures, participation, ecology, the design of common and public areas etc.) in order to include individual ideas and needs – sometimes with support of external experts. In addition, a concept for participation within the co-operative was developed by the managing board, describing the different forms and structures of co-operative participation that would be incorporated.

Many members conceive the group explicitly to be not only a housing co-operative, but a network of civil society members shaping their neighbourhood, including various other associations and institutions. This is echoed in several statements that the co-operative as an organisation as well as its individual members should actively contribute to integrating people with less money and to reducing poverty, social neglect and unemployment locally. But they are also aware that their current make-up, with a majority of senior citizens, might constrain a diversification of their member structure. Despite the high levels of participation among members, the daily running of the co-operative business is still delegated to the executive and the supervisory board. Some conflicts emerged between members and the managing board because of differing ideas on how much time would be needed for implementation and on how much money would be spent on specific measures.[35]

Since, at time of writing, the co-operative has not yet started to build the neighbourhood, the extent to which its ambitious aims will be realised is unclear. The general public's reception of the project, however, can be described as positive. According to some members' statements the varied methods of communication have already triggered learning processes among members, the executive board and local politicians. This communication has also increased the quality of discussions and the members' dedication to the project.

Solidary capacities

Members of this housing co-operative defined solidarity as the production of collectively owned material and immaterial values that couldn't be created by individuals. A prominent topic in meetings and discussions is the relation of collective approaches to climate protection and to social inclusiveness, as several members emphasised the importance of barrier-free neighbourhoods and the integration of people with less money in co-operative structures and ecofriendly lifestyles, as well as a general need to reduce resource consumption.

Examples given for collectively-owned material values were joint investment in larger electrical devices (e.g. washing machines), sharing cars and providing services for both members and neighbours (such as children's daycare). In order for residents to relate to their neighbourhood, the co-operative has already opened a meeting space for both members and non-members, where monthly energy counselling services are offered and group meetings can take place. Appreciated intangible values are meeting friends and neighbours; working together; lending money in order that others might join the co-operative; a barrier-free culture of communication, respect and awareness; the ability to give and receive criticism; exchanging knowledge on various matters; and networking. Some members of the co-operative whom the authors interviewed during a research project mentioned that the level of positive personal communication they experience could only be possible within a co-operative. Others remarked that they prefer not to have too many personal contacts within the co-operative, and that a limiting factor to actual solidarity could be the growing number of members.

Conclusions

While the German co-operative movement is in many aspects different from those in other countries, these three short illustrations of housing co-operatives provide insight into today's co-operative housing landscape – and into challenges experienced while implementing participatory and solidary structures in the context of local climate protection. With a traditionally strong focus on economic activities, a growing number of small and larger German housing co-operatives already implement environmentally sustainable solutions. One major challenge for a transition towards a sustainable future though is the systematic connection of economic, social and environmental sustainability while dealing with diversity and complexity. In consequence, it is quite difficult to provide standardised recommendations for a co-operative transition towards sustainability.

Individual contributions to participation and solidarity within a co-operative are not necessarily a consequence of its size or age. But we can identify some crucial aspects that facilitate participatory and solidary structures for local climate protection. Raising awareness for issues of sustainability within a member-based organisation is clearly related to the objectives of the co-operative and to the interests of its members. In addition, providing different opportunities for communication and participation is crucial, as they allow for informal and formal exchange of opinions, knowledge, concerns and decisions. These opportunities may range from local meeting spaces to consultation processes and workshops about specific climate-related topics, and to establishing network structures with other, climate-aware organisations.

While it has to be stated that the institutionalised structure of a co-operative is not the only form of organisation to successfully implement local climate protection measures, linking co-operatives' values such as participation and solidarity to climate protection might be a major asset – especially if a co-operative as an entity engages in climate protection. Nonetheless, in order to achieve results in climate protection, co-operatives need to network with politics, the economy and civil-society groups. While many larger housing co-operatives (particularly in eastern Germany) are already working closely with municipalities, smaller co-operatives tend to not be perceived as potential partners for local climate protection at this time. In any case, personal contacts with politicians and excellent public relations are indispensable. But there are many small co-operatives with unpaid executive boards and limited resources who are struggling for their existence on a day-to-day basis, with not much time left for networking and lobbying. Nonetheless, with an already stronger emphasis on sustainability and climate protection, co-operatives have the potential to develop long-term solutions for their members' benefit, as well as to promote new, more sustainable behavioural and social patterns of action for individuals, civil society, policy-makers and economic actors.

Notes

1 Intergovernmental Panel on Climate Change (IPCC), *Climate Change 2014: Synthesis Report, Contribution of Working Groups I, II and III to the Fifth Assessment Report of the Intergovernmental Panel on Climate Change* (Geneva: IPCC, 2014); see also IPCC, *Fourth Assessment Report on Scientific Aspects of Climate Change for Researchers, Students, and Policymakers* (Geneva: IPCC, 2007).

2 Climate protection in this context refers to actions taken to reduce greenhouse gas emissions, while adaptation to climate change refers to behavioural and structural adjustment to changing conditions of the environment.

3 E. Ostrom, 'Nested externalities and polycentric institutions: must we wait for global solutions to climate change before taking actions at other scales?', *Economic Theory* 49:2 (2012), 353–69.

4 N. W. Adger, *Social Capital and Climate Change*, Tyndall Centre Working Paper 8, (Norwich: University of East Anglia, 2001), p. 1.

5 J. Röpke, 'Wirtschaftlicher Wandel und genossenschaftliches Unternehmertum' [Economic change and co-operative entrepreneurship] in Marburg Consult, ed., *Genossenschaftliche Selbsthilfe und Struktureller Wandel* [Co-operative self-help and structural change] (Marburg: Marburg Consult, 1992), pp. 13–33.

6 B. Flieger, *Produktivgenossenschaft als fortschrittsfähige Organisation: Theorie, Fallstudie, Handlungshilfen* [Productive associations as progressive proof organisations: theory, case study, practical aids] (Marburg: Metropolis Verlag, 1996), p. 33; International Co-operative Alliance (ICA), 'Statement of co-operative identity, values and principles' (1995), http://ica.coop/en/whats-co-op/co-operative-identity-values-principles (accessed 15 February 2016).

7 C. Sanchez Bajo and B. Roelants, *Capital and the Debt Trap: Learning From Cooperatives in the Global Crisis* (Basingstoke and New York: Palgrave Macmillan, 2011); T. Brockmeier and U. Fehl, eds, *Volkswirtschaftliche Theorie der genossenschaftlichen Kooperation* [Economic theory of co-operative co-operation] (Göttingen: Vandenhoeck und Ruprecht, 2007); and R. Greve, *Globalisierung der Wirtschaft: Auswirkungen auf lokale Unternehmen* [Globalisation of the economy: impact on local businesses], Münsteraner Diskussionspapiere zum Nonprofit-Sektor Münster Nr. 4 [discussion papers for

the nonprofit sector No. 4] (2000), http://nbn-resolving.de/urn:nbn:de:0168-ssoar-373851, accessed 20 January 2016, p. 7.

8 F. Braudel, *Civilization and Capitalism*, 3 vols, trans. S. Reynolds (New York: Harper & Row, 1979).

9 M. Patera, 'Genossenschaftliche Förderbilanz' [Co-operative funding balance] in J. Laurinkari, ed., *Genossenschaftswesen: Lehr- und Handbuch* [Co-operative studies: teaching and manual] (Munich: Oldenbourg, 1990), pp. 285–301, p. 287.

10 UN Habitat, *Cities and Climate Change: Global Report on Human Settlements* (London: UN Habitat, 2011).

11 V. Beuthien, T. Brockmeier and H. Klose, *Materialien zum Genossenschaftsgesetz, Band V: Genossenschaftsrecht der SBZ und DDR 1945–1990* [Materials for Co-operatives Act, Volume V: co-operative law of SBZ and DDR 1945–1990] (Göttingen: Vandenhoeck & Ruprecht, 1997).

12 C. Schröder and H. Walk, *Genossenschaften und Klimaschutz: Akteure für zukunftsfähige, solidarische Städte, Buchreihe 'Bürgergesellschaft und Demokratie'* [Co-operative and climate protection: sustainable solidarity cities, for 'Civil Society and Democracy book series'] (Heidelberg: Springer, 2014).

13 C. von Blanckenburg, 'Genossenschaftliche Partizipationsstrukturen als Teil der besonderen Handlungsmöglichkeiten im Klimaschutz: Partizipation in Genossenschaften und im Nachhaltigkeitsdiskurs' [Co-operative participation structures as part of the special opportunities for action on climate change: participation in co-operatives and the sustainability discourse] in Schröder and Walk, *Genossenschaften und Klimaschutz*, pp. 257–83.

14 Ibid.

15 Schröder and Walk, *Genossenschaften und Klimaschutz*.

16 W. Vogt, *Genossenschaften – eine andere Form des Wirtschaftens: Ein Reader der Parlamentarischen Linken in der SPD-Bundestagsfraktion* [Co-operatives – another form of economic activity: a reader of the Parliamentary Left in the SPD parliamentary group] (Berlin, 2011), p. 30 fn.

17 H. Bonus, *Das Selbstverständnis moderner Genossenschaften: Rückbindung von Kreditgenossenschaften an ihre Mitglieder* [The self-image of modern co-operatives: back donation of credit unions to their members] (Tübingen: C. B. Mohr, 1994), pp. 45–6; Vogt, *Genossenschaften*, p. 22.

18 S. Gherardi and A. Masiero, 'Solidarity as a networking skill and a trust relation: its implications for co-operative development', *Economic and Industrial Democracy* 11 (1990), 553–74, p. 554.

19 C. Schröder, 'Neue Formen städtischer Solidarität: Das Beispiel Genossenschaften' [New forms of urban solidarity: the example of co-operatives] in Schröder and Walk, *Genossenschaften und Klimaschutz*, pp. 73–91.

20 Vogt, *Genossenschaften*.

21 W. Hardtwig, '"Genossenschaft" in der deutschen Geschichte: Wirtschafts- und Lebensformen' ['Co-operative' in German history: forms of economy and ways of life] in H. J. Rösner and F. Schulz-Nieswandt, eds, *Beiträge der genossenschaftlichen Selbsthilfe zur wirtschaftlichen und sozialen Entwicklung*

[Contributions of co-operative self-help to economic and social development], Teilband 1, Neue Kölner Genossenschaftswissenschaft Band 5 (Sub-band 1, New Cologne Co-operative Science vol. 5) (Berlin: LIT Verlag, 2009), pp. 27–48.

22 M. Stappel, *Die deutschen Genossenschaften 2009: Entwicklungen – Meinungen – Zahlen (Sonderthema: Nach der Krise)* [The German co-operatives 2009: developments – opinions – numbers (special issue: after the crisis)] (Wiesbaden: DG-Verlag, 2009).

23 D. Atmaca, 'Produktivgenossenschaften: Zwischen Utopie und Realismus' [Producer co-operatives: between utopia and realism] in T. Brockmeier and U. Fehl, eds, *Volkswirtschaftliche Theorie der (genossenschaftlichen) Kooperation: Marburger Schriften zum Genossenschaftswesen* [Economic theory of co-operation, Marburgers' writings on the co-operative system], Vol. 100 (Marburg: ifG Marburg, 2007), pp. 837–46.

24 DZ Bank Research, *Konjunktur und Kapitalmarkt: Genossenschaften in Deutschland* [Economic and capital markets: co-operatives in Germany] (Frankfurt am Main: DZ Bank Research, 2011).

25 S. Elsen, 'Genossenschaften als transformative Kräfte auf dem Weg in die Postwachstumsgesellschaft' [Co-operatives as transformative forces on the way to the post-growth society] in Schröder and Walk, *Genossenschaften und Klimaschutz*, pp. 34–47.

26 Those amendments made it easier to establish co-operatives, as the necessary number of founding members was reduced from seven to three and the compulsory auditing period for smaller co-operatives was extended from annual to biannual auditing.

27 F. Pollich, *Die Auswirkungen der Genossenschaftsrechtsreform von 2006 auf die Neugründungen von Genossenschaften* [The effects of the co-operative law reform of 2006 on the establishment of new co-operatives], Arbeitspapiere des Forschungsinstituts für Genossenschaftswesen an der Universität Erlangen-Nürnberg [Working Papers of the Research Institute of Co-operative Studies at the University of Erlangen-Nuremberg] 36 (Nuremberg: Universität Erlangen-Nürnberg, 2009).

28 B. Flieger, 'Energiegenossenschaften: Eine klimaverantwortliche, bürgernahe Energiewirtschaft ist möglich' [Energy co-operatives: a climate responsible, community-based energy economy is possible] in S. Elsen, ed., *Ökosoziale Transformation: Solidarische Ökonomie und die Gestaltung des Gemeinwesens* [Eco-social transformation: the solidarity economy and the design of the community] (Neu-Ulm: Ag Spak, 2011), pp. 315–38.

29 J. R. Müller and L. Holstenkamp, *Zum Stand von Energiegenossenschaften in Deutschland: Aktualisierter Überblick über Zahlen und Entwicklungen zum 31.12.2014* [On the state of energy co-operatives in Germany: an updated overview of pay and developments to 31.12.2014] (Lüneburg: Leuphana Universität Lüneburg, 2015).

30 H. Klemisch, 'Energiegenossenschaften als regionale Antwort auf den Klimawandel' [Energy co-operatives as a regional response to climate change] in Schröder and Walk, *Genossenschaften und Klimaschutz*, pp. 149–66, p. 150.

31 A. Zimmer, 'Genossenschaften als zivilgesellschaftliche Organisationen?' [Co-operatives as civil society organisations?], in H. J. Rösner and F. Schulz-Nieswandt, *Beiträge der genossenschaftlichen Selbsthilfe zur wirtschaftlichen und sozialen Entwicklung* [Contributions of co-operative self-help to economic and social development] (Berlin: LIT Verlag, 2009), pp. 143–56; H.-H. Münkner and G. Ringle, eds, *Neue Genossenschaften und innovative Aktionsfelder: Grundlagen und Fallstudien* [New co-operatives and innovative fields of action: principles and case studies] (Baden-Baden: Nomos Verlagsgesellschaft, 2010).

32 D. Atmaca, 'Genossenschaften in Zeiten raschen Wandels: Chancen einer nachhaltigen Organisationsform' [Co-operatives in times of rapid change: chances for a sustainable organisation] in Schröder and Walk, *Genossenschaften und Klimaschutz*, pp. 49–72.

33 Sanchez Bajo and Roelants, *Capital and the Debt Trap*, p. 107.

34 Bundesministerium für Verkehr, Bau und Stadtentwicklung (BMVBS), ed., 'Aktivierung von Potenzialen genossenschaftlichen Wohnens: Evaluierung der Empfehlungen der Expertenkommission Wohnungsgenossenschaften im Forschungsprogramm 'Experimenteller Wohnungs- und Städtebau (ExWoSt)' [Activation of potential co-operative housing, an evaluation of the recommendations of the Commission of Experts on housing co-operatives in the research programme 'Experimental Housing and Urban Development (ExWoSt)'], BMVBS online publication No. 25 (Berlin: BMVBS, 2010), www.bbr.bund.de/BBSR/DE/Veroeffentlichungen/BMVBS/Online/2010/DL_ON252010.pdf?__blob=publicationFile&v=2 (accessed 15 February 2016); BMVBW, *Wohnungsgenossenschaften: Potenziale und Perspektiven, Bericht der Expertenkommission Wohnungsgenossenschaften* [Housing co-operatives: potential and prospects, report of the Expert Commission on Housing Co-operatives] (Berlin: BMVBW, 2004).

35 von Blanckenburg, 'Genossenschaftliche Partizipationsstrukturen', p. 161.

Further reading

W. Neil Adger, 'Social capital, collective action, and adaptation to climate change' in M. Voss, ed., *Der klimawandel: Sozialwissenschaftliche Perspektiven* [Climate change: social science perpectives] (Wiesbaden: VS Verlag für Sozialwissenschaften, 2010), pp. 327–45.

G. Alber, 'Die sozialen Dimensionen von Klimawandel und Klimapolitik' [The social dimensions of climate change and climate policy] in C. Schröder and H. Walk, eds, *Genossenschaften und Klimaschutz: Akteure für zukunftsfähige, solidarische Städte* [Co-operatives and climate protection: actors for sustainable, solidarity cities] (Berlin: Springer VS, 2014), pp. 109–33.

D. Atmaca, *Kooperation im Wettbewerb: Kontinuität im Wandel. Identität und Erfolg der produktivgenossenschaftlichen Organisationsform* [Co-operation in competition: continuity in change – identity and success of producer co-operative structures] (Aachen: Shaker Verlag, 2002).

C. von Blanckenburg, 'Co-operatives and climate protection' in O. Renn, A. Reichel and J. Bauer, eds, *Civil Society for Sustainability: A Guidebook for Connecting Science and Society* (Bremen: Europaeischer Hochschulverlag GmbH, 2012), pp. 107–25.

C. von Blanckenburg, 'Genossenschaftliche Partizpationsstrukturen als Teil der besonderen Handlugnsmöglichkeitne im Klimaschutz', in C. Schröder and H. Walk, *Genossenschaften und Klimaschutz: Akteure für zukunftsfähige, solidarische Städte* [Co-operatives and climate protection: actors for sustainable, solidarity cities] (Berlin: Springer VS, 2014), pp. 257–83.

K.-W. Brand and G. Warsewa, 'Lokale Agenda 21: Perspektiven eines neuen Politiktypus' [local Agenda 21: perspectives on a new policy type], *GAIA* 12:1 (2003), 15–23.

B. Flieger, 'Genossenschaften auf dem Vormarsch: Bürgerliche Energieerzeuger entdecken die Vorteile einer bisher ungenutzten Rechtsform' [Co-operatives on the rise: civil energy producers are discovering the benefits of a previously unused legal form], *Photon* 2 (2009), 78–84.

M. Hanisch, ed., *Genossenschaftsmodelle: Zwischen Auftrag und Anpassung* [Co-operative models: between order and adjustment] (Berlin: Institut für Genossenschaftswesen der Humboldt-Universität zu Berlin, 2002).

M. Hunecke, *Verantwortung, Lebensstile und Umweltverhalten* [Responsibility, lifestyles and environmental behaviour] (Heidelberg: Asanger, 2000).

D. Keppler, H. Walk, E. Töpfer and H. L. Dienel, *Erneuerbare Energien ausbauen! Erfahrungen und Perspektiven regionaler Akteure in Ost und West* [Expanding renewables! Experiences and perspectives of regional actors in East and West] (Munich: Oekom, 2009).

K. Kern and H. Bulkeley, 'Cities, Europeanization and multi-level governance: governing climate change through transnational municipal networks', *Journal of Common Market Studies*, 47:1 (2009), 309–32.

M. Olson, *The Logic of Collective Action: Public Goods and the Theory of Groups* (Cambridge, MA: Harvard University Press, 1965).

E. Ostrom, 'Nested externalities and polycentric institutions: must we wait for global solutions to climate change before taking actions at other scales?', *Economic Theory* 49:2 (2012), 353–69.

Projekt 100% Erneuerbare Energie Regionen (Project 100% – renewable energy regions), *Schriftliche Befragung von Erneuerbare-Energien-Regionen in Deutschland: Regionale Ziele, Aktivitäten und Einschätzungen in Bezug auf 100% Erneuerbare Energien in Regionen* [Written survey of renewable energy regions in Germany: regional objectives, activities and assessments based on 100% renewable energy in regions] (Kassel: Universität Kassel, 2009).

A. Smith, *Multi-level Governance: Towards an Analysis of Renewable Energy Governance in the English Regions*, SPRU Electronic Working Paper, Series 153 (Brighton: SPRU, 2006).

G. Spaargaren and A. Mol, 'Greening global consumption: redefining politics and authority', *Global Environmental Change* 18 (2008), 350–9.

P. Späth, M. Koblmüller, K. Kubeczko, F. Faber, J. Bärnthaler, H. Bergmann, C. Luttenberger and A. Breisler, '"EnergieRegionen": Wirksame Leitbildprozesse und Netzwerke zur Gestaltung des sozio-technischen Wandels' ['Energy regions': effective mission statement processes and networks for the design of socio-technical change], *Projektbericht im Rahmen der Programmlinie Energiesysteme der Zukunft im Auftrag des österreichischen Bundesministeriums für Verkehr, Innovation und Technologie* [Project report in the framework of the program for energy systems of the future on behalf of the Austrian Federal Ministry for Transport, Innovation and Technology] (2007).

I. Stieß and D. Hayn, *Ernährungsstile im Alltag: Ergebnisse einer repräsentativen Untersuchung* [Eating patterns in everyday life: results of a representative study], Ernährungswende-Diskussionspapier 5 [Foodways discussion Paper 5] (Frankfurt: Institut für sozial-ökologische Forschung, 2005).

United Nations Task Team on Social Dimensions of Climate Change, *The Social Dimensions of Climate Change: Discussion Draft* (2011), www.iom.int/jahia/webdav/shared/shared/mainsite/activities/env_degradation/cop17/SDCC-Social-dimensions-of-climate-change-Paper.pdf (accessed 20 January 2016).

H. Walk, *Partizipative Governance: Beteiligungsformen und Beteiligungsrechte im Mehrebenensystem der Klimapolitik* [Participatory governance: forms of participation and participation rights in a multi-level system of climate policy] (Münster: VS Verlag für Sozialwissenschaften, 2008).

G. Wendorf and C. Wemheuer, 'Wohnungsgenossenschaften als städtische Akteure im Klimaschutz' [Housing associations as urban actors in climate change] in C. Schröder and H. Walk, eds, *Genossenschaften und Klimaschutz: Akteure für zukunftsfähige, solidarische Städte* [Co-operatives and climate protection: actors for sustainable, solidary cities] (Berlin: Springer VS, 2014), pp. 167–201.

Wissenschaftliche Beirat der Bundesregierung Globale Umweltveränderungen [German Advisory Council on Global Change, WBGU], *Welt im Wandel: Gesellschaftsvertrag für eine Große Transformation* [World in transition: social contract for a great transformation] (Berlin: WBGU, 2012).

13

The co-operative identity: good for poverty reduction?

Rowshan Hannan

Introduction

As discussions crystallise on the ways in which co-operatives reduce poverty, an important question emerges as to whether this is their purpose.[1] Indeed, the definition of co-operatives emphasised by global bodies, such as the International Co-operative Alliance (ICA) and the International Labour Organization (ILO), recognises their identity as enterprises that provide economic opportunities for members rather than referring to any role in reducing poverty. It has been argued that, unlike some other community-based mechanisms, 'co-operatives are not designed to help the poor'[2] and that they are not 'instruments for development'.[3] Münkner argues that co-operatives and the poverty reduction agenda do not necessarily go hand in hand. In some countries, the growing acknowledgement of co-operatives as businesses within the private sector places them in the category of 'wealth creators and not poverty reducers'.[4] This means that unlike some bodies, such as non-governmental organisations, co-operatives may not be focused so much on reducing poverty as generating wealth. Does this mean that co-operatives have no place in poverty-reduction debates? Other authors have argued that although co-operatives should not be seen as instruments for reducing poverty, they are a means through which groups of people can gain advantages that they could not do individually.[5] If this approach is adopted, Birchall asserts, co-operatives have the potential to reduce poverty 'more effectively than other forms of economic organization'.[6]

In this chapter I discuss whether and how the identity of co-operatives allows for an important contribution to reducing poverty, irrespective of their actual intention in this area. I explore this identity through a set of core values, and discuss why this means that co-operatives are more likely to engage in multiple activities that are important to members, their families and communities. These multiple activities can combine to reduce poverty, particularly in member households. This was an in-depth case-study research undertaken with dairy farmers in Kenya. It contributes research-based evidence linking co-operatives to poverty reduction at the household level, as well as improving understanding of how dairy farmer co-operatives raise household milk income.[7]

I begin by exploring the co-operative identity and the extent to which it is 'good' for poverty reduction. I then present the case-study research in Kenya, exploring the links between co-operative identity and poverty reduction through a case-study co-operative and village. I discuss the different areas of activities in which the case-study co-operative engages, and how these multiple activities combine to impact poverty in co-operative member and non-member households. Finally, I present some conclusions, drawing on the importance of a co-operative identity for allowing engagement in multiple activities that can reduce poverty.

The co-operative identity and its advantages in reducing poverty

The co-operative identity is based on six internationally recognised values:

- Self-help: in co-operatives people help each other whilst helping themselves by working together for mutual benefit.
- Self-responsibility: individuals within co-operatives act responsibly and play a full part in the organisation.
- Democracy: a co-operative will be structured so that members have control over the organisation.
- Equality: each member will have equal rights and benefits (according to their contribution).
- Equity: members will be treated justly and fairly.
- Solidarity: members will support each other and other co-operatives.[8]

These values emphasise co-operatives' nature of self-help and self-responsibility, and are core to their functioning as enterprises that meet the needs of their owner members. This includes bringing people together to take charge of their own situation and organising themselves for improved outcomes. Co-operative values also emphasise their democratic nature, where members are central to the decision-making processes that control and direct the way co-operatives operate. The democratic structure and processes, which the values embed, allow members to articulate their priorities and take them forward through their co-operative. This directs ownership of development processes to the people themselves, allowing them control of decisions that affect their lives, solving their own problems through the co-operative and being the agents of their own development.[9] Co-operatives' identity is also based on values of equality, equity and solidarity, where members participate equally in the co-operative, enjoy its benefits in a fair way and work together to support each other. It emphasises the importance of the way members participate in the co-operative, which can support or undermine its operations. Where members participate equally (such as women and men, the young and old) and support each other, its benefits may be disbursed more widely and enjoyed in an equitable way within the membership. The way members and co-operative leaders (such as board directors) embed these six values and take them forward through the co-operative's organisational structures and processes is important here.

This identity, based on their core values, means that co-operatives often have both economic as well as social goals, giving them a 'dual nature'.[10] Economic goals emphasise the economic interests of members and others in the wider community, which includes activities that help generate greater income and other financial benefits. It might also include activities that are not directly linked to the business of the co-operative, but nonetheless promote the economic interests of individuals. Social goals look beyond individual or co-operative economic needs to wider social benefits within and beyond the membership, to incorporate a perception of co-operatives as associations that also 'build social and human capital'.[11] In pursuing their social goals, co-operatives may work to meet member priorities in areas such as education or training, or support the communities where they live in other ways. This dual nature means that co-operatives often have multiple objectives,[12] some linked to their economic identity and some to their social identity. In pursuing these multiple objectives co-operatives might engage in multiple areas of activity, allowing them to play an important role in reducing poverty.

Case study research and methods

This research explored how the co-operative identity provided distinct advantages in reducing poverty through a case-study co-operative and in case-study households. It focused on aspects of the co-operative identity around values of self-help and responsibility, which required meeting owner-member needs in various areas. It also focused on exploring the link between the co-operative's democratic nature and poverty reduction. The other values of equality, equity and solidarity emphasise how members participate in and benefit from co-operatives, and are also important in understanding how they reduce poverty. However, the limited time and resources for the research kept my exploration to the three former areas.

The research involved fieldwork in 2012, within a district in the semi-arid Eastern province of Kenya.[13] Over 60 per cent of the population in the district lives below the poverty line,[14] compared to the national average of between 34 per cent and 42 per cent.[15] In the district over 90 per cent of households are engaged in livestock rearing, with the dairy industry identified as the key source of livelihood.[16] The research included working with a case-study co-operative in the dairy sub-sector. The co-operative was established in 1976, and now has over 2,000 members across a number of villages in its surrounding area. Approximately 200 members are active, of which one-third are women. The main requirement for membership is the ability to deliver milk regularly to the co-operative. The co-operative has a nine-member board of directors, directly elected by the membership for three-year terms. The research also included working with a case-study village, which had 123 homesteads (or 984 people) and a total of fifteen members from the case study co-operative (eight male and seven female).

The main business of the case-study co-operative was to 'bulk' the individual milk of its members, market it and pay members at the end of the month according to their milk deposits. It operated in a competitive environment, with many private milk traders in the local area. These traders also bought milk directly from smallholder farmers, but (unlike the co-operative) paid them cash on delivery. The case-study co-operative did not have any explicit intentions to reduce poverty, with objectives in these areas not outlined in its strategic planning documents. Instead its vision and mission statements focused on improving the quality of life of members and the community by being lead processors and marketers of dairy products. Its main objectives were to support farmers to improve milk supply through a range of services including training, veterinary and farm inputs, and credit facilities.

The empirical study was largely carried out at the local level with co-operative members, non-members and others within the household, as well as with staff and board directors of the co-operative. This was a qualitative in-depth study that focused on understanding the perspectives of research participants, using semi-structured interviews as well as different participatory methods. Fourteen households participated in the research, seven member and seven non-member households.[17] Amongst the member households, there were five that were active (i.e. regularly delivering milk to the co-operative) and two that were inactive (i.e. had not delivered milk for a consecutive six-month period). A total of fifteen individual interviews were carried out, which included eight co-operative members (this included two people from a dual-member household),[18] and seven non-members. Five different participatory exercises were carried out with each household, which allowed exploration of household dynamics and strategies. These were

- household matrix scoring on changes to income;
- household matrix scoring on access;
- household matrix scoring on expenditure;
- household decision-making scale; and
- household exercise on milk yields.[19]

Wherever possible the exercises were undertaken with two adults, usually the person interviewed and their spouse or daughter-in-law. All exercises at the village and household levels were designed to be accessible to illiterate or semi-literate people, with minimal writing used in exercise materials (often just dates or numbers).

The empirical study captured data retrospectively at various points over a five-year period. Many of the participatory exercises asked for details on how things had changed from 2007, to 2009–10 and to 2012 (for example, changes to milk yields over these three 'snapshots').[20] The 2009–10 snapshot allowed the research to capture changes during the drought that occurred over this period in the case-study area, and to better understand the extent of recovery within households and villages. Much of the analysis focused on a comparison between active member households and non-member households.

The multiple activities of the case-study co-operative

I show here how the co-operative identity, specifically based around values of self-help and self-responsibility as well as democracy, meant that the case-study co-operative pursued both economic and social goals. This resulted in it engaging in a number of different activities beyond milk marketing. I discuss two important activity areas of the co-operative, delivery of farm inputs and services as well as of member training, examining how these activities emerged and developed to meet the needs of members and their families.

The importance of co-operative inputs and services

Alongside its main milk marketing business, the case study co-operative ran a farm inputs store supplying agricultural and veterinary products to members as well as non-members. The co-operative competed directly with a number of other input suppliers in the local area. It also provided credit (with no interest charged) to active members against purchases at the store, which was deducted from their milk payments at the end of the month. This was a unique feature that the private inputs stores did not provide to their customers.

The majority of participants in the village confirmed that they regularly used the farm inputs store at the co-operative, and that prices there were competitive.[21] A non-member described the service he receives at the store:

> I go there because they always advise me. They tell me what portions of feed I should give my cattle, also the type of feed. The minute you go to the store they ask you many questions – is it a bull, a heifer, size of cow, is it local or hybrid? These are the questions they ask you before they sell you feed for your cow – so you get the right type of powder [supplementary feed].[22]

He describes here a personal advisory service that was available to him at the store, even as a non-member, to ensure that he bought appropriate feeds for his dairy cows. Another non-member referred to the type of products he was able to access from the store: 'They select the right seeds for the farmers. Location X[23] is amongst the dry areas, so they choose the better seeds that are drought resistant and mature in two months, and bring them down to farmers.'[24]

The advisory support, as well as careful seed selection, shows the co-operative supporting values of self-help and self-responsibility amongst farmers, and meeting needs that they might have to improve farm productivity. This shows the co-operative not just pursuing economic goals (by improving milk productivity of members and milk deposits to the co-operative) but also wider social goals through advice to non-members as well as bringing appropriate inputs (including agricultural inputs) to the general area. Of the fifteen case-study participants, all thirteen who regularly used the farm inputs store could not recall a time when it did not have all the inputs they required within the 2007 to 2012 study period, including through the 2009 drought:[25] 'very rare that the society store does not have what you need'.[26]

The provision of credit at the store to active members can be seen to deliver economic goals around improving milk production as well as store revenue. However, the way credit was delivered suggests that wider considerations were also taken into account. A member describes a flexible credit mechanism where 'your bill at the store might be carried forward to the next month'[27] if you are not able to pay it. The manager at the co-operative talked confidently about finding payment solutions through communication, when members found it difficult to repay: 'We follow-up, write letters, call them to the office. We make arrangement on how to pay by other means, such as payment by cash ... can also agree to use their dividends or bonuses.'[28] The two statements by the member and the manager suggest that the delivery of a flexible credit service at the store helped to ease member access to essential farm inputs, including through the 2009 drought.

Values of self-help and self-responsibility can also be found in the co-operative's direct provision of artificial insemination (AI) services to dairy farmers to help improve dairy cow breeds: 'When you need a doctor for AI and you don't have the money, you can get it from the society and pay at the end of the month.'[29] Although this service would have helped to improve members' milk delivery to the co-operative (supporting economic goals), its provision on credit (accessible to members throughout the 2007 to 2012 study period) shows the co-operative recognising member access constraints and easing this by reducing the need for cash (thus pursuing social goals). Members also talked about being able to access a veterinary doctor, in a similar way, through the co-operative.[30] The co-operative's engagement in these multiple areas of activity meant that these important services were available to members (as well as non-members in some areas), and were free at the point of access.

Training: a potent combination for poverty reduction?

The research found evidence of the case-study co-operative using its democratic nature to understand the training needs of farmers, and striving to meet them. The manager at the co-operative talked about a 'consultation process with farmers', referring to five different methods:

1. talking to members to identify needs;
2. identifying production trends;
3. analysing data from member surveys carried out by a partner;[31]
4. during Annual General Meetings (AGMs), trying 'to understand the problems that members face'; and
5. having board members 'who are the elected representatives from the grassroots'.[32]

These five areas outline the different ways that the co-operative uses its democratic structure to understand member needs. It suggests that the manager recognised the members' control and direction of the co-operative, and sought out mechanisms to gather their views. This included using the AGMs as well as elected representatives (i.e. board directors). The board director representing the case-study village talked of how he used meetings, organised by himself in his electoral zone with members from the case-study village as well as others, to arrange separate farmer-to-farmer training sessions for his area: 'Most of the time I let the community identify what kind of training they want.'[33]

This all led to the co-operative taking a holistic approach to training, working with extension officers from both the Ministry of Livestock Development and the Ministry of Agriculture, as well as private inputs suppliers. It facilitated training in a wide range of areas important to members and their families, meeting both social and economic goals. This included training on agricultural farming to fuel-efficient stoves and fruit farming.[34] With private farm input suppliers the manager explained how they do not just accept the training that the suppliers are offering, but consider what is needed through board directors who 'represent their members' and 'the person at the [co-operative's farm inputs] store knows the complaints and needs of members'.[35] Out of a total of eight training sessions organised with private suppliers in 2012, four had been initiated by the co-operative and four by suppliers.[36] This shows the co-operative promoting areas important to members by using its democratic structures and values to seek out the perspective of farmers and direct services accordingly.

Although the majority of training sessions facilitated through the co-operative were open to non-members, only approximately 20–25 per cent of attendees were from this group (this included training sessions organised by the board director representing the case-study village).[37] This is, perhaps, not surprising given that the co-operative's direct interaction with communities is largely through members. The remainder of this section focuses specifically on dairy farming, to allow exploration of how training in this area contributed to changed practices.

Training on dairy farming was reported to have changed the way farmers feed and look after their cattle, as well as the use of AI. Participants talked in these sessions of how they: 'Also learned about digging holes and planting napier[38] grass. Also trained that if there's dry land where nothing grows we can plant grass and make it useful.'[39] The participant discussed how dairy farming training helped him to change land use, and increase on-farm production of animal feeds. Others talked of the impact of changed feeding practices: 'Earlier on, after harvesting we would leave [maize] stalks to be eaten by ants. We were taught that this could be used as feed during dry season. So now we store them in sacks.' When asked if this helped, the participant responded, 'Yes, a lot. They increase the milk yields of the cows.'[40]

The majority of the training that participants described did not include follow-up activities or distribution of inputs. However, members in the case-study village talked of being able to access all their farm input needs through the co-operative's store and veterinary services.[41] This suggests that, following training, members in the village would have had access to inputs on credit (such as seeds or AI) to support changed practices in many of the training areas.

Impacting poverty in member/non-member households

So far I have discussed the link between co-operative identity, as understood through the core values, and poverty reduction. I explored how this identity led to the co-operative engaging in multiple activities (e.g. farm inputs, veterinary services and training) to meet the economic and social needs of its owner-members and others. I now examine whether and how these multiple activities improved dairy farming to impact poverty, comparing member and non-member households. Although these activities also impacted other areas, such as agricultural farming, I look specifically at dairy farming to provide a more focused discussion of the links to poverty reduction.

Changes to dairy cow ownership

In the case-study village members and non-members talked about the size of their dairy cow herd increasing gradually over the years. Four out of the five active member households, and the same number in non-member households (only five of the seven non-member households owned dairy cows in 2007), confirmed a growing herd: '2006 – got one [dairy cow]. Registered at co-operative, then bought another two. Then they started giving birth. We don't sell the dairy cows – just sell the male calves.'[42] This statement describes a breeding and buying/selling process where, despite the 2009 drought and the dairy cows lost over this period, the herd of one dairy cow in this household in 2006 increased to eight by 2012. Across participant member and non-member households, overall dairy-cow ownership increased from 2007 to 2012 (Table 13.1).

Table 13.1: Participant household dairy cow ownership from 2007 to 2012

Household type	Number of dairy cows owned		Percentage increase/decrease of total herd	Percentage of dairy herd deaths in 2009 drought
	2007	2012		
Active members	14	27	93%	14%
Non-members	5	12	140%	38%

The data in Table 13.1 is based on member and non-member interviews from the fourteen case-study households, with data amalgamated for each of the two household types. It shows that the percentage increase in dairy cows over the five-year study period was higher for non-member households than member households. I return to this issue below, showing how non-members were increasing their ownership of indigenous dairy cows, whereas members were more likely to invest in smaller herds of cows of higher-quality breeds. The co-operative was directly linked to increases in dairy-cow ownership, particularly by active members: 'Someone who's not a member – those that don't even have cattle, the society is encouraging them to acquire dairy cows and improve their lives.'[43] The director representing the case-study village explains this further: 'Many farmers have started dairy farming because of the society – they learnt that they can sustain their households through dairy farming'.[44]

This suggests that the co-operative identity, based on values of self-help and self-responsibility, helped it to portray dairy farming as an economically viable option to households.

Members and non-members also talked about dairy cows dying during the 2009 drought. Data collected in this area showed that member households performed better than non-members, with only 14 per cent of the active member herd lost compared with 38 per cent of the non-member herd (see Table 13.1). The co-operative's provision of farm inputs and services can help to explain these findings. I discussed above how the co-operative ensured a steady provision of agricultural and veterinary products through the farm inputs store to meet the needs of members and other customers, including through the 2009 drought. Although non-members could also purchase inputs from the store, they were not able to do this on credit, as members were able to. This would have reduced the latter's need for cash during this harsh period. The co-operative also provided veterinary services to members over this period, indicating that if cows fell sick then members in the village would have had access to a veterinarian on credit. This suggests that the co-operative's multiple activities in these areas, through farm inputs and services (including the provision of credit), would have helped to lower dairy-cow deaths in the member households.

Breed improvement of dairy cows

Members in the village talked about how they had been able to change from indigenous cows to hybrid ones. All five active members confirmed that they use either AI or hybrid bulls to improve the breed. This compared with only one out of the six non-member households in the village that owned mature dairy cows in 2012. Non-members talked of how they 'can't afford'[45] to use AI, and that instead they used a 'local bull'.[46] During the interviews, data was collected on the breed of dairy cows owned by participant households. The entire active member herd was identified as purebred or hybrid, compared with 16.5 per cent of the non-member herd. Members directly linked improved dairy-cow breeds to the co-operative: 'It has helped us change from local breeds to hybrids. Many people in the village have been able to do this. People have been motivated to get better breeds, and improve their dairy farming.'[47] Another member continued to explain how the co-operative has 'motivated' people in this area: 'It is conducting more training now to educate farmers and many have benefited from them ... Badilisha Kailu[48] will help those with local cows to get better breeds.'[49]

This statement directly links training in breed improvement, facilitated through the co-operative, to improvements in dairy-cow breeds. However, as discussed above, training sessions were largely attended by members, suggesting that the co-operative was predominantly improving dairy-cow breeds within the membership through this activity. In addition to training, members in the village also directly linked breed improvement to the AI service provided on credit to members by the co-operative: 'Even when people have local cows they can use AI and transform them to better breeds – when you need a doctor for AI and you don't have money, you can get from the society and pay at the end of the month.'[50]

These two participant statements suggest that the co-operative was helping to improve dairy cow breeds in member households through a combination of its activities in training as well as veterinary services.

Household milk productivity

I have shown, so far, how dairy-cow ownership improved in both member and non-member households over the five-year study period. The co-operative's multiple activities in training as well as farm inputs and services also helped members to improve dairy-cow breeds better than non-members. I now look at what all this means for household milk productivity.

During the household matrix scoring exercise on milk yields, all five active member households confirmed that they normally milk at least one dairy cow. For non-members, this was six out of the seven households. Although a lower number of member households were actively engaged in dairy farming, they were found to milk more cows than non-members (Table 13.2). Four out of the five active member households talked of how 'milk has increased' or 'production gone up'.[51] In contrast

Table 13.2: Combined household daily milk production

Household type	Total number of cows milked	Milk production per day (litres)	
		Dry season	Rainy season
Active members	8	28.5	86.5
Non-members	7	17.5	51

to this, none of the four non-member households who were milking over the 2007–12 period confirmed that milk production had increased. Instead they talked of how yields had gone down.[52]

During the interviews, I collected data on average household milk production in the dry as well as the rainy seasons.[53] Although active members were milking only one extra dairy cow than non-members, they showed significantly higher daily milk production – a combined 28.5 litres during the dry season, and 86.5 litres during the rainy season. This is compared to 17.5 litres for non-members in the dry season, and 51 litres in the rainy season (see Table 13.2). The household matrix scoring exercise on milk yields collected data on perceived changes to milk production over the five-year study period. Participant households were given ten seeds and told that this represented all the milk from all their cows in 2012, and asked to allocate seeds comparing their milk production in 2007 and 2009–10. This allowed me to collect data on milk produced per cow,[54] and elaborated on the extent to which productivity was changing over the five-year period as well as exploring any reasons for this. The scores from this exercise then allowed me to generate average percentage differences in production for the seven or eight milk-producing cows in each participant group. Active member households increased milk production per cow more than non-member households, an 82 per cent increase over the five-year period. In contrast to this, non-members showed a decrease in milk production per cow of 10 per cent over the five-year period.

Members made direct links between dairy farming training and higher milk production overall as well as per cow: 'In 2007 we were not much trained. But in 2010 we had more knowledge … From the training we learnt that you can have two cows now and produce more milk than from the many cows we had earlier.'[55] The only non-member in the village who regularly attended dairy farming training facilitated through the co-operative also stated: 'The society has been training us nowadays on that [changing to hybrid dairy cows]. We should stop investing in so many cattle that produce nothing, and invest in cattle that can produce milk.'[56]

These two statements capture the link between the co-operative's activity in training and higher household milk production. The majority of non-members, however, described a different situation: 'There's no pasture. It is a local cow, so when there's no pasture it dries up.'[57] In contrast to this situation I have shown how members attended training that helped them to produce their own on-farm feeds as well as upgrade to cows of higher-quality breeds. I have also shown the importance of member access to inputs on credit to support milk production, which would have reduced their dependence on pasturelands during the dry season. The above two participant statements also further explain the findings discussed above on why active member households were increasing their dairy cow ownership at a slower rate than non-members. They indicate the importance of greater investments in dairy cows, rather than just striving to increase herd size.

The findings here suggest that the co-operative helped to improve household milk production as well as milk yields per cow through its multiple activities in farm inputs, veterinary services and training. This helped to boost milk production more in member households than non-member households.

Household milk income and use

What does the higher member milk production compared to non-members actually mean for the case-study households? Active members identified two main sources of household income: financial support from children or other family members engaged in waged employment, and income from milk.[58] All five active member households mentioned dairy farming as an important source of income in 2012. In contrast to this, only two out of the six non-member households that were engaged in dairy farming in 2012 even mentioned income as a benefit of dairy farming.[59] In these households dairy farming largely provided milk for household consumption. Four out of the five active member households also talked of an increasing income from dairy farming over the five-year study period: 'we're doing well on the side of dairy farming'.[60] This indicates the growing importance of milk income to these households.

During the interviews, I asked both members and non-members how they used milk income. The growing milk income for member households suggests that impact in these areas were improving, compared to non-member households. All five active members reported using milk income for domestic purposes, primarily for purchasing basic foodstuffs (such as cooking oil, sugar and vegetables) that supported household food intake. Three out of the five member households also talked of using milk income to cover health-care and education costs.[61] Non-members who reported having some income from milk for at least part of the year (three out of the seven non-member households) talked of using it mostly to purchase food.[62] Only one non-member also mentioned using 'some for [school] fees'.[63] The findings here suggest that milk income primarily sustained 'domestic activities', in particular supporting food intake, with positive impacts also on health care and education. The greater importance of milk income to member households compared to non-member households suggests that the co-operative was able to impact these areas more in the former group.

Conclusion

The findings discussed here directly link co-operatives to poverty reduction, providing research-based evidence in this area to complement other project-based studies.[64] I have shown that the issue is not whether co-operatives are 'designed to help the poor'[65] or are 'wealth creators and not poverty reducers'.[66] It is instead about how the co-operative identity can help to improve people's lives. Although the primary purpose of the case-study co-operative was to market milk, with no explicit intentions in reducing poverty, I have shown how the co-operative identity (based on values of self-help, self-responsibility and democracy) led to engagement in multiple activities, many of which reduced poverty in areas important to members, their families and communities in the case-study village.

The multiple areas of co-operative activity, in farm inputs and services as well as in training, combined to support dairy cow ownership in both member and non-member households. In member households, these multiple activities also supported greater dairy-cow breed transformation as well as helping to lower dairy-cow deaths during the 2009 drought. The findings showed that the co-operative was not only able to promote hybrid cow ownership in member households, but also to ensure that they were better able to maintain them. This adds new understanding to how hybrid-cow ownership and maintenance can be improved in smallholder dairy-farming households,[67] providing important insights into the role that co-operatives can play in this area.

Higher dairy-cow ownership and better breeds in member households compared to non-member households meant higher overall milk production in the former group, as well as higher milk production per cow. This resulted in a growing milk income for member households compared to non-member households. Milk income was used to improve access to a number of areas important to families including food, access to health care and education. This complements other findings in the literature discussing the importance of milk income to dairy-farming households,[68] and provides new evidence of how co-operatives improve household milk productivity.

Although this was a case-study research project, looking at a specific co-operative sector in a specific locale, the findings point to a general link between the co-operative identity and the economic and social goals that co-operatives pursue through engagement in multiple activities to meet member needs. I showed how these multiple activities impacted multiple areas, which came together to reduce poverty in ways that were important to members, their families and communities in the case-study village (e.g. improved farm production led to increased household income, which was used to access food, education and healthcare). Further research, exploring links between the co-operative identity and poverty reduction, would strengthen understanding of the role co-operatives in other sectors and in other parts of the world can play in reducing poverty. As the co-operative movement revives and grows across the globe, it is important to ensure that a strong co-operative identity develops with it. With this identity co-operatives can help to carve a better position for smallholder farmers and their families.

Notes

1 J. Birchall and R. Simmons, 'The role and potential of co-operatives in the poverty reduction process: a research agenda', *Journal of Co-operative Studies* 40:1 (2007), 43–51; Department for International Development (DFID) *Eliminating World Poverty: Building our Common Future* (London: DFID, 2009); International Labour Organization (ILO) and International Co-operative Alliance (ICA), *Cooperatives and the Sustainable Development Goals* (Geneva: ILO and ICA Policy Brief, 2014).

2 H. Münkner, *Co-operation as a Remedy in Times of Crisis* (Marburg: Institute for Co-operative Research, Philipps University, 2012), p. 15.

3 H. Münkner, 'Rediscovery of co-operatives in development policy', ICA/ROAP subregional workshop on co-operative policy reforms, 13–16 January 1991, Kathmandu, p. 1.

4 I. Pollet and P. Develtere, *Development Co-operation: How Co-operatives Cope. A Survey of Major Co-operative Development Agencies* (Leuven: Higher Institute for Labour Studies, 2005), p. 62.

5 J. Birchall, *Rediscovering the Co-operative Advantage: Poverty Reduction through Self-Help* (Geneva: ILO, 2003).

6 Ibid., p. 4.

7 This chapter discusses findings from my PhD project based at the University of Leeds, and undertaken in close collaboration with the Co-operative College, Manchester.

8 Co-operatives UK (2004), cited in P. Somerville, 'Co-operative identity', *Journal of Co-operative Studies* 40:1 (2007), 5–17, p. 7.
9 T. Allen and A. Thomas, *Poverty and Development into the 21st Century* (Milton Keynes: The Open University, 2000).
10 Canadian Co-operative Association (CCA), *Co-operatives: An Enterprise Approach to Fighting Poverty* (Ottawa: CCA, 2004) and R. O. Odeke, 'Co-operative governance in Africa: a study of the Uganda co-operative movement', in *Co-operative Development in Africa: Prospects and Challenges*, International Cooperative Research Conference for Africa, Moshi (26–28 September 2011), pp. 214–21.
11 CCA, *Co-operatives*, p. 1.
12 B. Emana, *Cooperatives: A Path to Economic and Social Empowerment in Ethiopia*, CoopAfrica Working Paper No. 9 (Geneva: ILO, 2009) and P. Mooney, 'Democratizing rural economy: institutional friction, sustainable struggle and the cooperative movement', *Rural Sociology* 69:1 (2004), 76–98.
13 Names at the local level (including of the district, case-study village and co-operative) have been anonymised to encourage open discussion by participants, as well as to protect sensitive data that emerged.
14 Ministry of State for Planning, *X District Development Plan, 2008–2012* (Nairobi: Republic of Kenya, 2008), p. 34.
15 World Bank, *Kenya Economic Update: Time to Shift Gears* (Nairobi: World Bank, 2013), p. iv.
16 Ministry of State for Planning, *X District Development Plan*, p. 12.
17 Although the research also explored wider village-level findings, these are discussed elsewhere; see R. Hannan, 'Good co-operative governance: the elephant in the room with rural poverty reduction', *Journal of International Development* 26:5 (2014), 701–12.
18 A dual-member household is where both the wife and husband are separate members of the case-study co-operative.
19 R. Hannan, 'Participatory co-operative research: for the people, by the people, with the people', *Development in Practice* 25:4 (2015), 490–502.
20 M. Saunders, P. Lewis and A. Thornhill, *Research Methods for Business Students*, 6th edition (Harlow: Pearson Education, 2012), p. 190.
21 Member and non-member interviews in case-study village.
22 Non-member interview. All participants at the local level were anonymised to protect sensitive data that emerged. More information on the reasons for this and on individual participants can be found in R. Hannan, 'Co-operative governance: pathways to poverty reduction? The case of Kenya' (unpublished PhD thesis, Sustainability Research Institute, University of Leeds, 2014).
23 This is the anonymised name given to the location where the case-study co-operative operates.
24 Non-member interview.
25 Member and non-member interviews in case-study village.
26 Non-member interview.
27 Member interview.

28 Interview with manager of case-study co-operative.
29 Member interview.
30 Ibid.
31 The partner, We Effect (formerly known as the Swedish Co-operative Centre), had been working with the case-study co-operative for a number of years, supporting activities such as member training.
32 Interview with manager of case study co-operative.
33 Member interview (board director representing case-study village).
34 Member and non-member interviews in case-study village.
35 Interview with manager of case-study co-operative.
36 Ibid.
37 Member interview (board director representing case-study village).
38 Napier grass is given to dairy cows to improve milk production.
39 Member interview.
40 Ibid.
41 Ibid.
42 Ibid.
43 Ibid.
44 Ibid.
45 Non-member interview.
46 Ibid.
47 Member interview.
48 Badilisha Kailu is the name of a recent initiative at the co-operative, which aims to gradually transform indigenous cows to hybrids through awareness-raising among farmers and through AI support.
49 Member interview.
50 Ibid.
51 Ibid.
52 Non-member interviews.
53 The rainy season in Kenya lasts for three to four months a year.
54 To facilitate data collection in this area it was assumed that each cow being milked within the same household produced an equal amount of milk.
55 Household matrix scoring exercise on milk yields.
56 Non-member interview.
57 Household matrix scoring on milk yields.
58 Household matrix scoring exercises on changes to income.
59 Non-member interviews in the case-study village.
60 Household matrix scoring on changes to income.
61 Member interviews.
62 Non-member interviews.
63 Ibid.
64 Food and Agriculture Organization (FAO), *Agricultural Co-operatives: Key to Feeding the World* (Rome: FAO, 2012); and I. MacPherson, C. Johnston and J.-E. Imbsen, *Promise the Future: A Collection of Essays on Co-operatives and Poverty* (Ottawa: CCA, 2001).

65 Münkner, *Co-operation as a Remedy*, p. 15.
66 Pollet and Develtere, *Development Co-operation*, p. 62.
67 C. Leksmono, J. Young, N. Hooton, H. Muriuki and D. Romney, *Informal Traders Lock Horns with the Formal Milk Industry: The Role of Research in Pro-poor Dairy Policy Shift in Kenya*, Working Paper 266 (London and Nairobi: Overseas Development Institute and International Livestock Research Centre, 2006) and C. F. Nicholson, P. K. Thornton and R. W. Muinga, 'Household-level impacts of dairy cow ownership in coastal Kenya', *Journal of Agricultural Economics* 55:2 (2004), 175–95.
68 A. Espinoza-Ortega, E. Espinosa-Ayala, J. Bastida-Lopez, T. Castaneda-Martinez and C. M. Arriaga-Jordon, 'Small-scale dairy farming in the highlands of Central Mexico: technical, economic and social aspects and their impact on poverty', *Experimental Agriculture* 43:2 (2007), 241–56; and J. Hoorweg, P. Leegwater and W. Veerman, 'Nutrition in agricultural development: intensive dairy farming by rural smallholders', *Ecology of Food and Nutrition* 39:6 (2000), 395–416.

14

What do we really know about workers' co-operatives?

Virginie Pérotin

Introduction

The idea that employees can run firms sounds unrealistic to many people. Even if they accept that businesses owned and managed by their employees exist, most people still think of those enterprises as unlikely businesses. Worker co-operatives have traditionally been viewed as small, specialised and undercapitalised organisations that only thrived in unusual conditions and could not possibly constitute a serious alternative to conventional firms. This view has long been shared by many economists studying labour-managed firms, on the basis of economic theory and relatively limited empirical observation.

Since the 1990s, data on large, representative samples or whole populations of worker co-operatives and conventional firms have become increasingly available internationally. As a result, a growing number of international economic studies present comparative analyses of the two types of firms using extensive information on their characteristics and behaviour. In this paper, I present new descriptive evidence using information provided in these studies and other aggregate data to examine whether received ideas about worker co-operatives seem verified. I also briefly review international findings about pay and employment behaviour, productivity, investment and firm survival among conventional businesses and worker co-operatives. I argue that together these different types of evidence suggest that we should urgently revise our 'stylised facts' about worker co-operatives and focus research and policy on learning from the most successful worker co-operative movements in Italy and Spain.

For the purposes of this paper, a firm is regarded as a worker co-operative if it has the following characteristics:[1] All or most of the capital is owned by employees (members) whether individually and/

or collectively (capital ownership arrangements vary). All categories of employees can become members; and most employees are members. Following international co-operative principles, members each have one vote, regardless of the amount of capital they have invested in the business. The worker co-operatives I look at in this paper normally are for profit, though profit aims may be mitigated to various degrees by other aspects of members' interests including, for example, employment, social or ethical considerations and goals. Worker co-operatives represent a very small proportion of all firms in most countries. However, they are more numerous than is usually thought: at least 25,000 can be found in Italy, about 17,000 (employing some 210,000 people) in Spain, 2,600 (employing 51,000 people) in France and about 500–600 in the UK.[2]

In the following section, I present descriptive statistics about the size of worker co-operatives and their industry distribution in comparison with those of other businesses. International evidence about the compared patterns of firm creation and survival patterns, capital intensity and investment is summarised in the third section; and findings on the compared productivity, and employment and pay adjustments of labour-managed and other firms are briefly reviewed in the fourth section, followed by some conclusions.

New descriptive evidence on the characteristics of worker co-operatives

Are worker co-operatives smaller than other firms?

Perhaps the most common received idea about worker co-operatives is that they must be small, because they are thought to be financially constrained and/or because a small size is regarded as a condition for workplace democracy to function. Standard economic theory also predicts that labour-managed firms that pursue maximum profit per member will be smaller than conventional firms in the short run (though not in the long run). In addition, the theory argues that labour-managed firms do not have the same incentives to grow indefinitely as conventional firms, as maximum profit per member may be independent of scale.[3] People will also commonly remark that very large worker co-operatives are extremely rare. The worker co-operative group the Mondragon Corporation in Spain does employ some 80,000 people around the world,[4] and the employee-owned John Lewis Partnership in the UK (which operates slightly differently) counts around 90,000 partner employees, but these two cases may just be exceptions.[5]

What is not widely understood is that most firms actually are very small: among the firms that have at least one employee, around 90 per cent have fewer than twenty employees in the UK (93.7 per cent) the US (89.6 per cent) and France (90.4 per cent) and fewer than ten employees in Spain.[6] Large firms are very rare: only 0.3 per cent of the firms that have employees have 500 employees or more in the UK and the US, 0.2 per cent in France and 0.1 per cent in Spain.

Where we have data for workers' co-operatives we observe that the co-operatives are actually larger than other firms. Pencavel et al. use a data set covering 2,000 worker co-operatives and 150,000 other firms in Italy, observed over thirteen years.[7] They find that both the average and the median numbers of employees are larger for the co-operatives than for the other firms (for example, in 1994, the last year for their sample, average employment was 284 in the co-operatives and 228 in the other firms, and median employment 153 and 72 respectively in the two groups of firms). Similarly, the data presented by Craig and Pencavel on the plywood industry in the US Pacific northwest indicate that the worker co-operatives are larger than the other firms – on average over all the years in their sample, firms employed 233 people in the industry, but among these the co-ops employed 257 on average.[8] In Spain, firms with employees had 9.2 on average in 2014, but worker co-operatives were reported to have 12.6 employees on average.[9] For France and Uruguay, we can compare the size distributions of worker co-operatives and firms generally. Using data on all firms in Uruguay provided in Burdín and Dean and data available from the French statistical office Insee on firms with at least one employee and from the French worker co-operative federation CG-SCOP, we can use the same breakdown by size groups in the two countries.[10] This information is presented in Figures 14.1 and 14.2. In both France and Uruguay, it is clear that a lower share of worker co-operatives are micro-firms than of other firms. The co-operatives are more often found in the larger size groups.

A more detailed breakdown of the population of French firms by size group, available for 2006, shows the difference persists if we select a higher cut-off point for firm size. Among French firms with at least one employee, 0.04 per cent had 2,000 employees or more that year; this proportion was 0.05 per cent among French worker co-operatives (see Figure 14.3). Given the small number of worker co-operatives, such a percentage represents a very small number of firms, which is why it is very rare to see a large worker co-operative. However, worker co-operatives clearly seem to be larger than conventional firms overall, principally because there are proportionally fewer micro-firms

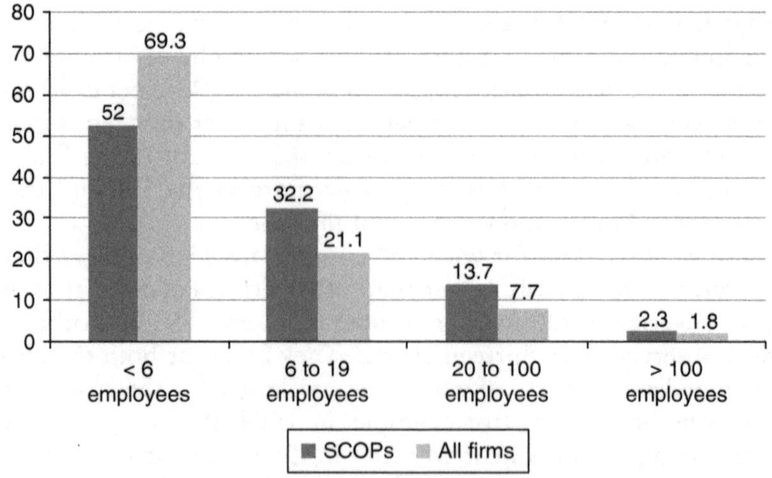

Figure 14.1: Compared size distributions of worker co-operatives (SCOPs) and other firms with employees, France 2007 (per cent of firms)

Source: Elaborated from Confédération Générale des Sociétés Coopératives et Participatives (CG-SCOP) and Institut national de la statistique et des études économiques (Insee) data.

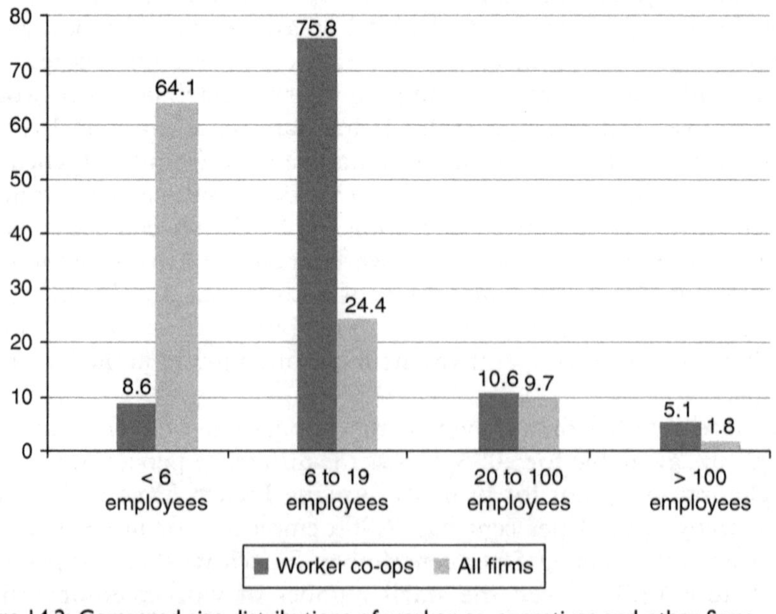

Figure 14.2: Compared size distributions of worker co-operatives and other firms, Uruguay 2005 (per cent of firms)

Source: Elaborated from data presented in G. Burdín and A. Dean, 'New evidence on wages and employment in worker cooperatives compared with capitalist firms', *Journal of Comparative Economics* 37 (2009), 517–33.

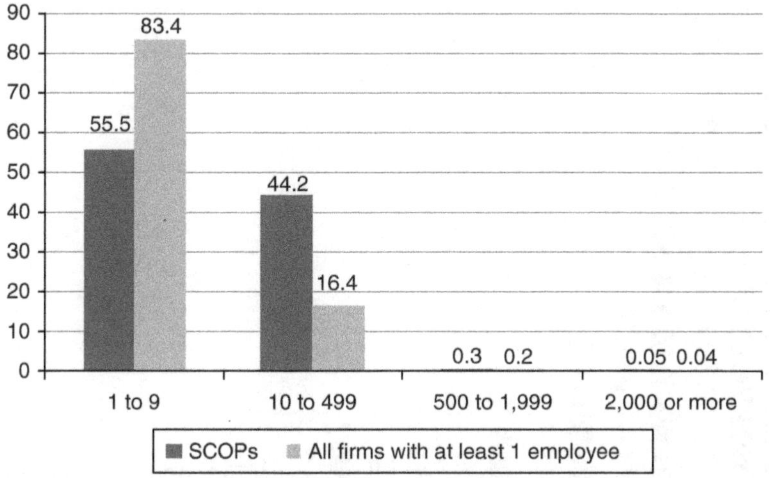

Figure 14.3: Compared size distributions of worker co-operatives (SCOPs) and other firms with employees, France 2006 (per cent of firms; number of employees)
Source: Elaborated from Insee and CG-SCOP data.

Table 14.1: Compared size distributions of worker co-operatives (SCOPs) and other firms with employees, France 2013 (per cent)

	1–9 employees	**10–49 employees**	**50–249 employees**	**250 employees or more**
SCOPs	64.1	27.6	7.2	1.1
			50–200 employees	**200 employees or more**
All firms with employees	82.9	14.2	2.2	0.7

Source: Author's computations from CG-SCOP and Insee data.

among the co-operatives. The most recent data for France (shown in Table 14.1) suggest that the pattern remains the same, with a larger proportion of worker co-operatives than of firms in general in the larger size groups.

Worker co-operatives could be larger because they are created larger, or because they grow faster and/or survive longer than conventional firms. Arando et al. present data from the Basque country in Spain that suggests that worker co-operatives are created larger than other firms (see Figure 14.4).[11] Worker co-operatives were created with an average of four members in 2013 in Spain as a whole, which is likely to be substantially higher than the average new firm's employment, given

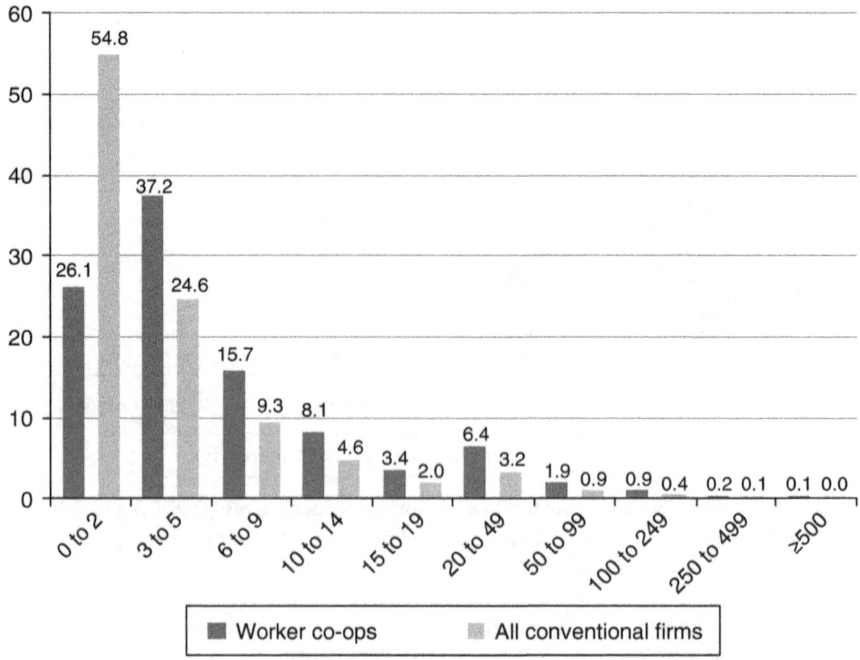

Figure 14.4: Size distribution of newly created firms, Basque country (Spain), 1993–2003 (per cent of firms; initial number of employees)

Source: Elaborated from data presented in S. Arando, I. Peña and I. Verheul, 'Market entry of firms with different legal forms: an empirical test of the influence of institutional factors', *International Entrepreneurship and Management Journal* 5 (2009), 77–95.

that 56.7 per cent of all firms with employees had one or two employees in Spain in that year,[12] and many firms are created with only one employee. It should be noted that the reason for the difference in size at creation is unlikely to be that the co-operatives are more often set up by workers taking over their employer firm, since this origin seems less common among worker co-operatives than among other firms (see below). However, in many countries, the law specifies, or specified until recently, a minimum number of members necessary to create a worker co-operative. This, and the fact that a co-operative is necessarily a collective enterprise, may explain the difference in initial sizes with conventional firms.

Are worker co-operatives found in different industries from other firms?

Another commonly held idea is that worker co-operatives are only suited to particular industries – for example, industries with low capital intensity or low capital requirements. It is often thought that

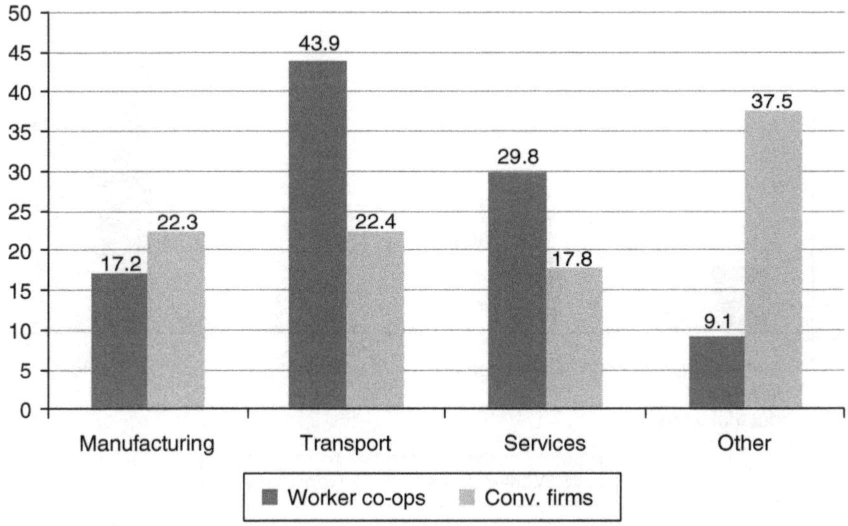

Figure 14.5: Compared sector distributions of worker co-operatives and other firms, Uruguay 2005 (per cent of firms)
Source: Elaborated from data presented in Burdín and Dean, 'New evidence'.

labour-managed firms will not thrive in such industries, because of limited access to capital and/or because employee control is better suited to industries in which skills are most important to firm performance (yet, at the same time, many people seem to think few co-operatives will be found in high-tech industries, where human capital is often essential). In practice, worker co-operatives can be found in most industries. Figure 14.5 shows the compared distributions of conventional firms and worker co-operatives by broad sector using data presented by Burdín and Dean for Uruguay in 2005.[13] The distributions are clearly different, with proportionately more co-ops than conventional firms in transport and services, and fewer in manufacturing. The sector distribution of the two groups of firms also is different in France (Figure 14.6). However, in that country, worker co-operatives are more often found in manufacturing and less often in services than other firms. So the differences vary across countries.

Figure 14.7 shows the compared shares of employment in each of the broad sectors between Spanish worker co-operatives and conventional firms, based on the data presented by Clemente et al. for 2007.[14] This graph is not directly comparable with the charts for Uruguay and France, which use the share of firms rather than employment, because the average scale varies across sectors. However, it suggests that the two groups of firms have quite similar sectoral distributions in Spain.

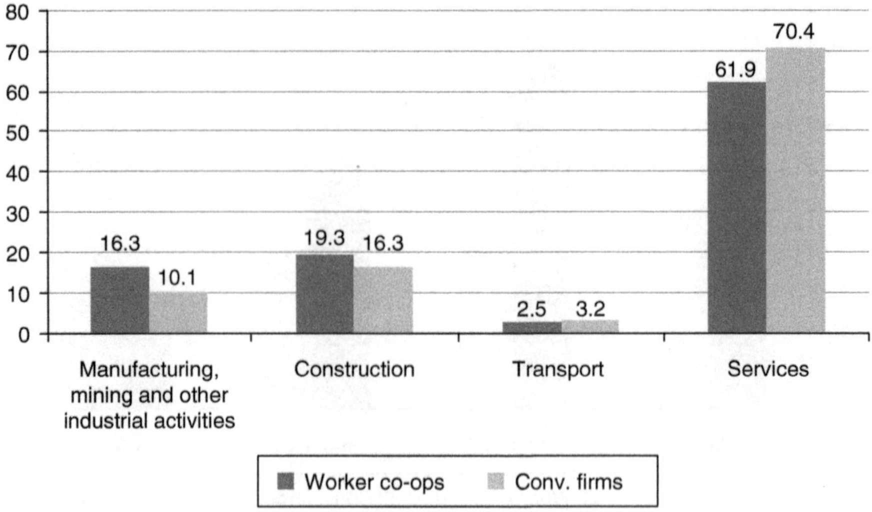

Figure 14.6: Compared sector distributions of worker co-operatives (SCOPs) and other firms with employees, France 2013 (per cent of non-agricultural firms)
Source: Elaborated from Insee and CG-SCOP data.

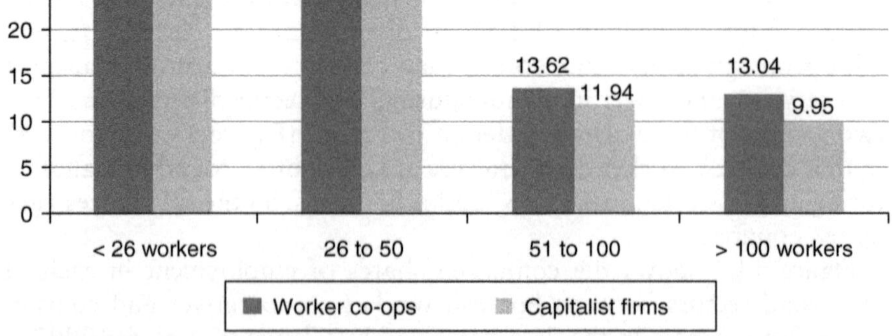

Figure 14.7: Compared sector distributions of worker co-operatives and conventional firms, Spain 2007 (per cent employment)
Source: Elaborated from data presented in J. Clemente, M. Díaz-Foncea, C. Marcuello and M. S. Navarro, 'The wage gap between cooperative and capitalist firms: evidence from Spain', *Annals of Public and Cooperative Economics* 83:3 (2012), 337–56.

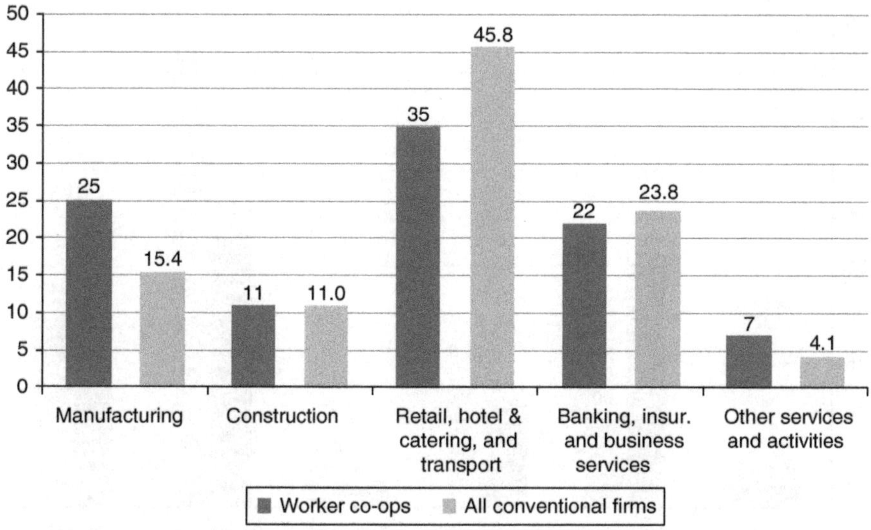

Figure 14.8: Sector distributions of newly created firms, Basque country (Spain), 1993–2003 (per cent of firms)
Source: Elaborated from data presented in Arando et al., 'Market entry of firms'.

The industry distribution of firms observed at a given time comes from the distribution of firm creations across industries and the extent to which they survive in each industry. Arando et al. provide data on the industry distribution of newly created firms in the Basque country in Spain, which show some differences between worker co-operatives and other firms in manufacturing (a greater share of co-ops than of other firms) and some services, but no or little difference in the proportions of new firms to be found in construction or financial services (see Figure 14.8).[15] Data presented by Podivinsky and Stewart for the UK in the period 1976–85 shows a different pattern again, with a comparatively higher share of labour-managed firms created in manufacturing but a lower share in construction than the corresponding proportions of conventional firm creations (see Figure 14.9).[16]

If worker co-operatives were only suited to a small group of special industries, we would expect a clear pattern common to different countries in the ways worker co-operatives' distribution across industries compares with that of other firms. The absence of any such pattern suggests the differences between the two groups are more complex. One way to investigate the role of different factors in creating these patterns is to look at the effect of industry characteristics on firm creation and survival for worker co-operatives and other firms.

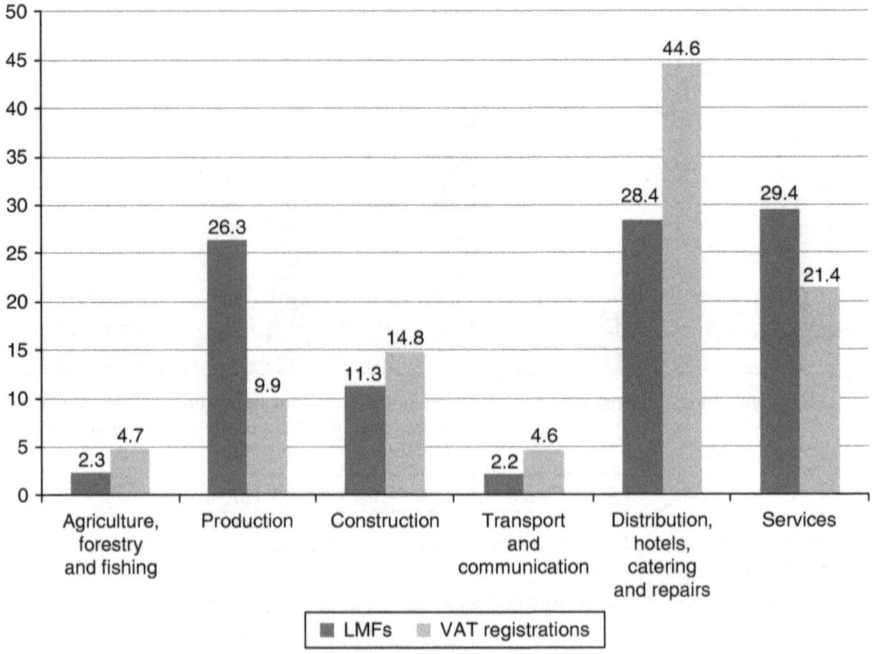

Figure 14.9: Compared sector distributions of newly created labour-managed firms (LMFs) and other firms, UK 1976–85 (per cent of firms)

Source: Elaborated from data presented in J. Podivinsky and G. Stewart, 'Why is labour-managed firm entry so rare? An analysis of UK manufacturing data', *Journal of Economic Behavior and Organization* 63 (2007), 177–92.

International findings on firm demography and investment

Firm creation and survival

Using UK manufacturing data for the early 1980s, Podivinsky and Stewart examine the factors that explain the proportion of new firms that are labour-managed in each industry.[17] They find that, as predicted by theory, a lower share of newly created firms are worker co-operatives in industries that have high capital intensity and high risk (measured by the variance of profits in the industry). Studying the effect of individual firm characteristics on the survival of worker-managed firms in Uruguay, Burdín attributes to issues of capital requirements the fact that the co-operatives' survival advantage over conventional firms is greater in services than in manufacturing and transport.[18] However, he does not find that co-ops do less well in these sectors: in manufacturing and transport the risk of closure is the same in the two groups. Worker co-operatives survive longer than other firms overall when industry, starting

Table 14.2: Firm creation and failure rates, France, 1979–2009

1979–98	Birth rate	Death rate
Worker co-operatives (SCOPs)	0.16	0.11
All French firms	0.12	0.11
1993–2009		
SCOPs	0.104	n.a.
All French firms	0.104	n.a.

Source: Derived from CG-SCOP and Insee data.

wage, size and year of creation are taken into account, and this is due to their much lower closure risk (hazard), all else being equal, than conventional firms' in services.[19]

Burdín's finding is consistent with less rigorous evidence on other countries suggesting that labour-managed firms survive at least as well as other firms.[20] It is not uncommon for worker co-operatives to survive for well over a century. The aggregate data available for France (Table 14.2) show identical failure rates for the two groups of firms in the long run, and more volatile creation rates for labour-managed firms.

Some of the differences between the industry distributions of labour-managed and other firms may also be due to historical factors that resulted in clusters of co-operatives set up in certain industries. Podivinsky and Stewart observe that in the early 1980s labour-managed firm creation was more concentrated than firm creation in general in the UK.[21] A higher proportion of co-operatives were created in the footwear and clothing industry and in paper, printing and publishing – two industries, they note, highlighted by Estrin et al. as being traditional for worker-managed firms in the UK.[22] Similarly, France has traditionally had concentrations of worker co-operatives in printing and publishing following a historical tradition of anarchist co-ops, and in the construction sector as worker co-operatives benefited from preferential treatment over comparable bids in government contracts. With data on the Basque country in Spain, Arando et al. show that agglomeration effects cause more worker co-operatives to be formed in industries where more co-operatives exist.[23] The paucity of information available in most countries about worker co-operatives creates barriers to entry, as entrepreneurs will often have little idea of what a co-operative is or how to create one. Existing worker co-operatives provide an example, and show to would-be entrepreneurs that labour-managed firms can be viable businesses. Familiarity with labour-managed firms where more are in operation also accounts for some of the geographical distribution of worker co-operatives. Where there are labour-managed firms, local banks are more likely to be familiar with the business form, and co-operatives themselves may form supporting agencies if they are sufficiently numerous. In the US, Israel, France and Spain, the number of new worker co-operatives that are created is positively related to the density of existing firms of the same type in the area.[24]

Worker co-operative creations are more clearly counter-cyclical than conventional firm creations in the US, Israel, France and Spain. The counter-cyclicality of new co-operative formation is related to increased unemployment,[25] which may, out of necessity, create a greater pool of potential entrepreneurs, but also create opportunities, as redundancy payments and sometimes unemployment benefit may be used with some tax advantage to set up new firms in some countries.[26] However, it does not seem that new co-operatives massively result from worker rescues of failing firms, as has been hypothesised.[27] Although rescue takeovers by employees are often widely publicised during recessions, this way of forming a co-operative appears relatively rare. At least in France, for which data are available, creations resulting from rescue takeovers are less common for worker co-operatives than for other firms. Table 14.3 shows that over the period 1993–2001 the overwhelming majority of worker co-operatives newly formed in that country were created from scratch. The proportion of co-operatives resulting from a takeover, whether of a failing or a sound firm, was 16.0 per cent, less than half that of French firm creations in general with that origin (36.5 per cent). In 2014, the proportion of new worker co-operatives created as rescues of failing conventional firms still was only 12 per cent (as against 6.6 per cent in 1997–2001) in France, despite the financial crisis and its aftermath.

Although they are created more counter-cyclically than other firms, worker co-operatives have not been found to close down in recoveries, as had been hypothesised by Ben-Ner.[28] In France at least, the effect of the business cycle on firm closures is the same among worker co-operatives and other firms.[29] More generally, as we have seen, the existing evidence suggests that labour-managed firms survive at least as well as conventional firms. It should be noted, however, that much of the

Table 14.3: Firm creations by origin, France, 1997–2001 (per cent of firms)

	From scratch	Conversions	Rescues
SCOPs	84.0	9.4	6.6
All creations	63.5	16.1	20.4

Source: Derived from CG-SCOP and Insee data.

evidence on survival comes from countries where worker co-operatives are set up with constitutions that preclude the two forms of failures identified by economic theory – death by degeneration[30] or by underinvestment.[31] Degeneration and demutualisation (when the co-operative is turned into a conventional firm as it is floated on the stock market or sold to a conventional owner) have often been observed,[32] and some of the provisions against these problems were introduced into French co-operative law, for example, at the request of the co-operative movement.[33] Unsurprisingly, Estrin and Jones find no evidence of degeneration in France. The evidence available also does not support the other failure hypothesis proposed by economic theory: underinvestment.[34]

Capital intensity and investment

Several studies find that the average capital intensity of worker co-operatives is lower than that of conventional firms.[35] However, Pencavel et al. find that in Italy the median capital–labour ratio is higher in worker co-operatives.[36] In addition, they find that the values of the ratio are more dispersed for the co-operatives, which have higher proportions of firms with both very low and very high levels of capital intensity than conventional firms. The comparisons in France by Fakhfakh et al. by broad industry group show conventional firms' capital intensity is higher than that of worker co-operatives in three industry groups,[37] but there is no statistically significant difference between the two types of firms in the four other industry groups (see Table 14.4).

The underinvestment hypothesis predicts that worker co-operatives that are collectively owned by their employees and depend on internal finance will underinvest because members' property rights are truncated – when they leave the firm they do not keep a claim on future profit as they would with shares that appreciate in value and reflect the present value of future profit if capital markets are efficient.[38] One of the solutions proposed for this problem has been to require the co-operative to retain a minimum percentage of profit annually.[39] Such a provision exists in France and Italy and in the Mondragon group, in all of which a substantial proportion of capital is collectively owned. However, in practice worker co-operatives plough back significantly more profit than required, perhaps as a form of insurance against job losses in downturns.[40] This suggests that the hypothesised underinvestment process itself does not apply in practice. No evidence of underinvestment has been found in French worker co-operatives or in Italian ones.[41] Table 14.4 shows that in all the industry groups looked at by Fakhfakh et al. investment, measured as the growth of fixed assets, is either the same in both types of firms (three industry groups) or faster

Table 14.4: Compared mean characteristics, worker co-operatives (SCOPs) and representative sample of conventional firms with twenty employees or more,[a] France, 1987–90

Industry (max n)	Capital goods (SCOPs 157; Conv. 3,217)			Consumer durables (SCOPs 128; Conv. 2,588)			Consumer goods (SCOPs 272; Conv. 3,678)		
	SCOPs	Conv. firms	*t*-test	SCOPs	Conv. Firms	*t*	SCOPs	Conv. firms	*t*
L	64	61	NS	79	63	NS	**71**	51	***
K	1,668	**2,718**	***	4,401	1,649	NS	1,600	1,319	NS
K/L	20.8	**31.3**	***	20.2	19.0	NS	20.5	20.2	NS
ΔK%	**10.0**	7.2	*	**13.5**	7.3	**	5.1	5.2	NS

***, ** and *: means are significantly different at the 1%, 5% and 10% levels respectively; NS: difference is not significantly different from zero; L: average number of employees; K: capital stock (fixed assets); K/L: capital intensity (fixed assets per employee); ΔK: investment (annual growth in fixed assets).
[a] Observations on conventional firms weighted by inverse strata sampling probabilities; financial variables in €1,000s.
Source: F. Fakhfakh, V. Pérotin and M. Gago, 'Productivity, capital and labor in labor-managed and conventional firms', *Industrial and Labor Relations Review* 65:4 (2012), 847–78.

in the co-operatives (four industry groups).[42] This pattern is confirmed by their compared estimations of returns to scale, which show no evidence that labour-managed firms operate at a smaller, inefficient scale as the underinvestment hypothesis would imply.

Other international findings

Productivity

A handful of international studies have compared the total factor productivity of worker co-operatives and other firms, by estimating production functions.[43] These studies concern groups of employee-owned firms that are set up quite differently, so that some of the financial incentives provided by co-operative organisations are much stronger in one group of co-operatives than in the others. In the plywood industry of the Pacific northwest US, members have shares that appreciate in value and are partly tradable; but in Italy and France a large part of capital is owned collectively by members, dividends on individual shares are low and shares are paid back at their nominal value, at most adjusted for inflation. In all cases, the findings imply that worker co-operatives organise production differently from other firms: the production function is not the same for the two groups.

Table 14.4: (cont.)

Construction (SCOPs 645; Conv. 925)			Transport (SCOPs 71; Conv. 1,702)			Business services (SCOPs 71; Conv. 2,788)			Consumer services (SCOPs 47; Conv. 1,412)		
SCOPs	Conv. firms	*t*	SCOPs	Conv. firms	*t*	SCOPs	Conv. Firms	*t*	SCOPs	Conv. firms	*t*
61	**93**	***	40	**66**	***	47	**56**	*	**108**	66	*
958	**1,220**	***	1,113	**1,933**	***	561	**1,891**	***	539	**1,538**	***
14.1	14.1	NS	25.7	**32.7**	**	17.1	16.7	NS	9.8	**18.7**	***
8.8	6.2	***	8.6	5.9	NS	**18.6**	9.7	***	11.0	7.7	NS

***, ** and *: means are significantly different at the 1%, 5% and 10% levels respectively; NS: difference is not significantly different from zero; L: average number of employees; K: capital stock (fixed assets); K/L: capital intensity (fixed assets per employee); ΔK: investment (annual growth in fixed assets).
[a] Observations on conventional firms weighted by inverse strata sampling probabilities; financial variables in €1,000s.
Source: F. Fakhfakh, V. Pérotin and M. Gago, 'Productivity, capital and labor in labor-managed and conventional firms', *Industrial and Labor Relations Review* 65:4 (2012), 847–78.

Two studies – Craig and Pencavel, and Fakhfakh et al. – apply both of the estimated production functions to the current inputs of each group of firms.[44] Both studies find that on average overall firms can produce more with the technology of employee-owned firms. In other words, the way worker co-operatives organise production is more efficient. Fakhfakh et al. show that in several industries conventional firms would produce more with their current inputs if they adopted the employee-owned firms' way of organising production, whereas worker co-operatives would always produce at least as much with their own technology as with conventional firms.[45]

Employment and pay adjustments

Four studies compare the responses of employee-owned and other firms to changes in market conditions. Craig and Pencavel look at the plywood firms of the US Pacific northwest in 1968–86 in two studies; Pencavel et al. examine a very large sample of Italian conventional and co-operative firms in 1982–94; and Burdín and Dean study all firms (worker co-operatives and others) in Uruguay in 1996–2005.[46] Despite the differences in co-operative constitutions between these countries, their findings are remarkably consistent. Conventional firms are found to adjust employment in response to changes in product prices and to demand shocks (in the Uruguayan study they also adjust pay). Worker co-operatives adjust pay and not employment in response to product price changes (in Uruguay, only members' pay changes and the change is much greater than pay changes in conventional firms). In response to demand shocks, the co-operatives adjust pay much more than employment, and their employment adjustment is slower and more limited than other firms. These findings imply that worker-managed firms may hire less than other firms in periods of growth, but importantly may also preserve jobs better in downturns.

It should be noted that no conclusion can be drawn from these results about the relative pay and employment levels in worker co-operatives and other firms, since pay includes profit in worker co-operatives. Anecdotal evidence also indicates that in Italy and in France worker co-operatives first draw from accumulated retained profits in order to preserve both jobs and pay when business is bad, before cutting pay. Relative pay levels in the two sectors are therefore likely to depend on the stage in the business cycle. This possible variability may explain the contradictory findings of the very few studies comparing pay in worker co-operatives and conventional firms, with some studies observing higher pay in the co-operatives[47] and others equal hourly wages in the two groups of firms[48] or lower pay in the co-operatives.[49] Burdín on Uruguay, Magne on France, and to a certain extent Clemente et al. on Spain also observe that worker co-operatives are more egalitarian than conventional firms.[50]

Conclusion

Since the 1990s, the availability of large, comparative datasets has made systematic comparisons between worker co-operatives and other firms possible. In this chapter, I have started to make use of these data to revisit what were thought until now to be 'stylised facts' about worker co-operatives. The evidence presented in this chapter paints a rather different picture from the received view of worker co-operatives as small, specialised, undercapitalised and rather unlikely businesses. We need to revise our stylised facts. Worker co-ops are larger than other firms and not necessarily less capital intensive, although they may be created more often than other firms in less capital intensive industries, all else being equal. They are present in most industries, and differences in industry distributions with conventional firms vary from one country to another.

International evidence also suggests that worker co-operatives survive at least as well as other firms, even in capital-intensive industries.

Labour-managed firms are probably more productive and may preserve jobs better in recessions than conventional firms, creating more sustainable jobs. Promoting worker co-operatives could thus improve local communities' employment, and therefore health and social expenditure, and tax revenue.[51]

The most unusual feature of worker co-operatives – worker control – may be key in explaining the findings I have outlined about productivity, investment, employment and pay. Employee control is thought to increase productivity, and in a labour-managed firm adjusting pay to preserve jobs is incentive compatible: worker-members make the decision to adjust pay and they get the future profits (whereas it is more difficult for a conventional firm to elicit agreement for pay cuts in exchange for job preservation, since the firm has an incentive not to increase pay when business recovers). A job in a worker co-operative is particularly valuable, since it is a job in which the employee has a say in decisions that affect employment risks. Employees' focus on job security may explain worker co-operatives' accumulation of collectively-owned capital by profit plough-backs well above the minimum required by law in Italy and France or by the co-operatives' constitution in Mondragon. Those reserves can be drawn on for preserving pay and jobs. As a result, worker co-operatives keep more profit in the firm than conventional businesses.[52]

Some of the evidence presented in this chapter concerns a small number of countries or particular phases in the business cycle and needs to be further replicated. Yet it is consistent in suggesting that far from being a niche business form only appropriate in special circumstances, worker co-operatives constitute a serious alternative for the twenty-first century: a high-performing firm type suited to all or a very broad range of industries, and possibly more sustainable than conventional businesses. However, worker co-operatives represent a very small part of the business sector, because too few are created. In order to design strategies to overcome this obstacle, we need to examine in more depth the successful experiences of Italy and Spain, where the worker co-operative sector reaches a different scale altogether from the UK and French sectors, employing hundreds of thousands of people. It is possible that the support structures in place, the co-operative funding options and the dissemination of information concerning co-operatives among mainstream would-be entrepreneurs are better organised in these countries. Worker co-operative entrepreneurship still is poorly understood, but may hold the key to making sure this otherwise high-performing firm type takes pride of place among mainstream business forms.

Notes

Earlier versions of this paper were presented to the International Association For the Economics of Participation Congress in Paris, France; the European Association of Elected Regional Assemblies in Trento, Italy; the Co-operative Education Trust for Scotland in Edinburgh; the Mainstreaming Co-operation conference in Manchester; the URPE session on Worker Cooperatives at the ASSA meetings in San Diego, USA; the Conference on Workplace Democracy of the Franco Swedish Programme on Philosophy and Economics in Paris; and the Seminar of the White Rose Employee Ownership Centre in Leeds. Participants' comments are gratefully acknowledged.

1 In this chapter I use the terms 'worker co-operative', 'labour-managed firm' and 'employee-owned firm' interchangeably unless otherwise specified in the text.

2 The estimate for Italy was communicated to the author by Alberto Zevi in 2012. The estimate for Spain includes the *cooperativas de trabajo asociado* (16,664 is the figure given for 2012 by the Confederation of Spanish worker co-operatives in Confederación Española de Cooperativas de Trabajo Asociado (COCETA), *Memoria de actividades 2012* (Madrid: COCETA, n.d.), www.coceta.coop); but not *sociedades laborales*, in which employees own at least 50.01 per cent of the capital but voting is proportional to capital. In 2013 there were 11,322 *sociedades laborales* (Ministerio de Empleo y Seguridad Social, *Avance: resumen situación empresas de economía social y sus trabajadores en situación de alta en la seguridad social* (31 December 2014), www.empleo.gob.es/es/sec_trabajo/autonomos/economia-soc/EconomiaSocial/estadisticas/SociedadesAltaSSocial/2013/indice.htm (accessed 16 February 2016)). The French figure is for 2014 and includes 2,222 *sociétés coopératives et participatives*, or SCOPs, and 408 *sociétés coopératives d'intérêt collectif*, or SCICs (Confédération Générale des SCOP). See CG Scop, *Les chiffres-clés* (2015), www.les-scop.coop/sites/fr/les-chiffres-cles (accessed 16 February 2016). The UK estimates includes firms that identify themselves as workers' co-operatives and other employee-owned firms that meet the definition provided in this chapter.

3 See J. Vanek, *The General Theory of Labor-Managed Market Economies* (Ithaca: Cornell University Press, 1970) and D. Schweickart, *Against Capitalism* (Boulder: Westview Press, 1996).

4 Mondragon's employment figure includes non-co-operative subsidiaries, so that only 40.3 per cent of Mondragon's employees are members. The percentage is considerably higher in the birthplace of the group in the Spanish Basque country (the group has engaged in a 'cooperativisation' process for some of the non-co-operative parts of the group; see Mondragon Corporation, *Experiencia cooperativa/FAQs* (2015), www.mondragon-corporation.com/experiencia-cooperativa/faqs (accessed 16 February 2016).

5 The John Lewis Partnership has more than 93,000 permanent employees or 'partners' (see John Lewis Partnership [2015] www.johnlewispartnership.co.uk/about.html). It has a unique constitution organising the sharing of power between senior management and the other employees (see www.johnlewispartnership.co.uk/about/our-constitution.html (accessed 16 February 2016)).

6 Unless otherwise specified, aggregate figures in this section come from the author's computations from data provided respectively by: the UK's Office for National Statistics (ONS), 'Analysis showing the count of VAT and/or PAYE based enterprises in the United Kingdom by UK SIC 2007', provided at the author's request on 31 March 2015, concerning 2014; and for large firms by Department for Business Innovation and Skills (BIS), *Business Population Estimates for the UK and Regions 2012*, BIS/12/92 (October 2012, available at www.gov.uk/government/statistics/bis-business-population-estimates) concerning 2012; the US Census Bureau, *Statistics of US Businesses (SUSB) Main* (2015), www.census.gov/econ/susb/ for 2012; France's Institut national de la statistique et des études économiques (Insee), 'Unités légales selon le nombre de salariés et l'activité en 2013', Table NATTEF09203 (Sirene: REE, 2015), www.insee.fr/fr/themes/tableau.asp?ref_id=nattef09203 for 2013, except for the share of firms with fewer than twenty employees, Insee, Table NATTEF09203 for 2007 (2009); and Spain's Instituto Nacional de Estadística (INE), 'Empresas por estrato de asalariados y condición jurídica' (2015), www.ine.es/jaxiT3/Tabla.htm?t=299, for 2014 (all accessed 16 February 2016).

7 J. Pencavel, L. Pistaferri and F. Schivardi, 'Wages, employment and capital in capitalist and worker-owned firms', *Industrial and Labor Relations Review* 60:1 (2006), 23–44.

8 B. Craig and J. Pencavel, 'The behavior of worker cooperatives: the plywood companies of the Pacific Northwest', *American Economic Review* 82:5 (1992), 1083–105.

9 The averages are for firms registered with the Seguridad Social system (Ministerio de Empleo y Seguridad Social, *Resumen Situación de Empresas de Economía Social*, 2014). Only about half of worker co-operatives belong to this system, with the others operating under a different regime (*autónomos*). However, the figure for total employment in worker co-operatives given by COCETA, *Memoria de actividades*, seems to use the average size for Seguridad Social worker co-operatives.

10 G. Burdín and A. Dean, 'New evidence on wages and employment in worker cooperatives compared with capitalist firms', *Journal of Comparative Economics* 37 (2009), 517–33.

11 S. Arando, I. Peña and I. Verheul, 'Market entry of firms with different legal forms: an empirical test of the influence of institutional factors', *International Entrepreneurship and Management Journal* 5 (2009), 77–95.

12 Figures computed from data provided by INE, 'Empresas por estrato de asalariados' (2015) and Ministerio de Empleo y Seguridad Social, *Resumen situación de empresas de economía social* (2014). Data available from the same source allow computation of the initial average number of members for newly-created *sociedades laborales*, which is identical to that of worker co-operatives.

13 Burdín and Dean, 'New evidence'.

14 J. Clemente, M. Diaz-Foncea, C. Marcuello and M. S. Navarro, 'The wage gap between cooperative and capitalist firms: evidence from Spain', *Annals of Public and Cooperative Economics* 83:3 (2012), 337–56.

15 Arando et al., 'Market entry of firms'.
16 J. Podivinsky and G. Stewart, 'Why is labour-managed firm entry so rare? An analysis of UK manufacturing data', *Journal of Economic Behavior and Organization* 63 (2007), 177–92.
17 J. Podivinsky and G. Stewart, 'Modelling proportions: random effects models of UK firm entry', *Singapore Economic Review* 54:3 (2009), 367–77.
18 G. Burdín, 'Are worker-managed more likely to fail than conventional enterprises? Evidence from Uruguay', *Industrial and Labor Relations Review* 67:1 (2014), 202–38.
19 Ibid.
20 For a review, see G. K. Dow, *Governing the Firm: Workers' Control in Theory and Practice* (Cambridge: Cambridge University Press, 2003).
21 Podivinsky and Stewart, 'Modelling proportions'.
22 S. Estrin, D. C. Jones and J. Svejnar, 'The productivity effects of worker participation: producer cooperatives in Western economies', *Journal of Comparative Economics* 11:1 (1987), 40–61.
23 S. Arando, M. Gago, J. Podivinsky and G. Stewart, 'Do labour-managed firms benefit from agglomeration?', *Journal of Economic Behavior and Organization* 84 (2012), 193–200.
24 R. Russell and R. Hanneman, 'Cooperatives and the business cycle: the Israeli case', *Journal of Comparative Economics* 16 (1992), 701–15; R. Russell, *Utopia in Zion: The Israeli Experience with Worker Cooperatives* (Albany: State University of New York Press, 1995); V. Pérotin, 'Entry, exit and the business cycle: are cooperatives different?' *Journal of Comparative Economics* 34 (2006), 295–316; Arando et al., 'Market entry of firms'; and M. Díaz-Foncea and C. Marcuello, 'Spatial patterns in new firm formation: are cooperatives different?', *Small Business Economics* 44 (2015), 171–87.
25 Pérotin, 'Entry, exit and the business cycle'; Arando et al., 'Market entry of firms'; and Díaz-Foncea and Marcuello, 'Spatial patterns'.
26 As for example in France and Spain at different times.
27 A. Ben-Ner, 'The life cycle of worker-owned firms in market economies: a theoretical analysis', *Journal of Economic Behavior & Organization* 10:3 (1988), 287–313.
28 Ben-Ner, 'Life cycle'.
29 Pérotin, 'Entry, exit and the business cycle'.
30 A. Ben-Ner, 'On the stability of the cooperative form of organization', *Journal of Comparative Economics* 8:3 (1984), 247–60; H. Miyazaki, 'On success and dissolution of the labor-managed firm in the capitalist economy', *Journal of Political Economy* 94:5 (1984), pp. 909–31. Degeneration describes a process by which the proportion of members gradually reduces until only a few members are left, with a much larger number of non-member employees.
31 E. G. Furubotn and S. Pejovich, 'Property rights and the behaviour of the firm in a socialist state: the example of Yugoslavia', *Zeitschrift für Nationalökonomie* 30:3–4 (1970), 431–54; J. Vanek, *The Labor-Managed Economy* (Ithaca: Cornell University Press, 1977).

32 J. Pencavel, *Worker Participation: Lessons from the Worker Co-ops of the Pacific Northwest* (New York: Russell Sage Foundation, 2001) and J. Pencavel, 'Worker cooperatives and democratic governance' in A. Grandori, ed., *Handbook of Economic Organization* (Northampton, MA: Edward Elgar, 2013).

33 In the Mondragon worker co-operatives, at least 75 per cent of workers must be members; in France, profit is shared with non-members as well as members; and in Italy tax incentives lead worker co-operatives to distribute surplus in the form of wage increases, which also benefit non-members (wage increases are costs and decrease taxable profit, which is entirely retained). All three practices are remedies against degeneration. In France as in the UK, Italy and Spain, worker co-operatives have also traditionally had an 'asset lock', by which in case of closure the net assets of the co-operative devolve to another co-operative, a co-operative institution or a charity. This provision prevents demutualisation. See I. Alzola, S. Arando, F. Fakhfakh, F. Freundlich, M. Gago, V. Pérotin and A. Zevi, 'Are labour-managed firms all the same? A comparison of incentives for growth, democracy and institutional sustainability in the constitutions of worker cooperatives in Mondragon, Italy and France', Paper presented at the 15th World Congress of the International Association for the Economics of Participation (IAFEP), Paris (July 2010).

34 S. Estrin and D. C. Jones, 'The viability of employee-owned firms: evidence from France', *Industrial and Labor Relations Review* 45:2 (1992), 323–38.

35 W. Bartlett, J. Cable, S. Estrin, D. C. Jones and S. C. Smith, 'Labor-managed and private firms in North Central Italy: an empirical comparison', *Industrial and Labor Relations Review* 46:1 (1992), 103–18; Pencavel et al., 'Wages, employment and capital'; O. W. Maietta and V. Sena, 'Shadow price of capital and the Furubotn–Pejovich effect: some empirical evidence for Italian wine cooperatives', *Applied Stochastic Models in Business and Industry* 24 (2008), 495–505.

36 Pencavel et al., 'Wages, employment and capital'.

37 F. Fakhfakh, V. Pérotin and M. Gago, 'Productivity, capital and labor in labor-managed and conventional firms', *Industrial and Labor Relations Review* 65:4 (2012), 847–78.

38 Furubotn and Pejovich, 'Property rights', and Vanek, *Labor-Managed Economy*.

39 Vanek, *Labor-Managed Economy*.

40 C. Navarra, 'How do worker cooperatives stabilize employment? The role of profit reinvestment into locked assets', Working Paper 1307, Department of Economics, Namur University (2013); Alzola et al., 'Are labour-managed firms all the same?'; A. Zevi, 'Il finanziamento delle cooperative' (The financing of co-operatives) in E. Mazzoli and S. Zamagni, *Verso una nuova storia della cooperazione* (*Towards a new history of co-operation*) (Bologna: Il Mulino, 2005), pp. 293–332.

41 S. Estrin and D. C. Jones, 'The determinants of investment in employee-owned firms: evidence from France', *Economic Analysis* 1:1 (1998), 17–28; Maietta and Sena, 'Shadow price of capital'.

42 Fakhfakh et al., 'Productivity, capital and labor'.

43 K. V. Berman and M. D. Berman, 'An empirical test of the theory of the labor-

managed firm', *Journal of Comparative Economics* 13 (1989), 281–300; B. Craig and J. Pencavel, 'Participation and productivity: a comparison of worker cooperatives and conventional firms in the plywood industry', *Brookings Papers: Microeconomics* (1995), 121–74; S. Estrin, 'Some reflections on self-management, social choice, and reform in Eastern Europe', *Journal of Comparative Economics* 15 (1991), 349–66; D. C. Jones, 'The productive efficiency of Italian producer cooperatives: evidence from conventional and cooperative firms' in S. Novkovic and V. Sena, eds, *Advances in the Economic Analysis of Participatory and Labor-Managed Firms*, vol. 9, *Cooperative Firms in Global Markets: Incidence, Viability and Economic Performance* (Oxford: Elsevier, 2007), pp. 3–28; Fakhfakh et al., 'Productivity, capital and labor'.

44 Craig and Pencavel, 'Participation and productivity', and Fakhfakh et al., 'Productivity, capital and labor'.

45 Fakhfakh et al., 'Productivity, capital and labor'.

46 Craig and Pencavel, 'Behavior of worker cooperatives'; B. Craig and J. Pencavel, 'The objectives of worker cooperatives', *Journal of Comparative Economics* 17 (1993), 288–308; Pencavel et al., 'Wages, employment and capital'; Burdín and Dean, 'New evidence'.

47 Bartlett et al., 'Labor-managed and private firms'; G. Burdín, 'Equality under threat by the talented: evidence from worker-managed firms', IZA Discussion Paper No. 7854 (Bonn: IZA, 2013).

48 N. Magne, 'Wage inequality in French worker cooperatives versus conventional firms', paper presented to the Congress of the European Association for Comparative Economic Studies, Budapest (2014).

49 Bartlett et al., 'Labor-managed and private firms'; Burdín, 'Equality under threat'; Magne, 'Wage inequality in French worker cooperatives'; Pencavel et al., 'Wages, employment and capital'; Clemente et al., 'Wage gap'.

50 Burdín, 'Equality under threat'; Magne, 'Wage inequality in French worker cooperatives'; Clemente et al., 'Wage gap'.

51 V. Pérotin, 'Worker cooperatives: good, sustainable jobs in the community', *Journal of Entrepreneurial and Organizational Diversity* 2:2 (2014), 34–47.

52 Zevi, 'Finanziamento delle cooperative'.

15

The impact of the co-operative ethos on the creation of shared value: a case study of Lincolnshire Co-operative Society

Phil Considine and Martin Hingley

This chapter examines the ways that a co-operative creates shared value for the community that it serves and works to define the concept of 'co-operative advantage' in a context where competitive advantage is more commonly discussed. Shared value has been defined as 'policies and operating practices that enhance the competitiveness of a company while simultaneously advancing the economic and social conditions in the communities in which it operates'.[1] Applied is a case-study approach of a local co-operative organisation – Lincolnshire Co-operative Society – that serves a wide and dispersed population in the county of Lincolnshire and areas of east Nottinghamshire, in the east Midlands of the UK. The chapter will consider the different approaches that the co-operative adopts, contrast this to the standard investor-owned firm (IOF) model and will draw conclusions as to the benefits of the co-operative model. It will try to give insight into what constitutes the co-operative advantage in creating shared value.

Introduction

There is an absence of extant research on the impact that the co-operative ethos has in the creation of shared value or indeed what constitutes the co-operative advantage. By examining the processes used to create shared value, this chapter provides an insight into how a new form of capitalism might be developed to the benefit of all stakeholders and not merely a small group of shareholders. We propose that the structure and culture of a co-operative facilitates the creation of shared value, and this in turn gives insight into how this business model might apply to the wider market.

Our study focuses on the Lincolnshire Co-operative Society (LCS). The co-operative is introduced through a description of the organisation's history, development and philosophy. The case-study approach follows the method outlined in Hingley[2] and Stake.[3] It can be seen as a typical case study of this type,[4] and the case-study technique gives a richness of detail by allowing input from the widest cross-section of co-operative staff. The case study is built using a series of interviews of staff ranging from the senior management team to customer-service operatives. The interviews follow a semi-structured format, and various themes and emergent categories have been identified that give insight into the underpinning values of the co-operative. The approach applies 'grounded theory' to investigate exactly what shared value means to employees of the co-operative and how this impacts the concept of the co-operative advantage. Analysis is then made of the interviews and interpretation drawn in order to derive meaning and sense-making. Following interpretation under key themes the chapter is concluded concerning the case-study co-operative, and understanding is derived concerning ethos and shared value.

Lincolnshire Co-operative Society

The key objective of LCS is to serve the community that it represents. This core value is a recurring theme of all of the interviews conducted with co-operative personnel and would seem to underpin all other decisions that are made by the society. This is not to suggest that commercial decisions are avoided – the society is acutely aware of the pillars of sustainability[5] and that without economic sustainability it would not be possible to discharge societal or environmental duties – but equally these elements are as central to the organisational values as the need to make profit.

The structure of LCS is that it is owned by its members and that the members elect a board of directors, who appoint the chief executive, who in turn appoints a management team. Each member has a single vote and any member is eligible to stand for election as a director. This means that the board and management team are motivated to ensure that the needs of the community and the best interests of the membership are fundamental to the organisational goals. This is a significant departure from the investor-owned model, as IOFs have a fiduciary duty to their shareholders with their expectations of profit maximisation as the key metric of organisational and management success. The need to meet the expectations of the owners is a common theme in both the IOF sector and with LCS – however, these expectations are significantly different. In a traditional IOF the owners are the shareholders and whilst in some cases the shareholders play an active part and have an important stake in the business beyond simply the financial, in many cases these owners are more accurately identified as investors or even in some cases gamblers.[6] The LCS in contrast is owned by its members, who are members of the local community that is served by the organisation and who have a very real and live stake in the organisation – not simply from the perspective of being customers. The LCS recycles all of its profits to the local community via community grants, dividends and support for local community activities, and being accountable to a board of directors from the local community gives the society a focus on this community that would not be possible in an IOF.

This local focus is a common theme throughout the case study, and at all levels of the organisation the importance of serving the local community is a constant theme. This does not negate the need to be commercial, and LCS is part of the Co-operative Retail Trading Group (CRTG) which represents all of the UK consumer societies and is responsible for the national buying strategy. However, the strength of the local focus has led LCS to source a range of local products and to support a sizable number of local suppliers who are not part of the CRTG process but with whom LCS now deals. In some cases CRTG products have been replaced with locally sourced ones with a view to developing and securing a local supply chain. The ability of an international IOF to support such local and long-term initiatives is more difficult to envisage.[7]

Part of the induction process for LCS involves ensuring that staff understand the history of both the society and the movement more generally. There is a strong sense that both the values of both the contemporary organisation and the historical values of LCS and the co-operative movement more generally are fully understood by staff, and that managers and leaders are seen to visibly model these values. The values of LCS are a direct translation of the International Co-operative Alliance (ICA) principles.[8]

The LCS now has over 200 outlets, employing around 2,700 staff. It can boast over 230,000 members from a county of fewer than 719,000 inhabitants and, in 2010–11, the dividend payout to members was £4.8 million.[9] Whilst this level of membership is slightly higher than the average, at 31 per cent of the population as opposed to a national average of 24 per cent, this is due, in part, to the isolated nature of much of the county of Lincolnshire and the fact that in many of the more rural parts of the county LCS is the only retailer. In 2013 LCS had a turnover of £288 million from a range of divisions comprising food stores and retail (including petrol stations), pharmacy, post office services, funeral services, travel and property services. All members of staff automatically become members. This is both desirable in terms of meeting the society's objectives of increasing membership but also pragmatic and practical because the IT system for LCS is a single system that requires membership to gain access, as it is on the same platform as the members' web access.

The LCS has a set of values, which are codified and explained in Box 15.1. In addition to the principles of business and the co-operative principles LCS promotes its 'Three Es theme' (3es), to provide a guide to staff: the theme is an abbreviation of Exceeding Everyone's Expectations. The 3es are positioned as an aid to success in delivery of employees' jobs and are generic enough to be relevant to all staff. Underpinning the metaphor of Exceeding Everyone's Expectations are a set of skills, competencies and behaviours. These are:

- communication skills;
- co-operative difference;
- customer care;
- motivation and initiative;
- planning and organising; and
- teamwork and support.

Managers have an additional two themes:

- continuous improvement; and
- leadership.

Methodological approach and the case study

The LCS can be seen as a typical case study[10] of a large local consumer co-operative. Interviews were carried out over a seven-year period (2007–13) to give a longitudinal study of the staff's understanding and perspectives on corporate social responsibility (CSR), shared value and the co-operative advantage. The research was carried out in two phases. Phase one involved a series of interviews with head office and divisional staff between 2008 and 2010, which were repeated for phase two between 2011 and 2013. The sampling strategy was that of purposive/theoretical sampling to ensure that a representative sample was achieved, and interviews were carried out until saturation.[11] The samples came from the LCS head office in central Lincoln and from a mix of staff from the divisions.

From 2008 onwards the UK economy went into its deepest postwar recession, with six consecutive quarters of negative growth, which had impacts on all sectors, especially the retail sector.[12] This led to

Box 15.1: Lincolnshire Co-operative Society ethical principles of business

Local sourcing	The 'Love Local' programme aims to ensure that local suppliers are favoured where possible. LCS deals with a wide range of local suppliers including Dennett's ice cream and honey, Myers of Horncastle plum loaf and tea bread, Lincolnshire Poacher cheese, Curtis' meats, free-range local eggs and a range of local beers and ales.
Fairtrade	LCS introduced fairtrade products in 1992 and since then has seen them grow to their current level, where LCS offers its own branded fairtrade products. In 2003 all own-brand coffee was made fairtrade, soon followed by own-brand tea. LCS champions fairtrade and promotes it in schools and the community through the Fairtrade Fortnight activities.
Community	The Community Champions scheme forms an important part of LCS's community initiatives. Local stores nominate local causes and every time a member shops at the store using their membership card, money is donated to the cause. In addition, LCS members nominate a Charity of the Year, and works with that organisation throughout the year. These have included Macmillan Cancer Support, Lincs and Notts Air Ambulance, and Help For Heroes. LCS runs a volunteering programme where staff are given two days per year to volunteer using their skills to help the local community – working on community projects or acting as school governors. LCS's volunteering programme won a Business in the Community award. LCS further supports education in the local community, where they have developed a set of learning materials for schools that they will also deliver to pupils using suitable qualified staff. There programmes combine national curriculum subjects such as mathematics with social and health education themes such as healthy eating and fairtrade.
Environment	LCS has several sets of key performance indicators monitoring energy usage, recycling and renewables. They financially support energy-saving initiatives and monitor all energy usage within their buildings and within their sphere of influence to reduce carbon usage. LCS's work in this area has been recognised by the Carbon Trust.
Family of businesses	LCS runs a range of divisions, as noted previously. The largest division is retail (food and non-food); however, pharmacy, funerals, pharmacy wholesale, travel and their forty post offices are all important business divisions. As per the ICA value of 'co-operation amongst co-operatives' all divisions try to encourage customers to interact with other divisions where possible.

Source: Lincolnshire Co-operative Society, 'Financial reports', www.lincolnshire.coop/about-us/financial-reports (accessed 29 February 2016).

uncertainty and to job losses in most organisations. In 2011 the second phase of interviews began. At this time, although trading conditions had changed significantly, LCS still employed the same level of staff and the turnover had grown every year except for a very small 0.7 per cent drop between 2011 and 2012, which was more than compensated for by a 2 per cent increase in 2012–13.[13] This meant that LCS managed to retain its size and staff numbers (around 2,700) over the course of the recession.

As a result of this all of the interview themes between 2008 and 2013 could be combined, as no new themes or comments were identified with the exception of several new open codes that were identified when the data was disaggregated. Once meaning was derived from these open codes[14] they were subsumed into the axial codes as they reflected the cycle that the economy generally had undergone and were not directly relevant to the ethical values or CSR activities that related specifically to LCS. The following section summarises the key themes from the interviews.

Key themes and findings

This section examines the key findings from the research with staff at LCS and represents the themes identified as underpinning the values and culture of the society.

Creation of meaning and sense-making

The LCS has a set of values and a mission, and through its 3es programme it has a set of guidelines for staff to understand what it expects in terms of their behaviours and the way that they add value and interact with stakeholders. The process that staff go through to make sense of these is more simplistic in LCS than in many other organisations. Most organisations have an approach whereby meaning is derived from a range of internal communications in an attempt to exert a form of control over the sense-making process, and in order that the dominant culture is controlled and is to the best interest of the organisation – so the organisation seeks to influence the paradigm;[15] and this takes place through a process of sense-giving.[16]

Sense-giving means to influence the sense-making and meaning construction of others towards a preferred definition of organisational reality.[17] Leaders and managers often engage in sense-giving behaviours when ambiguous or complex issues arise or when events involve numerous stakeholders.[18] This process can be seen in many organisations, and whilst there is evidence of it in LCS via initiatives such as the 3es this is a much less overt process than is often seen in larger organisations. However, the 3es are more of a customer-service mantra than a sense-making framework, and whilst the behaviours and competencies that support it might be viewed as an attempt by management to influence the sense-making process there was no evidence that staff felt this to be the case: 'I went on a training course about the 3es – it was really good because it explained what they mean but I found some of the parts more relevant than others. I liked the co-operative difference. I think it is important because as well as working here I am a member as are almost all of our customers.'[19]

Of far more importance from a sense-making perspective and from the creation of understanding was a much simpler message with which the society underpins all of its activities – that of serving the local community. The local community is central to everything LCS does: 'I use the 3es as the main way of understanding what is important – but I also speak to my manager and we get regular updates sent through so that we know what is important. It really comes down to serving the community.'[20]

The notion of community is a core value of LCS reflecting the fact that a high percentage of the Lincolnshire population are members of the society, as are all LCS staff. From a sense-making perspective Maitlis described four different forms of organisational sense-making based on two criteria: animation and control.[21] Animation is linked to the degree to which individuals are engaged in sense-making, while control refers to the extent to which the organisation or its leaders are involved in influencing the sense-making process. Maitlis categorises four types of organisational sense-making:

1. guided (high animation and high control);
2. restricted (low animation and high control);
3. fragmented (high animation and low control); and
4. minimal (low animation and low control).

The sense-making process in LCS would appear to be guided as organisational leaders provide clear guidance regarding the importance of the co-operative principles and the LCS values around serving the local community,[22] whilst the staff seem to be fully engaged in the process. There is a consistent level of understanding of the values throughout the organisation. The research would suggest that this is due to simple order generating rules[23] that provide the foundations for change and form part of the narrative that contributes to the sense-making process. These simple rules are anchored to a symbiotic relationship between LCS and the wider co-operative movement and in particular to the ICA update of the founding principles.[24] These values and principles are widely understood and each element is either measured or promoted within LCS.

This suggests that the ICA co-operative principles have taken on the form of an object in the sense-making process.[25] Blumer suggests that the nature of the object is 'constituted by the meaning it has for the person or persons for who it is an object'.[26] The ICA principles might not always be known verbatim but this gives them meaning in two ways. Firstly they are a physical object in that they exist and can be held, read and understood. But they are also abstract objects in that they also represent a metaphor for what it means to be a co-operative. This is evidenced by the fact that every member of staff spoken to was aware of the co-operative principles and knew that they formed the cornerstone of the LCS values; however, often they were unable to list them. This suggests that they use the principles as both an overarching set of values and as a symbolic metaphor. This in turn underpins their view of CSR, as can be seen in Box 15.2, as the principles help staff to understand the levels of affiliation and integration of any of the initiatives.

Definitions

At first sight the definitions of shared value and CSR by LCS are a relatively unimportant theme, as LCS do not consider themselves as engaged in CSR as a theme: 'We don't practise CSR – it is who we are and it is such an important part of what we do that it is not CSR it is DNA.'[27] This is not to say that definitions cannot be implied or indeed that an underlying definition is not applicable: one staff member commented: 'CSR is simply about working with our communities to make sure that they are in a better state tomorrow than they are today. That includes all aspects of what others see as the TBL [triple bottom line: economic, social and environmental elements].'[28] A customer service staff member added: 'I don't know about CSR but for us it is about local community work. We are part of the community; so are our members.'[29] A closer reflection of the LCS values lies in the Porter and Kramer definition of shared value: 'policies and operating practices that enhance the competitiveness of a company while simultaneously advancing the economic and social conditions in the communities in which it operates'.[30]

Porter's language is that of the IOF, and LCS may feel it requires some modification to be applicable. However, this definition would seem to be far more applicable than the traditional view of CSR that sees it as an outside-in approach.[31] The traditional views of CSR are premised on managing external factors and limiting the more negative impact of running businesses. The LCS seems to adopt an inside-out strategy grounded in the identity and underlying values of both LCS and the

Box 15.2: International Co-operative Alliance (ICA) principles

1. Voluntary and open membership

Co-operatives are voluntary organisations, open to all people able to use their services and willing to accept the responsibilities of membership, without gender, social, racial, political or religious discrimination.

2. Democratic member control

Co-operatives are democratic organisations controlled by their members – those who buy the goods or use the services of the co-operative – who actively participate in setting policies and making decisions.

3. Member economic participation

Members contribute equally to, and democratically control, the capital of the co-operative. This benefits members in proportion to the business they conduct with the co-operative rather than on the capital invested.

4. Autonomy and independence

Co-operatives are autonomous, self-help organisations controlled by their members. If the co-operative enters into agreements with other organisations or raises capital from external sources, it is done so based on terms that ensure democratic control by the members and that maintain the co-operative's autonomy.

5. Education, training and information

Co-operatives provide education and training for members, elected representatives, managers and employees so they can contribute effectively to the development of their co-operative. Members also inform the general public about the nature and benefits of co-operatives.

6. Co-operation among co-operatives

Co-operatives serve their members most effectively and strengthen the co-operative movement by working together through local, national, regional and international structures.

7. Concern for community

While focusing on member needs, co-operatives work for the sustainable development of communities through policies and programmes accepted by the members.

Source: Adapted from International Co-operative Alliance (ICA), 'Statement of co-operative identity, values and principles' (1995), http://ica.coop/en/whats-co-op/co-operative-identity-values-principles (accessed 17 February 2016).

co-operative movement. Jonker suggests that these values will underpin the organisation's mission and that from this is likely to stem a 'leading mission based on historical "roots" interwoven with corporate values'.[32] The historical roots of LCS and the wider co-operative movement play a significant role in the identity and definition of the CSR activity of LCS. As one manager put it: 'I'm not convinced that CSR is an issue for us. It is not an addition, it is what we have always done – all the way back to the pioneers.'[33]

The co-operative principles are important to LCS and to its staff, and whilst many staff members may not be able to list them all accurately they are all aware of the core values that they represent – especially the principles and values connected to voluntary and open membership, democratic member control, members' participation, education and training, co-operation among co-operatives, and above all concern for community. These principles give LCS staff the dominant narrative that allows them to operate without a formal definition of what it means to be a socially responsible organisation or for an explicit definition to be necessary.

Activities and focus

The activities and focus of LCS are centred on the needs of its members and the local community. This does not mean that other stakeholders are marginalised – all staff are members and as such are fully involved in decisions and in the decision-making process. Table 15.1 identifies a CSR activity matrix, in which we can see the key activities and focus. The table illustrates the degree to which the activity might be seen to be aligned to the organisational mission and values (integration) and shows us those activities where the employees feel a strong sense of identity with the cause (affiliation), even though it might not be strongly aligned to the organisational mission, such as one-off television appeals. This does not mean that LCS has an isolationist view of being a good

Table 15.1: CSR activity matrix

3. Cause related Charity of the year Reading groups Social activities	1. Strategic CSR Supply chain activities Local food sourcing Business mentoring Education Healthy habits Health care fund Volunteering	High **Affiliation**
4. After-profit activities Donations Sponsorship	2. Relevant activities National Group activities Local development initiatives	Low
Low	**Integration** High	

corporate citizen or an insular view of activities. Fairtrade is a major theme for the organisation, and there is a sense of being at the forefront of fairtrade in Lincolnshire. 'We were one of the first organisations to embrace fairtrade. Most of the fairtrade suppliers are workers' co-operatives so it is something that we can all relate to and we know that.'[34] Where possible LCS try to combine activities to maximise benefits: 'The great thing about fairtrade is that we go into schools to talk about it and this means that we engage with school kids from an early age. We can then talk about what it means to be a co-operative and introduce some of our learning packages. It also means that staff engage with schools and can lead to volunteering and people becoming school governors.'[35]

This form of 'benefit stacking' adds considerable value by linking different elements of what might be seen as the CSR value chain. Benefit stacking simply refers to the deliberate maximisation of benefits to all stakeholders and could be defined as a deliberate process of adding value to as many activities as can be connected. One of the most frequently identified manifestations of the LCS commitment to the local community was in its support of businesses too small to contract with due to a lack of security in the supply chain. Examples were given where LCS would actively work with local business start-ups and small independent businesses supporting growth and giving direct access to their expertise and facilities – for example, transporting and distributing products whilst delivering to local stores.

Beliefs

In common with most constituent members of The Co-operative Group, the history, stories and narrative that accompany being a co-operative are important parts of the LCS story: 'We have been around since 1861 so during that time we have built up an understanding of the community that means we are seen by them as much more than just a local employer – we are part of them.'[36] Another manager offered his assessment:

> LCS is independent with its own membership but we are part of CRTG, it's our buying group so our whole supply chain relies on them so every single co-op in the country is a member of the buying group. There is no way that a small independent could do the type of deals with the Coca-Colas of this world that the buying group can.[37]

Paradigm and shared values

Johnson et al. suggest that a paradigm is the set of assumptions shared by all staff in an organisation, and that paradigms are reinforced by a range of additional factors within the cultural web of the organisation.[38]

This web consists of the stories, symbols, rituals, systems and structures (power, control and organisational) that underpin the organisation. In LCS these are transparent and are discussed by all staff.

Shared value creation focuses on identifying and expanding the connections between societal and economic progress. The concept rests on the premise that both economic and social progress must be addressed using value principles. Value is defined as benefits relative to costs, not just benefits alone. Value creation is an idea that has long been recognised in business, where profit is revenues earned from customers minus the costs incurred. However, businesses have rarely approached societal issues from a value perspective but have treated them as peripheral matters. Shared value suggests that organisations can create economic value by creating societal value. There are three distinct ways to do this: by reconceiving products and markets, redefining productivity in the value chain and building supportive industry clusters at the company's locations. Porter and Kramer suggest that each of these is part of the virtuous circle of shared value; improving value in one area gives rise to opportunities in the others.[39]

The LCS is active in all three of these areas. Firstly, it reconceives products and markets by seeing its customer as a member of the society. It also identifies its market as the local community and not by the usual socio-demographic segments. This means that all stages of the LCS value proposition are linked to the development of the local community, and whilst there is a clear understanding that all activities are premised on commercial success the financial rewards of this success are used to improve the local communities: 'I think that for me it means looking after the local community – after all they are the members and that means they are the owners. We work with schools and the local community to volunteer.'[40]

The LCS redefines productivity in the value chain in a number of ways. In their supply chain they actively promote and support local businesses. LCS is part of the national CRTG; however, they support local businesses that, for reasons of supply-chain security, would be unable to contract with the CRTG category managers. Further, LCS actively supports fledgling local businesses with access to the LCS logistics and distribution operation: 'We bring their product to our distribution centre when we are coming back. So that lets them look at their costs and get a little more competitive as they did not have all of the costs that they thought they were having to put into the business.'[41]

Finally, the building of supportive clusters at the company's locations is very clearly being met by the support and partnerships being built with the local university (University of Lincoln). In 1995 the board of

LCS was authorised to make contributions of up to £1 million over a ten-year period to support the university's move from Hull to Lincoln. This has transformed the city by increasing economic activity, bringing jobs and creating a talent pool of graduates for Lincolnshire. This partnership has led to the 2012 announcement of a £14 million collaboration between LCS and the university to set up the Lincoln Science and Innovation Park.[42] In addition to these, LCS supports a range of other local businesses, charities and social enterprises through its health-care, development and education funds.

Structure and configuration

At LCS, co-operative structure is seen as being central to their ethos and values: 'I think that being a co-operative is fundamental to what we do. It gives us our values and it gives us our culture. All members are equal and all staff are members so it certainly has an impact.'[43] The co-operative ownership model places the interests of the members ahead of the short-term financial interest of the organisation. LCS also manages to leverage its closeness to the membership to serve them better.[44]

In exchange for placing members interest ahead of short-term commercial interest LCS has seen membership grow to over 230,000 members – this equates to over one in four of the population of the county. The structure of LCS is supported by nine members' groups throughout the county. These groups meet four times per year and consist of approximately thirty people each. The members' groups have a range of roles: they act as consumer panels testing new products, they are the mechanism by which the Community Champion awards are made – making awards to local charities and community groups – and they influence the choice of Charity of the Year.

'The importance for our members who are also our customers, [is that] they are all shareholders. All the staff are shareholders. I am a member; I have one vote, same as everyone else does.'[45] This means that LCS has a 'proximity advantage'[46] in several respects, including the following examples. Firstly, in a geographically dispersed county it remains close to its members via the members' groups and it has a closer relationship to its customers. Additionally, the structure allows the differing divisions to benefit from the member groups and so the usual organisational silos are less problematic than in other organisations. Further, the ICA principles that are generally well known and accepted by staff include 'co-operation among co-operatives', which encourages staff to gain an understanding of other aspects of the business. The structure of LCS means that the owners are members, and as members they participate in the process of setting direction via the members' groups.

The organisational strategy is aligned to the needs of the members and of the local community. Additionally, the fact that staff are members and therefore owners gives them a strong sense of belonging to the organisation and of ownership of LCS. This is not possible in a public company or investor-owned firm with the primacy of shareholder returns.

Business case and measures

As a society LCS measures performance using a ten-indicator balanced scorecard developed by Co-operatives UK, and all employees are aware of the importance of meeting the range of key performance indicators that the society measures. In addition to these key performance indicators the individual business units have financial performance targets and budgets to ensure that they are operating effectively and efficiently. The LCS uses another tool, LM3, to measure the financial impact that it has on the local economy. The LM3 is a tool developed by the New Economics Foundation (NEF) to measure the multiplier effect of spending in the local economy. The LM3 report estimated that £5m a year, which would go to external investors in a PLC goes to the LCS members, staff and suppliers. The LM3 analyses wages paid, the dividend given to members and the donations made to good causes. It gives an analysis of the impact of money spent with local businesses, such as the 'Love Local' food suppliers. However, it also considers more transactional elements of the supply chain, such as the contractors that build and refit stores or who print posters and leaflets, as well as professional firms such as solicitors and accountants. The LM3 also examines how much the suppliers then spend locally (the total in 2012–13 was estimated to be around 75 per cent of their revenue). The NEF suggests that 'a higher proportion of money re-spent in the local economy means a higher multiplier effect because more income is generated for local people'.[47]

LCS uses this information to encourage members to engage with their business:

> Did you know that for every £1 spent with Lincolnshire Co-op, an extra 40p is generated for the local economy? We've taken part in some research which looked at where money goes once it is spent in our outlets. We were really excited by the results. It showed that cash spent in our outlets passes through local people's hands five to eight times.[48]

Culture and leadership

In their book *The Leadership Challenge*, Kouzes and Posner suggest that leadership in an organisation is not a positional responsibility; rather, it is about 'mobilizing others to want to work towards shared aspirations'.[49] They suggest that there are five traits or behaviours that underpin this. Quotations are added to these points to show possibility of alignment with LCS staff views:

1. Model the way

To model the behaviours expected from others it is necessary to be clear about guiding principles and values. Effective leaders are aware that their behaviours must reflect their rhetoric and that credibility is only possible if words and deeds are aligned.

'I feel that the values and principles are clear and we can see them being lived and they are not just something on the wall.' There were numerous comments from staff, such as this from a retail assistant, that pointed to the fact that the senior management team clearly believe in the values and principles of the co-operative movement and in the LCS mission and objectives. These are underpinned by the performance management systems and measures that quantify the impact that LCS has on the local community, the way that it creates shared value and, through the fairtrade scheme, how its ethical trading claims are verified.

2. Inspire a shared vision

Leaders have a responsibility to engage others in tying their 'personal dreams' to the aspirations of the group to create a shared vision. Leaders inspire this shared vision through 'vivid language and ... uplift others with their infectious enthusiasm and excitement to strive towards achieving the groups goals for the greater good'.[50] 'What always impresses me is that it's not just values that are passed down from the top – they also make sure that we see them adhering to them.'[51]

3. Challenge the process

Much of the role of the leaders involves managing change. In their seminal work on change management McCalman and Paton suggest that a 'systems approach' to change is required to effectively manage change.[52]

LCS's stated values include the notion of a 'family of businesses', which is designed to combat the silo mentality the divisional structure can encourage. The values provide a framework for staff to understand the importance of taking a 'whole-business' approach to LCS, and although the retail arm is the largest no one part is seen as being any more important than another. There are very strong links between pharmacy and retail; however, there is a weaker link between the funeral business and the rest of the group. By putting in place the organisational structures to promote the less visible parts of LCS the leadership team are breaking down the silos and challenging the process.

4. Enable others to act

Kouzes and Posner suggest that leadership is a team effort that requires trust and strong relationships. That these exist in LCS is evidenced repeatedly in the research.

> We all have to take responsibility for bringing the best out of each other. I think our commitment to education is probably the most important thing that we do – it shows that we are serious about developing communities but it starts with us – we invest in our own people's education and that shows that it's not just about looking good – we actually do it.[53]

5. Encourage the heart

This involves putting into practice the principles and actions that create a sense of community. In LCS this is done through the co-operative values and the consistent communication of what is important to the society.

> In terms of culture – it is part of our job to make sure that everyone understands the values and that they are lived and breathed. Do we create the culture – no we do not. The staff create the culture but what we do is to provide the structures where that culture comes to mean something. We must be visible in doing this.[54]

Organisational culture has been defined by Schein as a pattern of basic assumptions invented, discovered or developed by a given group as it learns to cope with its problems of external adaptation and internal integration.[55] The employees of LCS explain the culture in a consistently uniform way. The importance of a local agenda combined with the grounding principles of the wider co-operative movement and the values of LCS combine to evidence a very powerful dominant narrative that the staff use to help make sense of the essence of what it means to be a part of LCS. The fact that all staff become members and that the members are the owners of the society helps to create a culture of 'members first',[56] where LCS manages to create member loyalty and to grow its member base. Member loyalty is an important factor in the creation of the LCS culture as this would appear to underpin other elements of the cultural web of the society.

Conclusions

This chapter has investigated the practices, values and culture of a regional co-operative. The case study has taken a longitudinal approach, and the organisation was revisited on several occasions between 2008 and 2013. The key findings are that staff at the LCS show a very high degree of awareness of the benefits that the values and structures of the co-operative movement, and more importantly LCS, bring. Whilst they do not use the standard language of CSR they have a very strong sense of what being responsible means to the society and there is a very strong level of engagement in its values and objectives.

Meaning is created through a range of different processes – symbolic interactionism plays a role and in the case of LCS there are abstract objects but also concrete objects. The interaction between the staff and members plays an important role in this process, as does the relationship between staff in the different divisions and between staff and managers and the top leadership team.

The majority of the society's activities are focused around local initiatives. It has a very strong relationship with one local school, and education is a constant theme that runs through all activities and is reflected in the beliefs and values of the society. The local focus does not mean an overly insular approach to CSR, and indeed a significant element of the LCS activities is to ensure there is an understanding of the logic behind, and benefits of, fairtrade. The LCS paradigm centres on the creation of shared value, and this is reinforced repeatedly throughout the case study. Shared value is created by adapting the organisational processes and structures to ensure not only that they benefit the society but also that the local community is a significant beneficiary. This is not just an aspiration, however: through the performance management system and by using the LM3 tool the benefit to the local community can be quantified in financial terms.

The leadership team in LCS provide much of the context through which sense is made and their behaviours and alignment of their actions to the values and mission of the society creates much of the context for LCS. Ultimately, LCS has a focus on its local community and the members, and in doing so it brings all of the experience and capabilities available in the society to enhance and develop these stakeholders. By developing local businesses it stimulates the economy, by investing in community groups it enhances the community, and its focus on environmental activities encourages the local community to consider the impact of their activities and actions on the planet and to ensure sustainability is a value that, whilst not necessarily explicitly codified, guides all of their activities.

Porter and Kramer suggest that 'The concept of shared value resets the boundaries of capitalism. By better connecting companies' success with societal improvement, it opens up many ways to serve new needs, gain efficiency, create differentiation, and expand markets.'[57] LCS would appear to be at the vanguard of this change.

Notes

1 M. E. Porter and M. R. Kramer, 'Creating shared value', *Harvard Business Review* 89:1/2 (January/February 2011).
2 M. Hingley, 'Networks in socially embedded local food retailers: the case of retail co-operatives', *Journal of Business Marketing Research* 4:3 (2010), 111–28.
3 R. E. Stake, *The Art of Case Study Research* (Thousand Oaks: Sage, 1995).
4 R. Yin, *Case Study Research: Design and Methods* (London: Sage, 2014).
5 A. B. Carroll, 'A three-dimensional conceptual model of corporate performance', *Academy of Management Review* 4:4 (1979), 497–505.
6 C. Handy, 'What's a business for?', *Harvard Business Review* (December 2002).
7 Hingley, 'Networks'.
8 International Co-operative Alliance (ICA), 'Statement of co-operative identity, values and principles' (1995), http://ica.coop/en/whats-co-op/co-operative-identity-values-principles (accessed 17 February 2016).
9 Lincolnshire Co-operative Society (LCS), 'What is a co-operative?', http://lincolnshire.coop/about-us/what-is-a-co-operative? (accessed 29 February 2016).
10 Yin, *Case Study Research*.
11 J. Corbin and A. Strauss, *Basics of Qualitative Research* (London: Sage, 2008).
12 C. Campos, A. Dent, R. Fry and A. Reid, *Impact of the Recession: Regional Trends 43* (London: Office for National Statistics, 2011).
13 LCS, 'Financial reports', www.lincolnshire.coop/about-us/financial-reports (accessed 29 February 2016).
14 Corbin and Strauss, *Basics of Qualitative Research*.
15 G. Johnson, R. Whittingham and K. Scholes, *Exploring Strategy: Texts and Cases* (Harlow: Pearson, 2011).
16 D. Gioia and D. Chittipeddi, 'Sensemaking and sensegiving in strategic change', *Strategic Management Journal* 12:6 (1991), 433–48, and J. Miles, *Management and Organisational Theory* (San Francisco: Jossey Bass, 2012).
17 Gioia and Chittipeddi, 'Sensemaking and sensegiving'.
18 S. Maitlis and T. B. Lawrence, 'Triggers and enablers of sense-giving in organizations', *Academy of Management Journal* 50:1 (2007), 57–84.
19 Food retail store worker.
20 Dispensing manager.
21 S. Maitlis, 'The social processes of organizational sense-making', *Academy of Management Journal* 48:1 (2005), 21–49.
22 Ibid., p. 32.
23 R. MacIntosh and D. MacLean, 'Conditioned emergence: a dissipative structures approach to transformation', *Strategic Management Journal* 20:4 (1999), 297–316.
24 ICA, 'Statement of co-operative identity'.

25 H. Blumer, 'The methodological position of symbolic interactionism' in *Symbolic Interactionism: Perspective and Method* (Englewood Cliffs: Prentice-Hall, 1969), p. 68.
26 Ibid., p. 69.
27 Store manager.
28 Pharmacy dispenser.
29 Customer service assistant.
30 Porter and Kramer, 'Creating shared value', p. 66.
31 J. Jonker and A. Marberg, 'Corporate social responsibility *quo vadis*', *Journal of Corporate Citizenship* 27 (2007), 107–18.
32 Ibid., p. 16.
33 Head office manager.
34 Store worker.
35 Head office manager.
36 Ibid.
37 Supply chain manager
38 Johnson et al., *Exploring Strategy*.
39 Porter and Kramer, 'Creating shared value'.
40 Pharmacy worker.
41 Supply chain staff.
42 University of Lincoln, 'Multi-million pound science and innovation park announced' (2 August 2012) www.lincoln.ac.uk/news/2012/08/544.asp (accessed 17 February 2016).
43 Membership officer.
44 McKinsey and Company, *McKinsey on Cooperatives* (n.p.: McKinsey and Company Industry Publications, 2012).
45 Sales assistant.
46 McKinsey and Company, *McKinsey on Cooperatives*.
47 NEF Consulting, 'Local multiplier 3 (LM3)' (n.d.), www.nef-consulting.co.uk/our-services/evaluation-impact-assessment/local-multiplier-3-lm3 (accessed 17 February 2016).
48 Head office manager.
49 J. Kouzes and B. Posner, *The Leadership Challenge* (San Francisco: Wiley, 2011), p. 1.
50 Ibid., pp. 100–1.
51 Retail manager.
52 J. McCalman and R. Paton, *Change Management: A Guide to Effective Implementation*, 3rd edition (London: Sage, 2008), p. 101.
53 Human resources officer.
54 Learning and development manager.
55 E. H. Schein, *Organisational Culture and Leadership*, 4th edition (San Francisco: Jossey-Bass, 2010).
56 McKinsey and Company, *McKinsey on Cooperatives*.
57 Porter and Kramer, 'Creating shared value'.

16

Learning to swim against the tide: crises and co-operative credibility – some international and historical examples

Anthony Webster, Linda Shaw, Rachael Vorberg-Rugh, John F. Wilson and Ian Snaith

The year 2013 was intended to be a celebratory one for The Co-operative Group, as the organisation once known as the Co-operative Wholesale Society (CWS) marked 150 years since its founding. Instead, 2013 became an *annus horribilis*, marked by the greatest financial crisis in the Group's history. Losses for the 2013 financial year totalled £2.5 billion, and the Group lost 70 per cent of its ownership stake in The Co-operative Bank.[1] As events unfolded, leadership and governance failures at the Group took centre stage in an increasingly public debate over whether the UK's largest co-operative was fit for purpose. Although the crisis was initially confined to the financial pages, in the autumn of 2013 it made lurid tabloid headlines when former chairman of The Co-operative Bank Paul Flowers was exposed for incompetence, financial impropriety, and involvement in drugs and prostitution.[2] As 2013 came to a close, a parade of former Group and Bank leaders testified before the Treasury Select Committee in Parliament, and financial regulators opened investigations into the problems at the Bank.[3] In April 2014, when Sir Christopher Kelly published an independent report, he roundly condemned the Bank's management and the Group's poor governance procedures. A further review by Lord Myners, investigating governance at The Co-operative Group, was published in May 2014. The Myners Review pulled no punches, castigating the Group's governance procedures, citing the lack of professional expertise on its elected Board, critiquing the inability of members to hold the Board directly to account through an annual general meeting (AGM), dismissing the existing tiered governance system as unwieldy, and highlighting the longstanding dominance of elected positions by a clique of member governors. Myners suggested a series of reforms, including the appointment of a PLC-style board, coupled with the establishment of a directly elected national membership council charged with safeguarding co-operative values and holding the board and executive management to account.[4]

Although many expressed concerns over the impact of such reforms,[5] by summer 2014 the elected members of the Group found themselves in a serious predicament. Amidst the UK's greatest co-operative crisis in living memory, surrounded by concern over what its creditors might do if reforms were rejected, and a great deal of uncertainty over the nature and extent of member involvement in the future, the Group's elected members were asked to approve a radical reorganisation plan based largely on Myners' suggestions.[6] On a damp Saturday in early September 2014, a specially convened Special General Meeting (SGM) voted for major changes in the governance of the organisation. The vote ensured that in future the board would be dominated by qualified business professionals, with a much diminished role for elected members. This represented a major compromise of the long tradition of lay leadership within consumer co-operation. By October 2014 the Group had put interim arrangements in place, with the new governance set to begin full operation in May 2015 (see Box 16.1).[7] Meanwhile, the devastating financial impact of the crisis led the Group to introduce extensive cost-cutting measures and, to reduce its debt burden, sell off some of its long-established subsidiary businesses, including The Co-operative Pharmacy (established in 1945 as National Co-operative Chemists) and The Co-operative Farms (established in 1896).[8]

These reforms arguably arose from the serious failure of co-operatives to accept the problems faced by any stakeholder group in maintaining control of a business where managers who are business professionals have control of all the information flowing to the board. The problem of the division of ownership from control, first identified by Berle and Means in their seminal 1930s book,[9] applies to large co-operatives with millions of members who have little financial stake in the society and an easy option to exit by trading elsewhere. The Group was just such a co-operative. The 2014 reforms to The Co-operative Group's governance addressed that issue by the use of the nonexecutive director system as it applies in listed PLCs. It will be interesting to see how far other large consumer co-operatives move in a similar direction by abandoning tiered delegate board structures in favour of direct election by members with the appointment of external nonexecutive directors vetted for competence by a nominations committee.[10]

While such a chain of events would have been catastrophic for the UK co-operative movement at any time, the context in which they arose amplified their impact. In the wake of the international economic slump

Box 16.1: The Co-operative Group: governance changes

2003–14

Board of directors: 20 directors (15 elected by regional boards, considered non-executive; 5 elected by independent societies).

Membership structure: 48 area committees (members elected by geographical region), who elect representatives to 7 regional boards.

Values and principles (V&P) committees: National V&P committee (4 group board directors; 1 banking group board director; 1 elected from each of 7 regional V&P committees; 1 representative of diversity working group; 1 representative of independent societies).

2015

Board of directors: 7–11 directors, of whom up to 3 may be member-nominated directors. Independent non-executive directors retain a majority, and are appointed on recommendation of nominations committee; no more than two executive directors (including the chief executive) may also be appointed.

National members council: 100 councillors, whose role is to act as guardian for the Group's purpose and principles, and to hold board and executive management to account:

- 15 representatives of independent societies
- 85 individual member representatives, elected via one member, one vote:
  - 76 geographic representatives (South West, 11; North West, 10; Scotland, 9; South East, 9; Yorkshire & Humber, 8; East of England, 6; London, 5; Cymru Wales, 5; East Midlands, 4; West Midlands, 4; North East, 3; Northern Ireland, 2)
  - 9 special representatives (to address shortfalls in diversity, 4; members 25 or under, 3; Co-operative Young Members' Board representative, 1; Isle of Man resident, 1)

Senate: a steering committee of the council, comprising 10–15 councillors, 2–3 of whom must be representatives from independent societies. Serves as conduit between council and board.

Sources: 2003–14: J. F. Wilson, A. Webster and R. Vorberg-Rugh, *Building Co-operation: A Business History of The Co-operative Group* (Oxford: Oxford University Press, 2013), p. 349; The Co-operative Group, *Sustainability Report* (2011), www.co-operative.coop/Corporate/sustainability-report-2012/downloads/Co-op-2012_LINKED.pdf (accessed 29 February 2016), p. 9.

2015: A. Murray, 'Drafting in the changes: the Co-op Group's new governance structure', *Co-operative News* (8 August 2014), and A. Voinea, 'Nominations open for council and board elections at the Group', *Co-operative News* (8 February 2015).

of 2008, up until 2013 all the signs were that the Group had enjoyed a 'good crisis', which, if anything, had enhanced its reputation. This was a period of expansion for the Group, particularly following the 2007 merger with United Co-operatives and former United chief executive Peter Marks' ascension to the top post at the Group. However, effectively appointing a CEO without open competition by engineering a merger of societies may be neither an appropriate procedure for the selection of the best candidate to run a major business nor an expression of the co-operative value of openness. It also left something to be desired in terms of equal opportunities best practice.[11]

In 2009, the Group purchased the private retail chain Somerfield for £1.6 billion, seeking to expand its market share via acquisition. Similar moves were afoot with The Co-operative Bank, notably through its 2010 merger with Britannia Building Society.[12] At that point, the Bank was publicly regarded as a success story, showing a 17.7 per cent increase on profits over the previous year – notwithstanding the progression of its merger.[13] In fact, ambitions were growing, with the emergence of an audacious plan to catapult the Bank into the charmed circle of leading high street banks by acquiring 600 or more branches of the troubled Lloyds/TSB. 'Project Verde', as it became known, signalled an attempt to re-establish the Group and the co-operative movement as a major force in British business. Not only would it enhance the co-operative presence on the high street, a larger Co-operative Bank promised to become the financial hub for a wider revival of co-operatives of all kinds in the UK, promoting start-ups and facilitating the scaling-up of existing co-operative operations. The Co-operative Group had already made initial moves in this direction, with the creation of its own Co-operative Enterprise Hub in 2009 (although it was suspended due to funding issues in 2014).[14] The Group's status from 2011 as the preferred bidder for the Project Verde branches had the express backing of the Chancellor of the Exchequer, a significant development signalling in part the Conservative Party's belated embrace of co-operation and social enterprise as part of its 'Big Society' initiative. This in itself was indicative of a wider acceptance of co-operation as a legitimate business form by those on the political right who had been implicitly hostile to it, traditionally regarding it as essentially a leftist project.

Indeed, the nadir of co-operative fortunes globally had come in the last twenty years of the twentieth century, at a time of major failures of consumer co-operatives in Western Europe, widespread rejection of co-operation in Eastern Europe as it emerged from communist rule, and an aggressive neoliberal economic orthodoxy in the Anglo-Saxon world which asserted that the investor-owned firm was the only rational form of business organisation – an ideology which spawned new legal regimes and business cultures which facilitated and promoted widespread demutualisation.[15] In Britain this had seen the demutualisation of a large tranche of building societies, and even an attempt to buy the CWS, in the abortive 'Lanica' takeover bid led by Andrew Regan in 1997.[16] After 2008, however, this ideological antipathy towards co-operation had receded, and many of the extensive demutualisations were increasingly regarded as premature, and in some cases counter-productive. Co-operatives, together with social enterprises more generally, were seen after the crisis as a viable alternative to some of the excesses of investor-led capitalism, especially in the financial sector. Such a revisionist view was apparent not only in political initiatives such as the 'Big Society', but also in emerging European Union (EU) economic policies, which emphasised 'social innovation' and a strong 'third sector' of social enterprises as key components in the European economies of the twenty-first century. From this perspective, The Co-operative Group's troubles came at a moment of renewed hope and ambition for the UK and global co-operative movements. The ramifications of the Group's crisis for these aspirations, however, remain unclear at this point. In this capacity, it should be noted that, while as the largest co-operative in the UK the Group's crisis clearly impacted public perception of co-operatives, there are more than 6,000 co-operative enterprises in the UK at time of writing in 2014.[17]

This chapter is concerned with how co-operatives cope with arguably the greatest threat to staking a claim to the economic mainstream: the crises which emerge from time to time within co-operatives and events which threaten to undermine the credibility of co-operation as a viable economic, business and social model. Inevitably, the problems of the British consumer co-operative movement will loom large in this chapter, but other examples will be explored in brief. Co-operative failure has a long history, and the outcomes of particular crises have varied – some resulting in regeneration or stabilisation, others in oblivion. The principal aims are to identify key problems which have undermined co-operative practice and strength in a range of contexts, and to assess the effectiveness of attempts either to rectify such shortcomings or to facilitate recovery. It is thus concerned with common weaknesses and vulnerabilities in co-operation as a model, external enemies and threats to the idea, and the effectiveness of strategies to stave off failure or effect revival.

While such an essay has great obvious potential value for the British consumer movement at the present moment, the aim is to offer some general observations which might guide co-operative movements of all kinds that experience difficulties. The threat inherent in co-operative failures or crises to co-operation as an idea should not be underestimated. Co-operation has many ideological enemies – on both the neoliberal right and the statist left – and failures present opportunities for those enemies to exploit. If co-operation is to re-establish itself in the mainstream, coping with crisis swiftly, effectively and publicly is absolutely essential. The way in which the very title 'co-operative' has become a sullied title to be avoided – the term 'mutual' seems now to be the preferred title for aspiring co-operatives – since the onset of the Group's travails in 2013, is just one indication of the extreme damage conspicuous co-operative failure can inflict upon the idea itself.[18]

As Krampfer shows, the nature of co-operative failure is itself a challenge, for co-operatives can fail in one or both of two senses.[19] Of course, they can go under commercially just as any investor-led business can; but because their organising principles seek to provide an alternative to capitalism they are also ideologically damaged by business and leadership failures. Independently of commercial performance, they can also lose belief and support for co-operative ideas, leading to conversion to investor-led organisations (demutualisation). Such a development might be the result of a complex range of factors, including loss of membership or membership commitment to co-operative ideals, self-interested managers seeking greater rewards and status, or the need for capital either to facilitate expansion or avoid failure.[20] The central point, however, is that co-operation has a capacity for crisis or failure on an ideological as well as a commercial front; success in the market, though essential for co-operative survival, is not enough in itself. The conclusion will bring together some general observations on generic reasons for co-operative crises and failures, and the strategies adopted for overcoming them.

In respect of the crisis in British consumer co-operation in 2013, inevitably much of the focus of the media coverage, the investigative reports of Kelly and Myners, and indeed of those now struggling to cope with its aftermath, is on the immediate short-term reasons for the Group's difficulties. Particular attention is being paid to key events such as the Group's acquisition of Somerfield stores, the merger between The Co-operative Bank and Britannia, and the commercial strategies associated with the recent leadership of the Group, especially those of Peter Marks (CEO from 2008 to 2013), and the board with which he worked at the time. This is, of course, an essential preoccupation with those tasked with explaining and addressing the immediate and catastrophic capital shortfalls of The Co-operative Bank, and other emerging inefficiencies in the Group's commercial practices.[21] But the historian's longer-term perspective arguably offers more important insights into the fundamental causes of the crisis, especially in respect of problems of democracy and governance, as well as longer-term commercial challenges. It is the contention here that it is an error to see 2013 as a particular moment of crisis for a business recovering rapidly after a period of earlier crisis and difficulty in the late twentieth century. Rather, the most fruitful approach is to see 2013 as one episode in a deeper and longer-term crisis unfolding since the middle of the twentieth century: a long-term malaise only partially and unsuccessfully addressed by several major attempts at reform since the 1950s. Until recently the reforms of the 1990s and 2000s were thought to have finally reversed the fortunes and tackled the underlying problems of British consumer co-operation. As we shall see below, this assessment was premature, and some of the most serious problems facing the movement remain unresolved.

As is analysed in greater detail in Wilson, Webster and Vorberg-Rugh's recent history of The Co-operative Group,[22] the problems of the modern British consumer co-operative movement can be traced back to at least the 1950s, when several major socio-economic trends threatened what had become a dominant position in British retail. The first and most obvious issue was a rapidly changing commercial environment. With remarkable speed, private retailers consolidated their operations into large regional, and later national, chains, and became public companies that were able to access City finance to modernise their operations and construct larger, more attractive and more conveniently located stores.[23] These actions reflected a further issue: the radical restructuring of the urban geography and sociological context within which British consumer co-operation had flourished. Between 1950 and the mid-1970s, postwar reconstruction and the democratisation of motor transport altered the landscapes of towns and cities in ways that were inimical to co-operative interests. The shift of population to the suburbs, combined with full unemployment and unprecedented levels of prosperity, severely disrupted many of the working-class communities within which local co-operative societies and their stores were embedded. As these communities dispersed and reformed, the spatial distribution of co-operative stores in many regions was no longer appropriate for their memberships and markets. Centralised managerial decision-making in the private retail chains, and their access to capital through the City, made it relatively easy for them to respond effectively to these changes by building new and larger stores in locations which reflected changing population patterns and transport technologies.

Although the co-operative movement represented Britain's largest retailer in the 1950s, it faced two significant challenges in responding to this shifting commercial environment. The first of these was structural. In the 1950s, the British movement was made up of 1,000 or so independent co-operative societies, loosely tied together through federal arrangements. Central organisations like the Co-operative Union had little authority to enforce decisions made at national Co-operative Congresses, and the CWS dealt with each individual society as a separate commercial unit. Thus, there was no central authority within the movement which could compel societies to merge into more economic units, or work out collaborative strategies to reconfigure and relocate their stores to better suit the changing commercial environment. A second, related issue was access to capital, in order to finance store relocations and modernisation schemes. Unlike their private counterparts, co-operatives were unable to fund capital expansion through market share offerings, and many small societies had inadequate member capital to fund improvements. The lack of co-ordination in governance was mirrored in the difficulty in mobilising capital resources, and while there was some consolidation of capital in federal bodies like the CWS and its Scottish counterpart, it was inadequate to address the full scope of the need for capital investment at local and national levels.[24]

This is not to say that there was no will for change. As early as 1906, when J. C. Gray surprised the Birmingham Co-operative Congress by proposing a single national co-operative society, there was widespread discussion of the challenges of co-ordinating the disparate movement and consolidating its capital. A few years later, the General Co-operative Survey Committee of 1914–20 reignited these debates, albeit with limited results in terms of policy.[25] In 1941, R. H. Palmer, leader of the Co-operative Union, argued for the establishment of district societies: federal organisations of ten to fifteen societies in a particular area, intended to improve collaboration between those societies and lead ultimately to amalgamations. Larger societies would then have the resources and strategic direction needed to adapt to a changing market.[26] While a similar prescription for amalgamation was offered by the Co-operative Independent Commission (CIC) in 1958, neither initiative was taken up by the societies themselves. When amalgamations of societies did start to gather pace from the 1960s, it was an uncoordinated response to commercial failure, as impoverished societies either merged with each other to maximise resources, or were taken over by Co-operative Retail Services (CRS), the 'ambulance service' of the movement. As will be seen, the co-operative society 'merger mania' beginning in the 1960s was to create its own problems and arguably exacerbated rather than eased the evolving crisis. The key question, however, is why were so many societies so obdurately resistant to change until it was forced upon them by deteriorating circumstances?

Two main factors seem to have been instrumental here. Firstly, British consumer co-operation had long been characterised by the fierce independence of its constituent societies. The highly competitive context within which British consumer co-operation emerged in the late nineteenth century forged powerful loyalties to the local society amongst members, taking the form of strong cultural and social attachments as well as economic self-interest.[27] An important consequence of this was a stubborn resistance to perceived overbearing attempts to direct the movement by its national leadership. The CWS, as a secondary co-operative whose members were the many retail societies, was often in the midst of conflict over tensions between societies' local interests and different perceptions of the national movement's needs. For example, although CWS was intended as the main source of goods and services for retail societies, it was unable to take the loyalty of member societies for granted. Most societies insisted on their freedom to source produce from wherever they wished, and proved largely immune to demands for loyalty from CWS's national leaders.[28] Local societies proved just as suspicious of top-down efforts at reform in the decades after the Second World War as they had been previously. This became evident in the years following the publication of the CIC report in 1958, when societies resisted all efforts to implement its recommendations.[29]

These difficulties were also compounded by a second development. Like many membership-based organisations in postwar Britain, the co-operative movement suffered from a decline in, first, member participation in co-operative democracy and, in due course, by the 1960s a decline in membership.[30] While the reasons for this still require careful research, it is clear that it was, in part, a symptom of wider trends in declining political and social participation within British society. It did not go unnoticed within the co-operative movement itself, nor were its national leaders oblivious to its dangers. In the mid-1950s, a study was commissioned by the Co-operative College from two academics, J. A. Banks of the University of Liverpool and E. N. Ostergaard of the University of Birmingham, into the state of internal consumer co-operative society democracy in Britain. A sign of the extent of the concern was the fact that just a few years later the two produced a second report on the same issue. Both reached essentially the same conclusion: membership engagement was severely on the wane.[31] Walton shows that by the 1970s even the 'optimistic' assessments of membership in society records revealed an unequivocal decline.[32]

The atrophy in the membership base of British consumer co-operation is difficult to overestimate as a source of the movement's subsequent problems. There were several long-term consequences which hamper the movement to this day. Some are well recorded. Conversations with many people over the age of fifty from working-class origins perhaps most eloquently spells out the obvious problem. 'Divi' numbers are remembered by many such people, and implicit in those memories is a lost world of local loyalties, local communities and an almost automatic perception of the local co-operative as the source of most everyday – and long-term – needs. While the loss of such a powerful tradition of brand loyalty was inevitably damaging for the movement, there were other consequences which, especially in the light of the most recent debates about governance and the role of the membership, were arguably even more corrosive in their effects on the ability of the movement to recover from its problems. One of the reasons why resistance to change was so intransigent within societies was the withering away of challenge from below. Throughout the latter half of the twentieth century, the British movement struggled to attract new and younger members, whose circumstances and concerns were markedly different from those of the prewar generations. The weakness, and in some cases absence, of an active younger generation of co-operators impeded the movement's ability to redefine what co-operation might mean in the context of Britain's postwar 'long boom'. As membership declined, so too did the generational diversity of its members; nor was the movement able to attract members from outside of its traditionally white working-class base. In these circumstances, many societies became the fiefdoms of well-established elites and managers, convinced of the rightness of increasingly outdated practices, and aggressively vigilant against potential challenges from below.

As societies' economic performance declined, the relative power of managers – increasingly divorced from, and sceptical of, principles of co-operation and co-operative democracy – grew, paradoxically. The essential argument, presented most forcibly in the 1958 CIC report, that the co-operative movement's problems were ones of commercial 'backwardness', of not mimicking the commercial strategies of the private sector, became the mantra of co-operative society managers, and eventually of the national leadership itself. Perhaps maddeningly for the authors of the CIC report, it took another ten years of severe decline before most of its essential arguments were accepted – far too long for the report to have the anticipated galvanising impact. When the national leadership opted for 'Operation Facelift' in the late 1960s, many societies were beginning to run into trouble, prompting a wave of mergers. While this weakened some of the resistance to change, making at least some reform possible, the basic culture of resistance to central authority remained – and indeed became strengthened, as newly enlarged regional societies emerged, with illusions of even greater independence. Again, this was anticipated and feared by some of the architects of reform. Fred Lambert, Head of the CWS Market Research Bureau, an advocate of reform since the 1955 commission, and a moving force behind the CWS reorganisation of 1965 and many of the changes associated with Philip Thomas' brief reign as CEO in the later 1960s, anticipated that larger regional societies would result in even less cohesion within the national movement, as these societies felt large enough to 'go it alone' and dispense with their links with CWS.[33] Lambert contended that unity could only be strengthened by changing the role of CWS in its relations with societies; by CWS becoming a buying agency for the movement, rather than a producer which sold to societies in a competitive context. This would eventually come to pass – but not until the establishment of the Co-operative Retail Trading Group (CRTG) in the mid-1990s, such was the prolonged resistance to the 'centre' within the movement.[34]

An additional problem was that the process of mergers and takeovers by CRS was shaped by the fact that the movement's residual membership, activists and managers involved in mergers were predominantly concerned with securing comparable positions of influence and power in newly formed regional societies. In this respect, reform and reorganisation were distorted by the self-interested machinations of a declining membership and a managerial elite intent on protecting its own interests. At a basic level, newly emergent regional societies were dominated by political and commercial leaders who already had a track record of failure. This was also especially true of CRS, which grew from being a small department of CWS into, by the 1980s, essentially a rival organisation. As it took over struggling society after society, it not only acquired a large portfolio of shops and other assets, it also incorporated into its decision-making structures former society members, managers and leaders who brought with them many of the negative and self-interested attitudes which had flourished in their former societies. In this respect, the roots of the long-term crisis of British consumer co-operation were not merely commercial. They stemmed from a declining membership and activist base, which tilted the balance of power in favour of managers who increasingly saw themselves as commercial managers first and promoters as co-operative principles a very poor second.

In addition, the failure to appreciate that the concept of the separation of ownership and control applied to large consumer co-operatives prevented any serious consideration of other strategies to improve managerial accountability in the absence of the involvement of well-informed members. The existing elected board and committee members always resisted the use of experienced independent nonexecutive directors at board level to critically appraise management performance and proposals. Recommendations of the 1994 Co-operative Union Governance Working Group, regarding the inclusion of both the Chief Executive and the Finance Director as board members, and in both the 1994 and 2005 Corporate Governance Review Group reports for consideration of the inclusion of appointed outside directors, if additional skills were needed in the board room, were largely ignored by societies.[35]

Of course, mergers and CRS takeovers were, in many cases, the inevitable consequence of commercial failure, and CWS found itself supporting these wherever they seemed the only way forward. The pressures were considerable. In the late 1960s CWS became especially concerned about the impact of society failures on the confidence of members in societies generally, who had sums invested in those societies, if only in the form of accumulated dividends. The fear was that in an age of declining membership participation, society failures would trigger a national departure of younger and less committed society members – effectively a run on co-operatives – which could destroy the movement very quickly indeed. So serious were these worries by 1970 that Alfred Wilson, then CEO of CWS, even approached the Chancellor of the Exchequer, Anthony Barber, alerting him of the danger which publicity of society failures could have on a membership whose loyalty to the movement had been weakened by a range of cumulative factors.[36] Wilson claimed that so serious might the situation become that at some point help from the City of London or even from government might be required. By February 1971, so severe were these worries that two senior CWS officials approached the Registrar of Friendly Societies to persuade them to spell out the problems to the Treasury on their behalf. The officials pointed out that withdrawals of funds from societies had resulted in a decline of withdrawable capital from societies, reaching an unprecedented level of 10–12.5 per cent per annum. Their fear was that eventually some societies would either go out of business or would be forced to stop withdrawals, with incalculable consequences in terms of a national collapse of confidence in the movement as a whole. They cited in particular some extremely serious negative publicity for the movement, notably a BBC documentary into the failures of the Millom Society, *Ghosts of Millom*.[37]

While ultimately the Heath government took no action on the reports, it showed clearly that the collapse of society membership was recognised by national leaders of the movement as a serious threat to its commercial fortunes. It is little wonder that mergers and CRS takeovers were so unquestionably accepted as the best, if not only, solutions to these problems. When in 1973 the Scottish CWS (SCWS) experienced a major crisis as a result of catastrophic investment decisions by its bank, the takeover of that organisation by the English CWS was the overwhelming choice of solution – supported not only by the movement, but also by the Bank of England.[38] While the merger averted short-term disaster, however, it merely exacerbated the increasingly fractious relations within the co-operative movement, as CWS inherited SCWS' chain of retail outlets, bringing it into direct competition with its customers and the regional societies, as well as the CRS. Relations within the movement continued to deteriorate, and the market share of British consumer co-operatives plummeted. In the grocery trade, market share held by the co-operative movement halved from 20.5 per cent in 1976, to 10.1 per cent in 1992.[39]

Another by-product of the use of mergers to consolidate the movement was the absence of the discipline of the threat of corporate insolvency as a check on managers and directors responsible for business failure and decline in co-operative societies. Indeed, both groups often secured positions of responsibility in the society into which the failing society merged. This added to the absence of effective member voice or any substitute for it to create a lethal recipe for large organisations competing in the market with PLCs run by boards made up of independent nonexecutives and subject to the disciplines of market and press scrutiny, major disclosure requirements, and the threat of insolvency. In 2014, legal reforms applied insolvency rescue processes to co-operative societies for the first time. Previously liquidation or the appointment of a receiver by secured creditors (usually banks) was the only remedy. Now that societies have the administration procedure available, it may be appropriate to see insolvency processes as a distinct possibility for societies that fail.[40]

As we have already seen, the British consumer co-operative movement had long been dysfunctional in many of its internal relations.[41] There had always been tension between societies and CWS over commercial loyalty of the former to the latter. The Co-operative Union and the CWS frequently clashed. For decades, consumer co-operation and worker co-operatives were estranged, stemming from problems experienced by the former in its relations with the latter in the 1880s and carried forward by the dominant economic position of the consumer societies. These tensions worsened during the crisis years of the 1960s–80s, as CRS expanded and became a competitor to CWS, and as larger regional societies developed illusions of greater independence. A factor in this scenario of deteriorating internal relations was undoubtedly the pressured self-interest of the dwindling number of activists and society managers, who desperately sought survival and retention of authority as societies merged, activities were contracted and labour (active members and managers) were all shed. In this context, the corrosive effect on co-operative democracy and values, as well as on democratic governance, of decline in members and activism was amplified, as self-interest trumped co-operative behaviour. The manifestation of this deteriorating co-operative spirit took many forms – self-interested resistance to collaboration between co-operative institutions such as CRS and CWS, CWS and regional societies, as well as The Co-operative Bank and CIS. Corruption among officials and co-operative managers also became a problem, with a number of damaging scandals emerging in the late 1980s and early 1990s.[42]

In these circumstances, the problems of the movement by the 1980s seemed to vindicate contemporary neoliberal beliefs that co-operation was a movement whose day was rapidly passing. Major national failures of consumer co-operative movements in Europe, continuing loss of market share by the British movement and the success of demutualisation by the mid-1990s all served to reinforce the notion that its days were numbered. Nevertheless, demise was averted in the 1990s by several factors and influences which for a time gave the impression that the underlying problems of the movement were at last being addressed. These apparent solutions to co-operative problems included a mixture of changing circumstances, a widening appreciation within the movement of the severity of the problems faced, structural reforms and also, for a time, leaders who genuinely aspired to an ethical and democratic as well as a commercial revival. Up until fairly recently, it was all too easy to overestimate the success of the changes which the decade brought. However, it is important first to note what these were before assessing their limitations.

Perhaps the most important initial development was a realisation within the movement and its managers by the end of the 1980s that if divisions within the movement continued, its demise was assured. By then the number of independent societies had been reduced to a few score, and a strategy for their merger into one large national body began to gather momentum. Up to then most mergers or takeovers of societies had taken place as a response to commercial crises, rather than as positive strategy. A turning point was the decision of North East Co-operative Society to merge with CWS in 1990, a decision based on strength rather than weakness.[43] Despite resistance from CRS, the idea began to gather momentum. In the mid-1990s, a Co-operative Governance Working Group attempted to address the problems of corruption and lack of democratic engagement in the movement, contributing to a major Co-operative Union Congress series of resolutions in 1994, and a code of best practice in 1995.[44] In 1995, the International Co-operative Alliance (ICA) also produced a new set of principles and values, to which the incoming CEO of the CWS,

Graham Melmoth, committed his organisation to adopt in a proactive way. A major training initiative was launched through the Co-operative College to secure senior membership and managerial buy-in to this new attempt to 'go back to co-operative basics'. On a structural level, as we noted earlier, the creation of CRTG to buy for subscribing societies and the CWS marked a major breakthrough in the campaign for unity.

Crucially, though, it was the abortive attempt by Andrew Regan's Lanica consortium in 1997 which resulted in an apparently decisive swing of power in favour of Melmoth and his supporters within management and the membership. More than anything, the attempt brought home to members and managers alike just how vulnerable so many co-operative organisations potentially were, creating political momentum within the movement for further change. It provided the basis for the Co-operative Commission of 2001, the merger between CRS and CWS, and between CIS and the Bank, and the formation of The Co-operative Group, intended by Melmoth to become a 'Family of Co-operative Businesses'. It was no less than an attempt to revitalise the movement in both an ethical and commercial sense. The dividend was restored (in a modified form), and major new national initiatives to stimulate individual membership of the Group were undertaken. Membership initiatives built on the growing ethical consumer orientation of the 1980s and 1990s, as growing numbers of British consumers responded to crises of confidence in PLCs and their ability to address concerns such as social welfare, environmental impact and animal cruelty.[45] The optimism of the Melmoth years seemed to bear fruit, with a marked recovery in retail and other areas of Group business in the first decade of the twenty-first century as well as an expanding membership. The mergers with Somerfield, Britannia and the vaunting ambition of Project Verde all seemed to presage a new golden age for co-operation, especially given the changing ideological climate of 'Big Society' and social innovation. However, one effect of the CRS/CWS merger, the later United mergers and the subsequent constitutional review had been to leave The Co-operative Group board dominated by directors without business or management experience, who were expected to control a CEO appointed without any effective selection process, and who had no mechanism to assess or critique business plans or a strategy that ran up ever-increasing levels of debt.

The events of 2013 were to prove that the long-term crisis of the British movement had only temporarily receded. The deep-seated problems had not been resolved, although the effort to address them in the late 1990s was sincere and seemed to make some progress at first. Several aspects of the 1990s reform movement clearly did not achieve success in their objectives. Melmoth's determination that Group managers and elected officials should be steeped in co-operative values and principles, as well as equipped with the technical and democratic skills to create a successful business, proved fleeting. Supporters of reform in key institutions such as the Co-operative College always maintained that education of the membership and managers in co-operative values required persistent and high-powered programmes which would be sustained and further enhanced, to ensure that there was in fact an ongoing 'co-operative cultural revolution' which would embed values, principles and methods in successive generations of co-operative leaders. The same people recognised that the complexities of modern business required the emergence of an activist base which contained the expertise to hold managers truly to account. Nevertheless, after Melmoth the momentum behind this cultural initiative quickly stalled, and successive CEOs were noticeably less zealous about the centrality of co-operative values. A second problem was that the member and managerial elites which had come to dominate the merged societies in the late twentieth century continued to dominate the new structures of the Group, and their preoccupation with self-interest and position seems to have continued. A self-interested elite of member governors and officials with limited business training and a persistently weak commitment to co-operative principles was to figure prominently in both the Kelly and Myners reports as key reasons for the problems publicised in 2013. Those problems arose from a long-standing failure to acknowledge that the practical use of member 'voice' in consumer co-operatives is difficult, while 'exit' is easy. As a result, mechanisms such as the appointment or election of directors with business skills and experience enabling them to challenge management during strategic decision-making were not deployed until the investor stakeholder group from whom enormous amounts had been borrowed was able to force such changes on the Group after the crisis had struck. Neither managers nor those participating in the delegate system had any interest in such reforms while the Group could survive with a lower level of accountability to members, and the wider movement had ignored the calls of the Governance Reports of 1994 and 2005 for this issue to be addressed.[46]

Things had simply not changed enough. Nor had sufficient progress been made in rebuilding an active national membership, notwithstanding the sincere efforts of membership officials at the area, regional and national levels. Part of the problem here was that the modern retail experience had long ago lost the strong local and social attributes which had been so central to the rise of co-operative activism and commitment. Recreating it in a twenty-first-century context was never realistic. Some in the movement recognised this, and looked to other aspects of co-operative activity (banking, finance, funerals, childcare, pharmacies and health services) to play a more prominent role in twenty-first-century co-operation; but its national leaders were frequently slow either to take advantage of opportunities or to articulate a clear vision for the future of the Group, notwithstanding laudable initiatives such as the Co-operative Enterprise Hub and the efforts to establish The Co-operative Bank as a national player. Such moves as the latter seem to have been driven more by the perceived commercial advantages of greater size and market share than any wider vision of what would be best to resurrect a large active membership and a thriving co-operative democracy. The gloss of the new Co-operative brand, with its new shop frontages and television commercials themed to Bob Dylan's 'Blowing in the Wind', were ultimately more image than substance. Part of the problem was that the mergers with societies continued, and the one between the Group and United in 2007, which saw Marks become CEO and Flowers the Chair of the Bank, saw considerable dilution of the Melmoth vision as well as the culmination of a long-term failure to deal with the absence of mechanisms for effective management accountability for societies with elected 'lay' directors who were not subject to any competence requirement before election.

The Co-operative Group reforms of 2014 have dealt with the competence requirements. However, a more radical approach to the weakness of the commitment of most consumer members might be to question the viability above a certain limited scale of co-operative societies with a limited member stake or interest. Since consumers can easily decide to use other retailers, their stake in their society is minimal in economic terms unless they are required to hold some significant capital stake. Employees, on the other hand, have a strong interest in ensuring that their employing society thrives. Could a process developing an employee voice on the basis of employee membership be a way forward? Perhaps workplace organisation with trade union involvement would protect such a structure from the obvious risk of management influence over employee members. It has long been the case that the groups most likely to be active in a consumer co-operative were the employees (as consumer members) and those with an ideological commitment to co-operation.[47] That might point to a move towards restructuring consumer societies as worker co-operatives or at least hybrids.

It is hard not to conclude in 2015 that the last half-century of British consumer co-operation has been a long process of crisis and decline, punctuated by false dawns of resurrection and revival. Above all, what would appear to have been lacking is a combination of, on the one hand, a genuine and widespread commitment to co-operative values and principles across the Group and, on the other hand, a viable strategic orientation that adopted best practices from other co-operatives and large-scale retailers. While the first point has been made amply in the text above, it is essential to emphasise the need to rebuild the organisation as a member-driven operation, with a mission that is visibly manifested in the actual corporate governance mechanisms of the Group. Linked to this restoration process is the elaboration of a twenty-first-century membership benefits package, imitating what has been done in Scandinavian co-operatives with considerable success. At the same time, serious consideration ought to be given to the strategic orientation of the many components of The Co-operative Group, providing greater focus that reflects the interests of members and thereby generating the kind of cohesion that has been lacking for over fifty years. While implementing these changes will take some time and impose resource challenges, the Group needs to think more creatively about its future strategy and structure if it is to survive in the post-crisis era.

When considering the travails of The Co-operative Group in Britain, it is instructive to compare its strategies for recovery with those of its European peers. Many of the problems experienced by the UK consumer movement in the later twentieth century were not unique. Many European co-operatives faced similar difficulties in attracting and engaging members in the face of an increasingly individualistic consumer orientation and a general decline in participation in a variety of social and political organisations. The challenges posed by emergent retail-chain, PLC-style organisations were faced by consumer co-operatives in Austria, France, Germany, Italy and the Scandinavian countries. A number of national and comparative studies make sobering reading for any spectator of the problems of The Co-operative Group. Perhaps the best of the comparative analyses comes from Espen Ekberg, whose work on consumer co-operatives across a range of European countries offers some instructive observations.[48] Ekberg notes that what characterised the response of co-operative movements to the challenge of the retail chains was its striking diversity: different national movements adopted different strategies.

At one extreme were those countries which responded by unifying their many societies and by seeking to concentrate resources into few and larger organisations. This happened most notably in Austria and Germany. Following the Second World War, the movement began to rebuild through a centralised organisation of twenty-eight district co-operatives, organised through a holding company, the General Austrian Consumer Co-operative (AÖKG); 95 per cent of consumer co-operative members were under its umbrella. In her survey of the Austrian movement,

Gabriella Hauch notes that character of the Austrian movement changed markedly from its pre-*Anschluss* period, focusing on modernisation and rationalisation and seeking to maintain social and political neutrality.[49] In 1978, all of the Austrian retail societies voted to subsume themselves in a new, national organisation, Konsum.[50] However, the period between 1978 and 1990 was one of 'concealed scandal', in which rising deficits were hidden behind complex sale and leaseback arrangements, combined with a further weakening of co-operative identity. By the early 1990s, Konsum's fragile state became widely known, and despite an abortive attempt to create a transnational alliance with the Swiss co-operative Migros, in 1995 Konsum entered bankruptcy and its assets were sold off.[51] In West Germany, as Brett Fairbairn notes, consumer co-operatives after 1945 faced the dual challenge of rebuilding their distribution, retail and production system with few assets, and of adapting to the rapid changes of postwar retailing; in East Germany consumer and housing co-operatives were subsumed by the state.[52] Although it made considerable strides in the 1950s, by the late 1960s it faced growing difficulties, including the need for increased capital and for greater efficiencies and centralisation. By the late 1970s, most West German co-operatives were reorganised into regional amalgamations and converted into share companies, under a centralised national company, Coop AG. By 1984 the Coop AG group included about two-thirds of the nation's consumer co-operatives. However, by the late 1980s Coop AG was in financial difficulties and suffered a scandal when several leaders were convicted of embezzlement, leading to its ultimate failure. In his analysis, Fairbairn notes the failure of the West German consumer movement to provide a credible alternative to the increasingly individualistic, opportunistic consumer culture of the postwar era, or to adapt to the decentralised, flexible, grassroots orientation of the 'new social movements' of the 1980s.[53] Thus, in the German and Austrian cases, moves towards centralisation ended in failure. It is notable that Ekberg's analysis describes the evolution of The Co-operative Group as following a similar pattern of lengthy decline and increased centralisation, though not in such a complete and radical fashion, most notably since it effectively created a 'mixed membership' model in which individuals became members as well as the remaining independent retail societies which had once constituted the CWS.[54] For Ekberg, The Co-operative Group represented a kind of 'hybrid model' between centralisation and continuing federal structures.

Ominously, Ekberg contends that while there have been successful examples of merged, non-federal societies in Europe (notably in Switzerland), it has not proven to be the most effective response to the challenge of the multiples. Ekberg singles out Finland, Norway and Italy as examples of consumer co-operative movements meeting the challenge by reforming but maintaining the federal character of the movement. In these countries, local or, increasingly, regionally-based retail societies maintained their independence from national wholesale organisations, albeit with some regional mergers to facilitate advantages of scale and scope combined with major reforms in warehousing strategies. Probably the most successful of these examples was in Norway, where the reforms above were combined with careful co-ordination between the roles of NKL (the national wholesaling organisation) and the regional societies. In essence, NKL took over the buying function of the movement, procuring goods for the regional societies. For their part, while the regional societies retained autonomy and independence, they also followed NKL discipline and guidelines in terms of standardising the consumer's experience across Norway and through common marketing strategies. In other words, a balance was struck between national co-ordination and the retention of a high degree of local autonomy.[55] Similar developments occurred in Finland, where financial problems for societies in the 1960s led to widespread mergers and the emergence by 2002 of the 'S' Group, in which SOK, the central body, provides advice and support for the twenty-eight or so local and regional co-operatives, which run the stores and retain their own membership structures. In 2014, SOK held a 45 per cent market share.[56] In Italy, a strong federal approach has also brought success since the 1970s. The Italian structure features overlapping collaborative networks of retail societies and wholesale societies, which work in concert and have been remarkably successful in holding their own in the market. CoopItalia remains the top Italian mass retailer.[57] Federalism has also remained a core element in successful financial co-operatives. Desjardins, one of Canada's largest financial institutions, has grown based on a network of *caisses* (credit unions) and local business centres owned by the *caisses* in that area.[58] What is striking about these international examples is the extent to which continuing federalism seems to have proven to be a strength. Commercially, it appears to have combined local market knowledge with the advantage of an overarching central strategy and provision of support services, made possible by reasoned, co-operative relationships emerging between societies, and between them and the centre. Simultaneously, the preservation of regional societies – albeit in amended form through mergers – assisted significantly in maintaining member democratic engagement.

The long history of tension between the component parts of the British movement made a similar development impossible to achieve in Britain during the critical period of decline from the 1950s to the 1990s. While there were mergers to create larger regional societies, these did not facilitate the collaborative relationships evident in Italy and the Scandinavian countries – for a time they actually seem to make the dysfunctionality of the British movement even more of a problem, as regional societies saw themselves as powerful independent entities, and the CWS as at best an irrelevance and at worst a rival. When recovery came it was the result of cumulative loss of market share and retail society failure, precipitating a 'fall to the centre' by the 1990s that created The Co-operative Group and the peculiar patchwork of remaining independent societies coexisting with individuals as members of the Group. Comparisons between the Group and the European examples above suggest that finding an effective balance between centre and locality remains a key concern, both in terms of business adaptability and member engagement. In this respect, the example of the Lincolnshire Co-operative Society as an illustration of shared value, discussed in Considine and Hingley's chapter 15 in this volume, may prove instructive to the Group, despite the differences in size, scope and structure between the two societies.

Where to go from here? The return of the Group to profit in April 2015 was a moment of relief in what have been arguably the most difficult years in the history of the movement. But a heavy price has been paid. The loss of pharmacies and farms and the effective loss of the Bank have narrowed options to reconstruct a new, more attractive membership offer based on activities other than retail. Diversification into health, finance and legal services seemed credible alternatives before the crisis, but no longer appear so, given the contraction into the Group's core retail activities. Maintaining and building an active membership on the basis of retail alone would be a very tall order indeed, given the ferocity of the competition and the much diminished membership advantages of being a member of a retail society. The governance reforms of 2014, regardless of their commercial advantages, appear to many members to be a watering-down of the member offer, diminishing the political clout of members in the running of the Group. There are real fears that the destination might prove to be eventual demutualisation as the active membership is hollowed out. In short, while the Group's short-term survival now seems assured, its future as a co-operative entity seems less certain. The loss to co-operation in general would be deeply damaging. The success of the Group's Enterprise Hub between 2009 and 2014 is eloquent testament to the powerful role the Group has played in revitalising and mainstreaming the co-operative model. If British consumer co-operation is to survive to celebrate its bicentenary, urgent questions of how to rebuild a new business portfolio and a new membership offer for the twenty-first century need to be answered soon. There is not a moment to lose.

Notes

1 J. Quinn, 'Co-op's £2.5bn loss is just the start of the bad news', *The Telegraph* (17 April 2014). The Co-operative Group's ownership share subsequently fell to 20 per cent as the Bank sought further capital from other investors; prior to 2013 The Co-operative Bank had been a wholly owned subsidiary of the Group. A. Bell, '£400 million lifeline for the Co-op', *Manchester Evening News* (11 May 2014).

2 J. Armstrong, 'Disgraced Co-op Bank chairman Paul Flowers fined after admitting drugs charges', *Daily Record* (7 May 2014).

3 J. Treanor, 'Regulators launch investigations into Co-op Bank's £1.5bn capital shortfall', *The Guardian* (6 January 2014).

4 C. Kelly, *Failings in Management and Governance: An Independent Review of The Co-operative Bank* (30 April 2014), www.co-operative.coop/corporate/the-kelly-review (accessed 17 February 2016); P. Myners, *The Co-operative Group: Report of the Independent Governance Review* (7 May 2014), www.co-operative.coop/Corporate/PDFs/Myners/Report_of_the_Independent_Governance_Review.pdf (accessed 17 February 2016).

5 For example, see 'Reforming peer quits Co-op board', *Belfast Telegraph* (10 April 2014); G. Swarbrick, 'Second thoughts: the Co-operative can have both a corporate strategy and mutual values', *The Guardian* (14 May 2014).

6 G. Evans and K. Pilling, 'Co-op members back four-point resolution on governance reforms', *Evening Standard* (17 May 2014).

7 A. Murray, 'What's next? The Co-operative Group's transition arrangements', *Co-operative News* (8 August 2014), www.thenews.coop/88570/news/consumer/whats-next-the-co-operative-groups-transition-arrangements (accessed 17 February 2016); R. Harvey, 'Group's transitional board named as new rules registered', *Co-operative News* (1 October 2014), www.thenews.coop/90423/news/business/groups-transitional-board-announced-as-new-rules-registered (accessed 17 February 2016).

8 'Co-operative sells pharmacies to Bestway in £620m deal', *The Guardian* (18 July 2014); J. Moulds and J. Treanor, 'Co-op sells farms business to Wellcome Trust', *The Guardian* (4 August 2014); S. Farrell, 'Co-operative Group sells Sunwin security business', *The Guardian* (2 September 2014).

9 A. Berle and G. Means, *The Modern Corporation and Private Property* (New York: Transaction Publishers, 1932).

10 See I. Snaith and R. E. Amass, 'Corporate governance in co-operatives: lessons and contrasts', *Corporate Governance International* 1:3 (1998), 4–15, for a comparison of the governance issues between listed companies and large consumer co-operatives.

11 See International Co-operative Alliance (ICA), 'Statement of co-operative identity, values and principles', http://ica.coop/en/whats-co-op/co-operative-identity-values-principles (accessed 17 February 2016).

12 See J. F. Wilson, A. Webster and R. Vorberg-Rugh, *Building Co-operation: A*

Business History of The Co-operative Group (Oxford: Oxford University Press, 2013), chapter 9.

13 J. Myers, J. Maddocks and J. Beecher, 'Resting on laurels? Examining the reliance of co-operative values in times of calm and crisis', in A. Webster, L. Shaw, J. K. Walton, A. Brown and D. Stewart, eds, *The Hidden Alternative: Co-operative Values, Past, Present and Future* (Manchester: Manchester University Press, 2011), pp. 306–26, p. 308.

14 M. C. Kidd, 'Co-operative Enterprise Hub suspends operations', *Co-operative News* (27 March 2014) www.thenews.coop/64229/news/development/co-operative-enterprise-hub-suspends-operations (accessed 17 February 2016).

15 In respect of these trends, see Kramper, 'Why cooperatives fail: case studies from Europe, Japan, and the United States, 1950–2010', and P. Battilani and H. G. Schröter, 'Demutualization and its problems' in Battilani and Schröter, eds, *The Co-operative Business Movement, 1950 to the Present* (Cambridge: Cambridge University Press, 2012), pp. 126–49 and pp. 150–74.

16 For details of this see J. Wilson, 'Co-operativism meets City ethics: the 1997 Lanica takeover bid for CWS' in Webster et al., *Hidden Alternative*, pp. 16–36; also see Wilson et al., *Building Co-operation*, pp. 325–41.

17 See Co-operatives UK, *The Co-operative Economy 2014: Untold Resilience* (Manchester: Co-operatives UK, 2014), www.uk.coop/resources/uk-co-operative-economy-2014-untold-resilience (accessed 20 January 2016).

18 Historically, co-operatives have sometimes distanced themselves from the 'co-op' name at times of particularly negative public perceptions. For example, during the 1970s–90s, CRS branded some aspects of its business without reference to co-operation, including Leo's supermarkets, Stop & Shop convenience stores, and the non-food chains Living and Home World.

19 Kramper, 'Why cooperatives fail'.

20 Battilani and Schröter, 'Demutualization and its problems'.

21 For example, see A. Murray, 'Big deals led to "neglect" of Co-operative Group's core focus', *Co-operative News* (28 March 2014), www.thenews.coop/71118/news/consumer/big-deals-led-neglect-co-operative-groups-core-focus (accessed 17 February 2016).

22 See Wilson et al., *Building Co-operation*, chapters 5–9.

23 J. Birchall, *Co-op: The People's Business* (Manchester: Manchester University Press, 1994), pp. 159–60.

24 For more detail, see *Co-operative Independent Commission Report* (Manchester: Co-operative Union, 1958), particularly 'Part III: The Capital Position'.

25 See Wilson et al., *Building Co-operation*, pp. 137–42 and pp. 170–7.

26 'The District Society: plan for a complete co-operative consumer service', *Co-operative Review* 15 (9 September 1941); based on an address given by Palmer to co-operative managers in Manchester.

27 See P. Gurney, *Co-operative Culture and the Politics of Consumption in England 1870–1930* (Manchester: Manchester University Press, 1996).

28 A. Webster, 'Building the wholesale: the development of the English CWS and British co-operative business, 1863–90', *Business History* 54:6 (2012), 883–904.

29 L. Black, '"Trying to sell a parcel of politics with a parcel of groceries": The Co-operative Independent Commission (CIC) and consumerism in post-war Britain' in Black and N. Robertson, eds, *Consumerism and the Co-operative Movement in Modern British History* (Manchester: Manchester University Press, 2009), pp. 33–50.
30 J. K. Walton, 'The post-war decline in the British retail co-operative movement: nature, causes and consequence' in Black and Robertson, *Consumerism and the Co-operative Movement*, pp. 13–33.
31 The Ostergaard and Banks study was published as a Co-operative College paper. Both studies were highlighted in J. Bailey, 'A declining democracy', *Co-operative Review* (March 1963), p. 67.
32 Walton, 'Post-war decline', p. 23.
33 F. Lambert, 'CWS in the 20th century: notes on the basic problem', held in a bundle of documents entitled 'The Role of the CWS', National Co-operative Archive (NCA).
34 In 2015, at time of writing, the CRTG is being reorganised as Federal Trading Services. See A. Voinea, 'Group moves from CRTG to Federal Trading Services', *Co-operative News* (11 March 2015), http://www.thenews.coop/93982/news/co-operatives/group-moves-from-crtg-to-federal-trading-services (accessed 17 February 2016).
35 Co-operative Union (CU), *The Report of the Corporate Governance Working Group* (April 1994), recommendations 19, 20 and 21; see also Snaith and Amass, 'Corporate governance', 11–12; Co-operatives UK, *Report of the Corporate Governance Review Group* (May 2005), pp. 8–9 and *Corporate Governance Code of Best Practice* (May 2005), Recommendation B2, particularly B2.4 and B2.5.
36 L. P. Davies, Privy Council Office to W. S. Ryrie, Private Secretary to the Chancellor of the Exchequer (5 August 1970), Treasury File T326/1303. 'The Future of the Co-operative Wholesale Society', National Archives (NA).
37 Registry of Friendly Societies to B. E. Fensome, Treasury (2 February 1971), NA.
38 Wilson et al., *Building Co-operation*, pp. 258–66.
39 Ibid., p. 259.
40 See I. Snaith, ed., *Handbook to Co-operative and Community Benefit Society Law* (London: Jordan Publishing, 2014), section 12.8.
41 Ibid. This is also a central argument of Wilson et al., *Building Co-operation.*
42 The NCA holds a 'scandals file' documenting the extensive local and national press coverage of governance failures in consumer co-operatives in this period.
43 Snaith, *Handbook*, p. 307.
44 Ibid., pp. 310–14.
45 See Wilson et al., *Building Co-operation*, pp. 316–25.
46 Co-operative Union (CU), *The Report of the Corporate Governance Working Group* (April 1994), recommendations 19, 20 and 21; see also Snaith and Amass, 'Corporate governance', pp. 11–12; Co-operatives UK, *Report of the Corporate Governance Review Group*, pp. 8–9 and *Corporate Governance Code of Best Practice*, Recommendation B2, particularly B2.4 and B2.5.

47 See I. Snaith, *The Law of Co-operatives* (London: Waterlow, 1984), pp. 189–93.
48 E. Ekberg, 'Organization: top down or bottom up? The organizational development of consumer co-operatives', in Battilani and Schröter, *Co-operative Business Movement*, pp. 222–42.
49 G. Hauch, 'From self-help to Konzern: Consumer Cooperatives in Austria 1840–1990' in E. Furlough and C. Strikwerda, eds, *Consumers against Capitalism? Consumer Cooperation in Europe, North America, and Japan, 1840–1990* (Lanham: Rowman & Littlefield, 1999), pp. 191–213, pp. 211–12.
50 R. Schewidy, 'The decline and fall of Konsum Austria', *Review of International Co-operation* 89:2 (1996), 62–8.
51 Ibid., and Hauch, 'From self-help to Konzern', pp. 212–13.
52 B. Fairbairn, 'The rise and fall of consumer cooperation in Germany' in Furlough and Strikwerda, *Consumers against Capitalism?*, pp. 267–302.
53 Ibid., pp. 296–8.
54 J. Birchall, *The Governance of Large Co-operative Businesses* (Manchester: Co-operatives UK, 2014), pp. 40–2.
55 E. Ekberg, 'Consumer co-operation and the transformation of modern food retailing: the British and Norwegian consumer co-operative movement in comparison', in Black and Robertson, *Consumerism and the Co-operative Movement*, pp. 51–68.
56 Birchall, *Governance*, pp. 39–40.
57 T. Menzani and V. Zamagni, 'Co-operative networks in the Italian economy', *Enterprise & Society* 11:1 (2010), 98–127. See also Pellervo, 'Cooperation in Finland 2012', http://pellervo.fi/kielet/english/power-point-presentations (accessed 14 September 2015).
58 See Desjardins, 'How cooperatives work', www.desjardins.com/ca/about-us/desjardins/governance-democracy/how-cooperatives-work/index.jsp (accessed 14 September 2015).

Index